Library of
Davidson College

The Habsburg
Empire
and the Sea

ARCHDUKE FERDINAND MAX

Commander of the Austrian Navy, 1854–1864
Emperor Maximilian of Mexico, 1864–1867

Courtesy Bettmann Archive

The Habsburg Empire and the Sea

Austrian Naval Policy, 1797–1866

Lawrence Sondhaus

Purdue University Press
West Lafayette, Indiana

Copyright 1989 by Purdue Research Foundation, West Lafayette, Indiana 47907. All rights reserved. Unless permission is granted, this material shall not be copied, reproduced, or coded for reproduction by any electrical, mechanical, or chemical processes, or combination thereof, now known or later developed.

Published in 1989
Printed in the United States of America

Book design by Greg Corrigan
Maps and jacket design by Anita Noble

Library of Congress Cataloging-in-Publication Data

Sondhaus, Lawrence
    The Habsburg Empire and the sea : Austrian naval policy, 1797–1866
  / Lawrence Sondhaus.
      p. cm.
    Originally presented as the author's thesis (Ph. D.—University of Virginia, 1986)
      Bibliography: p.
      Includes index.
      ISBN 0-911198-97-0
    1. Austria. Kriegsmarine—History—19th century.
2. Sea-power—Austria—History—19th century. 3. Austria—History, Naval—19th century. 4. Austria—Military policy. I. Title.
    VA473.S66 1988
    359′.009436—dc19   88-24028
                                                                    CIP

CONTENTS

	Abbreviations in Notes	ix
	Preface	xi
One	The Unlikely Marriage	1
	• Austria and the Sea (to 1797)	2
	• The Navy under Thugut (1797–1801)	5
	• The Navy under Archduke Charles (1801–1806)	11
	• The "Second Trieste Navy" (1806–1809)	18
Two	Austria Returns to the Sea	29
	• The Reconquest (1813–1814)	29
	• The Italian Inheritance: Personnel	36
	• The Italian Inheritance: Materiel	40
	• Expanding Horizons: The Navy and Merchant Marine (1814–1821)	46
Three	Success and Failure in an "Era of Big Spending"	57
	• Humiliation and Indecision: The Early 1820s	57

	• Promise and Frustration: The Paulucci Era (1824–1833)	67
Four	In Defense of Morality and the Austrian Lloyd	**86**
	• Complacency and Economy: The Paulucci Era (1833–1839)	86
	• The Founding of the Austrian Lloyd	94
	• Triumph and Treason: The Paulucci Era (1840—1844)	101
Five	The Catastrophe	**118**
	• Deserters, Patriots, Martyrs: The Bandiera Brothers (1844)	118
	• The Navy under Archduke Frederick (1844–1847)	127
	• Toward Revolution (1847–1848)	136
Six	Out of the Ashes	**150**
	• Picking up the Pieces (1848)	150
	• The Navy under Dahlerup (1849–1851)	158
Seven	The Frustrating 1850s	**172**
	• Austria and the Revolution in Naval Technology	172
	• The Navy under Wimpffen (1851–1854)	177
	• The Era of Ferdinand Max: The Early Years	181
	• "A Long and Painful Summer": The War of 1859	190

Eight	The Italian Challenge	**200**
	• The Adriatic and the Unification of Italy (1859–1861)	200
	• Expansion and Ironclads: The Great Naval Debate (1860–1862)	206
	• The Italian Ironclad Program (1861–1864)	219
	• The Era of Ferdinand Max: The Final Act (1862–1864)	222
Nine	The Adriatic Secured	**237**
	• Baptism of Fire: The Danish War (1864)	237
	• Intermezzo (1864–1866)	242
	• "Hearts of Iron": The Lissa Campaign (1866)	252
	Epilogue	**265**
	Maps	**270**
	• Europe and the Mediterranean	270
	• The Adriatic	272
	• The Lissa Campaign (1866)	273
	Appendix A	**275**
	• Sailing Ships of the Austrian Navy	275
	Appendix B	**277**
	• Steam-powered Ships of the Austrian Navy (through 1866)	277

Appendix C	**279**
• Comparative Strength of the Austrian and Italian Fleets, 1866	279
Appendix D	**281**
• Commanders and Leading Personnel of the Austrian Navy, 1797–1866	281
Glossary	**285**
Bibliography	**287**
Index	**299**

ABBREVIATIONS IN NOTES

Archival Material

HHSA   Haus- Hof- und Staatsarchiv, Vienna

- Adm. Reg.   Administrative Registratur
- Archiv Max von Mexiko   Archiv Kaiser Maximilians von Mexiko
- PA   Politisches Archiv
- StK.   Staatskanzlei
    - Prov.   Provinzen

HKA   Hofkammerarchiv, Vienna

- Kommerz, 4.   Kommerz, 4. Litorale, 1749–1813

KA   Kriegsarchiv, Vienna

- CK   Centralkanzleiakten
- HKR   Hofkriegsrat Akten
- MA   Marineakten
    - A/j   Administrative Akten (judicial)
    - M/c   Militärische Akten
    - T/c   Technisches Archiv
- Ms/Ma   Manuskripte (Marine)

General Abbreviations

a.d.   an der/dem
AOK/AOKdo.   Armee-Ober-Kommando
Fasc.   Fascicle
FMLt.   Feldmarschalleutnant
fol.   folio
FZM.   Feldzeugmeister

Abbreviations in Notes

HKR Hofkriegsrat
Korr. Korrespondenz
MOK/MOKdo. Marine-Ober-Kommando
1797–1802, etc. Installments of the official history of the Austrian navy (after first note, cited by author and year only); if used with the term *MS*, the work is an unpublished draft in the Kriegsarchiv, Vienna.

PREFACE

In 1797 the Treaty of Campoformio confirmed the death of the Venetian Republic, the ancient mistress of the Adriatic. Austria's inheritance included the bulk of Venice's territory, navy, and merchant marine, a tremendous windfall that added a new dimension to her strategic horizons. During the decades that followed, the Austrians came to appreciate the advantages of sea power, but it was not an easy transition for a state whose traditional interests, geography, and role in the European balance of power dictated a land orientation. Habsburg leaders ultimately concluded that command of the Adriatic Sea was essential to the overall security of the empire. This service could be provided only by a navy worthy of a great power, one that was also strong enough to show the flag in more distant waters, both to defend commerce and to represent Austria in the dawning era of "gunboat diplomacy."

By the 1860s, Austria had become a regional naval power in the Adriatic and a major maritime commercial force in the Eastern Mediterranean. But the formative years of the Habsburg navy included no turning point as dramatic as Peter the Great's promotion of Russian sea power in the early 1700s or the German naval buildup begun by Alfred von Tirpitz in the 1890s. Whereas other European land powers experienced sudden, dramatic changes in attitude toward the sea, the process in Austria was long and tedious. The navy had to endure the opposition of a series of government ministers, from Baron Thugut in the 1790s to Count Rechberg in the 1860s, most of whom considered it a needless luxury that a financially strapped Habsburg state could ill afford. The transformation came because of the intervention, at crucial points in time, of interested members of the imperial house and the army hierarchy, the traditional bastions of Habsburg power. Foremost among them was Archduke Ferdinand Max, more famous as the ill-fated Emperor Maximilian of Mexico. Francis Joseph's dynamic younger brother, laboring three decades before the publication of Alfred Thayer Mahan's *The Influence of Sea Power upon History* (1890), won approval for a modern battle fleet by applying many of the same arguments used later by Tirpitz in Germany. Thanks largely to his efforts, the Habsburg fleet was able to play a central role in forcing Italy to abandon her extensive war aims in the Adriatic in 1866. The great naval victory of that year preserved Austria's outlet to the sea and made possible the further development of her overseas interests.

The fascinating history of the formative years of Austrian sea power has not received its due either from naval historians or from general students of the Habsburg monarchy. Within Austria, the navy has attracted the attention only of military historians; elsewhere, it has been largely ignored. Professor Anthony Sokol of Stanford University, a former Habsburg naval officer, wrote the first—and to date, only—English-language monograph on the subject, *The Imperial and Royal Austro-Hungarian Navy* (Annapolis, Md., 1968). A richly illustrated overview of the navy's history, it is of little use to the serious scholar. Nevertheless, its appearance sparked an interest in the Austrian fleet in the United States and, after its translation into German in 1972, a popular revival of the subject in Austria itself.[1] Unfortunately, Habsburg maritime enthusiasts, both professional and amateur, have focused almost exclusively upon the modern Austrian navy of the early twentieth century, producing technical studies of its last generation of warships or accounts of operations during the First World War. The earlier years of Austria's maritime experience have been virtually overlooked.

Discounting a number of semi-scholarly works, the core of the literature on the navy today still consists of an incomplete official history begun in 1882. This *Geschichte der k.u.k. Kriegsmarine* (title and subtitles vary) remains the most valuable published resource on the history of the Habsburg fleet. Written by Austrian naval officers, its volumes contain a wealth of information on naval operations but little, if any, commentary on the place of sea power or overseas interests in the general history of the empire. Only four installments were completed before the fall of the monarchy: Josef Rechberger von Rechkron's *Vorgeschichte*, published in 1882, covering the period 1500–1797; Josef von Lehnert's volume (1891) from 1797 to 1802; Jerolim Benko von Boinik (1884) on the years 1848 and 1849; and Josef Fleischer (1906) on the war of 1866. Artur von Khuepach's volume on 1802–14 (1942) appeared during a revival of scholarly interest in the fleet in the wake of the *Anschluss* of 1938. A second installment by Khuepach, filling the gap from 1814 to 1847, was postponed by World War II, and eventually revised and edited by Heinrich von Bayer for publication in 1966. Hans Hugo Sokol, who in 1930 wrote the definitive work on the Habsburg navy during World War I,[2] attempted to complete the series fifty years later. His volume *Des Kaisers Seemacht* (1980), covering the period 1848–1914, is subtitled the *Abschlussband des Geschichtswerkes der k.u.k. Kriegsmarine*. A broad overview of an extensive period of time, it lacks the meticulous detail of the earlier volumes and is of little help to the serious historian.[3] Dr. Lothar Höbelt's section on the navy in *Die Habsburgermonarchie 1848–1918*, volume 5: *Die bewaffnete Macht* (Vienna, 1987) appeared after the present manuscript was submitted for publication.

Of the periodical literature only a handful of articles merit mention. An administrative history of the navy from 1856 to 1918 by Walter Wagner (1961) and a somewhat deficient account of Austrian naval policy under Archduke Ferdinand Max by Antonio Schmidt-Brentano (1977) have been published in the *Mitteilungen des österreichischen Staatsarchivs*.[4] In the United States, an article by Louis A. Gebhard (1968–69) on the political battle over Austria's dreadnought squadron in 1911 and a recent piece by Franz Szabo (1981–82) on attempts to organize a Habsburg navy in Maria Theresa's time have appeared in the *Austrian History Yearbook*.[5] Since 1974, the Arbeitsgemeinschaft für österreichische Marinegeschichte has published *Marine—Gestern, Heute*, a quarterly journal of maritime affairs with a special interest in the history of the Habsburg navy and merchant marine.

In 1980 the military museum in Vienna devoted a volume of the *Schriften des Heeresgeschichtlichen Museum (Militärwissenschaftliches Institut) in Wien* to the navy.[6] This collection of essays includes a historiographical piece by Johann Christoph Allmayer-Beck in which the author points out the inadequacy of existing studies of the Austrian navy and Habsburg maritime policy. Citing the need for a break with the traditional "Branchengeschichte," he calls for a broadening and deepening of historical investigation into the field with special attention to the place held by the navy and the sea in the overall history of the Habsburg Empire. The present work represents an attempt to fill at least part of this gap in the literature.

This study originated as a doctoral dissertation at the University of Virginia. I owe a great debt of thanks to Professor Enno E. Kraehe for his supervision of the original work and critique of subsequent revisions. I am also grateful to Volker R. Berghahn of Brown University for kindling my interest in the political side of naval armaments questions during his semester as visiting professor at Virginia. A number of scholars have provided valuable criticism, advice, and encouragement at various stages of the project. They include Professors Hans A. Schmitt of the University of Virginia, Hugh Ragsdale of the University of Alabama, Paul W. Schroeder of the University of Illinois, and John D. Treadway of the University of Richmond.

I conducted most of my research in Austria at the Kriegsarchiv in Vienna, where *Oberrat* Dr. Peter Broucek, *Amtssekretär* Herr Karl Rossa, and *Marine Referent* Herr Peter Jung were always patient and helpful. I would also like to thank Dr. Anna Benna and her staff for help and guidance provided during my months of work at the Haus- Hof- und Staatsarchiv, and the staff of the Hofkammerarchiv for similar consideration during my short time there. I am grateful to Jean F. Preston, Curator of Manuscripts at Princeton University Library, for permission to use the Papers of Prince Eugene de Beauharnais and for her help and kindness during my two visits to Princeton. The collections of the library of the Kriegsarchiv and the Nationalbibliothek in Vienna, the Library of Congress in Washington, D.C., and Alderman Library at the University of Virginia all were invaluable to my secondary research. My work in Vienna was made possible by a Fulbright-Hays Training Grant from the U.S. Department of Education. The Society of Fellows of the University of Virginia provided a Forstmann Fellowship to help support the months of preliminary research.

Finally, I would like to thank family and friends for years of encouragement and moral support. Most of all I thank my parents, to whom this book is dedicated.

NOTES

1. This review of the literature is based in part on Johann Christoph Allmayer-Beck, "Die Geschichte von Österreichs Seemacht als historiographisches Problem," *Schriften des Heeresgeschichtlichen Museums (Militärwissenschaftliches Institut) in Wien*, vol. 8: *Österreich zur See* (Vienna: Österreichischer Bundesverlag, 1980): 7–21.

2. Hans Hugo Sokol, *Österreich-Ungarns Seekrieg 1914–1918* (Vienna: Amalthea Verlag, 1930).

3. The manuscript collection of the Kriegsarchiv in Vienna holds a number of unpublished installments of the official history, competing works that were not accepted for publication or abortive projects to rewrite or replace existing volumes. These were often more helpful than the published works, but they too were all written by active or retired naval officers and share the same fundamental shortcomings. They include manuscripts by Theodor Braun on 1500–1797 (1944) and 1797–1802 (n.d.); Josef Fleischer on 1802–1848 (1911); and Peter Handel-Mazzetti on 1850–1866 (n.d.).

4. Walter Wagner, "Die obersten Behörden der k.u.k. Kriegsmarine 1856–1918," *Mitteilungen des österreichischen Staatsarchivs*, Ergänzungsband 6 (1961); Antonio Schmidt-Brentano, "Österreichs Weg zur Seemacht: Die Marinepolitik Österreichs in der Ära Erzherzog Ferdinand Maximilian (1854–1864)," *Mitteilungen des österreichischen Staatsarchivs* 30 (1977): 119–52.

5. Louis A. Gebhard, "Austria-Hungary's Dreadnought Squadron: The Naval Outlay of 1911," *Austrian History Yearbook* 4–5 (1968–69): 245–58; Franz Szabo, "Unwanted Navy: Habsburg Naval Armaments under Maria Theresa," *Austrian History Yearbook* 17–18 (1981–82): 29–53.

6. See note 1 above.

CHAPTER

1

The Unlikely Marriage

On 17 October 1797 envoys of the Habsburg emperor and the French Republic met at the Venetian town of Campoformio, just down the post road from Udine, to conclude six months of acrimonious negotiations. An armistice the previous spring had brought an end to five years of warfare, but even in defeat the Habsburgs drove a hard bargain. The final agreement gave France the Austrian Netherlands and recognized her right to annex the left bank of the Rhine; a French satellite, the Cisalpine Republic, was to receive Habsburg Lombardy. In return, Austria was awarded the bulk of the lands of the Venetian Republic.

The Habsburg plenipotentiaries could congratulate themselves on a job well done. Under the prevailing circumstances Austria was powerless to deny France the Rhine frontier. As for Belgium and Lombardy, both were isolated possessions and the former had long been considered a strategic liability. The fact that French armies were already occupying all three areas made their concession a mere formality. In contrast, Austria's spoils came courtesy of General Napoleon Bonaparte, whose army had toppled the last of the great Italian republics during the course of his recent campaign. For decades Habsburg statesmen had coveted Venetia, Istria, and Dalmatia; in addition to being contiguous to the rest of the crown lands, these provinces would provide Austria with a far more extensive outlet to the sea. At the same time, her acquisition of the remnants of the Venetian navy and merchant marine suddenly made her a maritime power, if only a second rate one. Except for a brief separation later in the Napoleonic era, the unlikely marriage of Austria and the sea was to last until the collapse of the Habsburg monarchy.

Austria and the Sea (to 1797)

Prior to the Treaty of Campoformio the Habsburg possessions had been all but landlocked. Austria won her first foothold on the Adriatic in 1382 when the free city of Trieste, fearful of Venetian aggression, placed itself under Habsburg protection. In the centuries that followed, little was done to expand or exploit this tiny outlet to the sea. According to Fernand Braudel, Trieste was an "annoyance" for Venice but nothing more. Venetian merchantmen handled much of Trieste's direct traffic with overseas ports, and an even greater share of Austrian trade passed through Venice itself.[1]

In decades of warfare against the Turks, the Habsburgs provided the Christian alliance with its land power and left naval matters to the Venetians. But the Austro-Venetian partnership was born of necessity rather than friendship, and in 1718, after the eclipse of the Turkish threat, the republic adopted a policy of strict neutrality that lasted until its death at the hands of Napoleon. After the breach, Emperor Charles VI challenged Venice's traditional domination of the Adriatic by making Trieste a free port and expanding the Neapolitan navy he had acquired, along with the kingdom of the Two Sicilies, as a result of the recent War of the Spanish Succession. The new status of Trieste provided the groundwork for its future prosperity, but the first "Austrian" navy did not fare as well. After the Spanish Bourbons conquered Naples and Sicily in 1735, the emperor disbanded the fleet and abandoned his maritime goals.[2]

Trieste remained in the shadow of Venice throughout the reign of Charles's successor, Maria Theresa. In 1767, after a half-century of free port status, the city registered a total volume of trade (imports and exports) worth only ten million florins. Even more alarming were figures from the following year which revealed that Venetian merchantmen still handled 75 percent of Trieste's overseas commerce.[3] Vienna chartered an Austrian East India Company in an attempt to promote direct trade between Trieste and the Orient, but it folded after only ten years.[4] Still, the gradual growth of Austria's seagoing trade forced her to take measures to protect ships flying the imperial colors. In the late 1760s two frigates were build at Porto Ré (Kraljevica) on the Croatian littoral, and Chevalier Jean Charles de Meaussé of the French navy was hired as commander. This promising project soon died, however, amid arguments between court commercial officials, the *Hofkriegsrat* (court war council), and local authorities in the Adriatic littoral, none of whom wanted to be responsible for maintaining warships.[5]

An Austrian navy was finally established two decades later during the eventful reign of Joseph II. In 1786 pleas from Trieste for protection against pirates moved the emperor to transfer two small ships from the Austrian Netherlands to the Adriatic. The vessels were administered by port authorities rather than the *Hofkriegsrat* in Vienna, evidence of Joseph's view that this "Trieste navy" was not only a local institution but a non-military one as well. To underscore the fact that the new flotilla was not an organ of the Holy Roman Empire, Joseph devised a naval ensign featuring horizontal bars of red, white, and red, a design eventually adopted as the flag of the modern Austrian state.

The "Trieste navy" reflected the melting pot of influences and resources that were to be a feature of every Habsburg navy to come. Three of the six original officers were British; non-commissioned officers and other skilled personnel hailed from such diverse places as Ireland and the Philippines. Half of the common sailors were Italians or Croats from the Adriatic littoral, while half were South Slav soldiers from the Croatian Military Border.[6] Because of their Belgian origin, the original ships had French names, but later additions bore Italian names. Italian, the trading language of the Adriatic and Mediterranean, was also the language of command.

The original ships, supplemented by a number of small gunboats, quickly demonstrated their worth as a coast guard and deterrent to piracy; in 1789 the volume of trade of Trieste reached thirty-seven million florins, an unprecedented high.[7] But Joseph's subsequent intervention in the Russo-Turkish war of 1787–1792 brought a sudden halt to the economic boom and almost killed the "Trieste navy." The *Hofkriegsrat* assumed control over the flotilla, concluded that it could have no influence on the course of the war in the Balkans, and transferred most of its officers to gunboats on the Danube. After Joseph's death in 1790, Emperor Leopold II sued for peace, cut expenditure, and all but abolished the navy, reducing its active force to a pair of gunboats, one each at Trieste and Rijeka. Upon his accession to the throne in 1792, Francis II also favored a coastal rather than seagoing defense for Austria's modest littoral territory.[8]

The "Trieste navy" proved to be more durable than its predecessors, surviving as a pitiful reminder of the low priority Austria continued to give to maritime affairs. Over the first ten years of its existence (to 1797) it was allocated only 400,000 florins, compared to a sum two thousand times greater (800 million) for the Habsburg army.[9] The navy played no role in Austria's first war against revolutionary France and was not even mobilized until March 1797, when Bonaparte's troops besieged Trieste and occupied the adjacent Küstenland province. Thereafter, it helped evacuate the city by sea but saw no action against enemy warships. One month later, after the Franco-Austrian armistice of Leoben, French troops took possession of the entire Adriatic coastline between Ancona and Rijeka.

During the six months of negotiations leading up to the Treaty of Campoformio, Bonaparte and the French army remained active throughout the Adriatic region. After dragging his feet on a promise to evacuate Trieste, the general sent an expedition to occupy the Venetian Republic's last Greek possessions, the Ionian Islands, and ordered the removal or destruction of the naval stores and resources of the port of Venice.[10] The French annexation of the Ionians would enable them to control the mouth of the Adriatic even after conceding much of its coastline to Austria, and their activity in Venice reduced significantly the value of the old Venetian fleet. The award at Campoformio in October 1797 was a tremendous windfall for the Austrians, the more so in light of their military defeat at the hands of France. But because the Venetian inheritance also came through French hands, they were in no position to challenge the circumstances of the transfer or the condition of the goods.

The Navy under Thugut (1797–1801)

By the Treaty of Campoformio, the Habsburg Empire gained new territories for which the possibilities seemed limitless. The Duke of Gallo, one of the Austrian negotiators, outlined the advantages in a letter to Emperor Francis: Austria would gain a large navy, "decisive" influence in the Levant, and "incalculable" commercial advantages far outweighing those lost in the cession of Belgium to France.[11] But the emperor's chief minister, Baron Franz Amadeus Thugut, did not share these insights. He thought of the gains solely in terms of the immediate income the taxation of Venetia could provide for the depleted court treasury.[12] After Campoformio, Thugut was named minister plenipotentiary in charge of the former Venetian lands and the navy that came with them. In the years that followed, his narrow vision of the value of the inheritance was to prevail over calls for a broader exploitation.

On 18 January 1798 Austrian troops under *Feldzeugmeister* Count Olivier Wallis joined a flotilla of the "Trieste navy" in taking possession of the city of Venice and the wharves of its famed Arsenal. This ancient shipbuilding facility, mentioned by Dante in the *Inferno*, had served as the arena for some of Galileo's first observations of the laws of physics; for the next half-century it was to be the launching site for every new vessel of the Habsburg fleet. The commander of the "Trieste navy," Lieutenant Colonel James Ernest Williams, was overwhelmed by the prizes that had fallen into his hands: ten ships of the line, seven frigates and corvettes, and dozens of gunboats and smaller vessels, roughly half of the Venetian navy of 1797.[13]

Most of the larger ships were damaged or in disrepair, since the French had taken the best ones for themselves and left behind only what they could not use or destroy. Williams knew that he had more warships on his hands than Austria could possibly use, but even if only a fraction of them were repaired and put into service, the new fleet would be many times larger and stronger than the one corvette and twenty gunboats of his old "Trieste navy." Thugut, however, refused to sanction repairs for any of the Venetian ships; he also took steps to limit Williams's authority and, in general, complicated matters in every conceivable way. In February 1798 he chose a Venetian aristocrat, Andrea Querini, to command the navy but did not bother to fire Williams. Querini's appointment was purely political, a reward for a recent mission to secure Dalmatian acquiescence to Austrian rule, and the military authorities in Venice refused to take it seriously. Count Wallis, as military and civil governor of Venetia, continued to treat Williams as the head of the navy even after Thugut, in March, officially subordinated him to Querini. Thereafter, Williams was supposed to be in charge of the "Trieste navy," while Querini administered the ex-Venetian navy and the Venice Arsenal and answered to Thugut for all naval matters.[14] For his part, Williams as late as November 1798 still referred to himself as the "Marine Commandant" in correspondence with Vienna.[15] The confusion did not come to an end until the spring of 1799, when Williams was given command of a flotilla on Lake Constance, leaving Querini in undisputed control of the coastal and seagoing navy.

Amid the confusion, both Williams and Querini pleaded with Thugut to make the Venetian vessels the foundation of a larger Austrian navy. In May 1798 Querini informed the minister that four frigates and two cutters left undamaged by the French could be overhauled and put into service within four months. In June Williams proposed to arm the same six ships plus a number of gunboats and submitted a plan for a navy of six frigates, six brigs, and ninety smaller vessels. He estimated that such a fleet would cost 77,260 florins per month to maintain, a sum that must have seemed exhorbitant to Thugut, especially since the budget of the "Trieste navy" had averaged a mere 40,000 florins per year. The plans were rejected, and the navy continued to operate with the old Trieste corvette and some smaller coastal craft. Williams resubmitted his project later in 1798, arguing to Thugut that its ultimate goal would be "nothing other than a purely defensive navy." Williams's projected fleet would have been powerful enough to dominate the Adriatic, but he assumed that nothing less could assure a successful defense.[16]

Austria's neutrality in the ongoing Anglo-French war left little justification for a Habsburg navy capable of offensive action against another European power. But lacking command of the Adriatic, the Austrians could not even communicate with, much less defend, Dalmatia or the hundreds of coastal islands they had acquired along with it. Of greater concern was the security of Venice, the principal prize of the recent treaty; Colonel Anton von Zach, chief of staff of the Austrian army in Italy, lamented that "Venice without a fleet" was just "a very poor fortress."[17] The stakes were even higher for the large Venetian merchant fleet, now sailing under Austrian colors. Prior to 1797, the Venetian Republic had mounted the occasional campaign against pirate sanctuaries but relied mostly upon regular payments of tribute to the North African rulers to keep the predators in check. After rejecting Williams's appeals for more warships, Thugut also discontinued these payments, leaving the Barbary pirates with no reason to respect the Austrian flag. In 1798 and 1799 North African corsairs made a fortune on Habsburg prizes, the six richest cargoes having a combined value of some two million florins. Late in 1799 the merchants of Trieste, victimized along with those of Venice, petitioned the emperor for protection at sea. Their appeal listed losses of 1.25 million florins at the hands of the Algerians alone.[18]

Had Thugut considered such figures, Williams's fleet plan, costing just under one million per year, no doubt would have appeared more reasonable. The plan certainly promised to provide forces strong enough to deter such attacks. Of the six frigates and six brigs, two vessels of each type would have cruised on a line from Cattaro (Kotor), at the southern tip of Dalmatia, to the central Mediterranean island of Malta. Another brig and two frigates were allocated for the mouth of the Adriatic between Cattaro and Otranto, on the heel of the Italian peninsula. Meanwhile, a force of one frigate, two brigs, and a dozen gunboats would have cruised the Adriatic, catching any corsairs that slipped through the first two lines of defense. As for the protection of the coast, Williams had called for a brig and sixty gunboats to be stationed in the lagoon at Venice; the sixth frigate would have been kept in reserve at Trieste and the remaining gunboats scattered along the coast from Trieste to Cattaro.[19] It was a sound plan which, unfortunately, never stood a chance of being adopted. The navy had no friends among the government ministers to counter Thugut's opposition, and the archdukes of the imperial house had yet to take notice of it. In the army hierarchy, the naval cause had no supporters above the rank of colonel.

The perils facing Habsburg merchantmen increased still more after March 1799, when France again declared war on Austria. Since allies Britain, Russia, Naples, and Turkey all had fleets in the Mediterranean theatre, Thugut saw no need for an Austrian one, and Habsburg sea power played no more of a role in the War of the Second Coalition than it had in the first. Following the transfer of Williams to Lake Constance, the navy conducted patrols of the Adriatic under the command of Captain Nicolo Pasqualigo, a former Venetian officer. His forces were so weak, though, that French privateers operating out of Ancona soon were able to join the Barbary pirates in attacking Austrian commerce with impunity. Chevalier Joseph L'Espine, a French émigré naval officer in Habsburg service, lamented that "the navy is in its current condition . . . insignificant. The corsairs of Ancona venture out to ravage our commerce and one can do nothing against them."[20] Relief finally came when the Russians occupied the Ionian Islands, then sent a squadron into the Adriatic to blockade Ancona. In July 1799 the French base was closed; the Austrian navy, too weak to make a significant contribution, played no part in the operation.

Austria's land forces fared much better in the war, but by the fall of 1799 mutual Austro-Russian mistrust led Tsar Paul to recall all Russian forces and seek a peace with France. The maritime side of the animosity exploded at Ancona, where an Austrian siege on land complemented the Russian blockade at sea. In mid-November, when the city finally capitulated, the Austrians resorted to a coup to keep the thirty ships in its harbor (among them three former Venetian ships of the line) out of Russian hands. Under cover of night the Habsburg naval adjutant, the Chevalier L'Espine, secured the docks and had the Austrian flag raised on all the vessels; at dawn the Russians were presented with an infuriating fait accompli. Coming after the general Russian withdrawal but at a time when Paul may have been having second thoughts, the so-called "Flag Affair" of Ancona is considered by some historians to have been the final straw in Russia's exasperation with his allies.[21]

The captured warships made a triumphal entry into Venice, heartening the discouraged personnel of the navy and leading some to hope that better times were coming. But Thugut viewed the "Flag Affair" as a minor diplomatic problem, certainly not the coup that naval officers considered it to be. He experienced no change in thinking and was no more inclined to press these ships into service than he had been to use those gained two years earlier at Venice. In the campaign of 1800 Habsburg forces saw little action at sea, and the navy remained as weak as it had been before.

The fighting on land took a dramatic turn against the allies when the Russian withdrawal coincided with the return of Bonaparte from Egypt. After becoming First Consul of the French Republic, he took the field in Italy and defeated the Austrians in the decisive Battle of Marengo in June 1800. At the end of the year Austria once again sued for peace; the Treaty of Lunéville (9 February 1801) restored most of the provisions of Campoformio and, equally important, brought the fall of Thugut.

By the end of the war Austria was completely inactive at sea. Early in 1801 the French regained their foothold on the Adriatic by making the Austrian evacuation of Ancona a prerequisite to the Lunéville agreement. A treaty with Naples two months later gave France the right to occupy the Adriatic ports of Brindisi and Otranto, securing her direct control over the heel of Italy and effective domination of the entire west coast of the sea. Meanwhile, at the mouth of the Adriatic, a Russo-Turkish convention transformed the Ionian Islands into the Septinsular Republic, a self-governing state under Ottoman "suzerainty" and Russian protection.

Thus the Habsburg Empire came away from the War of the Second Coalition with its territorial holdings intact but in a situation far bleaker than after Campoformio. The French now had the bases necessary for a campaign to control the Adriatic, the Russians still had garrisons in the Ionian Islands, and the Austrian navy, as a fighting force, remained inconsequential. In the three and a half years since Austria first stumbled into the ranks of the maritime powers, the indifference of Thugut and the traditional land orientation of Habsburg strategists kept her from exploiting more than nominally the vast potential benefits of the Venetian inheritance. Thugut's ouster, followed by the elevation of Archduke Charles to the post of "minister of war and navy," brought hope for a brighter future.

The Navy under Archduke Charles (1801–1806)

Emperor Francis reacted to the defeats of 1800 by appointing his brother Charles president of the *Hofkriegsrat* with a mandate to investigate and reform the armed forces. In September 1801, at the archduke's suggestion, Francis restructured the hierarchy of the imperial government to include a *Staats- und Konferenzministerium* consisting of ministers of the interior, foreign affairs, and war and navy, Charles himself taking the latter post.[22] In the meantime, the archduke started reorganizing the navy, benefiting from the advice of his general adjutant, the French émigré Count Louis Folliot de Crenneville. An officer in the French navy from 1780 until 1791, Crenneville had served with royalist troops on the Rhine during the war of the First Coalition. He entered Austrian service in 1795, was assigned to Charles's personal entourage, and went on to become his lifelong friend.

The archduke's first step was to replace Querini, the Venetian aristocrat, with a true seagoing commander. In the fall of 1801 he appointed Baron Lelio Spannochi, a Tuscan with experience in the British and Neapolitan navies, to the post of *Marine-Kommandant*. The French émigré L'Espine, architect of the "Flag Affair" at Ancona, became his second-in-command, no doubt benefiting from Crenneville's influence. When the baron was unable to assume his new post, L'Espine was the logical choice to take his place. Meanwhile, Charles named Crenneville head of the Marine Bureau in Vienna, the executive body of a new naval administration. In January 1802 Querini formally stepped down, clearing the way for the reform of the navy.

The new *Marine-Kommandant* enjoyed the full confidence of Charles and the emperor. His background was almost identical to that of Crenneville, but L'Espine had more experience at sea. He had served in the French navy from 1775 to 1791, then with royalist forces along the Rhine, before obtaining a commission in the Austrian army. While with an allied flotilla on the Rhine, L'Espine met Williams, on temporary assignment there from the "Trieste navy," and was persuaded to transfer to the Adriatic. He had been on active duty with the Austrian navy since 1797 and knew well the men and materiel at his disposal. As commander, he placed in service the Venetian ships that Williams and Querini had failed to have armed earlier and also won authorization for a fleet of eight frigates, four brigs, four schooners, and forty gunboats.[23]

Under L'Espine the protection of commerce remained the greatest concern for the navy, especially since Austria's withdrawal from the war did little to decrease the attacks against her merchant marine. The French remained at war with Britain and, after Lunéville, quickly reestablished their corsair fleet at Ancona. Vienna protested in vain against the indiscriminate piracy practiced in the Adriatic under French letters of marque; Paris sent apologies but offered no guarantees that the situation would change.[24] Relief finally came after the Treaty of Amiens (27 March 1802) ended Anglo-French hostilities and left France with no justification for further privateering.

Notwithstanding the continuing warfare and piracy, the commercial health of the littoral remained relatively sound. The annexation of the Venetian Republic, far from hurting Trieste, brought unprecedented prosperity. The empire's oldest seaport handled sixty-five million florins worth of goods in 1800, compared to thirty-seven million in 1789. Because Austria did not grant Venice the status of a free port, foreign goods bound for the city or the Venetian interior up the Po were often brought to Trieste first, then transshipped to their final destination. At the turn of the century, transit trade accounted for 40 percent of both the imports and exports of Trieste. Forty-nine percent of its total exports went either to former Venetian ports or up the Po, whereas these markets accounted for a mere 18 percent of imports. Many Venetian merchants, eager to take advantage of the privileges of the free port, abandoned their home city and registered their ships in Trieste.[25]

The end of the Anglo-French war presented L'Espine with an opportunity to build up the fleet and provide safer conditions for Austria's seagoing commerce. But much to the chagrin of the navy and the merchants, the government decided to use the return of peace to bring the court finances back under control. By 1803 budget cuts left L'Espine's fleet with a core of only three frigates, one corvette, and four brigs instead of the authorized eight frigates and four brigs. Meanwhile, economies in personnel reduced by half the active naval officer corps. Crenneville and L'Espine, backed by Archduke Charles, pursued a policy of retaining French émigrés while furloughing men of all other nationalities, particularly veterans of the Venetian navy. In 1802 the corps was 60 percent Italian, 18 percent South Slav, 12 percent French, and 7 percent German, 53 percent of the officers (South Slavs as well as Italians) having served in the Venetian navy. By 1805 the composition was 53 percent Italian, 21 percent French, 14 percent South Slav, and 6 percent German, and only 45 percent of the whole were Venetian veterans.[26]

There is no evidence, however, of a campaign by Charles to "de-italianize" the navy. The navy continued to be commanded in Italian, and after the opening of the *Scuola dei cadetti di marina* in Venice during May 1802, Italian became the language of naval education as well. When designing the curriculum of the academy, the Austrians relied upon standard French mathematics and navigation texts but had them translated into Italian.[27] As for his prejudices in favor of Frenchmen, Charles apparently considered them more trustworthy than former Venetian officers and better trained than officers of the old "Trieste navy." Furthermore, owing to their social background and education, the French émigrés typically knew both German and Italian and thus were able to communicate easily with Austrian military officials and with their predominantly-Italian crews. In contrast, none of the Venetian officers could speak German and most were considered unsuitable for Habsburg service.[28]

In April 1803, when the sultan of Morocco unleashed his corsairs on Habsburg commerce, it came as no surprise that a French émigré, Count Charles Mogniat de Pouilly, was assigned to command the response. Austria took the unprecedented step of deploying regular warships outside the Adriatic, sending Mogniat to the coast of Morocco with two brigs in order to give "the most active protection" to her merchantmen in the area. The count soon found that the modest size of his force precluded any action other than showing the flag in Moroccan waters while plenipotentiaries negotiated a peace treaty with the sultan. The navy had to maintain its brigs off the coast for two years, from November 1803 until November 1805, before the Moroccans finally came to terms.[29] Hardly a smashing success, the mission did little to inspire confidence among Austrian merchants. Still, it represented Austria's first attempt to use sea power as an instrument of foreign policy.

During the course of the Moroccan venture, Austria's position both at sea and on land changed dramatically. In May 1803 war resumed between France and Britain, and the following year Bonaparte proclaimed himself emperor of the French, prompting Francis to write off the moribund German *Reich* and proclaim the Austrian Empire. Faced with the likelihood of renewed fighting in the Adriatic, the Habsburg government explored the possibility of arming merchantmen as an inexpensive supplement to the regular navy; the plan had to be abandoned, though, after a survey of the available ships found the prospects less than promising.[30] At the beginning of 1805 the Austrian fleet still had the same nucleus of three frigates, one corvette, and four brigs, all refurbished ex-Venetian warships. The rest of the vessels inherited in 1797 or captured later at Ancona lay rotting at the Arsenal in Venice, where only two new ships, both brigs, had been laid down by the Austrians. When the Anglo-French war intensified, Austrian merchantmen found themselves victimized by French and Italian corsairs and discriminated against in the Adriatic ports under French control. Complaints from Archduke Charles about the privateering led Vienna to raise the issue through diplomatic channels; Paris apologized, as it had before, and even promised to pay damages for lost cargoes, but did nothing to stop the attacks.[31]

If L'Espine had had the eight frigates promised in the program of 1802, the navy would have been more than strong enough to protect the neutrality of Habsburg merchant shipping. The French, no longer in control of the Ionian Islands, could not send regular naval units into the Adriatic to support their makeshift privateering campaign and would have had to respect even a modest show of force. Unfortunately, Charles was of little help to the cause of Austrian sea power at this crucial stage. He had had good intentions regarding the navy, had organized its administration, and had placed the best men he could find in charge of it. But in the face of financial limitations he was unable to do more, and as minister of war in addition to the navy, he could devote only a small part of his attention to the fleet. To make matters worse, Charles was besieged by intriguers at court, implacably at odds with a coalescing war party, and in no position to broaden his concern for naval affairs. At a time when no other imperial prince or high army leader had even the slightest appreciation for sea power, the lack of active support from the archduke left navy leaders with little hope for the future.

After concluding a defensive alliance with Russia in November 1804, the Austrian Empire moved slowly toward involvement in the war against France. Charles opposed the drift away from neutrality and argued that the army needed more time to prepare, but to no avail. In the spring of 1805 foreign minister Count Johann Ludwig Cobenzl engineered the rise to power of the headstrong general Baron Karl Mack von Leiberich. The emperor allowed Charles to keep his title of war and navy minister, but with diminished authority. As the archduke's protégés throughout the military gradually lost their jobs, his influence decreased accordingly. The country, meanwhile, continued to prepare for war, since Napoleon's assumption of the crown of Italy (in May 1805) on top of his French imperial dignity of the previous year made a confrontation seemingly inevitable. An Anglo-Austrian subsidy treaty, concluded in August 1805, sealed the Habsburg commitment to the alliance. The War of the Third Coalition began the following month.

Predictably, war caught the Austrian navy unprepared. Over the summer of 1805 Crenneville agitated for preparations on land and at sea, but nothing was done prior to the start of hostilities. As Austria committed herself to fight, he found that there were not even enough seamen on active duty in Venice to man a squadron of one corvette, two brigs, and a schooner, the minimum needed to ensure "the security of trade." Forced to resort to an involuntary levy in Venice to fill 500 vacancies, Crenneville cautioned that the men should be screened for their political beliefs to avoid disciplinary problems later.[32] But the rest of the war moved much faster than the navy's belated preparations and soon made them irrelevant. October 1805 witnessed the British triumph over the French and Spanish fleets at Trafalgar and the equally crushing defeat of Mack's Austrian army at Ulm. Archduke Charles, in command of the Habsburg Army of Italy, sensed disaster in the news from Germany and began an orderly retreat from Venetia. The French followed him to the Isonzo before breaking off the pursuit, then occupied the Veneto unopposed. The Austrians left behind only a garrison at Venice.

For the navy, the repercussions of Charles's political fall struck home at the worst possible time. Days before the war started, Crenneville lost his position as head of the Marine Bureau. L'Espine was called to Vienna to succeed him, leaving the post of *Marine-Kommandant* vacant and the navy without a seagoing commander. L'Espine's second-in-command, veteran Venetian seaman Count Sylvestro Dandolo, took over as *Marine-Kommandant,* and Nicolo Pasqualigo, perhaps the best of the younger Venetian officers in Habsburg service, moved into Dandolo's old job to give the Austrian navy an all-Venetian command for the first, and only, time in its history.

Charles and his circle also lost out to the Habsburg leadership on the vital issue of allied naval cooperation. Following his evacuation of Venetia, he hoped for a Russian landing at Venice to harass the French rear, but Cobenzl, wary of encouraging tsarist ambitions in the Adriatic, rebuffed Russian overtures for joint action at sea and even refused to open Austrian ports to their warships.[33]

In November 1805 Britain and Russia finally combined their resources for a meaningless landing at Naples. In the meantime, the Austrians, harassed by French and Italian corsairs operating out of Ancona and Rimini, had only one corvette, two brigs, and a schooner at sea in the Adriatic. Their remaining brigs had yet to return from the Moroccan mission, and the three Austrian frigates were still at Venice, one of them too unseaworthy to be refurbished and armed. With the war on land going badly, Charles finally sent L'Espine to the littoral on a special mission and in early December ordered him to move the headquarters of the navy from Venice to Senj on the Croatian coast. Austria then armed six merchantmen and delivered an eleventh-hour appeal to the Ionian Islands for Russian naval help.[34]

Napoleon's subsequent victory at Austerlitz made these last-minute measures meaningless. As peace talks got underway at Pressburg, Habsburg leaders assumed that this time around most of the gains of Campoformio would be lost at the negotiating table. In mid-December Charles informed Francis that L'Espine had already removed all of the arms and stores from Venice that could be moved. French troops, meanwhile, tightened their siege of the city and occupied Trieste. The Treaty of Pressburg (26 December 1805) granted all of the Habsburg Empire's former Venetian territory, including Istria and Dalmatia, to Napoleon's kingdom of Italy. The Austrians were required to turn over all ships originally built by the Venetian Republic and release from their service all officers and men of Venetian origin. Venice itself was to be evacuated by the end of January 1806.[35]

The "Second Trieste Navy" (1806–1809)

On 19 January 1806, eight years and one day after their arrival, Habsburg troops completed their evacuation of Venice. French forces occupied the city in the name of the kingdom of Italy; in the Arsenal and lagoon they took possession of the navy's frigates and corvette, as well as three of the six brigs, the bulk of the gunboats and smaller vessels, and the old Venetian hulks the Austrians had never done anything with. When the former Austrian-Venetian personnel were given the option of retiring or joining the Royal Italian navy, most decided in favor of the latter. L'Espine once again became *Marine-Kommandant*, in charge of a force that, because of its similarity in size and purpose to the one originally created by Joseph II, was dubbed the "Second Trieste navy."[36]

After the empire returned to its pre-Campoformio coastline, even Archduke Charles ceased to champion the cause of the navy. In March 1806 he admitted to the new foreign minister, Count Johann Philipp Stadion, that a larger fleet was no longer justifiable since Austria had lost not only most of her littoral holdings but the majority of her merchant marine as well.[37] The Trieste registry listed only sixty-two ships in 1806, compared to 537 a year earlier. The dramatic decline came when the merchants of Venice, who had transferred their ships to Trieste to take advantage of its favored status when both cities belonged to Austria, once again registered their vessels in their true home port. There were also far fewer Austrian merchantmen on the high seas, especially on the heavily traveled eastern route to Constantinople and Odessa where, in 1806, their numbers were only one-tenth of 1803 levels.[38]

Throughout 1806 and much of 1807, the continuing struggle between France and the Anglo-Russian alliance kept the "Second Trieste navy" busy. In March 1806 Russia seized Cattaro and other strategic points in southern Dalmatia to prevent the French from occupying them. Napoleon demanded action, protesting that by the terms of Pressburg, Austria was obligated to turn over all ceded territories directly to France. Vienna, eager to avoid the appearance of collusion with St. Petersburg, sent L'Espine with a flotilla and 2300 troops to dislodge the Russians from Cattaro. Upon arriving, the commander realized that his forces were hopelessly outnumbered and decided to await a diplomatic solution. In February 1807 a special Austrian mission to Napoleon's headquarters in Warsaw finally obtained French approval for the recall of the expedition. L'Espine returned to Trieste in April 1807, ten months after his departure, without ever actually fighting the Russians.[39]

Tsar Alexander, embroiled in a new war with Turkey since the fall of 1806, ceded the Ionian Islands to France under the Treaty of Tilsit (July 1807) and ended Imperial Russia's bid to become a Mediterranean naval power. In the process he sacrificed the Russian Mediterranean fleet, which because of the Turkish war and British anger over the Franco-Russian peace could not return home to the Black Sea or the Baltic. Most of the ships made a run for the Atlantic, only to be interned by the British at Lisbon; six of them made for Trieste. These warships—four ships of the line, one frigate, and one corvette—were many times more powerful than the whole of the "Second Trieste navy" and would complicate matters for Austria once she returned to war.[40]

After Tilsit, the Austrian navy stood aloof from the continuing Anglo-French hostilities and lapsed into relative inactivity. A brig, purchased in 1806, brought its total number to four, but L'Espine's flotilla—it could hardly be called a fleet—had no larger ships and scarcely two dozen smaller ones. The navy did little other than protect the harbors of Trieste and Rijeka, leaving what remained of the empire's seagoing commerce, according to one observer, to suffer "a thousand insults and a thousand confiscations" at the hands of the belligerents. The total trade of Trieste, valued at a record seventy-five million florins in 1803, plummeted to just under fourteen million for 1809.[41] Despite a number of appeals from suffering merchants, the imperial government took no action and did nothing to prepare the navy for the next war. Indeed, when the country began to arm for yet another conflict with France, L'Espine and his ships were completely ignored in the planning.

In 1808, following news of the first French setbacks in Spain, a war party began to form in Vienna around the foreign minister, Stadion, and Archduke John; by the fall of the year Charles and Francis were converted to the cause. The grand strategy of the Habsburg leadership disregarded the south and the sea. War plans hinged on early victories in the north to stir German patriotic fervor and neglected the Italians and South Slavs of the Adriatic hinterland, where the war also would have to be fought. John, after being appointed commander of the southern army early in 1809, promptly informed L'Espine that there would be no extraordinary expenditure for naval preparations. The *Marine-Kommandant* was to assist the operations of the British fleet in every way possible but to make no attempt to use his own overmatched navy. In early April the commandant of Trieste was ordered to open the port to British warships and arrange a deal with his Russian "guests" to let Austrian troops occupy their vessels.[42]

Shortly thereafter, John invaded northern Italy and forced a Franco-Italian army to retreat from Venetia. But after the defeat of Archduke Charles's main army in Germany and Napoleon's march on Vienna, John was forced to abandon his campaign without fighting a major battle. The Austrian retreat soon became a rout, with disastrous consequences for the littoral. Trieste fell to the French in mid-May before the British navy could arrive. The French Army of Dalmatia then defeated the Croatians at Gospić and occupied the ports of Senj and Rijeka, cutting off the Austrian interior from possible British aid. For the first time ever, the entire Adriatic coastline lay in French hands.

In early June Commodore William Hargood arrived off Trieste with three ships of the line, the most powerful squadron Britain had ever sent to the Adriatic. When the French and

Italians showed no signs of coming out of Venice to fight, Hargood's main concern became the Russian ships of the line in Trieste harbor; after they, too, remained at anchor, he felt free to do what he could to help the Austrians. L'Espine, still on the littoral, soon approached him with a proposal to retake Trieste. Plans were made to bring in supplies via Rijeka, where the French had left only a light garrison, but in early July the *Marine-Kommandant* had to cancel the operation for want of troops. Subsequent Anglo-Austrian contacts were both spotty and confused, leaving the British navy sailing to and fro among Venice, Trieste, and Rijeka, seeking in vain to support Austrian land attacks that never materialized.[43] Hargood blamed L'Espine for the breakdown of cooperation and overlooked the fact that the imperial government, with Napoleon already in Vienna, hardly considered the retaking of coastal cities its top priority. The Austrian commander, whose refusal to give up on the littoral deserved the highest commendation, ultimately saw his naval career ruined by British vindictiveness.

Napoleon's victory at Wagram (5–6 July 1809) sealed the defeat for Austria. By the Treaty of Schönbrunn (14 October 1809) she became a landlocked country; France annexed Trieste, Rijeka, the Croatian littoral and all of Croatia south of the Sava River, all of Carniola, and part of Carinthia. The French also acquired the former Venetian-Austrian provinces of Istria and Dalmatia from their own satellite kingdom of Italy and incorporated these with the new gains to form the "Illyrian Provinces."[44] A month before Schönbrunn, L'Espine had received orders to transfer all shipbuilding personnel to Pest on the Danube. The marine infantry and artillery moved to Zagreb in Croatia and took with them all the cannon and supplies that could be moved. Upon receiving word of the peace treaty, Commodore Hargood turned over his patrol to a squadron of frigates under Captain William Hoste. The new British commander, suspicious that Austria would turn her navy over to the French, promptly seized the largest Habsburg warships, the four brigs, and took them to Malta. There they were sold to the highest bidders, two of them going to a

Prussian merchant, the other two to Americans. The proceeds, some 150,000 florins, were sent to Vienna.[45]

To complete the liquidation of the navy, coastal gunboats and other smaller vessels were sold to Italian and Dalmatian merchants and all seamen were dismissed on two weeks' pay. The officer corps presented another problem, in part because the French, in contrast to their position of 1805, did not demand the release from Austrian service of all officers from the ceded provinces. As of 1809, 44 percent of the naval officers were Italian, 22 percent South Slav, 15 percent German, and 10 percent French émigrés. Since roughly two-thirds hailed from the littoral lands surrendered under the terms of Schönbrunn, Austria decided to release all of them from their oaths of loyalty, leaving them free to enter French service. Only one ensign availed himself of this option; a few of the officers retired, but most of the rest wanted to remain active under Habsburg colors. In December 1809 Francis relented and agreed to take L'Espine and forty-five other officers and cadets into the Austrian army. Representing almost 90 percent of the officer corps of the "Second Trieste navy," they provided a trained and loyal nucleus for the future, when Austria would return to the Adriatic.[46]

The eighteenth century witnessed a definite awakening of Austrian interest in the Adriatic and in maritime affairs as a whole, but, except for the grandiose schemes of Charles VI, efforts at establishing a navy were motivated exclusively by the need to protect the empire's growing overseas commerce. It was no coincidence that Charles's navy came into existence during the years that Austria controlled Naples and temporarily held a much larger share of coastal territory: notwithstanding the encouraging growth of Trieste, Austria's oldest port and the adjacent coastline could neither support a substantial navy nor justify the existence of one. Only with the acquisition of Venice did the need for a larger, more permanent fleet come under discussion.

After 1797 the Austrian navy still had as its main purpose the protection of commerce but was faced with the far greater responsibility of safeguarding the vast ex-Venetian merchant marine. By maintaining a naval force whose strength did not correspond to its purported responsibilities, Austria unwittingly contributed to the maritime lawlessness that destroyed an enormous number of Adriatic merchantmen, the "infrastructure" of her trade. This in turn handicapped the economy of Venice, Trieste, and Rijeka for years to come and caused permanent damage to many of the smaller Dalmatian ports. The decision to let the ships of the Venetian navy rot at anchor in itself constituted a waste of resources overshadowed only by the resulting losses of the merchant marine. Unfortunately, after the fall of Thugut, time was too short for much to be salvaged before renewed warfare took away the gains of Campoformio. At the same time, with Britain as an ally in three successive wars, Austria did little to develop the offensive capabilities of the navy, and few Habsburg strategists even considered its potential as an auxiliary force to the army. Yet Austria was not to remain landlocked for long. Regardless of whether or not she deserved a second chance, the fall of Napoleon would allow her to resume her unlikely marriage with the sea.

NOTES

1. Fernand Braudel, *The Mediterranean and the Mediterranean World in the Age of Philip II*, trans. Sian Reynolds, 2 vols. (New York: Harper & Row, 1972), 1:127, 129.

2. In its only battle, in 1734, Charles VI's navy defeated a small Spanish squadron off Naples, then prudently fled to the Adriatic before the bulk of the Spanish fleet arrived. See Josef Rechberger von Rechkron, *Geschichte der k.k. Kriegsmarine,* part 1: *Österreichs Seewesen in dem Zeitraume von 1500–1797* (Vienna: Verlag des k.k. Reichs-Kriegs-Ministeriums, Marine-Section, 1882), pp. 25–33.

3. Figures from Attilio Tamaro, *Storia di Trieste*, 2 vols. (Rome, 1924; reprint, Trieste: Edizionini Lint, 1976), 2:165.

4. Fulvio Babudieri, *L'espansione mercantile austriaca nei territori d'oltremare nel XVIII secolo* (Milan: Dott. A. Giuffré editore, 1978), pp. 93–162, gives the most detailed account of this venture. The head of the company was William Bolts, a veteran of the British East India Company. See also Fernand Braudel, *Civilization and Capitalism, 15th–18th Century*, vol. 2: *The Wheels of Commerce*, trans. Sian Reynolds (New York: Harper & Row, 1982), p. 222.

5. Szabo, "Unwanted Navy," pp. 35–52.

6. The navy's original officers included three Britons, one Dutchman, one from the Austrian Netherlands, and one Italianized Croat from Ragusa (Dubrovnik). The twenty-nine non-commissioned officers and other skilled personnel included seven South Slavs, four non-Adriatic Italians, three German Austrians, three Britons, two Irishmen, two Italians from Trieste, two Dalmatian Italians, one Venetian, one Dutchman, one Swede, one Frenchman, one German from Hanover, and one Spaniard from the Philippines. The seamen included thirty-two Italians and Croats from the Adriatic littoral, thirty-two South Slavs from the Croatian Military Border, and one Briton. Figures from Theodor Braun, *Geschichte der k.u.k. Kriegsmarine*, part 1: *Österreichs Seewesen in dem Zeitraume von 1500–1797* (MS, Vienna, 1944), Vienna, Kriegsarchiv (hereafter cited as KA), Ms/Ma 1, pp. 290–91.

7. The boom was fueled by Austrian involvement in the new Russian grain trade. See Patricia Herlihy, "Russian Grain and Mediterranean Markets, 1774–1861" (Ph.D. diss., University of Pennsylvania, 1963).

8. Theodor Braun, *Geschichte der k.u.k. Kriegsmarine*, part 2, vol. 1: *1797–1802* (MS, n.d.), KA, Ms/Ma 2, p. 112; Rechberger, *1500–1797*, pp. 157–224 passim.

9. Figures from Josef von Lehnert, *Geschichte der k.u.k. Kriegsmarine*, part 2: *Die k.k. österreichische Kriegsmarine in dem Zeitraume von 1797 bis 1848*, vol. 1: *Geschichte der österreichisch-venetianischen Kriegsmarine während der Jahre 1797 bis 1802* (Vienna; Gerold & comp., 1891), p. 4.

10. Roberto Cessi, *Campoformido* (Padua: Editrice Antenore, 1973), p. 274. Cessi uses the proper Italian spelling "Campoformido"; the traditional "Campoformio" has been used throughout the present text.

11. Gallo to Francis, Udine, 13 September 1797, text in Cessi, pp. 325–30.

12. See Karl A. Roider, Jr., *Baron Thugut and Austria's Response to the French Revolution* (Princeton, N.J.: Princeton University Press, 1987).

13. Lehnert, *1797–1802*, pp. 66–68. In 1797 the Venetian navy (counting ships under repair or construction) consisted of some twenty-one or twenty-two ships of the line, fifteen frigates and corvettes, a half-dozen brigs and cutters, and over a hundred gunboats and other small vessels. It was roughly half as large as the French navy and one-fifth the size of the British. See Cesare Augusto Levi, *Navi da Guerra construite nell'Arsenale di Venezia dal 1664 al 1896* (Venice: by the author, 1896), pp. 38–44 passim.

For army officers' ranks, the closest English equivalent will be used, except in cases where a suitable one does not exist (e.g., *Feldzeugmeister, Feldmarschalleutnant*). Williams and other officers of the early navy were given army ranks, but German equivalents of the traditional Italian naval ranks were introduced after 1798. Throughout the text, grades of captain and lieutenant (e.g., *Linienschiffskapitän, Fregattenkapitän, Linienschiffsleutnant, Fregattenleutnant*, etc.) have been simplified to "captain" and "lieutenant," respectively. "Ensign" has been used for *Fähnrich*.

14. Braun, *1797–1802 MS*, pp. 12, 117–21.

15. Ibid., pp. 123–25; Williams to Thugut, Venice, 14 November 1798, Vienna, Haus- Hof- und Staatsarchiv, Staatskanzlei (hereafter cited as HHSA, StK.), Notenwechsel HKR, Carton 293, fol. 177–91.

16. Braun, *1797–1802 MS*, pp. 126–28; Williams, "Specificierter Ausweis," Venice, 24 June 1798, HHSA, StK., Notenwechsel HKR, Carton 293, fol. 194, and "Dislocations-Tabelle," same date, ibid., fol. 195; Williams to Thugut, 14 November 1798, ibid., fol. 177–91.

17. Zach to Count Louis Folliot de Crenneville, n.p., May 1798, quoted in Braun, *1797–1802 MS*, p. 134. Austria owned no Adriatic islands prior to Campoformio.

18. Ibid., p. 383; petition to Francis, Trieste, 22 December 1799, Vienna, Hofkammerarchiv, Kommerz, 4. Litorale 1749–1813, (hereafter cited as HKA, Kommerz, 4.), Fasc. 134 (no. 687).

19. Williams, "Specificierter Ausweis" and "Dislocations-Tabelle."

20. Quoted in Braun, *1797–1802 MS*, pp. 164–65.
21. See Lehnert, *1797–1802*, pp. 289–94, and Hugh Ragsdale, *Détente in the Napoleonic Era: Bonaparte and the Russians* (Lawrence, Kans.: The Regents Press of Kansas, 1980), p. 52.
22. Gunther E. Rothenberg, *Napoleon's Great Adversaries: The Archduke Charles and the Austrian Army, 1792–1814* (Bloomington: Indiana University Press, 1982), p. 67.
23. Lehnert, *1797–1802*, p. 356; Artur von Khuepach, *Geschichte der k.u.k. Kriegsmarine,* part 2: *Die k.k. österreichische Kriegsmarine in dem Zeitraume von 1797 bis 1848,* vol. 2: *Geschichte der k.k. Kriegsmarine während der Jahre 1802 bis 1814* (Vienna: Staatsdruckerei Wien, 1942), p. 17.
24. Champagny (French ambassador) to Ludwig Cobenzl, Vienna, 28 frimaire X (18 December 1801), HKA, Kommerz, 4., Fasc. 135 (no. 690), fol. 137–38.
25. Figures from anonymous report on trade of Trieste, dated 14 December 1802, HKA, Kommerz, 4., Fasc. 39 (no. 537). In 1803 Trieste's trade reached a record value of seventy-five million florins. See Fulvio Babudieri, *Industrie, commerci e navigazione a Trieste e nella regione Giulia* (Milan: Dott A. Giuffré Editore, 1982), p. 125.
26. Statistics compiled from Khuepach, *1802–1814,* pp. 294–317 and KA, Nachlass Folliot de Crenneville, B/216, no. 3, fol. 118–21. The Austrian navy did not compile statistics of the nationality of its officers and men until the 1880s. Figures cited here and in subsequent chapters are based on rosters of officers in various published and unpublished sources, the ethnic groupings deduced from surname and place of birth. In some cases personnel records were consulted to determine the languages spoken by the officer in question.
27. Peter Salcher, *Geschichte der k.u.k. Marine-Akademie* (Pola: Carl Gerold's Sohn, 1902), p. 40.
28. Braun, *1797–1802 MS,* p. 78.
29. Khuepach, *1802–1814,* pp. 51–60; Mogniat de Pouilly to Crenneville, Tangier, letters of 13–14 June 1805 and 15 August 1805, KA, Nachlass Folliot de Crenneville, B/216, no. 6, fol. 160–1, 163–7.
30. Count Carl Palffy (Hungarian court chancellor) to Hofkammer, Vienna, 19 October 1803, ibid., fol. 242–75; Sebastian Alberti, (captain of port of Cattaro) to Hofkammer, Cattaro, 26 November 1803, ibid., fol. 503–29; and Federigo Carlo d'Assezky to Hofkammer, Trieste, 3 June 1803, HKA, Kommerz, 4., Fasc. 110

(no. 624), fol. 507–25, give extensive reports on the merchantmen of the Croatian littoral, the Bocche di Cattaro, and Trieste and Rijeka, respectively.

31. Charles to Ludwig Cobenzl, Vienna, 17 November 1804, HKA, Kommerz, 4., Fasc. 109 (no. 622), fol. 1087–88; Charles to Count Karl Zichy (HKR president), Vienna, 28 February 1805, ibid., Fasc. 135 (no. 690), fol. 778; Philipp Cobenzl to Count Franz Colloredo, Paris, 20 March 1805, ibid., fol. 810.

32. Crenneville, "Projet sur la défense maritime de Venise," (n.d.—1804 or 1805), KA, Nachlass Folliot de Crenneville, B/216, no. 9, fol. 183–212; Crenneville to Count Maximilian Baillet de Latour (HKR president), Venice, 6 July 1805, ibid., fol. 233–36; Crenneville to HKR, Vienna, 28 August 1805, B/216, no. 11, fol. 277–78.

33. Piers Mackesy, *The War in the Mediterranean, 1803–1810* (Cambridge, Mass.: Harvard University Press, 1957), p. 84; Count Andreas Razumovsky to Ludwig Cobenzl, Vienna, 7 October 1805, HKA, Kommerz, 4., Fasc. 109 (no. 622), fol. 1533–34.

34. Khuepach, *1802–1814,* pp. 108–9; Mackesy, *War in the Mediterranean,* pp. 80, 83; HKR to Trieste Gubernium, Vienna, 7 November 1805, HKA, Kommerz, 4., Fasc. 135 (no. 690), fol. 938–41.

35. Khuepach, *1802–1814,* pp. 132–33. In addition to losing her Venetian inheritance, Austria also ceded the Tyrol to Bavaria.

36. Ibid., pp. 133–34.

37. Charles to Stadion, Vienna, 23 March 1806, in ibid., p. 177.

38. Khuepach, *1802–1814,* pp. 181–83; figures on commerce from Ludwig Cobenzl to Hofkammer, Vienna, 22 April 1804, HKA, Kommerz, 4., Fasc. 125 (no. 673), fol. 213, and P. S. Thom (consul-general) to Hofkammer, Odessa, 30 November 1806, ibid., fol. 470.

39. Khuepach, *1802–1814,* pp. 158–67.

40. See D. Fedotoff White, "The Russian Navy in Trieste During the Wars of the Revolution and the Empire," *American Slavic and East European Review* 6, no. 18–19 (1947): 33–34.

41. Antonio de Giuliani (commercial chargé, Trieste) to Francis, Vienna, 17 January 1808, HKA, Kommerz, 4., Fasc. 135 (no. 690), fol. 1125. Trade figures for 1809 from Tamaro, *Storia di Trieste,* 2:213.

42. Khuepach, *1802–1814,* pp. 192, 214–217.

43. Capt. William Hoste to his father, off Lucie [sic] 4 June 1809, *Memoirs and Letters of Capt. Sir William Hoste,* 2 vols. (London:

Richard Bentley, 1833), 1:338; Mackesy, *War in the Mediterranean*, pp. 321–23.

44. Italy received the southern Tyrol, since 1805 the property of Bavaria, as compensation for the losses; Bavaria received Salzburg.

45. Khuepach, *1802–1814,* pp. 241–42; Hoste to father, off Lussin, 15 November 1809, *Memoirs and Letters*, 2:8. The Russian warships at Trieste fell into French hands, but aside from one corvette the vessels were beyond repair and had to be scrapped. Their crews were finally repatriated to Russia in March 1810, after spending two and a half years in Trieste. See White, "The Russian Navy in Trieste," p. 40.

46. Khuepach, *1802–1814,* pp. 242–43; statistics compiled from appendix of same, pp. 406–25.

CHAPTER

2

Austria Returns to the Sea

The Peace of Pressburg was more of a watershed for the Adriatic region and Austria's maritime interests than the Peace of Schönbrunn. After 1805 the Habsburgs retained a small foothold on the sea but also saw almost all of their navy pass into the hands of the Napoleonic kingdom of Italy. It was this fleet, vastly improved and expanded, that Austria reacquired in 1814 to provide the basis for a new start as a sea power. Because most of the personnel, all of the materiel, and much of the character of the post-1814 Habsburg fleet were inherited from Napoleon's royal Italian navy, it was in many ways the true precursor of the Austrian navy.[1]

The Reconquest (1813–1814)

For Austria, Napoleon's Russian debacle made a return to war with France no longer unthinkable. Count Clemens von Metternich, minister of foreign affairs since 1809, temporarily kept the Habsburg Empire out of the struggle, refusing to join Russia and Prussia in the spring of 1813 for the campaign in Germany. Instead, he worked toward a general armistice, signed by the belligerents in early June, then offered armed mediation.[2] It was a courageous course when one considers that Austria had only just emerged from bankruptcy; her finances and resources were exhausted; and her military strength, despite almost four years of peace, left much to be desired. Metternich, wary of replacing French continental hegemony with Russian, sought to negotiate Napoleon out of central Europe while buying more time for Austria, and the allies in general, to organize for a renewal of warfare.

Like his predecessors, Metternich thought first and foremost in terms of Germany; however, he did not ignore the importance of the littoral and the sea. Throughout his first years as foreign minister he repeatedly raised the question of the restoration of an Austrian outlet to the Adriatic, and during the course of the armed mediation he demanded the Illyrian provinces as partial payment for an Austrian intervention on the side of France. Metternich made his first overtures on the matter in July 1810 while in Paris following the wedding of Napoleon and the Archduchess Marie Louise. Napoleon, in the spirit of the moment, assured him that "all can be restored; these points are not worth a hair to me," but proceeded to offer only the annexation of Serbia.[3] The foreign minister later succeeded in gaining a commercial mission for Austria at Rijeka but lamented that Trieste was "destined to ruin" because of the French intention to make the city "an exclusively military post."[4] In December 1811 Napoleon, eager for Austrian help in his upcoming campaign against Russia, conceded that "Illyria must sooner or later go back to Austria; the port of Trieste is necessary to her; they can, therefore, serve for matters of exchange." Under the Franco-Austrian treaty of 14 March 1812, which provided a Habsburg auxiliary corps for Napoleon's Grand Army, Austria secured the option to trade Galicia for Illyria at any time.[5] In the summer of 1813, however, the French emperor reacted so harshly to Metternich's demands for Illyria that the foreign minister did not include the province in his final peace proposal, although he did reserve for Austria the right to claim it in a future, general settlement.[6]

Well before the expiration of the armistice on 10 August, it became clear that France would not be brought to terms. Austrian preparations for war proceeded in earnest, and with the archdukes Charles and John both out of favor, Emperor

Francis appointed Field Marshal Prince Karl zu Schwarzenberg to head Austria's main field army in Bohemia. Thanks to Metternich's insistence, the prince was also named supreme allied commander. Meanwhile, in the south, *Feldmarschalleutnant* Baron Johann Hiller took charge of a 70,000-man army in Inner Austria. His objectives, like his forces, were far more modest than Schwarzenberg's: he was to protect the existing southwestern border of the Habsburg Empire, avoid at all costs a clash in the Alps with the Bavarians (whose defection to the coalition was a key element in Metternich's strategy) and, if possible, reconquer territories lost in 1809.

One of Hiller's subordinate commanders, Major General Count Laval Nugent, called for a major push to the Adriatic as soon as hostilities began. An Irish émigré with years of service under Habsburg colors, Nugent had the support and respect of the British, with whom he had corresponded largely on his own initiative since early 1813, proposing various schemes to subvert French rule in the Illyrian provinces. Hiller, however, did not attach much importance to a drive toward the coast and refused to commit troops to it on the grounds that it would leave his main army too weak against the Franco-Italian forces in Venetia. He placated Nugent by sending him along with a detached corps to retake Croatia.[7]

The kingdom of Italy, exhausted by years of contributing to Napoleon's legions, was hardly capable of a war effort worthy of Hiller's fears. The viceroy, Prince Eugene de Beauharnais, resolved to defend the line of the Julian Alps with 57,000 inexperienced troops, but his bold confidence on land had no counterpart at sea. The Franco-Italian fleet, largely inactive since the beginning of 1812, remained in harbor throughout the campaign despite having four new ships of the line completed and ready for action.[8] Meanwhile, a British squadron under Rear Admiral Thomas Fremantle recaptured several of the Dalmatian islands and launched a raid on Rijeka before Austria even entered the war. France's shaky hold on the eastern Adriatic littoral collapsed completely as soon as the continental armistice expired. The detached Austrian corps made such easy progress in Croatia that Nugent decided to disobey Hiller's orders and press on immediately to the Adriatic coast. On 26 August, after a three-day march, a small detachment from his brigade reached Porto Ré unopposed; later the same day, the Austrians entered Rijeka.

At the end of the month, Habsburg troops occupied the city of Trieste and besieged its citadel. Count L'Espine, recently promoted to *Feldmarschalleutnant,* came to the littoral shortly thereafter to take over the "leadership of naval affairs." The pace of the campaign slowed after the first two weeks, when Eugene's stubborn resistance in the Alps forced Nugent and the detached corps to move inland to support Hiller. With all other resources committed to the showdown with Napoleon in Saxony or to coordinating operations with the British to retake Dalmatia (now completely isolated from the rest of the French empire), little more could be done in Trieste or Rijeka.

Once the allied victory at Leipzig (16–19 October) relieved most of the tension in Vienna, the president of the *Hofkriegsrat,* Field Marshal Count Heinrich Bellegarde, fired the lethargic Hiller and personally took command in the southern theater. By then, Bavaria's defection from the Napoleonic cause had compromised Eugene's left flank, and Joachim Murat's negotiations to bring Naples over to the allies were threatening to do the same to his right. The viceroy retreated to the Adige, leaving the entire Veneto in Austrian hands. Habsburg troops laid siege to Venice from the land side, complementing a British naval blockade that had been in place since early October.

On 29 October the citadel of Trieste finally capitulated, outdueled by the guns of Fremantle's ships of the line. The end of the two-month siege enabled L'Espine at last to start building a new Austrian navy. Nugent soon joined him in Trieste to supervise the arming of four small gunboats, which on 14 November participated in an Anglo-Austrian amphibious landing at Goro on the Italian Adriatic coast south of the mouths of the Po. A modest mission, escorted the entire way by British warships, it nevertheless marked the return to the high seas of the Austrian flag.[9]

Lacking materiel, trained personnel, and the cooperation and confidence of his British counterparts, L'Espine subsequently encountered obstacles on almost every front. In evacuating Rijeka and Trieste, the French destroyed or sold to local merchants most of the ships, boats and naval stores that might have been of use to him, and the Austrian provisional governor of Illyria, *Feldmarschalleutnant* Baron Christian Lattermann, sought to sell the rest in order to raise funds for his own administration. The Austrian army, meanwhile, was reluctant to grant transfers to former officers of the "Second Trieste navy," many of whom, as members of the *Pontonierbataillon*, currently were responsible for getting Schwarzenberg's troops across the major rivers of Germany. To make matters worse, the British, remembering Commodore Hargood's experience in 1809, were skeptical of both the efficacy of an Austrian navy and the choice of L'Espine as commander.[10]

The British were the greatest of L'Espine's problems, at least according to A. L. Adamić. A wealthy Austrophile merchant and, by virtue of his position in the timber export trade of Rijeka, an invaluable source of information for Vienna, Adamić reported in December 1813 that "the nomination of General L'Espine to the command of Trieste has not pleased the Rear Admiral [Fremantle]." The British commander's main complaints concerned the *Marine-Kommandant*'s "French origin" and the fact that he "got along very poorly in the last war [1809] with Commodore Hargood." Fremantle "would have preferred to give to Colonel Konig [August de Conninck, commander of the *Pontonierbataillon*] the command of the navy, and to General L'Espine that of the city [fortress] of Trieste." Vienna did not immediately abide by Fremantle's wishes, but soon had to recognize that he was the true power broker in the Adriatic. Without the broadsides of his ships of the line, Austrian land assaults against the French fortresses of Dalmatia would be futile, and without the approval or cooperation of the Royal Navy, it would be impossible for an Austrian navy to return to the seas. Fremantle punctuated his views on L'Espine by conceding nothing to the Austrians following the capture of Zara (Zadar) in December. Adamić noted that "the English seized everything which could be of use to the navy" and delivered the gloomy prediction that "the same will happen in Ragusa and, in time, in Ancona and Venice."[11]

Emperor Francis, determined to do nothing that might compromise the future terms of peace, refused to take formal steps to reestablish the navy until Austria officially regained her coastline by treaty. This suspended for a time the question of L'Espine's fate. Over the winter of 1813–14 the *Marine-Kommandant* busied himself by organizing flotillas on the Po and Lake Garda in support of Bellegarde's army, still deployed along the Adige pending the outcome of diplomatic efforts to secure Eugene's defection to the allies. Beauharnais refused the overtures, however, even as Murat's desertion, in January 1814, took Naples into the allied ranks and virtually sealed the fate of the Napoleonic kingdom of Italy. In February Bellegarde resumed the campaign, took Verona, and forced Eugene to withdraw to Lombardy. Meanwhile Murat's Neapolitans, within weeks of changing sides, occupied most of central Italy, including the port of Ancona. The Austrians overestimated Eugene's ability to make a last stand and decided to invade Lombardy only in league with Murat. On 15 April, more than two weeks after Napoleon's defeat in France, the Neapolitans crossed the Po and entered southern Lombardy. The following day, at Schiarino Rizzino on the outskirts of Mantua, Eugene concluded an armistice.

Under the terms of the agreement the viceroy promised to return all of his French troops to France. His Italian forces were to remain in occupation of all territory not yet taken by the Austrian or Neapolitan armies (i.e., most of Lombardy). Isolated garrisons still holding out in Venetia (including Venice itself) were to surrender to the Austrians no later than 20 April. After the armistice was concluded the French naval commander in Venice, Vice Admiral Guy Duperré, noted that it did not specifically require him to surrender his ships. The Austrian negotiators, eager to avoid a repetition of the destruction of resources that had occurred in Venice after the Treaty of Campoformio, quickly drafted an additional article binding the French and Italians to turn over intact the forts, ships, and naval stores of the city. The first Austrian troops entered Venice on the twenty-second, and L'Espine arrived from Trieste the following day.[12]

The people of Venice, for seven months blockaded and besieged to the brink of starvation, welcomed the Austrians enthusiastically. The *Marine-Kommandant* found the Franco-Italian fleet in good order with many recently built ships of the line and frigates afloat in the lagoon and more vessels under construction in the Arsenal. In the weeks to come, however, the personnel, not the materiel, of the defunct Italian navy were to cause him the most headaches. Pending a general peace settlement, Schiarino Rizzino had preserved for Eugene a landlocked rump of the kingdom of Italy, including his capital, Milan. The additional article had called for the evacuation from Venice of all Italian as well as French naval personnel, the Italians to be transported up the Po and deposited behind the viceroy's lines in Lombardy. But on 20 April a revolt in Milan toppled Eugene's government and three days later, as L'Espine entered Venice, Bellegarde began to occupy the remainder of Lombardy. The Austrians entered Milan and restored order in the name of the allies, after which the viceroy renounced all claims to the kingdom and gave up his efforts to save the Italian crown. The personnel of the Italian navy never left Venice; having gone for several months without pay, they soon besieged L'Espine with appeals for pensions, salaries, and admission to Austrian service. The *Marine-Kommandant*, deprived of the full confidence of the emperor by the ill-concealed British displeasure over his appointment, set about the most difficult task of his career—incorporating the Italian navy into the Austrian or, more accurately, making an Austrian navy out of the Italian.

The Italian Inheritance: Personnel

Austria handled her reacquisition of a fleet in a haphazard manner reminiscent of her past record in naval affairs. L'Espine, embarking upon a process that was to determine the character of the service for decades to come, received no concrete guidelines from the government. Consequently, during his first weeks in Venice he merely took inventory of the ships and naval stores on hand and compiled lists of the Italian naval officers and administrators applying for positions in the Austrian service. The *Marine-Kommandant* personally felt these petitioners would be of little use to the new Habsburg navy, in part because his own efforts to obtain the transfers of old officers of the "Second Trieste navy" had finally started to bear fruit. He had no such doubts, however, about the rank and file of the defunct Italian navy and took their loyalty and utility for granted. At the end of April, in a hastily organized mustering out ceremony, the seamen dutifully recited the oath to the emperor in what could not have been a comforting sight, even to the most optimistic of observers. The total inactivity of the Italian navy during the last several months of the war had taken its toll on the appearance and military bearing of the crews. Though mostly Italian, their ranks included Frenchmen as well as a hodge-podge of conscripts from all over the former Napoleonic empire. To make matters worse, owing to a somewhat comical oversight, many of the seamen professed their new allegiance to the Habsburgs while sporting the red-white-green Italian cockade in their caps.[13]

The crews of the fleet were built primarily from personnel on hand in Venice but soon included large numbers of Croatians and Dalmatians whose reliability, unfortunately, was no more certain than that of the Italian veterans. In May 1814 the governor of Illyria, Baron Lattermann, began to press for the repatriation of the "significant number of Illyrians" taken into French service between 1809 and 1813 "mainly to serve on the French fleet at Toulon."[14] After their return to the littoral, many of these men found work in the rebuilding Adriatic merchant marine; others were taken directly into the Austrian navy. Habsburg officials apparently had no doubts about their loyalty.

As L'Espine set about the tasks of manning his ships and sifting through the petitions of ex-Italian officers, concerns in Vienna over his suitability for the job continued to undermine his authority. Keenly aware of British displeasure with the French *Marine-Kommandant,* the *Hofkriegsrat* finally resolved to replace him with Colonel August de Conninck, Admiral Fremantle's original choice for the position. A direct clash with Fremantle early in 1814 over the occupation of Cattaro was most likely the single event that sealed L'Espine's fate. Too young for retirement, he was reassigned to an army command in Galicia.[15]

In July 1814 Conninck formally assumed the duties of *Marine-Kommandant*. The issue of British approval aside, his experience made him the most logical candidate for the job. He had spent twenty-four years with the Austrian navy after coming to the Adriatic in 1786 as one of the original six officers of Joseph II's "Trieste navy." Conninck worked his way up to second-in-command during the years of the "Second Trieste navy" and on several occasions served as acting commander. He had headed the army's *Pontonierbataillon* from 1810 until earlier in 1814, when he was transferred to the littoral as a supervisor of shipbuilding. Since the Austrian navy had no senior naval ranks (such as admiral), Conninck, upon taking command, received a promotion to Major General.

The new *Marine-Kommandant* continued L'Espine's efforts to organize the navy, handicapped, as his predecessor had been, by indecision in Vienna over the size and scope of operations of the new fleet. The officer corps proved to be his biggest problem, reflecting the fact that by absorbing the former Italian navy, or in a sense being absorbed by it, the Austrian navy had acquired an Italian character even more overwhelming than that of earlier years. Gone were the trusted French émigrés, and because German Austria had been cut off from the sea in recent years, the number of Germans was as small as ever, alarmingly so among the younger officers. Notwithstanding L'Espine's earlier efforts, in 1817, the first postwar year for which statistics can be compiled, only about one-fourth of Conninck's 105 officers were veterans of the "Second Trieste navy." The rest had served in at least one non-Austrian navy, most of them in the Italian, and a quarter of the whole had changed allegiance a remarkable number of times during the past two decades: from the Venetian navy to the Austrian, to the Italian, and then back again to the Austrian. Italians made up 73 percent of the sea officers, South Slavs 18 percent, Germans a mere 5 percent. Of forty-five cadets, 62 percent were Italian and none German. In the land-based branches of the service—naval infantry, engineering and artillery—80 percent of the officers were Italian and none German.[16]

Conninck introduced German as the official written language of the navy but made no effort to "germanize" the service. Italian remained the language of command and of education, since the Austrians took over the Italian naval academy (founded by the French in 1810) virtually intact. A proposal in 1814 to introduce German there as an elective course was hardly the harbinger of an anti-Italian campaign; its proponents merely argued that the Italian-speaking students should learn German in order to facilitate future cooperation with the army.[17] Indeed, friction in the early post-Napoleonic navy was not between the Italians and German Austrians, but rather between the veterans of the "Second Trieste navy" and those taken in from the Italian navy, in particular the ex-Venetian officers who had served the Habsburgs between 1798 and 1806.

The controversy, cutting across lines of nationality and rank, stemmed from the government's decision to give seniority at every grade to the officers of the "Second Trieste navy." Eager to reward the men whose loyalty in the dark days after Schönbrunn had so moved the emperor, Vienna snubbed the officers who had passed into the Italian service from 1806 to

1814 and in many cases subordinated them to men who had once been their subalterns. The case of Conninck himself provides the best example of the implications of this seniority policy. Prior to 1806 he held a captain's commission, as did former Venetian officers Sylvestro Dandolo and Nicolo Pasqualigo, but ranked behind them on the seniority list drawn up after Campoformio. Dandolo and Pasqualigo then advanced to the roles of first and second in command, respectively, before the Treaty of Pressburg and their transfer to the Franco-Italian fleet. Upon returning to Austrian service, Dandolo and Pasqualigo were offered captain's rank and seniority inferior not only to Conninck but also to another Trieste veteran, Captain Matthew Flanegan, even though both men had been their subordinates in earlier years.

The Austrians, understandably, considered it the height of arrogance for these officers to expect their seniority to include years in which they had served in an enemy fleet, while the Italians could argue with equal justification that the terms of Pressburg had *required* their departure from Austrian service and that their transfers to the Italian navy were anything but voluntary. For Dandolo, whose loyalties the French apparently always doubted, the ruling was especially hard to accept, and, to make matters worse, it became clear from the outset that Conninck lacked the tact to handle this delicate situation. As early as January 1815 the *Hofkriegsrat* received reports of discontent with the new *Marine-Kommandant*, whose prowess in technical and theoretical matters failed to compensate for his lack of practical knowledge or insight into how to lead the navy through the difficult times ahead. Among other things, Conninck was criticized for his failure to explain adequately to the corps the "system of economy" under which the postwar navy was to be run.[18] The resulting misunderstandings over pay only exacerbated the bitterness of the former Italian officers.

In the first few years of their return to the littoral, the Austrians unwittingly laid the groundwork for the unreliability and disloyalty that were to paralyze the navy three decades later. Approaching the problem of personnel with no clear plan, they managed to alienate a significant number of Italians without accomplishing, or even attempting, a "de-italianization" of the service. In matters of education and administration, temporary measures were allowed to become permanent, enshrining the haphazard decisions of the immediate postwar months. But despite the bitter rivalry between Conninck's "Trieste" cohorts and the senior Venetian officers, the latter never wavered in their loyalty to the Habsburg crown. Pasqualigo, a genuine fighting seaman, was always a credit to the navy, and Dandolo, a true Venetian aristocrat, was guided throughout his long career by an impeccable sense of honor. At a time when Carbonari activity was casting a shadow over Italians in the army officer corps, navy men of the same generation, rank, and nationality showed no interest in revolutionary activity.[19]

The same was not to be true of the younger officers taken in from the Italian navy. As of 1817, about one-fourth of the entire officer corps consisted of men whose first commissions had been granted in the Franco-Italian fleet. Some had been cadets in the Austrian navy in the years between Campoformio and Pressburg, but most had never before served the Habsburgs and in 1814 were swearing allegiance to the emperor for the first time. They were to conduct their careers by their own code of honor, with no special feelings of loyalty toward Austria, and were anything but a credit to the navy when it faced its darkest hours thirty years later.

The Italian Inheritance: Materiel

In contrast to the personnel, the quality of the materiel inherited from the Franco-Italian fleet left little to be desired. There were ten ships of the line, eight frigates, over a dozen brigs, and countless gunboats and other craft. Of the larger vessels, however, all but four ships of the line and three frigates were still under construction.[20] Contrary to the predictions of Adamić, the British left the lot to the Austrians, claiming nothing for themselves. The spoils of 1814 were only slightly more than those of 1797 but potentially of much greater use since virtually the entire fleet had been built within the past eight years. The ships were an excellent base for the future of the navy, but the fact that there were far too many of them for Austria's needs led immediately to speculation and negotiation about their sale.

Count Stadion, since 1813 finance minister of the Austrian Empire, led the opposition to a large fleet. Other proponents of a smaller navy called for a force no larger than the Habsburg navy of 1804, the last peacetime year in which Venice had belonged to the empire. Francis at first seemed to favor a small navy or, at any rate, the sale of some of the larger ships. Metternich, eager to accommodate his wishes, in April 1814 arranged to sell to Denmark three ships of the line and one frigate. To facilitate a quick sale he proposed to accept 3,000 Holstein cavalry mounts as partial payment. The parties reached an oral agreement, but the king of Denmark, upon arriving in Vienna for the postwar congress, backed out on the deal. The Danish scheme was only the first of many attempts to sell vessels deemed superfluous by Vienna, but it was the only time that the government offered to trade warships for horses.[21]

There was no doubt about the need for some sort of navy. Without a fleet, Austria could not defend or even communicate with Dalmatia and its islands, and Habsburg commerce at sea would be as helpless as it had been before. As early as May 1814 the merchants of Trieste were reporting losses at the hands of the pirates of Algiers and Tripoli. The Austrian governor of Illyria complained on their behalf that an inquiry to the *Marine-Kommandant* had found that "the sailing of larger armed ships, in defense of Austrian trade, at present is not yet under discussion." Yet the return to sea was no simple matter since Austria had to weigh all factors, including the feelings of Great Britain. Adamić of Rijeka, while receptive to any efforts that would help to protect commerce, advocated the sale of some of the naval inheritance, noting that "the Arsenal of Venice presents a treasure, the plenty of which can be realized to the favor of the Austrian finances. . . ." He believed the empire could meet its needs by maintaining "a ship of the line with three frigates and three brigs, without entangling itself in major expenses and *Gelosie di Navigazione*."[22] Even though the British had not interfered in the surrender of Venice, Adamić feared that they would not approve of a larger Austrian navy. Given Britain's unquestioned control of the seas, any open disagreement on the issue would be detrimental to the future development of Habsburg sea power.

Once the Congress of Vienna left Austria formally in possession of the original gains of Campoformio, plus Lombardy, Francis finally permitted serious discussion of the fate of the navy. In 1815 a *Hofkriegsrat* commission recommended a fleet with a core of three frigates and three brigs to cruise the Mediterranean and four brigs or schooners for the Adriatic. Two brigs would perform harbor-watch duty and another would be kept in reserve at Venice.[23] Metternich and Stadion responded by rejecting a role for the navy outside the Adriatic. The foreign minister firmly believed that the British navy could be counted upon to defend Austrian interests overseas. When Britain gained a protectorate over the Ionian Islands in the postwar settlement and, consequently, the ability to close the mouth of the Adriatic with little difficulty, he dismissed the notion that this would be detrimental to Austrian strategic interests. "In what case would we ever find ourselves in a collision *at sea* with England?" he asked incredulously.[24] If Austria went to war allied with Britain, she would not need a navy of her own, and if she went to war against Britain, a challenge at sea would be out of the question. Stadion likewise observed that the British protectorate over the Ionians effectively made the Royal Navy "master of the Adriatic." Echoing both Metternich's confidence in Britain and Adamić's concern that Austria do nothing to offend her, the finance minister reasoned that since it was beyond the capabilities of the empire ever to build a navy stronger than Britain's, it would be "politically and militarily compromising" to maintain anything larger than a coastal flotilla.[25]

Swayed by these arguments, the emperor in February 1816 decreed that the navy should have only five brigs in service in peacetime, three to cruise the Adriatic and two for harbor-watch duties, along with several smaller coastal vessels. The two best frigates and another three brigs were to be disarmed and maintained in the Arsenal as a reserve force, and all other ships sold. The navy escaped this "death sentence" when the new president of the *Hofkriegsrat*, Prince Schwarzenberg, intervened and urged the emperor to reconsider his decision. In January 1817 Francis relented and raised the authorized active strength of the navy to two frigates and eight brigs, with a third frigate in reserve, thirty-three smaller vessels to patrol the coast, and additional gunboats to defend the lagoon at Venice.[26] The emperor did not set specific limits for future naval operations and, by authorizing a force larger than what was needed solely to police the Adriatic, left open the possibility of a Mediterranean role.

Like Archduke Charles before him, Prince Schwarzenberg viewed the navy as a branch of the common armed forces rather than a competing service. He interceded on its behalf and lobbied for a larger fleet with much the same conviction that he would have for a stronger army. Like Charles, he lacked personal experience with naval matters, and the duties of his office required him to devote most of his attention to the army. But Schwarzenberg's sympathy for the navy reflected a breadth of vision rare among Habsburg military leaders of his time. Unfortunately, his role as protector of the fleet was cut short by his early death in 1820. Future *Hofkriegsrat* presidents would not always share his views on the utility of sea power.

Even after the navy won its reprieve, Austria still had plenty of ships to sell: all of her ships of the line (eight, after two were destroyed by fire at Venice in the fall of 1814) and over half a dozen frigates. Most of the surplus brigs were sold locally in the Adriatic in advance of Francis's final decision. After Metternich's Danish deal collapsed at the Congress of Vienna, offers for the larger ships were solicited from Britain, Spain, Holland, Portugal, the United States, Sardinia-Piedmont, and even the Papacy. In addition to the general postwar austerity in military spending, a major problem in selling the vessels was that most of them were still under construction. Prospective buyers wanted finished ships, and completing the work would cost Austria a considerable amount of money. For example, the eight ships of the line were valued in 1815 at 5,474,900 florins, but appraisers estimated that readying them for sale would take an additional 3,382,167 florins, a sum almost three times the navy's entire budget of 1,171,195 florins and far more than the government was willing to spend on the project.[27]

Frequent changes in the emperor's attitude toward the navy only complicated Conninck's efforts to impose order on the material chaos of the Venice Arsenal. Neither Francis nor Metternich had any firm convictions about sea power, other than that Austria should leave its exercise, whenever possible, to the other great powers. In the first three postwar years the emperor made two extensive southern tours, from October 1815 to May 1816 in Italy and the Croatian littoral, and from February to May 1818 to the Croatian coastline and Dalmatia. On both occasions he came into close contact with the navy and the sea, and on the second trip he even seemed to develop an interest in maritime affairs. On another visit to Italy in 1819, Francis conducted inspection tours of the harbors of Venice and Naples, the latter including visits to British and American ships of the line anchored in the port. The emperor seemed impressed, but, as before, any interest he may have felt at the time failed to evolve into genuine enthusiasm. Afterward, he did nothing to raise the limits of his decree of January 1817 or stop the sale of the ships at Venice.[28]

After the failure of the initial round of efforts to sell the ships, Metternich narrowed the scope of the campaign and pressed for a deal which, if not so lucrative financially, might achieve some constructive diplomatic end. By 1819 Spain, rebuilding her navy and struggling to retain her rebellious Latin American colonies, emerged as the leading prospective buyer. The wily Adamić of Rijeka, involved since 1816 in private schemes to purchase the ships for resale abroad, offered his services as an agent for the transaction. Arguing forcefully that Spain "really could make the best use" of the vessels, Adamić sought to prevent the financial problems of the Spanish government from wrecking the negotiations and even suggested that Vienna accept payment in kind—colonial goods from Mexico or elsewhere—in exchange for the ships.[29] Haggling over price and method of payment dragged on until early 1820 when Metternich, in the wake of the Spanish revolution, ordered a halt to the talks on the grounds that "in the present circumstances" a sale would be highly imprudent.[30]

In subsequent attempts to dispose of the ships, Austria weighed the political consequences as well as financial considerations. Metternich remained eager for a sale but did not hesitate to block one that might cause the vessels to fall into the wrong hands. In April 1820 he supported a proposal to sell the ships to Portugal, calling it perhaps the "last hope" for a deal, but acquiesced when the *Hofkriegsrat* advised against it.[31] Four months later, after the revolution in Naples had joined Spain on his growing list of concerns, the foreign minister rejected the offer of a Tuscan trading house to buy a ship of the line and two frigates, ostensibly for resale to Egypt, and noted that the volatile international situation precluded "unconditional sales" of ships to private firms.[32] The failure of the Tuscan bid marked the start of a year-long hiatus in the campaign to sell the surplus vessels, lasting until after Austria restored order in the Italian peninsula.

By 1821 the number of ships being marketed by Austria was dwindling. With the elements taking their toll on vessels under construction on uncovered slips, three of the six unfinished ships of the line had to be scrapped. Of the two completed ships of the line that survived the Arsenal fire of 1814, one was employed as the commander's flagship at Venice and the other stood at anchor, disarmed, in the Arsenal. Two frigates completed by the French were put to sea, and a third, finished in 1815, joined them to fill the quota of the imperial decree of January 1817. Four others, all still on the stocks, remained eligible for sale. In lieu of the prescribed eight brigs, the navy by 1818 had seven brigs and a corvette in service.

As the immediate postwar era came to a close, diplomatic considerations clearly overshadowed the question of ship sales. Metternich, for six years willing to approve any kind of deal, abruptly changed his tone when faced with the possibility that Austrian ships might end up in the hands of revolutionaries. Habsburg agents continued to have problems attracting buyers for ships still under construction, but the government, fearful of being left with finished vessels it could not use, stood by its policy of refusing to fund their completion. There remained, of course, the needs of the Austrian navy itself. In the years following 1814 the service demonstrated its utility in executing a variety of duties, slowly building a case for a fleet larger than the modest force Francis had authorized.

Expanding Horizons: The Navy and Merchant Marine (1814–1821)

Amid the uncertainty over Austria's postwar naval policy, the Habsburg fleet and the Adriatic merchant marine began putting ships to sea. In the months following the occupation of Venice, both expanded their sphere of operations; in a remarkably short period of time, they were sailing to parts of the world where the Austrian flag had never before appeared. The need to protect Habsburg merchantmen on the high seas and a new realization that the navy could be a valuable instrument of foreign policy helped fuel the debate over the importance of sea power in the empire's overall strategic concerns.

In the summer of 1814 a corvette and a brig were sent out to escort troop transports to the Bocche di Cattaro, the most distant of the Habsburg possessions in Dalmatia and the last to be occupied by Austrian forces. In the spring of 1815, after Napoleon's escape from Elba, the two ships and a half dozen smaller vessels formed a flotilla in the Adriatic under Captain Pasqualigo, the best seagoing commander in the service. As soon as Joachim Murat declared himself in favor of Napoleon, the ships began to prey upon Neapolitan commerce.

Fortunately for Austria, the renegade king's northward march, amid proclamations exhorting the people of Italy to rally around him and "liberate" the peninsula, had no similarly bold counterpart at sea. Fearing the overwhelming might of the British fleet, Murat made it clear that he did not wish to fight a naval war of any sort. In April 1815 he called for the Habsburg Empire to respect the freedom of commerce; in return for the release of ships taken by Pasqualigo, he promised to continue to respect the Austrian flag in Neapolitan ports and issue no letters of marque in the Adriatic.[33] Meanwhile, to support his advance on Lombardy and Venetia, he dispatched two frigates, a corvette, and a brig to the mouth of the Po, a location dangerously close to Venice. But malaria soon ravaged the Neapolitan crews and forced the squadron to withdraw to Ancona, where the British, assisted by Pasqualigo, kept it blockaded for the remainder of the war.[34]

After being stopped at the Po in early April, Murat withdrew to Ancona, then southward toward Naples. The retreat soon became a rout, and a hard Austrian pursuit brought the disintegration of the Neapolitan army. In mid-May Murat's ministers surrendered the rest of his fleet to a British squadron in Naples harbor; Austrian troops then entered the capital to pave the way for the restoration of the Bourbon King Ferdinand. Ironically, the triumph of Austrian arms on land had negative repercussions for the navy, overshadowing the modest activities of Pasqualigo's flotilla so completely that Vienna hardly took notice of its participation in the campaign. Despite the respectable showing at sea, the end of the Hundred Days brought a great reduction in the number of ships on active duty. The performance of the British fleet, which once again had carried the burden of the naval war, only reinforced the notions of Metternich, Stadion, and other Austrian leaders regarding the dispensability of Habsburg sea power.

Even after the British (in July 1815) returned the last of the Dalmatian islands to Austrian rule and withdrew their navy from the Adriatic, Vienna saw little need to fill the void with warships of her own. After 1809 the Royal Navy had supplemented its naval war against the French and Italians with a successful privateering campaign based on the island of Lissa (Vis) that, coming in the wake of the years of Austrian negligence, had all but destroyed the Adriatic merchant marine. The hundreds of damaged and destroyed ships represented a permanent loss of millions in invested capital and left fewer merchantmen flying the Austrian flag in 1814 than in 1805.[35] Thus, even though Austria's vessels were victimized by North African corsairs almost from the moment her flag returned to the high seas, her stake in the matter was deemed too small to warrant decisive action. In the immediate postwar years Vienna preferred to consider piracy an international rather than an Austrian problem and was content to let the larger naval powers of Europe take care of the North Africans. In the spring of 1816, when Britain invited Austria to participate in a blockade of the coast of Tripoli, the emperor declined on the grounds that the cost of the proposed Habsburg contingent would exceed the limits he had placed on naval spending.[36]

It took the marriage of an archduchess to persuade Francis to send Austrian frigates on an overseas mission. In the spring of 1817 his daughter Leopoldine was married by proxy to Dom Pedro, the heir to the throne of Portugal and future emperor of Brazil. Because the Braganzas had not yet returned to Lisbon from their colonial refuge of the Napoleonic years, the bride had to be delivered to Rio de Janeiro. The Portuguese navy had more than enough ships to accomplish the task, but Habsburg pride dictated that Austrian vessels make up at least part of the entourage.

The honors fell to Captain Pasqualigo and the warships *Austria* and *Augusta,* two of the three frigates put into service under the recent imperial decree. They reached their destination in November 1817, but only after absorbing considerable damages on a difficult four-month passage. The admirable behavior of the crewmen, both at sea and during their stay in Brazil, subsequently made the repair of the ships Pasqualigo's only real concern. The *Hofkriegsrat* at one point argued that the best solution would be to sell the two frigates to the Portuguese and have the crews transported home, but Portugal's refusal to buy the battered ships saved the remainder of the mission. Pasqualigo finally set sail for home in June 1818 and arrived at Venice three months later. Though entirely ceremonial in character, the voyage could be counted as a success. The Austrian flag made its first appearance in South American waters, the door was opened for future Austro-Brazilian trade, and, perhaps of greatest importance, the mission generated publicity and acclaim for the navy. Pasqualigo received several decorations and, the following year, the honor of escorting the emperor on his Italian tour.[37]

Shortly after the frigates returned from Brazil, plans were laid for a trade mission to China, the first for Austria since the collapse of Maria Theresa's East India Company in the mid-1780s. The disarmed frigate *Carolina* was chosen for the assignment, the command going to Captain Seraphim von Pöltl, a native of Graz and the first German Austrian to have reached captain's rank in the Habsburg navy. A naval officer since 1798, Pöltl spent the last years of the Napoleonic wars on special assignment with the British fleet and had probably logged more sea miles than anyone else in the corps. The *Carolina* left Trieste in September 1820 and proceeded to China via Rio de Janeiro, Capetown, and Singapore. Arriving off Canton after an eleven-month passage, the ship was denied permission to dock because the Chinese did not recognize its red-white-red flag, adopted by Joseph II only in 1787. In order to enter the port, Pöltl had to run up the old Habsburg standard, a black double-eagle on a gold field. After unloading half a million florins' worth of goods, including four tons of mercury, the most exotic raw material mined in the Austrian Empire, Pöltl set sail for home, leaving behind a permanent consul-general to facilitate future relations. The voyage of the *Carolina* would have been completely successful if not for the cholera that claimed the lives of many aboard, including the captain, who died in May 1822, a month before the ship reached Trieste.[38]

The opening of new markets helped bring the economy of the littoral back to life. In 1817 thirty-two million florins' worth of imports and exports passed through the port of Trieste, a dramatic improvement over the wartime low in 1813 of 2.4 million, but still well below 1789 levels.[39] Venice, once again denied the status of a free port, was slower to recover. During the emperor's visit to the city over the winter of 1815–16, Metternich raised the question of granting it such privileges, but the matter was soon dropped.[40] By the time Venice finally became a free port (in 1830), Trieste already had established itself as Austria's maritime commercial center.

Venice, meanwhile, remained the main base for the navy. The honor brought with it no fringe benefits since it was clear that Austria did not intend to maintain a fleet as large as that of the Napoleonic kingdom of Italy. The Venice Arsenal, bustling with activity during the war years, was transformed into a sullen resting place for the ships and hulks for which Vienna could find no buyer. The lot of the navy at sea was little better since aside from the cruises to Brazil and China, it did little after 1815 other than patrol the Adriatic.

In 1820, as the ambitious *Carolina* mission prepared to depart, the *Hofkriegsrat* forced upon the navy the rather humiliating chore of operating a packet-boat service between Trieste and Corfu (Kérkira). The new assignment came after Vienna reasoned that it would be cheaper to have the navy carry passengers and official mail to and from the Ionian Islands than to maintain enough warships to guarantee the safety of the route for unarmed packets which would have to be rented from private owners. The *Hofkriegsrat* ordered the navy to use brigs for the monthly runs, but after the first of the vessels capsized and sank off Zara, schooners handled the bulk of the service. The use of warships for the Trieste-Corfu packet duty set a precedent that was to prove hard to live down. For decades to come, the navy on numerous occasions was forced to acquiesce in having its ships used as ferries, packet-boats, or pleasure craft for dignitaries, withholding protest only because such duties were often the only alternative to rotting in port.

Over the summer of 1820, Austrian hostility toward the new liberal regime in Naples raised the possibility of a role for the navy in another war against the Neapolitans. After rebels forced Ferdinand I to grant a constitution, the governor of Venice, Count Carlo d'Inzaghy, expressed concern that merchant ships from Naples (a major trading partner of Austria) would be used to spread revolutionary Carbonari propaganda to Habsburg ports.[41] Metternich responded by declaring that ships flying the flag of "the insurgents in Naples" should not be recognized at sea by Austria.[42] Naval officials hastened to inform the foreign minister that the new policy would jeopardize Austro-Neapolitan relations, but his determination to use force to restore Ferdinand to full power soon made such observations irrelevant. In September, a month before the Congress of Troppau convened to discuss the situation, Francis ordered the preparation of a squadron for service against Naples, thus guaranteeing a place for the navy in the upcoming campaign.[43]

The return of Venice and the original gains of 1797 gave the Habsburg Empire a second chance to take advantage of strategic and commercial opportunities in the Adriatic. The addition of Lombardy, however, ensured that Austrian strategists concerned with the region would spend most of their time looking westward, away from the sea. Although Metternich's view of the littoral and its potential was not as narrow as Thugut's had been, he believed that Britain could be counted upon to protect Habsburg commerce at sea and took for granted that the British would defend Austria's coast as well. He would change his view only after the two powers experienced a definite parting of ways in their foreign policies.

Until then, Vienna's indecision made the role of Austrian sea power even more ambiguous than it had been in earlier years. On the surface, protection of seagoing trade was the main issue, but the devastating effects of war had left the ports of the Adriatic with far less native commerce for the restored navy to protect. In addition to dumping British goods and surplus Russian wheat on local markets, foreign merchantmen also assumed the bulk of the heavy carrying trade in the region. Showing the flag outside of the Adriatic, a new task for Habsburg warships, was hampered by Vienna's reluctance to maintain a fleet large enough to fill this more ambitious role. Meanwhile, the material gains from the former Franco-Italian fleet were handled only slightly better than the Venetian inheritance of 1797. Amid a negative postwar atmosphere in which the sale or disposal or "surplus" vessels was Austria's major concern, the navy continued to attract little attention as a potential auxiliary force to the army, despite having acquitted itself in the minor action against Murat's Neapolitans in the Italian campaign of 1815. The next phase of its history was to open with another sortie against the Neapolitan navy, this time with less pleasant results.

NOTES

1. Boxes 34 and 35 of the Papers of Prince Eugene de Beauharnais, Princeton University Library, contain the most com-

plete set of records of the navy of the Napoleonic kingdom of Italy and Napoleon's warship construction program at the Venice Arsenal.

2. On Metternich's armed mediation see Enno E. Kraehe, *Metternich's German Policy*, vol. 1: *The Contest with Napoleon, 1799–1814* (Princeton, N.J.: Princeton University Press, 1963), pp. 147–86.

3. Metternich to Francis, Paris, 9 July 1810, Clemens Lothar Wenzel von Metternich-Winneburg, *Memoirs of Prince Metternich*, ed. Prince Richard Metternich, trans. Mrs. Alexander Napier, 5 vols. (New York: Harper & Brothers, 1880–82), 1:595, no. 108.

4. Metternich to Francis, Paris, 5 September 1810, ibid., 614, no. 172.

5. Schwarzenberg interview with Napoleon, Paris, 17 December 1811, ibid., 657, no. 182; Kraehe, *German Policy*, 1:142–43.

6. Kraehe, *German Policy*, 1:180–81.

7. Khuepach, *1802–1814*, pp. 275–76; KA, Feldakten 1813, Fasc. 1: Feldzug in Istrien, Brigade Nugent I–X contains Nugent's correspondence with the British. Hoste, one of Nugent's greatest supporters, characterized him as "active, brave, and enterprising . . . and a very distinguished officer . . . equal to anything." See Hoste to father, Capo d'Istria, 22 September 1813, *Memoirs and Letters*, 2:175.

8. Eugene's navy fought its last battle in February 1812, losing the new ship of the line *Rivoli* in the upper Adriatic.

9. Nugent to Metternich, Trieste, n.d. (2d week of November 1813), HHSA, StK., Prov., Küstenland, Carton 4: Trieste, Varia 1723–1856, fol. 219–20; Khuepach, *1802–1814*, pp. 276–79.

10. Adamić to Hudelist, Rijeka, 22 December 1813, HHSA, StK., Prov., Küstenland, Carton 5: Fiume 1761–1846, fol. 3–4; Khuepach, *1802–1814*, p. 278.

11. Adamić to Hudelist, Rijeka, 22 December 1813, ibid.

12. For a text of Convention of Schiarino Rizzino see Artur von Khuepach and Heinrich von Bayer, *Geschichte der k.u.k. Kriegsmarine*, part 2: *Die k.k. österreichische Kriegsmarine in dem Zeitraum von 1797 bis 1848*, vol. 3: *Geschichte der k.k. Kriegsmarine während der Jahre 1814–1847* (Graz: Verlag Hermann Böhlaus Nachfolger, 1966), pp. 277–80.

13. Ibid., pp. 33, 41.

14. Lattermann to StK., Ljubljana, 5 May 1814, HHSA, StK., Prov., Illyrien, Carton 13: Illyrisches Gubernium, Korr. 1813–44, fol. 20–1.

15. L'Espine to Metternich, Trieste, 19 January 1814, HHSA, StK., Prov., Küstenland, Carton 2: Korr. Triester Guberniums 1797–1815, fol. 454–55, gives his account of the fall of Cattaro.
16. Statistics compiled from *Militär-Schematismus des österreichischen Kaiserthums* (1817).
17. Khuepach and Bayer, *1814–1847*, p. 47; Salcher, *Marine-Akademie*, p. 12.
18. (Anonymous report), Venice, 5 January 1815, KA, Hofkriegsrat Akten, Präsidialreihe (hereafter cited as HKR Akten, Präs.) 1815/8–11, fol. 2–3. The "Observations" in "Etat Nominatif des Officiers de la Marine Italienne," n.d. (1806–1808), The Papers of Prince Eugene Beauharnais, box 34, folder 5, charge Dandolo with "conduite susceptible."
19. See Hans Kramer, *Österreich und das Risorgimento* (Vienna: Bergland Verlag, 1963), pp. 198–99.
20. There has been some disagreement over the number of frigates inherited in 1814, the result of confusion over whether the ship *Carolina* was a frigate or a corvette. The most recent reappraisal is Karl Klaus Körner's "Die *Carolina* 1808–1832: Schicksal und Rekonstruktion," *Marine—Gestern, Heute: Die Zeitschrift der Arbeitsgemeinschaft für österreichische Marinegeschichte* 13 (1986). Journal cited hereafter as *MGH*.
21. Khuepach and Bayer, *1814–1847*, p. 61. Several sources contend that ships were indeed sold to Denmark.
22. Latterman to Hudelist, Ljubljana, 8 July 1814, HHSA, StK., Prov., Illyrien, Carton 13: Illyrisches Gubernium, Korr. 1813–44, fol. 38–45; Adamić to Hudelist, Rijeka, 10 May 1814, HHSA, StK., Prov., Küstenland, Carton 5: Fiume 1761–1846, fol. 11–12.
23. Khuepach and Bayer, *1814–1847*, p. 56.
24. Metternich to Hudelist, Venice, 16 December 1815, HHSA, StK., Acta secreta, Carton 1, no. 49. Underscoring in original.
25. Stadion to Francis, Vienna, 27 December 1815, in Khuepach and Bayer, *1814–1847*, pp. 65–66.
26. Khuepach and Bayer, *1814–1847*, pp. 66–70.
27. See Joseph Alexander Helfert, *Kaiser Franz I. von Österreich und die Stiftung des lombardo-venetianischen Königreichs* (Innsbruck: Verlag der Wagner'schen Universitäts-Buchhandlung, 1901), p. 411; Josef Fleischer, *Geschichte der k.u.k. Kriegsmarine,* part 2, vol. 2: *Die österreichisch-venetianische Kriegsmarine während der Jahre 1802–1848* (MS, Leitmeritz, 1911), KA, Ms/Ma 4, p. 42.

28. Khuepach and Bayer, *1814–1847*, pp. 169–76.
29. Adamić to Hudelist, Rijeka, 18 July 1816, HHSA, StK., Prov., Küstenland, Carton 5: Fiume 1761–1846, fol. 346–48; Adamić to Brenner, Rijeka, 6 March 1819, ibid., fol. 357.
30. Metternich to HKR, Vienna, 20 February 1820, KA, HKR Akten, Präs. 1820/134, fol. 2–3; HKR to StK., Vienna, 25 February 1820, ibid., fol. 1.
31. Metternich to HKR, Vienna, 8 April 1820, KA, HKR Akten, Präs. 1820/280, fol. 2–3; HKR to StK., Vienna, 11 April 1820, ibid., fol. 1.
32. Paulucci to HKR, Venice, 3 August 1820, KA, HKR Akten, Präs, 1820/600, fol. 2–3; Metternich to HKR, 25 August 1820, ibid., Präs. 1820/623, fol. 2–3.
33. Khuepach and Bayer, *1814–1847*, pp. 181–82; Murat's decree on commerce, Faenza, 17 April 1815, KA, HKR Akten, Präs. 1815/5–8, fol. 2.
34. Lamberto Radogna, *Storia della Marina Militare delle Due Sicilie (1734–1860)* (Mursia: U. Mursia editore S.p.A., 1978), pp. 70–71; Khuepach and Bayer, *1814–1847*, p. 182. Radogna contends that the British blockaded the ships at Brindisi, where they surrendered at the end of the war.
35. Igor Karaman, *Privreda i društvo: Hrvatske u 19. stoljeću* (Zagreb: Školska knjiga, 1972), p. 14. In 1814 the ocean-going Austrian merchant fleet numbered 504 ships, compared to 537 in 1805; see Khuepach and Bayer, *1814–1847*, p. 24.
36. Francis to Metternich, Vienna, 25 March 1816, quoted in Helfert, *Kaiser Franz I*, p. 411.
37. The Portuguese government praised the conduct of the Austrian sailors; "Trunkenheitsexzesse und Messerstechereien waren nicht vorgekommen," and hardly any of them deserted. See Khuepach and Bayer, *1814–1847*, pp. 182–85.
38. Körner, "Die *Carolina* 1808–1832," pp. 58–60; Frimont to Bellegarde, Naples, 24 June 1822, KA, HKR Akten, Präs. 1822/495, fol. 1–4. Owing to the need for an experienced crew with some knowledge of Portuguese, the trading language of the Far East, many veterans of Pasqualigo's trip to Brazil also went to China.
39. Figures from Tamaro, *Storia di Trieste*, 2:213, and Giuseppe Stefani and Bruno Astori, *Il Lloyd Triestino (1836–1936)* (Trieste: A. Mondadori, 1938), p. 7.

40. Metternich to Hudelist, Venice, 8 December 1815, HHSA, StK., Interiora, Fasc. 79, fol. 367–68.
41. Inzaghi to Frimont, Venice, 27 July 1820, KA, HKR Akten, Präs. 1820/564, fol. 3.
42. Metternich to Bellegarde, Vienna, 16 August 1820, ibid., Präs, 1820/608, fol. 2.
43. HKR circular, Vienna, 29 September 1820, ibid., Präs. 1820/734, fol. 10.

CHAPTER

3

Success and Failure in an "Era of Big Spending"

The liberal revolutions of 1820 prompted a decisive diplomatic and military response from Vienna. As the Congress of Troppau gave way to another meeting at Laibach (Ljubljana), Metternich turned his energies toward restoring order in the Italian peninsula. The subsequent campaign against Naples marked the start of what can be characterized as an "era of big spending" in Habsburg foreign policy that would last for just over a decade, through a second series of revolutions and intervention in Italy in 1831–32.

Humiliation and Indecision: The Early 1820s

For the Austrian navy, the new era began on a tragic note. In January 1821 its most prestigious seaman, Captain Nicolo Pasqualigo, died of a lung ailment only weeks after being named squadron commander. His sudden passing could not have come at a worse time. The congress had already reconvened in Ljubljana to approve Austria's intervention in Naples, and the army was scheduled to march in early February. Count Bellegarde, once again president of the *Hofkriegsrat,* ordered his foremost expert on naval affairs, Major General Marquis Amilcare Paulucci delle Roncole, to submit a list of candidates for the vacant position.

Because of his age and years away from the sea, *Marine-Kommandant* Conninck was not even considered for the assignment. The veteran Flanegan, though "a good seaman," was rejected on the same grounds. Dandolo, next on the list of seniority, was described as "a man in his best years." Captain Antonio Armeni, fourth in line after Pasqualigo's death and, like Dandolo, a veteran of Venetian, Austrian, Italian, and, since 1814, Austrian service once again, was the only other possibility. Bellegarde, however, did not want to present the emperor with a choice of two Venetians. Before forwarding the list to Francis at Ljubljana, he added Paulucci's name to it.[1]

At the end of January the emperor chose Paulucci to head the squadron. A native of Modena, the marquis had entered Austrian service in 1814 at the rank of major general after an eventful career in the Neapolitan, French, and Italian navies and the Italian army. Because of his experience at sea, which included a brief period as commander of the Italian navy, L'Espine at the time had asked for his transfer to the Austrian fleet. The request was denied, however, and Paulucci instead served as a brigadier in Bohemia from 1815 to 1818. After being transferred to a *Hofkriegsrat* post, the marquis in 1819 was commissioned to inspect the navy, an assignment that led to reforms of the Venice Arsenal, prison hulks, and naval education.[2] But despite his qualifications, the navy viewed Paulucci as an outsider. By selecting him as squadron commander, the emperor snubbed not just the officer corps as a whole but the Venetians in particular, whose leading candidates, Dandolo and Armeni, were handicapped neither by age nor infirmity.

The Austrian army's intervention in Naples went off as planned in early February. The invading force, under the command of Field Marshal Count Johann Maria von Frimont, had a nominal strength of over 70,000 men. In contrast the Neapolitan army, over 50,000 strong on paper, had only 20,000 regulars on the peninsula after the rest were sent to Sicily to suppress a rebellion against the new constitutional government. It was not such a mismatch at sea. Paulucci, after collecting his squadron at Ancona, moved down the Adriatic with two frigates, four brigs, and several schooners and smaller ships, including four transports. The Neapolitan navy had three ships of the line, only one of which could put to sea, five frigates, two of them usable, a corvette, two brigs, and a number of smaller craft.[3]

Paulucci's ships were to support Frimont's land operations from the Adriatic then round the Italian boot and sail to Naples itself. They probably would have encountered no resistance at all in the Adriatic if not for the implementation of Metternich's earlier guidelines against ships flying the flag of Naples. In early March 1821, when all of their merchantmen anchored in Austrian ports were interned, the Neapolitans responded by doing the same to Austrian vessels in their ports. Then, much to Paulucci's dismay, they sent a squadron of their own into the Adriatic. The Neapolitan fleet, which had recently assisted the army in putting down the Sicilian revolt, was known to have at sea one ship of the line and two frigates, a force strong enough to persuade the Austrian commander to put in at the island of Lissa rather than venture out of the Adriatic.[4]

Paulucci's subsequent defensive deployment sent two brigs to Ragusa and two smaller vessels to Ancona; the marquis kept his 44-gun flagship *Austria*, the second frigate, and two brigs with him at Lissa. The Neapolitan squadron appeared off the island shortly thereafter, and its commander, Baron Matteo Correale, blockaded the Austrians with his 74-gun ship of the line *Capri* and an escorting frigate. Realizing that it would be suicidal to challenge the broadsides of the *Capri*, Paulucci opened communications with Correale and learned (no doubt much to his relief) that the Neapolitan admiral had no intention of attacking. Given two sets of contradictory orders, one from the revolutionary government in Naples and the other from his king at Ljubljana, Correale decided to drop anchor and await news from the land campaign. Paralyzed by the standoff at Lissa, Paulucci implored Vienna to authorize the arming of merchantmen in Venice, Trieste, Rijeka, and Cattaro and asked when the frigate nearest to completion among the four under construction in the Venice Arsenal would be ready for sea.[5]

Even before the arrival of the bad news from Lissa, Vienna had authorized the arming of a second flotilla for use against Naples and even ordered the suspension of the navy's Trieste-Corfu packet boat service to free more ships for action. Bellegarde, upon receiving Paulucci's dismal reports, asked the emperor to approve sweeping defensive measures for Dalmatia and the littoral and a strengthening of the navy, including the arming of some of the ships of the line still on hand at Venice. Francis, unaware that Frimont's troops were already in Naples, instructed him to act without delay.[6] In contrast to the problems at sea, the opposition on land disintegrated after Neapolitan General Guglielmo Pepe invaded the Papal State on 7 March to attack the advancing Austrians at Rieti. Pepe's men, mostly militia and raw recruits, broke and ran following the first Austrian volley; the retreat quickly became a rout, and Naples itself fell two weeks later. Once he learned of the demise of the revolutionary government, Correale lifted the blockade of Lissa and let Paulucci proceed to his destination.

While the Habsburg army was pursuing the retreating Neapolitans toward their capital, a revolution in Piedmont complicated Austria's quest to restore order in the Italian peninsula. On the night of 9–10 March, liberal Sardinian army officers seized control of the fortress of Alessandria, inciting the garrison to mutiny and march on Turin. The rebels reached the capital two days later and demanded a constitution from King Victor Emmanuel I, who promptly abdicated in favor of his brother, Charles Felix. News of the revolution caused panic in Vienna and among the observers still gathered at Ljubljana; for the Austrian navy, the latest events kept alive the proposal to arm more ships. Sardinia had a smaller navy than that of either Naples or Austria, with a core of two 60-gun frigates, two corvettes, and four brigs and schooners, but the size and strength of the frigates made it a respectable force. Plans were made to put to sea the two ships of the line currently afloat in

Venice—the 74-gun *Severo*, since 1814 anchored in the lagoon as the commander's flagship, and the *Italiano*, disarmed but also with room for seventy-four cannon—as well as a frigate that was nearing completion.[7]

A quick resolution of the conflict on land ended the revolt in Piedmont before the Austrian navy could play any part. In early April, Habsburg troops under Count Ferdinand Bubna joined loyalist remnants of the Sardinian army to defeat a rebel force near Novara. Turin fell within days, and the threat passed. Nevertheless, in the midst of the crisis, it had become clear that the navy could not guarantee the defense of the Austrian coast against the Neapolitans, much less against the threat of a combined fleet from Naples and Sardinia. This unforseen scenario exposed a fatal flaw in the earlier arguments of Metternich and Stadion regarding the utility of Austrian sea power. The two statesmen had postulated two types of warfare, allied with Britain or against her, and argued that in either case, Austria would not need a navy. But in the latest campaign, Britain was neither a friend nor an enemy: the Royal Navy neither came forward to defend Austria's coastline or commerce nor brought its tremendous weight to bear against Paulucci's expedition. The events of 1821 demonstrated that there would be situations short of a general European war in which a stronger Austrian navy could be very useful. But the restoration of friendly regimes in Naples and Piedmont calmed fears over the security of the Adriatic, and the *Hofkriegsrat* concluded that a naval buildup was unnecessary. The plans for arming the two ships of the line were dropped later in 1821.[8]

In both of the vanquished states, Austrian armies of occupation guaranteed the stability of the restored order, remaining in Piedmont until 1823 and in Naples until 1827 at the expense of the host countries. In addition to supporting Habsburg troops on land, the Neapolitans were obligated to pay for a naval force of three frigates, four brigs, and several smaller vessels, more ships than Paulucci would ever actually have in his squadron. The Neapolitan division remained in existence until 1826, but aside from assisting in the suppression of a revolt on Sicily early in 1822, the ships saw action only as transports, ferrying troops home as the size of the occupying army fell from 54,000 in 1821 to a mere 12,000 men five years later. Nevertheless, the operation marked the first regular stationing of Austrian naval forces outside the Adriatic.[9]

Despite the fact that the occupied states paid for the operations of the Habsburg forces, the initial outlay for preparation upset the fragile imperial finances and undid much of Stadion's recent work to restore Austrian solvency and credit. Consequently, after the campaigns of 1821 the finance minister was more eager than ever to raise money from ship sales. He turned first to Britain in the hope that a favorable deal on the *Severo* and *Italiano* would help to temper the Austrophobia that had seized some circles in London during the invasion of Naples. But a number of influential members of Parliament had opposed the intervention, and the House of Commons soon demanded the repayment of old war loans contracted by Austria in the 1790s. In October 1821 Foreign Secretary Castlereagh reluctantly informed Metternich that Britain would pursue a settlement of the war debts. Stadion, undeterred, subsequently sought to include warships and naval stores as payment in kind for part of the bill. The British initially expressed interest in the two ships of the line but made known their preference for a combination of cash, ship timbers, and mercury. The *Severo* and *Italiano,* at 1.3 million florins worth only a fraction of the total amount owed, quickly disappeared from consideration. In late 1823 the parties finally agreed that Austria should pay a cash sum of £2.5 million, or approximately 25 million florins, the money to be borrowed from the Rothschilds in Vienna.[10]

Along with the accumulation of ever greater debts, domestic economic problems kept the Austrian state finances out of balance. The littoral economy in particular seemed unable to escape the post-Napoleonic doldrums. Far fewer merchant cargoes were lost to piracy after the allied action of

1816 against North Africa, but this alone failed to stimulate commercial activity in the Adriatic. In 1821 the slow economic recovery of the region was dealt a severe blow by the outbreak of the Greek revolution, which brought all commerce with the Black Sea to a virtual standstill and jeopardized what trade Austria had with the Levant.[11]

The Greek uprising, flaring up in the wake of Austria's successful restoration of order in Italy, posed an immediate danger to Habsburg security east of the Adriatic. Some have questioned whether Metternich at this stage feared a general collapse of Turkish rule in the Balkans,[12] but in any event there was little that the chancellor could do to organize a unilateral or collective response against the Greeks: too many Austrian troops were still tied down in Italy, and the wave of philhellenism sweeping Europe was too strong to overcome. Once the seamen of Greece resorted to piracy to finance the uprising, however, Metternich dispatched warships to defend Austrian commerce in the Aegean and Eastern Mediterranean, giving them free rein to battle the Greeks at sea and instructions to provide Vienna with first-hand accounts of the fighting on land. In July 1821 the frigate *Lipsia*, two brigs, and a schooner were sent to the Levant, to be joined early in 1822 by the *Austria*, two more brigs, and another schooner. By the fall of 1822 Austria's commitments in the Eastern Mediterranean forced her to reduce the Neapolitan division to one frigate, one brig, and a schooner, far less than what the government of Naples was committed to support. As the rebellion continued, freebooters from every corner of the Mediterranean flocked to the Levant to enter "Greek service," multiplying the number of vessels flying the rebel flag and blurring even further the distinction between patriot and pirate. Vienna responded by ordering still more ships to the Aegean and Eastern Mediterranean until the squadron numbered twenty-two vessels in all. To facilitate their operations, the Porte conceded the ships docking rights at Smyrna (Izmir) on the western coast of Turkey.[13]

The new responsibilities strained both the human and material resources of Austrian sea power and kept the navy among the active concerns of the *Hofkriegsrat,* thus assuring that questions raised by Paulucci's humiliation at Lissa would not simply disappear. Before revising his decree of 1817 or authorizing any further reforms of the navy, Francis ordered a special investigation to be headed by Count Folliot de Crenneville. Despite his continuing friendship with the ostracized Archduke Charles, Crenneville had not fared badly since his dismissal from the Marine Bureau in 1805. Over the years the former French seaman had held a series of army posts, finally rising to the rank of *Feldmarschalleutnant.* His earlier experience with naval matters made him a logical choice to review the navy for the *Hofkriegsrat,* especially since Paulucci, while never officially transferred to the fleet, clearly could no longer evaluate it from the perspective of an outsider. Because Paulucci's inspection tour of 1819–20 had already brought changes to the Arsenal, prison hulks, and naval college, Crenneville's mission focused more on the material resources of the navy than on its administration or personnel. His main task was to determine the feasibility of a recent proposal by Paulucci to cut down the *Severo* and *Italiano* from 74-gun ships of the line to large 56-gun frigates. Other duties included an inspection of damage to the frigate *Carolina,* only recently returned from its two-year voyage to China, and assessment of the condition of the ships still on the stocks at Venice. At the conclusion of his visit he was to make recommendations on the number of warships needed for the navy to handle its current duties.[14]

Crenneville's inspection tour, in November and December of 1822, came at a time of crisis for the navy. The fleet had been allowed to fall below its authorized strength of three frigates and eight brigs and could barely keep up its patrols of the Adriatic, not to mention the new duties in Neapolitan and Greek waters. The frigates *Lipsia, Austria,* and *Augusta,* begun by the French at Venice in 1810 and 1811 and put into service by the Austrians in 1814 and 1815, were all nearly useless despite having spent so few years at sea. The *Ebe,* launched in 1821 after ten years on the stocks, was the only truly seaworthy Austrian frigate, and the number of brigs in service had fallen to five. To complicate matters still more, on the eve of Crenneville's departure for Venice the financier Solomon Rothschild, head of the Vienna branch of his family's banking house, offered to back Trieste merchant Baron Joseph von Dietrich in a bid of six million florins for all of the ships of the line at Venice, including those still under construction, plus all of the frigates currently afloat (except for the *Ebe*), regardless of their condition. Metternich, while no doubt seeing the need for a navy to support Austria's present foreign policy in Italy and the Levant, opened negotiations for the sale. His fears that the ships might fall into Greek hands were dispelled by Rothschild's assurances that "no insurgents" would ever get them and that they would be resold only to European powers willing to disclose their future use.[15]

In late December Crenneville forwarded his report to the *Hofkriegsrat,* shocking Bellegarde with his recommendations. In addition to the *Severo* and *Italiano,* he called for two of the three ships of the line still unfinished at Venice to be completed as 56-gun frigates. Crenneville also concluded that the 44-gun *Ebe* should be joined in service by the three other frigates her size currently on the stocks, that the *Carolina* was not too damaged to repair, and that the navy should keep in service eight brigs and some eighty smaller vessels. In defense of the expense this would entail, he cited the millions of florins' worth of ships and cargoes lost by the Austrian merchant marine of 1798–1805 for want of adequate protection on the high seas. As for the strategic benefits, he argued that in the event of a Franco-Austrian war in northern Italy, a fleet of four large and four small frigates could blockade Genoa and harass troop transports out of Toulon. Even in its current state Crenneville thought the navy could hold its own against Spain, Portugal, Turkey, or the pirates of North Africa, although he had reservations about its superiority over the Neapolitan fleet because of the performance of 1821. Having already overstepped the limits of his mandate, he also gave his opinions on personnel and noted that the Venetians, in light of their maritime history and traditions, needed the navy as an outlet for their natural aspirations. He dismissed the idea that it was dangerous for Austria to have a navy so thoroughly Italian in character.[16]

Not surprisingly, Francis and Bellegarde rejected the appeal for an eight-frigate navy. Even though recent events had shown that Britain would not always be an ally of Austria, they could not imagine a French invasion of Italy that would not be part of a general European war, pitting France against the old anti-Napoleonic alliance. In their view, British sea power would be brought to bear in the Mediterranean in any war against France, leaving Austria with no need for the sort of offensive naval capability Crenneville advocated. Nevertheless, they heeded his advice on the *Severo, Italiano,* and *Carolina,* if for no other reason than the dire need for substitutes for the navy's three deteriorating frigates. Francis authorized the immediate conversion of the *Severo,* which joined the Levant squadron in 1824 as the frigate *Bellona.* Work on the *Italiano* was postponed until 1827, and to save money the *Carolina* was refitted as a corvette. Meanwhile, the government reserved the right to sell any or all of the ships if a suitable buyer made an offer. Francis approved the scrapping of one unfinished ship of the line but reserved judgment on two others and on the three frigates still on the stocks at Venice. Crenneville's bold proposals failed to provoke a decisive change in the government's attitude toward the navy. Vienna instead resorted to stop-gap measures designed to cover the bare minimum of its needs.[17]

After more than two years of active sea duty, Paulucci returned to his old post with the *Hofkriegsrat* and managed to salvage the navy's cause with the emperor and Bellegarde. The marquis spent the remainder of 1823 subtly lobbying for a peacetime strength of five frigates, one of which would be kept in reserve, an increase of two active frigates over the number authorized by the imperial decree of 1817. At the same time, he submitted budget recommendations that always seemed to promise change without increasing expenditure and, in general, tactfully pursued a personal campaign to replace the ineffective Conninck as *Marine-Kommandant*. On the touchy subject of the navy's future, Paulucci merely gave his "humble" opinion that the empire needed some sort of naval force "for the protection of its commerce and other considerations." But in a rare act of audacity he proposed that the navy, since 1814 technically under the jurisdiction of the army's Venetian *Generalkommando* at Padua, should have an independent position immediate to the *Hofkriegsrat* in Vienna. The change would transform the existing *Marinekommando* into a *Marine-Ober-Kommando,* with a corresponding elevation of the power and prestige of its head. To the surprise of all concerned, Francis concurred and in February 1824 ordered a reform of the naval administration. By then Paulucci had maneuvered himself into the position of heir apparent. In March 1824 the sixty-three-year-old Conninck was pensioned off, to live in retirement for another twenty years, the same length of time that Paulucci was to head the navy.[18]

Promise and Frustration: The Paulucci Era (1824–1833)

Paulucci capped his rise to power by implementing the new administrative reforms with an energy never shown by Conninck. He started his tenure with the complete confidence of the emperor and the *Hofkriegsrat*, either because they believed sincerely in his professional abilities or, perhaps, respected his demonstrated political skills. After all, he had evaded the blame for his squadron's impotent showing against Naples in 1821 (and rightly so, since he was hardly responsible for the material weaknesses of the fleet), then succeeded in convincing Vienna that he could improve the navy within the limits of the traditional restraints on spending.

Many were unimpressed by Paulucci's sleight of hand. Young Count Anton Prokesch, an army officer on temporary assignment to the fleet, characterized him as "a charlatan par excellence." The navy's strong Venetian element was even less kind and still regarded Paulucci as an outsider. His Modenese birth apparently did little to make him more acceptable than his Flemish predecessor, but it was some consolation to the Venetians that the new commander at least was not a veteran of the "Trieste navy." Indeed, after the departure of Conninck, the Venice-Trieste friction within the officer corps all but disappeared. Dandolo, once again passed over for a major appointment, was placated with active sea commands in the Neapolitan and Levant squadrons and acquitted himself in countless situations in which diplomatic tact meant as much as seamanship. Paulucci, on the other hand, followed Conninck's precedent of commanding the navy from Venice, returning to active sea duty only once (in the Levant, during 1826) after being named *Marine-Ober-Kommandant*.[19]

Paulucci failed in his campaign for the extra frigates, but by taking advantage of a change in leadership at the *Hofkammer*, he at least made certain that the fleet would get no smaller. The death of Count Stadion in May 1824, although a tragedy for Austrian finances, removed from the scene one of the greatest opponents of naval spending and a leading advocate of ship sales. The marquis moved quickly to court the favor of his successor, Count Mihaly Nádasdy. Barely two weeks after Stadion's death, the new finance minister gave the navy full control over the sale of surplus or obsolete warships. The *Staatskanzlei* acquiesced in the decision but subsequently urged the *Hofkriegsrat* to make sure that Paulucci pursued every possible opportunity for a deal.[20] Fortunately for the navy, the bid of Dietrich and Rothschild recently had been rejected after nearly two years of negotiations. An English ship broker, John Wilson, emerged as the central figure in future offers. An agent for the British East India Company, the Spanish government, and, if Vienna's suspicions were well founded, the Greeks as well, his untrustworthiness prompted even the *Staatskanzlei* to urge caution in negotiations with him.[21]

Spared for the moment from internal threats, Paulucci laid the groundwork for an expansion of the navy to a size commensurate with its duties. The 56-gun frigate *Bellona*, the 44-gun *Ebe*, and the *Italiano*, rebuilding at Venice, technically filled the three-frigate limit of the imperial decree of 1817, but the navy's corvette *Carolina* and five brigs fell below the eight brigs prescribed by the same law. In 1825 the marquis won permission for the construction of two new brigs by arguing that it constituted not an expansion but merely a restoration of strength. He then permitted discussion of deals on the obsolete frigates *Austria, Augusta,* and *Lipsia,* and allowed the two remaining unfinished ships of the line to be sold for scrap, all to divert attention away from the three frigates still on the stocks in Venice, which he viewed as insurance for the future.[22] Finally, out of deference to Metternich's strong desire to bolster the Turkish position against the Greeks, Paulucci prudently pursued an offer from the sultan's Egyptian ally, Mehemet Ali, to buy warships from the Austrian navy.[23]

Amid these efforts to increase the material strength of the navy, the marquis also pressed successfully for an expansion of the officer corps. The chronic shortage of qualified staff and other "*ober*" officers led the *Hofkriegsrat,* late in 1826, to propose to Metternich that Austria recruit experienced men from the British navy, promising that all candidates for imperial service would be required to meet strict "moral and political" standards.[24] The chancellor's apparent coolness toward the project, combined with the problems presented by the dearth of Italian-speaking English officers, effectively killed the idea, but the navy managed to meet its growing needs by hiring officers from the Adriatic merchant marine.[25]

Unfortunately, much to the detriment of discipline and morale, appropriations did not keep pace with the expansion of the corps. Salaries were so ridiculously low that officers often resorted to smuggling to supplement their incomes. The most celebrated incident of this type occurred in 1827, when the navy brig *Orione* was intercepted by an Austrian customs cutter while trying to smuggle a cargo of salt into Venice. True to the lenient standards he would follow throughout his tenure, Paulucci postponed a hearing for four years and ultimately let the officers and men involved go unpunished; he even authorized a promotion for the commander of the *Orione* while the case was still pending. Paulucci went so far as to change the name of the "tainted" brig in an effort to erase all memory of the event.[26] His light-handed approach to such cases, most likely out of appreciation for the strains caused by poor pay and conditions in the service, encouraged a deterioration in discipline that was to have the most serious consequences in the long run.

For the moment there were no doubts about the loyalty or efficacy of the Habsburg fleet. Nevertheless, the good showing of Dandolo and his subordinates in Greek waters went unrewarded. In 1826 the imperial government had a new frigate laid down in the Venice Arsenal for Mehemet Ali even though it refused to let the Austrian navy build any new ships larger than a brig. Adding insult to injury, Vienna subsequently agreed to sell the flagship *Bellona* to Egypt. Dandolo, reluctant to turn over this vessel, cited the need for reinforcements in the Levant and noted that the price (500,000 florins) was less than what it would cost Austria to build a replacement.[27] His recalcitrance soon worked to the favor of the navy. In May 1827 Metternich ordered the suspension of the *Bellona* deal, as well as plans to sell the corvette *Carolina* to the Egyptians, on the grounds that the present Levant squadron was already too weak to protect Austrian commerce. The chancellor also recognized that the concentration of British and French warships in the Eastern Mediterranean made it necessary to stay on a strong footing.[28]

With Ottoman forces on the verge of crushing the revolution, Britain, France, and Russia agreed to implement a naval blockade of the Greek coast and force a mediated settlement. Following the Treaty of London (6 July 1827) a Russian squadron joined the British and French fleets to intimidate the Turco-Egyptian fleet, which the allies eventually blockaded in Navarino Bay. On 20 October, "by accident rather than design," as one historian has noted,[29] the allies opened fire and destroyed the Ottoman ships, sustaining only light damage themselves but causing their governments a great deal of embarrassment.

The Austrian navy did not participate at Navarino or intervene directly in any engagements of the war. Dandolo executed Metternich's orders to the letter and behaved impeccably vis-à-vis the squadrons of the other powers and the Turks. The chancellor praised the fleet and later remarked to the emperor that "while the larger navies daily compromise themselves in the waters of the Levant," the Austrian squadron alone "knows how to maintain its honor and the common law."[30] With Metternich's blessing, Dandolo treated as pirates the captains who raided commerce indiscriminately under the Greek ensign, a flag Vienna did not recognize. His most serious clash with the Greeks came in the tense weeks before Navarino after two of their schooners seized four Austrian merchantmen and towed them to the Morean port of Spezzia, where they were condemned by a prize court of the provisional government of Greece. On 18 July the Austrian commander appeared off the port with the *Bellona* and six other warships and, according to the local Orthodox primate, "insisted on the surrender of the vessels, saying that he was prepared to recognize neither the Greek authorities, nor their admiralties, nor their sentences. . . ." After receiving no satisfaction, Dandolo on the following day "approached the entrance to our harbor, where the vessels of our fleet were anchored, and opened fire on them."[31] The Greek foreign minister, appealing later for British intercession against the Austrian squadron, noted that Dandolo "fired all kinds of ammunition against the fleet . . . and the town of Spezzia. He injured the ships, knocked down houses, and killed men; in short, perhaps he did what even the bloodthirsty Turk would not have dared to have done!"[32]

The British captains and diplomats on duty in the Levant routinely ignored such pleas. They had no complaints themselves against the Austrian squadron, especially since Dandolo as a rule assisted any merchantman victimized by the Greeks. Later in 1827 a British merchant captain reported that after his ship had been plundered by Greek pirates, an Austrian corvette arrived on the scene and gave him food and clothing for his crew, then an escort to Smyrna.[33] A record of similar acts of good will toward Turkish ships ultimately helped to spare Habsburg commerce from the backlash of Navarino. In early 1828 the Turks sent another fleet to the western coast of Greece that gained revenge for the losses of the previous fall by pillaging commerce in and around the Ionian Islands. By the end of March, the zealous raiders already had claimed some thirty prizes; because of their country's good relations with the Porte, Austrian merchantmen were not among the victims.[34]

By cutting off the Egyptian army in the Morea from supply and reinforcement by sea, the Battle of Navarino Bay had saved the Greek cause and, in the short run, prolonged the instability in Levantine and Greek waters. In April 1828 Russia added a new dimension to the hostilities by declaring war on Turkey, invading the sultan's domains not only along the lower Danube but also to the east of the Black Sea in the Caucasus. The naval forces of the two belligerents squared off in an equally wide variety of places, including the waters off Cattaro in the lower Adriatic, but did not fight a major sea battle. Because Austria wished to maintain cordial relations with both powers, Dandolo judiciously avoided running afoul of either of their navies. The imperial government, meanwhile, decided to postpone the delivery to Egypt of the new frigate *Egiziana,* recently completed in the Venice Arsenal at a cost of 425,000 florins.[35] The international situation cleared rapidly after the three Navarino allies, in the London Protocol of March 1829, agreed to the creation of an autonomous Greek state under Turkish sovereignty. The Russians, exhausted after only a year and a half of fighting, concluded the Treaty of Adrianople in September 1829 to end their war with the Turks. In February 1830 a second London Protocol established a completely independent kingdom of Greece. Austria was a spectator to all of these machinations and merely reacted to the developments as they occurred. After the First London Protocol Francis ordered the reduction of the Levant squadron to one frigate, two corvettes, and two smaller vessels; after the second, he abolished it entirely.[36] In the wake of the Adrianople settlement the navy delivered the *Egiziana* to the pasha of Egypt but dropped efforts to sell him the *Bellona* and other warships.

In addition to its various benefits for the Russians, the Treaty of Adrianople also compelled the Turks to recognize the right of all merchantmen to pass freely through the Bosporus and the Dardanelles, removing the requirement that their countries have commercial treaties with the Porte.[37] Except for the immediate post-Napoleonic years, the straits had been closed or trade with the Black Sea disrupted ever since 1806. Adrianople thus sparked a boom in the Russian grain trade since ships of all flags were now free to enter the Black Sea and load up with Odessa wheat. Unfortunately, the new conditions were disastrous for the economy of the Adriatic littoral and hinterland, whose traders and middle-men traditionally had brought Hungarian grain to the sea via the Danube, the Sava, and the overland caravan route across Croatia, supplying the needs of the coastal region and having enough left over for export via the Adriatic. The difficulty and cost of transporting Hungarian grain made it more expensive than Russian grain and susceptible to competition. After 1829 the influx of wheat from Odessa brought an almost total collapse of the Mediterranean market for Hungarian grain and caused a crisis in the balance of trade of the littoral, especially for the ports of the eastern Adriatic.[38]

If not for concurrent developments in the Croatian logging industry, the eastern hinterland would have fallen into a deep depression. By the late 1820s over three-quarters of the oak timber harvested in Croatia and Slavonia was being exported abroad through Rijeka and Senj, the ports hurt the most by the collapse of the Hungarian grain trade. The bulk of the exports were to Britain, mostly for ship timber, but in the 1830s the lumber mills shifted to the more lucrative business of providing barrel staves for the French wine industry.

This profitable trade continued unabated until the end of the century, more than compensating the harbors for their loss of grain exports.[39]

The developments in logging naturally provided a favorable basis for a shipbuilding industry, but, as we have seen, the Austrian navy already had more ships than it was able to use and the merchant marine, though depleted by the Napoleonic wars, had only modest needs. In the generally depressed postwar conditions, the small merchant fleet sufficed to handle the bulk of the trade of the Habsburg ports. Indeed, in the years after 1814 a consistent two-thirds of the goods coming into Trieste arrived under the Austrian flag.[40] But because few trading houses had the resources to maintain a fleet of their own ships, most of the vessels were owned by individual merchants. Their disadvantages became more acute after 1830 when an increasing number of foreign steamships began to call in Adriatic ports. The leading businessmen of Trieste soon realized that the future growth and prosperity of the littoral could be ensured only if a way were found for the Austrian merchant marine to harness this latest technology. The conditions were reasonably favorable; only the catalyst was missing.

Like the merchant fleet, the Habsburg navy was relatively small and not abreast of the latest technological developments. Still, its record during the Greco-Turkish war had been impressive, and in subsequent years Vienna never hesitated to dispatch a squadron when Austrian commerce was threatened. Such was the case in the summer of 1828 when, with tensions winding down in the Levant, the sultan of Morocco suddenly abrogated the treaty that had kept his corsairs away from Habsburg trade since 1805. After a Moroccan raider seized the merchant brig *Veloce,* Metternich ordered a naval demonstration to bring the sultan to terms. In early January 1829 Captain Francesco Bandiera, one of the best of the navy's younger officers, arrived off the coast of Morocco with two corvettes, a brig, and a schooner.

A cadet on Mogniat de Pouilly's Moroccan expedition of 1803–5, Bandiera took full advantage both of his knowledge of the waters and of his larger number of ships, attempting a full blockade of the coast while opening negotiations with the sultan's ministers. After months of fruitless dialogue, he sent ashore a small landing party under Ensign Ludwig Kudriaffsky. Once this group located and freed the crew of the *Veloce*, the captain suspended the talks and concentrated his ships off El Araisch (Larache), which he bombarded in early July. The imperial government subsequently felt compelled to remind Bandiera of the "purely defensive" nature of his mission, but at the same time it strengthened his hand with the new frigate *Medea*, launched just the year before, which became flagship over a reorganized squadron of two brigs and one corvette. Meanwhile, Austrian diplomacy brought Turkish pressure to bear on Morocco, and in January 1830 the sultan finally reopened talks with Bandiera. In March his envoys signed an agreement releasing the *Veloce*. The squadron remained in the area until the formal restoration of the Austro-Moroccan treaty that fall.[41]

The Moroccan expedition provided a great boost to the careers of Bandiera and Kudriaffsky and for the navy as a whole. Shorter and more dramatic than the recent years of cruising in Neapolitan and Levantine waters, the expedition called further attention to the utility of Austrian sea power, if only in the peacetime exercise of "gunboat diplomacy." The results of the expedition were admittedly modest but nonetheless compared favorably to the experiences of similar missions in the 1820s by navies with comparable resources. The Sardinian fleet, though expanded by Charles Felix and its commander Giorgio Des Geneys, had had little success pressing claims in 1822 against Morocco or in 1825 against the Bey of Tripoli. The Neapolitan navy, weakened by post-1821 purges of Muratists and liberals from its officer corps, was humiliated in 1828 by the Tripolitanians, who subsequently forced Naples to acquiesce in a tribute double the previous rate.[42] And while the *Veloce* episode with Morocco marked Austria's last real clash with a North African state, both Sardinia-Piedmont and Naples continued to have trouble with the pirates well into the 1830s. In March 1833 they finally concluded an alliance that provided for common action against the menace, and shortly thereafter a joint operation against Tunis gained restitution for attacks on Sardinian merchantmen. The Neapolitans took heart and in the summer of 1834 tackled Morocco on their own, forcing a great reduction in their tribute to the sultan.[43]

The Neapolitan and Sardinian fleets, though at this stage not formal rivals to the Austrian, were also second-rate navies and provide a good yardstick against which to measure the material progress of Habsburg sea power. The Neapolitan navy, in the eighteenth century a force second only to the fleets of the great powers, by the late 1820s had a core of two ships of the line, four frigates, and one corvette. After languishing under Ferdinand I (to 1824) and his successor Francis I (1824–30), the fleet was to see better days after 1830, when naval expansion became one of the favorite causes of the new king, Ferdinand II. Sardinia-Piedmont, starting from scratch after the Napoleonic Wars, by the end of the 1820s had eight frigates and two corvettes in its fleet, thanks largely to the building program of Charles Felix, who was responsible for five of the frigates and one corvette. By the early 1830s, however, the two Italian navies were moving in opposite directions. The indifference toward naval affairs of the new Sardinian king, Charles Albert, contrasted sharply with the strong maritime interests of Ferdinand II of Naples.

The Austrian navy, with no ships of the line and relatively few frigates, would have to be rated weaker than the fleets of Naples and Sardinia-Piedmont, despite its considerable growth under Paulucci. After returning to the levels prescribed by the imperial decree of 1817, the navy continued to increase in size and strength. True to the personal style of the marquis, however, expansion came slowly and without fanfare. The two brigs laid down in 1825 were redesigned on the stocks and in 1827 completed as corvettes, faster, three-masted vessels that could perform the same cruising duties as frigates at far less cost. The same year, an older brig was rebuilt as a corvette and in 1828 yet another corvette was begun in the Venice Arsenal, evidence of how popular this ship type had become. Paulucci at the same time recognized the need for larger, more powerful warships to replace the old *Austria, Augusta,* and *Lipsia* (all scrapped in 1826–27) and pressed for the completion of the three frigates still on the stocks at Venice. Laid down by the French between 1811 and 1813, they finally entered service years later, the *Medea* in 1828, the *Guerriera* in 1830, and the *Venere* in 1832. Sister-ships of the *Ebe,* they gave the Austrian fleet four homogeneous 44-gun frigates which were to remain its core for years to come. The larger frigates *Bellona* and *Italiano,* both cut down from ships of the line somewhat experimentally in the wake of the Crenneville mission, ultimately proved to be of little utility to the fleet. The *Bellona* was unseaworthy by 1830, after only six years of service, and the *Italiano* never left the lagoon at Venice, seeing duty first in reserve as a school- and harbor-ship, later as an artillery target. In the late 1820s the number of brigs dwindled to four, but in the 1830s Paulucci was to order the construction of five "brig-schooners," smaller brigs designed for the Trieste-Corfu packet service and other non-military duties, thus freeing the brigs-of-war for more important assignments. By 1832 the navy had attained Paulucci's goal, first proposed nine years earlier, of four active frigates with a fifth in reserve. Five corvettes, four brigs, and numerous smaller vessels rounded out the fleet, the greatest collection of Habsburg warships since the days of Charles VI.

The performance of the navy in the Levant and off Morocco inspired the confidence of Vienna and erased doubts raised by the embarrassing Neapolitan campaign of 1821 to such a degree that when Austrian troops again marched southward to crush an Italian revolution in 1831, the Habsburg leadership without hesitation assigned an active role to the fleet. In March of that year, only a month after rebels took control of Modena and the Papal legations, an Austrian army under Frimont crossed the Po and within days occupied Bologna, forcing the provisional government of central Italy to flee to Ancona. Bandiera, ordered to patrol the Papal coast with the new corvette *Abbondanza* and several schooners, at the end of the month intercepted a merchant brig with a hundred revolutionaries on board. Much to the relief of Vienna, the catch included Count Carlo Zucchi, a veteran of Napoleon's Italian army and, after 1814, a general in the Austrian army. The most wanted of the rebels, Zucchi had eluded Habsburg forces on land. The army, in the first hint of an inter-service rivalry, did not disguise its disappointment at seeing the navy take its quarry. Meanwhile, Bandiera's efforts won him the personal thanks of Metternich and the dignity of a hereditary baron of the Austrian Empire.[44]

Bandiera's capture of Zucchi provided the navy with unaccustomed, if ephemeral, prestige. After Austrian troops withdrew from the legations, the excesses of the Papal mercenaries taking their place provoked the populace to rise again. In January 1832 the Habsburg army in Lombardy-Venetia, under a new commander, Field Marshal Count Joseph Radetzky, occupied Bologna a second time. At Radetzky's request, Bandiera again was sent to the Papal coast but hastened back to home port when a French squadron appeared in the Adriatic. The new regime of Louis Philippe, having taken offense at Metternich's failure the previous year to respect French interests in the Italian peninsula, in late February countered the Austrian occupation of Bologna with a landing at Ancona. The French squadron, led by the 90-gun flagship *Suffren*, included a second ship of the line and at least three frigates larger than the 44-gun models that Austria had in service.[45] The ships deposited a regiment at Ancona, then roamed the upper Adriatic at will, calling at Venice, Trieste, and other Austrian harbors. Their conduct on occasion was outrageous; after French vessels put in at the Istrian fishing port of Pirano (Piran), the governor of the Küstenland, Prince Alphons

Porcia, complained to Metternich that sailors on shore leave overran the town and disturbed the peace with their "revolutionary songs" and bad behavior. The governor lamented that before such powerful "uninvited visitors" the littoral stood "completely unsupervised and defenseless."[46]

The navy could do nothing to challenge the French at sea. Though larger than ever before, it was only a fraction of the size of the French fleet. Even though Metternich had also ordered Radetzky to remain a safe distance from Ancona and avoid provoking hostilities on land,[47] the navy, unable to provide even the most rudimentary coastal defense, bore the brunt of the humiliation. The Habsburg Empire's first encounter since the Napoleonic era with the maritime might of one of the other powers of Europe strengthened the hand of the navy's domestic foes. As before, there was no question of Austria building an offensive fleet large enough to challenge the naval power of Britain, France, or Russia. Now, however, opponents could also argue that with the creation of an independent Greece and the French occupation of the Algerian coast in 1830, piracy was no longer such a problem and there was less need to patrol the sea in defense of commerce.[48] In the forthcoming years of austerity it would be difficult for supporters of a larger fleet to justify their cause. Once the search was on for budgets to cut, the navy emerged as a leading candidate for reduction.

After it became clear that the French would remain in Ancona and the Austrians in Bologna with neither side challenging the other, Austrian warships again ventured out to sea, but in smaller numbers than before. The cutback in naval operations reached such proportions that in late 1832, when arrangements were made to transport by sea some 3500 Bavarian troops accompanying Prince Otto of Bavaria to his new throne in Greece, Austria proposed to send only a brig and a schooner to escort the twenty-seven Greek and Austrian transports chartered for the occasion, and there was considerable debate over whether even these warships should be allowed to sail all the way to Greece or just to Brindisi at the mouth of the

Adriatic.⁴⁹ The concurrent eruption of the Near Eastern crisis, this time an attack on Turkey by the ambitious pasha of Egypt, Mehemet Ali, likewise brought no reactivation of the Levant squadron. Russia was quick to take advantage of Austria's apparent ambivalence and British and French preoccupation with crises in the Iberian peninsula. The tsarist empire put itself forward as protector of the Porte and in July 1833 concluded the Treaty of Unkiar-Skelessi, a defensive alliance with Turkey. Metternich responded by organizing a conference at Münchengrätz in Bohemia, where in September 1833 Austria and Prussia joined Russia in a guarantee not only of the integrity of the Ottoman Empire but also of the existing borders and institutions of Central Europe.

Metternich's relative inertia heralded the close of the active post-Napoleonic phase of Habsburg foreign policy. The new treaty was an attempt to salvage some good from a bad situation, since financial constraints made it impossible for him to act decisively in yet another international crisis. Unlike the occupation of Naples and Sardinia-Piedmont a decade earlier, the two incursions into the Papal legations were undertaken at an expense to Austria of some eighty million florins. Between March 1831 and February 1833 the Habsburg Empire floated three loans on unfavorable terms, incurring a debt of over 134 million florins for just over 108 million in cash. Once the bills were covered for the campaigns of 1831–32, Metternich's nemesis, interior minister Count Franz Anton Kolowrat, and other proponents of economy finally drew the line on spending. If one believes, as one historian has argued, that too little has been made of the role of Austria's financial weakness in her decline as a great power, there is certainly a case to be made for the year 1833 not just as the end of an era in Austrian diplomacy or naval policy but as a watershed in the history of the empire.⁵⁰

The conclusion of the Treaty of Münchengrätz found the Austrian navy operating under more uncertainty than usual. Paulucci ended the long campaign to sell warships and expanded the fleet to an unprecedented strength, but despite his efforts the era ended as it had begun, with Austria humiliated in the Adriatic by the stronger fleet of a foreign power. The hope once held by Metternich that Britain could be depended upon to defend Habsburg interests at sea had been dashed as the two countries went their separate ways in foreign affairs. Left to fill the breach on its own, the Austrian navy was able to defend the empire's maritime interests from Morocco to the Aegean—literally, from one end of the Mediterranean to the other—but could not deny the French Ancona or even challenge the Neapolitan navy, at best a second-rate force. Another two decades were to pass before anyone would attempt to answer the central question of whether Austria should have a fleet capable of offensive action against other navies.

NOTES

1. Bellegarde to Francis, Vienna, 24 January 1821, KA, HKR Akten, Präs. 1821/93, fol. 2–3.

2. Francis (decree), Ljubljana, n.d. [29 January 1821], ibid., fol. 4–5. Paulucci was captured at sea by the British in 1808 while serving as head of the active squadron of Napoleon's Italian navy. Imprisoned at Malta, he escaped in 1812 and served in the Italian army for the rest of the war. For a biographical sketch see Khuepach and Bayer, *1814–1847*, p. 299.

3. Khuepach and Bayer, *1814–1847*, p. 193; Radogna, *Storia della Marina*, p. 87.

4. Inzaghi decree, Venice, 1 March 1821, KA, HKR Akten, Präs. 1821/204, fol. 5; HKR to Bellegarde, Vienna, 2 March 1821, ibid., Präs. 1821/169, fol. 1–2; Stürmer to HKR, Vienna, 4 March 1821, ibid., Präs. 1821/173, fol. 2; Radogna, *Storia della Marina*, pp. 86–88. The decision to impound Neapolitan merchant ships drew criticism from Austrian commercial officials, who were not consulted by the *Staatskanzlei* or *Hofkriegsrat*.

5. Paulucci to HKR, *Austria* (Lissa), 13 March 1821, KA, HKR Akten, Präs. 1821/334–336, fol. 12; Paulucci to HKR, *Austria* (Lissa), 14 March 1821, ibid., fol. 10; Paulucci to Bellegarde, *Austria* (Lissa), 16 March 1821, ibid., fol. 6–8; Paulucci to Bellegarde, *Austria* (Lissa), 21 March 1821, ibid., fol. 16–22.

6. Küstenlandisches Gubernium to StK., Trieste, 21 March 1821, HHSA, StK., Prov., Küstenland, Carton 2: Korr. Triester Guberniums 1815–27, fol. 258–59; Bellegarde to Francis, Ljubljana, 24 March 1821, KA, HKR Akten, Präs. 1821/334–336, fol. 2.

7. HKR circular, Vienna, 6 April 1821, KA, HKR Akten, Präs. 1821/334–336, fol. 1, 58–62.

8. HKR circular, Vienna, 1 November 1821, KA, HKR Akten, Präs. 1821/998, fol. 1–4.

9. See Paul Schroeder, *Metternich's Diplomacy at its Zenith, 1820–1823* (Austin: University of Texas Press, 1962), p. 154; Khuepach and Bayer, *1814–1847,* pp. 193–94. Khuepach and Bayer do not even mention the humiliation the navy suffered at the hands of the Neapolitans.

10. HKR to Stadion, Vienna, 1 November 1821, KA, HKR Akten, Präs. 1821/996, fol. 1–3; HKR to Conninck, Vienna, 14 December 1821, ibid., Präs. 1821/1091, fol. 1–3. See also Karl Helleiner, *The Imperial Loans: A Study in Financial and Diplomatic History* (London: Oxford University Press, 1965), pp. 150–73.

11. Herlihy, "Russian Grain," p. 99; see budget statistics in Harm-Hinrich Brandt, *Der österreichische Neoabsolutismus: Staatsfinanzen und Politik 1848–1860,* 2 vols. (Göttingen: Vandenhoeck & Ruprecht, 1978), 2:1100.

12. Enno E. Kraehe, "Foreign Policy and the Nationality Problem in the Habsburg Monarchy, 1800–67," *Austrian History Yearbook* 3 (1967), pt. 3:19.

13. Khuepach and Bayer, *1814–1847,* pp. 193–95. The squadron reached its maximum size in 1826–27.

14. Bellegarde to Crenneville (instructions), Vienna, 7 November 1822, KA, Nachlass Folliot de Crenneville, B/216, no. 13, fol. 347–58.

15. Solomon Rothschild to Metternich, Verona, 12 November 1822, HHSA, StK., Notenwechsel HKR, Carton 293, a.d. HKR, Marine 1800–52, Teil 2.

16. Crenneville to Bellegarde, Vienna, 20 December 1822, KA, Nachlass Folliot de Crenneville, B/216, no. 14, fol. 361–70.

17. Bellegarde, Präsidial Vortrag, Vienna, 28 January 1823, KA, HKR Akten, Präs. 1823/139, fol. 2–17; Bellegarde to Francis, Vienna, 26 May 1823, ibid., Präs. 1824/108, fol. 2–99.
18. Paulucci to Francis, Vienna, 26 December 1823, HHSA, StK., Notenwechsel HKR, Carton 293, a.d. HKR, Marine 1800–52, Teil 2; Khuepach and Bayer, *1814–1847*, p. 78.
19. Prokesch quoted in Friedrich Engel-Janosi, *Die Jugendzeit des Grafen Prokesch von Osten* (Innsbruck: Universitäts-Verlag Wagner, 1938), p. 47; Khuepach and Bayer, *1814–1847*, pp. 299–300, 322.
20. Nádasdy to Bellegarde, Vienna, 31 May 1824, KA, HKR Akten, Präs. 1824/523, fol. 18; Stürmer to HKR, Vienna, 8 June 1824, ibid., fol. 24–26, 29. Stadion died on 15 May 1824 after eleven years as finance minister.
21. Pillersdorf to Bellegarde, Vienna, 7 May 1824, KA, HKR Akten, Präs. 1824/390, fol. 2; Stürmer to Bellegarde, Vienna, 16 August 1824, ibid., Präs. 1824/746, fol. 2–3.
22. Paulucci to HKR, Venice, 25 August 1824, ibid., Präs 1821/821, fol. 2–7.
23. Pietro Gioachino (agent for Egypt) to HKR, Vienna, 30 March 1825, KA, HKR Akten, Präs. 1825/356, fol. 4–5; Stürmer to HKR, Vienna, 7 April 1825, ibid., Präs. 1825/385, fol. 2–3.
24. HKR to Metternich, Vienna, 26 December 1826, ibid., Präs. 1826/1510, fol. 1–3.
25. Khuepach and Bayer, *1814–1847*, p. 82.
26. Fleischer, *1802–1848 MS*, p. 92.
27. Georg Hofmann (*Marine-Kriegs-Concipist,*) circular, Vienna, 6 January 1827, KA, HKR Akten, Präs. 1827/14, fol. 15–16; Dandolo to HKR, Smyrna, 16 February 1827, ibid., Präs. 1827/303, fol. 2–3; Hofmann circular, Vienna, 31 March 1827, ibid., fol. 1.
28. Metternich to Prince Friedrich zu Hohenzollern (HKR president), Vienna, 12 May 1827, ibid., Präs. 1827/450, fol. 101–3.
29. René Albrecht-Carrié, *A Diplomatic History of Europe Since the Congress of Vienna* (rev. ed. New York: Harper & Row, 1973), p. 45.
30. Metternich to Francis, Vienna, 4 March 1829, quoted in Engel-Janosi, *Prokesch von Osten*, p. 66.
31. Primate of Spezzia to Provisional Government, Spezzia, 21 July 1827, in Pitcairn Jones, ed., *Piracy in the Levant 1827–8*, vol. 72 of *Publications of the Navy Records Society* (London: Spottiswoode, Ballantyne & Co., Ltd., 1934), p. 133.

32. G. Glaraki (Greek foreign minister) to Stratford Canning (British ambassador to Turkey), Nauplia, 22 July 1827, ibid., pp. 135–36.
33. Report of James Hannah, Master of the brig *Nancy*, Smyrna, 17 September 1827, ibid., pp. 195–96.
34. FMLt. Baron Franz von Tomassich (governor of Dalmatia) to Hohenzollern, Zara, 30 March 1828, KA, HKR Akten, Präs. 1828/449, fol. 442–43.
35. Hofmann to Metternich, Vienna, 2 August 1828, ibid., Präs. 1828/1151, fol. 799–800.
36. Khuepach and Bayer, *1814–1847*, p. 196.
37. Herlihy, "Russian Grain," p. 101.
38. Karaman, *Privreda i društvo*, pp. 15–16.
39. Ibid., pp. 19, 28–29, 45.
40. Babudieri, *Industrie, commerci e navigazione*, p. 127.
41. See Fleischer, *1802–1848 MS*, pp. 80–87; Peter Handel-Mazzetti, "Vor 110 Jahren: El Araisch," *Marine Rundschau* 44 (1939): 747–54; Khuepach and Bayer, *1814–1847*, pp. 201–15.
42. C. Randaccio, *Le marinerie militari italiane nei tempi moderni (1750–1850)* (Turin: Artero e comp., 1864), pp. 28–32, 90–92; Radogna, *Storia della Marina*, pp. 93–95.
43. In addition to action against North Africa, both Sardinia and Naples maintained warships in the Levant during the Greek crisis, but their squadrons were not as large or as active as Austria's. See Radogna, *Storia della Marina*, pp. 97–100.
44. Bandiera to Metternich, Venice, 3 April 1831, HHSA, StK., Notenwechsel HKR, Carton 293, a.d. Marine 1800–52, Teil 2; Paulucci to Metternich, Venice, 3 April 1831, ibid.; Metternich to Bandiera, Vienna, 16 April 1831, ibid.; Metternich to Paulucci, 16 April 1831, ibid.; Frimont to Geppert, Milan, 31 March 1831, HHSA, StK., Prov., Lombardo-Venezien (hereafter cited as L-V), Carton 24: Berichte der kommandierenden Generäle l.v. Königreich Frimont und Radetzky 1826–1848, fol. 566–67.
45. Bandiera to HKR, Trieste, 16 March 1832, KA, HKR Akten, Präs. 1832/357, fol. 2–3.
46. Porcia to Metternich, Trieste, 14 March 1832, HHSA, StK., Prov., Küstenland, Carton 3: Korr. Triester Guberiums 1822–35, fol. 361–62.
47. Metternich to Radetzky, Vienna, 3 April 1832, HHSA, StK., Prov., L-V, Carton 24: Weisungen an die kommandierenden

Generäle l.v. Königreich Frimont und Radetzky 1826–1848, fol. 294–95.

48. Ronald E. Coons, *Steamships, Statesmen, and Bureaucrats: Austrian Policy Towards the Steam Navigation Company of the Austrian Lloyd, 1836–1848* (Wiesbaden: Franz Steiner Verlag, 1975), p. 22n, makes this point but gives it no emphasis.

49. Paulucci to HKR, Venice, 22 November 1832; KA, HKR Akten, Präs. 1832/1663, fol. 2–3; Ignaz von Hardegg (HKR president) to Francis, Vienna, 31 December 1832, ibid., Präs. 1832/1829, fol. 1–8; Paulucci to Hardegg, Venice, 16 January 1833, ibid., Präs. 1833/161, fol. 2–7; Nugent (military commander Küstenland) to Hardegg, Trieste, 16 February 1833, ibid., Präs. 1833/275, fol. 1–8.

50. Brandt, *Neoabsolutismus*, 1:102, suggests this but does not make a case for it, his work being concerned with a later period of Austrian history; see also ibid., 2:1104.

CHAPTER

4

In Defense of Morality and the Austrian Lloyd

As Austria entered a period of retrenchment in her foreign and domestic policies, the navy continued to restrict its regular duties to the Adriatic. Paulucci, after meeting his original goals for the size of the fleet, sought to preserve his accomplishments and, vis-à-vis the budget-cutting sentiments of Kolowrat and his circle, to prevent a further curtailment of the navy's activities. At the same time, the fleet was no longer threatened by schemes to sell warships and benefited from Metternich's growing conviction that, whenever possible, the ships on hand should be used to support Habsburg policy abroad. The chancellor's appreciation for the navy had been slow in coming, but by the late 1830s he developed firm ideas on the utility of sea power in demonstrating Austria's concern for "international morality" in crises far from her borders. The subsequent growth in the responsibilities of the navy increased still more in 1836 with the creation of the Austrian Lloyd, the Habsburg Empire's first seagoing steamship line.

Complacency and Economy: The Paulucci Era (1833–1839)

A tactful man with considerable political skills, Paulucci was well equipped to lead the navy through another period of austerity. But the success of his subtle maneuvering in the 1820s, which first brought him the job of

Marine-Ober-Kommandant, then a larger fleet to preside over, had made his personal position so secure that by the early 1830s he rarely showed the same energy that had characterized the first years of his tenure. His efforts were turned increasingly toward protecting both the earlier gains and his own scope of power, tasks which by their very nature encouraged complacency. Vienna did not lament the absence of dynamic naval leadership; the marquis knew when to avoid "rocking the boat" and was always able to make do with whatever funds he was given. For the most part he was left to his own devices and allowed to treat the navy as his personal domain. The navy, in turn, came to embody all of his best and worst personal characteristics.

The old tension within the officer corps between the Venetians and the veterans of the "Trieste navy" died out as more of the latter retired from service, but the natives of Venice remained sensitive about their status and were quick to take offense at perceived affronts to themselves and their city. As the senior Venetian officer, Dandolo assumed the role of self-appointed guardian of Venetian honor and at times took matters to ridiculous extremes. For instance, when Paulucci ordered the frigate *Bellona* scrapped at Trieste rather than Venice in 1830, Dandolo protested directly to Vienna that the decision was an insult to his city and its people.[1] Paulucci tried to rid himself of Dandolo, and the latter lived in fear that he would succeed in doing so, perhaps by assignment to a desk job in Vienna. The government chose to appease both men. In 1829, when admirals' ranks were finally introduced in the Austrian navy, the *Hofkriegsrat* went so far as to promote both Paulucci and Dandolo to rear admiral before making the marquis a vice admiral the following year. Despite their personal rivalry and differences of opinion on virtually every issue (including discipline, a matter in which Dandolo was especially critical of the commander), Paulucci had little reason to fear his Venetian adversary. Dandolo was older than he and, by the early 1830s, too old for active sea commands. His age also left him increasingly out of touch with the Venetian officers of younger generations, and his arrogance (he could boast of an 800-year lineage and a family tree that included four Doges) caused him to be disliked, if not disrespected, by all.²

In the 1830s the torch passed to the generation of men whose first experience as officers had been with the navy of the Napoleonic kingdom of Italy. After leading the operations against Morocco in 1828–30 and the Papal coast in 1831, Francesco Bandiera assumed command of the active squadron in the Adriatic when it ventured out again after the French occupation of Ancona. When Metternich sought to placate Louis Philippe by deporting to France a number of Italians taken prisoner in the Romagna, Bandiera received the call and in the summer of 1832 captained the frigate *Medea* on the mission from Venice to Marseilles and back. The chancellor was pleased with the success of the operation and turned to the navy once again to remedy a problem of far greater importance: the mass of refugees that had fled to Galicia from Russian Poland after the suppression of the Polish revolution of 1830–31.

The Poles were for the most part soldiers from the defunct rebel army, a source of great embarrassment for Metternich especially since he was attempting a rapprochement with Russia. In May 1833 Francis approved the chancellor's plan to deport them to the Americas on Austrian warships and in July put Bandiera in charge of planning the mission. After months of tedious negotiations between the *Polizeihofstelle* (imperial police office, in charge of the political internees) and the *Hofkriegsrat,* the first group of Poles left their refugee camps in Moravia to board the frigates *Ebe* and *Guerriera* at Trieste. Initial plans to sail first to South America were dropped in favor of a direct voyage to the United States. In November the two ships left for New York with 233 Poles on board.³

In March 1834 this first group of emigrants reached their destination; Bandiera sailed for home the following month and the frigates reached Trieste in June. By then a third warship, the corvette *Lipsia,* had left for New York with sixteen Poles, to return in November after a seven-month round trip. In February 1835 the corvette *Adria,* commanded by Lieutenant Giorgio Bua, a veteran of Pasqualigo's cruise to Brazil and Pöltl's to China, departed for America with another thirty-nine Poles. Its voyage to New York was the first for Ensign Attilio Bandiera, the oldest son of the esteemed captain; the ship returned home in August.

The cruises to New York marked the first appearance of the Austrian flag in North American waters. They provided invaluable training for officers and seamen alike, and the navy was more than happy to provide the service, especially since the voyages were not funded from its regular budget. But by 1835 wear and tear on the ships became a consideration. A vessel could be expected to take a beating during a transatlantic voyage (especially in winter) and naval authorities, with good reason, doubted that Vienna would authorize the construction of replacements if any of the existing warships were disabled. Attention was focused on possible alternatives, including shipping the refugees to Britain or France, both of which had already accepted great numbers of Poles but as yet none via Austria. As early as December 1833 the French had made overtures to Vienna for Polish officers, pledging to put them to work in North Africa.[4] In 1835 Metternich finally approved the scheme, and that summer Bandiera delivered sixty-eight Poles to Tangier aboard the *Guerriera.* In the fall of 1836 he took an additional eighty Poles to Toulon aboard the same ship, although on that occasion the French reneged on a deal to transport all of the men on to Algeria and allowed some to stay in France.

By 1836, at the navy's insistence, all deportations of Poles to America or Britain were carried out in chartered merchant ships. One further mission to New York, by the navy brig *Ussaro* from July 1836 to January 1837, involved the transportation of Federico Confalonieri and other Italian political prisoners, emigrants the imperial government considered too dangerous to be entrusted to civilian vessels. We may only speculate what influence these passengers may have had on the predominantly Italian crew of the *Ussaro,* but while in New York the ship suffered more desertions (five) than any of its predecessors had after carrying Polish exiles.[5]

Aside from the special voyages, the Austrian navy operated on a smaller scale than it had in the 1820s. Schooners were used for the Trieste-Corfu packet service and routine patrols of the Mediterranean, and far fewer ships stood watch in Levantine waters. The situation promised to worsen after the passing of Emperor Francis, who went to his grave in 1835 still resisting Kolowrat's calls for reductions in military and naval spending. Prior to his death, the emperor laid plans for a collective regency to govern the empire for his heir, the unfortunate Ferdinand. The council was to include Metternich, Kolowrat, and Archduke Ludwig, the least talented of his younger brothers. By the end of 1836, Kolowrat emerged as the victor in the power struggle that followed Ferdinand's accession to the throne and gained complete control over the domestic affairs of the empire, including finances. The following spring, he ordered deep cuts in the military and naval budgets. The new austerity program reduced the number of warships operating outside the Adriatic from one frigate, three corvettes, and two brigs to one frigate, one corvette, and one brig. In the future, the navy was to function within the limits of a new peacetime standard of eight active warships which included vessels as small as schooners.[6]

Metternich opposed Kolowrat's weakening of the imperial armed forces, but to no avail. Indeed, the two men were rarely in agreement about anything other than the need to continue Francis's policy of barring the more ambitious archdukes, especially Charles, from active participation in the affairs of state. To placate the disgruntled princes, the ministers commonly granted their wishes on matters of lesser importance. Charles, for instance, secured colonel's commissions for his two oldest sons, Albrecht and Charles Ferdinand, when they were still in their teens. When his third son, Frederick, expressed an interest in the sea, the archduke likewise met no resistance to his entry into naval service.

According to one of his tutors, Frederick at the age of fourteen decided on his own to pursue a naval career; his father approved, and two years later, in 1837, he became the youngest captain in the history of the Austrian navy. Charles no doubt influenced his son's choice. He had always been sympathetic toward the navy and must have reasoned that Frederick's opportunities at sea would be greater than in an army hierarchy already crowded with Habsburgs. The young archduke's first cruise, aboard the frigate *Medea* from July to October 1837, took him to Naples for a visit with his sister Maria Theresa, recently married to King Ferdinand II. He contracted typhus on the voyage and the following winter came so near death that Charles himself hastened to his bedside in Venice. The illness threatened to end his sea career, but by the summer of 1838 he had recovered enough to board the *Guerriera* for a cruise of the Western Mediterranean. Thereafter, his training progressed rapidly and on his third overseas voyage, to Greece in the summer of 1839, he commanded the corvette *Carolina*.[7]

Counting the vessels docked in reserve as a result of the budget cuts, the navy Frederick joined still had as its core four frigates and five corvettes; five large and five small brigs joined a number of lesser vessels to round out the fleet. By the late 1830s paddle steamers had become a common feature of the navies of Europe, but Austria had only one, the *Marianna*, launched at Porto Ré in 1836. Paulucci, like many older seamen, was wary of steam power and did not keep abreast of the latest developments in naval technology. In the absence of pressure from the top no one else in the naval hierarchy campaigned for a modernization of the fleet, and it was left to a soldier, *Feldmarschalleutnant* Nugent, to draft the first fleet plan to include steamships. The leader of the Austrian offensive to the coast in 1813, Nugent subsequently served for many years at Trieste as military commander of the Küstenland. After being the leading force behind the construction of the *Marianna*, he authored a plan for a fleet of three frigates and three corvettes, supported by four large and four small paddle steamers with another two dozen auxiliary steamers serving as transports or coastal defense ships. He argued that the cost of the steamships could be covered by selling the sailing ships they were to replace and by reorganizing the land-based branches of the service (naval infantry, artillery, and engineering) with an eye toward economy.[8] Needless to say, his proposals met the same fate as those of Crenneville in the early 1820s.

Nugent was not the only army leader with an interest in the navy. Field Marshal Radetzky, commander of the forces in Lombardy-Venetia since 1831, had a keen appreciation of the role sea power could play in a war in Italy. In the late 1830s he advocated concentrating the main force of the navy at an Istrian port, either Pola or Pirano, the dispersal of smaller vessels to guard the coast, and the use of steamers to improve communications in the upper Adriatic. Expounding a theory very much like the "fleet in being" of a half-century later, Radetzky argued that even if the stronger fleet of a major power entered the Adriatic (as the French navy had in 1832) the largest Austrian ships, if gathered in a single squadron at a port other than Venice or Trieste, would distract the adversary from a blockade of these harbors. Thus deployed, the fleet would contribute to the war effort even if forced to remain idle.[9]

The field marshal was not the first to suggest the construction of a naval base on the coast of Istria. Pola, a tiny fishing village on the site of an ancient Roman port, had drawn the attention of the French during the Napoleonic era. In 1814 Adamić recommended Pola instead of Venice as the main harbor for the navy, remarking that the "superb location of the port" made it "the best to handle the protection of all the rest of the Austrian coast." Pola was considered for use by the Austrian navy earlier in the 1830s but Paulucci, comfortable with the present state of affairs, vetoed the project and ensured that Venice would remain the principal anchorage of the fleet, at least for as long as he commanded it.[10]

When sketching plans for a possible Franco-Austrian war over Italy in the spring of 1839, Radetzky speculated that if

Austria were confronted by France on land and Britain at sea, she could hope to hold only Venice. On the other hand, if France were the only enemy at sea as well as on land, the field marshal thought the navy could attempt to take Ancona and defend the entire Adriatic coastline northward to Venice and Trieste. If Britain were neutral but potentially an ally of Austria, Radetzky thought it would be prudent for his "fleet in being" to deploy in the lower Adriatic at Cattaro or Lissa to impress the British with a gesture toward keeping the sea open to foreign commerce. Again rejecting Venice as a base for offensive operations, he reasoned that a southern location would facilitate the monitoring of enemy ships entering the Adriatic. He was especially intrigued with the notion of using steamships to transport large numbers of troops from the eastern coast of the Adriatic (presumably Croatians from the Military Border) to the western. He considered the Papal ports of Ravenna, Rimini, and Pesaro—all north of Ancona—invaluable landing sites and made their occupation a major goal of his war plans.[11]

By the late 1830s the navy had acquired a valuable network of political allies. Metternich, though not as powerful as he had once been, recognized the usefulness of an Austrian navy, as did Radetzky and Nugent, influential military men whose zones of command bordered the Adriatic. Ironically, aside from Kolowrat and his circle in Vienna, the navy's own commander was now the greatest impediment to its further development. Paulucci, like most old sailors of his generation, failed to appreciate the steamship as a potential weapon of war. Having accomplished his original goals for himself and for the navy, the marquis also lacked the desire to develop the capabilities of Austrian sea power to supplement the strategic needs of the army in Italy as envisioned by Radetzky. His refusal to cooperate with army leaders isolated the navy from an important base of support, and the technological backwardness of the fleet would in the long run frustrate other potential friends.

In the immediate future, however, Metternich's influence sufficed to guarantee the navy a role in the next clash of interests among the Great Powers, which came not in Italy, but in the Levant. The pasha of Egypt, supported by France, had intensified his long war with the sultan and by the summer of 1839 seemed on the verge of victory. After Egyptian troops crushed the Ottoman army, Turkish admiral Achmed Pasha deserted to Alexandria with most of the sultan's navy. As both Britain and France rushed ships to the Eastern Mediterranean, Metternich pressed for a meaningful Austrian naval presence in Levantine waters. In early August he got his wish. Frederick, just back from his cruise to Greece with the corvette *Carolina*, was given command of the frigate *Guerriera* and sent to Smyrna to join Bandiera, recently promoted to rear admiral and head of the reactivated Levant squadron.[12] The coming campaign was to bring the navy unprecedented international recognition and add even more momentum to the meteoric career of the young archduke.

The Founding of the Austrian Lloyd

The technological changes in shipbuilding threatened to render obsolete the sailing navies and merchant fleets of the world, but promised great benefits for the country willing to incorporate steamships into its navy or the entrepreneur daring enough to invest in ventures involving their commercial use. Whereas the Austrian navy failed to adjust to the new technology, the merchants of Trieste seized upon the opportunity it provided and in October 1835 founded a steamship line of their own. Their creation, the Steam Navigation Company of the Austrian Lloyd, was to form the catalyst for Austria's bid to become a commercial force in the Mediterranean.[13]

The Lloyd was the third steamship company to operate under the Austrian flag. In 1817 Vienna granted Englishman John Allen a concession to operate steamships between Trieste and Venice. His first steamer *Carolina*, built at the Panfilli shipyard in Trieste with an engine imported from Britain, was launched in November 1818, only months after Naples' *Ferdinando I* had become the first steamship in the Mediterranean.[14] Soon sold by Allen to other British investors, the line came to be known in the littoral as the "English Company." It remained a modest enterprise, never expanding beyond the Trieste-Venice route. Britons were also instrumental in founding Austria's second steamship line, the Danube Steam Navigation Company (Donau Dampfschiffahrtsgesellschaft, or D.D.S.G.), in 1829. After inaugurating regular service between Vienna and Pest in 1831, the Danube company grew rapidly and in 1834 expanded its operations into the Black Sea. Encouraged by Metternich (who was among the initial investors), the D.D.S.G. subsequently added routes from Constantinople to Smyrna, Beirut, Salonika (Thessaloniki), and Alexandria.

The founders of the Austrian Lloyd were all German or Italian businessmen based in Trieste, although few could claim it as their native city. Under the leadership of the energetic Carl Ludwig von Bruck, an insurance executive born in the Rhineland, the new firm sought to establish regular steamship service between Trieste and the sources of its most lucrative trade, the ports of the Levant.[15] Pressured by a French decision in July 1835 to create a fleet of steam packets in the Mediterranean, the Austrian government approved their plans and in August 1836 granted the company its first charter. The Lloyd budgeted a million florins for starting costs, most of it (780,000 florins) for the purchase of steam engines and the construction of six ships; initial projections were for an operating budget of just over a half million florins per year. The company raised its capital through a sale of stock, 60 percent of which was bought by Viennese banker Solomon Rothschild. His connections with the London House of Rothschild expedited the importation of ships and engines from Britain, enabling the Lloyd to start operations in May 1837.

A lucrative contract to carry the Austrian post to the Levant took effect in September 1837, guaranteeing the Lloyd a regular income from its voyages to Constantinople and Alexandria. The agreement also relieved the navy from the packet-boat duties it had performed since 1820, first on the Trieste-Corfu route and later to other ports in the Eastern Mediterranean. As far as the fleet was concerned, the creation of the Lloyd came in the nick of time since its only steamship, the brand-new *Marianna,* had just been assigned to carry mail to the Levant and Vienna was considering turning the vessel over to the Austrian postal administration for full-time packet duty.[16] There is no evidence that Paulucci or any other naval leader attached any special importance to the Lloyd in its early years, but strategists of greater insight, such as Radetzky, recognized that its steamers would be an asset in any future war effort since the government could charter the ships for use as troop transports or arm them as auxiliary naval vessels.

The company soon expanded its routes and its fleet. Four of the original six steamers were in service by the end of 1837, and a total of ten were operating at the end of the following year. The Lloyd gained access to Venice and a monopoly on the profitable Trieste-Venice passenger trade by buying out the "English Company" and took on the French line and a state-owned Neapolitan steamship firm in the Eastern Mediterranean.[17] Unfortunately, an international economic crisis in 1837 reduced the total trade of Trieste to sixty-one million florins, down from the previous year's peak of seventy million, and the Lloyd's rapid expansion of operations in the midst of the depression drove it dangerously close to bankruptcy. In the summer of 1838 the directors of the company suspended service to Alexandria and appealed to Vienna for financial help.

Metternich supported their pleas on the grounds that the Lloyd already was indispensable to Austria's interests in the Near East, but the court treasury was not so sympathetic. In September 1838 Rothschild intervened and offered the company a loan of 500,000 florins, provided the government guaranteed its repayment. Treasury officials balked at taking this unprecedented step, but Kolowrat's intervention in favor of the Lloyd ensured its approval. At the end of the year the emperor granted a package of minor concessions, and in July 1839 the contracts for the Rothschild loan were signed. Spared an early death, the steamship line contributed to a commercial recovery that saw the value of Trieste's trade increase to a new record of ninety million florins in 1839.

Because its chief foreign rivals were owned and operated by their governments, the Lloyd found it hard to obtain a solid share of the market in passengers and trade. It had long been the custom for countries to exempt their own navies and the visiting warships of foreign powers from all duties and quarantine regulations, and both France and Naples, which manned their steam packets with regular naval personnel, claimed that the vessels were warships entitled to the same privileges. The harbor taxes the Lloyd had to pay in Austrian as well as foreign ports added to its expenses, and the time its steamers had to spend in quarantine at the ports they visited made their service much slower than that of the competition. In its first year of operation the company petitioned Vienna for the "warship" status that would enable it to compete on equal terms with the steamers of France and Naples, but the president of the *Hofkriegsrat*, Count Ignaz von Hardegg, rejected the proposal. Nevertheless, when Naples made a bid to gain a share of the Adriatic trade for its commercial "warships," the Austrian government was forced to limit the privileges to genuine naval vessels on official business, thus guaranteeing that the Lloyd would not be at a disadvantage at least in the ports of its own country.

Just as Metternich had come to consider the navy a useful instrument of foreign policy, he saw in the Austrian Lloyd the potential salve for the strained Anglo-Austrian relations of recent years. In 1838 he encouraged the company to make a bid for the British–East India mail contract. The Austrian proposal was for the Lloyd to carry the mail between Egypt and Trieste and for coaches to handle the stretch from Trieste to the Channel coast via the German states and Belgium. The British, however, opted to let the French bring the Indian post to Marseilles, then by rail to Boulogne, a much faster route. Metternich was not discouraged by this failure, since he assumed (correctly, as it turned out) that Anglo-French tensions in the Near East would soon make Britain regret its decision. Meanwhile, his campaign for more cordial relations with the British remained closely intertwined with his aspirations for the Lloyd. Although he now accepted the Austrian navy as an asset to the empire, he had little confidence in its ability to protect the merchant steamers at sea against a hostile foreign power. In the event that the adversary were France, he believed that only the British navy could save the Lloyd from destruction.

In the end it was Metternich's diplomacy that worked to the benefit of the Lloyd's relations with the British, not vice-versa. In the summer of 1840, when the crisis in the Near East came to a head, the chancellor came down firmly on the side of Britain, which on this occasion was supporting Ottoman integrity, and against France's encouragement of Egyptian ambitions, which threatened to destroy the sultan's empire. An Austrian squadron was dispatched to the coast of Lebanon where, as we shall see, it drew praise for its performance in supporting the British fleet. After the crisis passed, many in London questioned the wisdom of leaving a link of the communications with India in French hands. In 1842 British Foreign Secretary Lord Aberdeen made overtures to Austria regarding a possible postal contract with the Lloyd.

The years of tedious negotiations that followed did not bring the Lloyd its coveted contract, but the process served other constructive purposes. On one hand, the increased dialogue between the two governments was in the spirit of the closer diplomatic ties that Metternich hoped for; on the other, in light of the fact that business and salesmanship had never been Austria's strong suit, the common action that united Vienna, the local authorities in Trieste, and the Lloyd in the campaign for the Indian mail provided an encouraging example for the future. Such cooperation between the central government, a provincial government, and a private company had no precedent in the history of the empire. Much to the Lloyd's benefit, this cooperation soon extended into areas other than the talks with Britain.

The two leading government figures in the interaction were both relatively new to their posts. Baron Carl Friedrich von Kübeck, a veteran treasury official whose liberal economic convictions were tempered by a pervasive pragmatism, was appointed president of the *Hofkammer* in 1840. Though he opposed government support for private businesses, Kübeck recognized the importance to the state of ventures such as the Lloyd and, on land, the railroads. Faced almost immediately with criticism from Venice over the privileges the government had granted to the Lloyd (and by implication, Trieste), he defended the company at the expense of his own free-trading principles. In 1841 the Lloyd gained another valuable ally when Count Franz Stadion, son of the former finance minister, was appointed governor of Trieste. Stadion was appalled by the previous administration's lack of support for the Lloyd and lobbied hard for the line and for improved communications between the littoral and the interior provinces of the empire. Even more pragmatic than Kübeck, he argued that "the theory of promoting competition in the public interest can hardly be applied to enterprises in which millions of florins are at stake."[18] In the first half of the 1840s both men took decisive steps to secure the future of the steamship company.

In order to strengthen the Lloyd vis-à-vis foreign rivals in the Levantine trade, Kübeck sought first of all to eliminate its Austrian competition. The D.D.S.G., in addition to its Danubian routes between Linz in Upper Austria and the mouth of the river, also reaped considerable profits from the Black Sea trade and its service from Constantinople into the Eastern Mediterranean, where in some cases it competed directly with the Lloyd. Kübeck first pressed the D.D.S.G. to reach some sort of accommodation with the Trieste line, but when this effort failed, he launched a campaign against the Danube company to force it to turn over its seagoing operations to the

Lloyd. By raising fears that the D.D.S.G. might sell these same routes to the Russians, Kübeck won an imperial order in January 1845 compelling it to limit its operations to the Danube. The Lloyd purchased the D.D.S.G.'s six seagoing steamships for a sum of 560,000 florins, gained rights to the routes in the Eastern Mediterranean it did not already serve, and subsequently extended its operations into the Black Sea.[19]

While Kübeck battled the D.D.S.G. on behalf of the Lloyd, the Trieste company continued to suffer from ever increasing debts and a shortage of capital. In order to attract new investors, it finally asked Vienna to guarantee annual dividends to its stockholders for a period of twenty years. Kübeck balked at this bold suggestion, but proposed to Stadion that Trieste itself undertake the obligation. The Lloyd, after all, was fueling the city's commercial boom as well as providing construction contracts for its shipbuilders, most notably the Panfilli firm. The municipal council of Trieste could hardly refuse. In February 1845, under heavy pressure from Stadion, it agreed to guarantee the dividends, thus publicly cementing the relationship between the city and the company. The guarantee was for the most part a symbolic act, especially since the imperial government at the same time pledged to provide the money if the city could not. A new government loan of one million florins to help cover past debts as well as the purchase of the six D.D.S.G. steamers and the cost of inaugurating service to the Black Sea was of far greater significance to the Lloyd than the guarantee.

Through the efforts of Kübeck and Stadion and the encouragement of Metternich and Kolowrat, the Austrian Lloyd by 1845 achieved the stability it needed to operate successfully. By demonstrating their clear commitment to the survival and prosperity of the Lloyd, the central, provincial, and local governments generated public confidence in the company and enabled it to attract the new investors essential to its quest for growth and independence. The creation of a private Austrian overseas steamship line opened cracks in the age-old wall dividing Vienna from the south and the sea. The decisions of the

Habsburg leadership to ensure the continued existence of the company were made primarily on strategic grounds and represented a significant departure from past indifference to the development of the empire's overseas interests. The Lloyd's rapid success in the Black Sea and Levantine trade attests to the fact that a share of this maritime commerce had been there for the taking all along. It was no small irony that these same routes had been dominated by Venetians prior to the destruction of the Venetian-Austrian merchant marine in the Napoleonic wars. In this light, it appears clear that the emergence of the Lloyd marked Austria's recovery of a share of trade lost over thirty years earlier when her defenseless merchantmen fell victim to pirates and privateers.

Triumph and Treason: The Paulucci Era (1840–1844)

The Near Eastern crisis of 1840 provided Metternich with a golden opportunity to improve Austria's relations with Britain. Throughout the 1830s the British foreign secretary, Lord Palmerston, had been the chancellor's nemesis in the international arena, but on the question of the preservation of the Ottoman Empire the two men shared the same views. In August 1839, well in advance of any formal international agreement, Austria increased its naval forces in Levantine waters by sending Archduke Frederick with an additional frigate to join the squadron recently reactivated under the command of the navy's most distinguished active seaman, Rear Admiral Bandiera.

The decision to give a frigate command to Frederick, now eighteen, apparently originated with Metternich himself, most likely under pressure from Archduke Charles. The young captain was hardly prepared for such an important assignment. Aside from his age, he had yet to finish his naval training and education, which was being supervised by Captain Johann Marinovich, appointed in 1837 as his personal companion and aide, and Colonel Wilhelm Lebzeltern of the army, one of his tutors since childhood. Fortunately, he was not put to the test upon his arrival in the Levant. In the quiet winter months of 1839–40, he had ample time for both practical and theoretical learning under the direction of Marinovich and Lebzeltern.[20]

The respite in the crisis came after both the British and French navies in January 1840 withdrew roughly half of their ships from the Eastern Mediterranean; their fleets were not to return to full strength until the summer. Despite the decreased tensions, Austria maintained a Levant squadron of two frigates and two corvettes throughout the winter although the number of brigs and smaller vessels accompanying them fluctuated over the months. By March 1840 the crisis had abated sufficiently to permit Frederick to sail first to Greece for a visit with King Otto, then to Constantinople for an audience with the sultan. He was sightseeing on land in Asia Minor when the Austrian squadron received word of an agreement concluded in London, aimed at forcing an end to the Turco-Egyptian war.

The Treaty of London (15 July 1840) committed Britain, Russia, Prussia, and Austria to a policy of armed mediation based upon the following terms: Mehemet Ali would become hereditary pasha of Egypt and ruler for life over southern Syria (Lebanon), but return to the sultan the remainder of Syria, the island of Crete, various Arabian conquests, and the Turkish fleet. Posed as an ultimatum, the points were rejected by the pasha, who counted on French support.[21] France, having backed Egypt prior to the crisis, was not a party to the London negotiations and reacted accordingly when the treaty was promulgated. Subsequent bellicose statements by Louis Philippe's prime minister, Adolphe Thiers, sparked a war scare along the Rhine while Radetzky rather cheerfully penned plans at his headquarters in Milan for the Italian theater of a continental war that would be fought under ideal circumstances. To fulfill Austria's obligations under the London agreement, the *Hofkriegsrat* on 17 July ordered Bandiera to place his squadron at the disposal of the British fleet for common action against Egypt.[22]

Bandiera and Frederick left Smyrna and in late August joined Admiral Robert Stopford's fleet off Alexandria. The two admirals paid a visit to the court of Mehemet Ali but failed to change his opinion of the Treaty of London. Following the expiration of an allied ultimatum, they resolved to use force to remove the Egyptian army from its coastal strongholds in Syria and Lebanon. British and Austrian warships joined loyal vessels of the Turkish navy in a bombardment of Beirut, destroying most of its fortifications, and on 15 September, at Lebzeltern's insistence, a nominal detachment of forty Austrians accompanied an Anglo-Turkish landing near the city. Five days later they marched inland for six hours but saw no action after an Egyptian force, attempting to relieve Beirut, withdrew rather than risk battle.[23]

The following week Frederick and his frigate *Guerriera* were among a squadron of ships detached for operations against Sidon, south of Beirut. After bombarding the city on 26 September, the allies sent landing parties ashore to take its citadel. Frederick personally led a detachment of seventy Austrians in the assault on the fort, which fell with little opposition. After the allies took Sidon, the local militias of the various Lebanese factions joined them in the campaign against Mehemet Ali's troops. On 10 October the allies occupied Beirut, and a week later it took only the appearance of the Austrian corvette *Clemenza* to bring the surrender of Tripoli. Allied forces subsequently took Haifa and Tyre, leaving Acre as the only Levantine city still under Egyptian control.[24]

Disagreements among the British commanders prevented immediate action against Acre, but after Stopford received a dispatch from Palmerston full of rumors of a French expedition to relieve Mehemet Ali, the decision was made to attack without delay. On 2 November Bandiera's flagship *Medea*, Frederick's *Guerriera,* and the corvette *Lipsia* joined seventeen British warships (including four steamers) and the Turkish flagship in the waters off Acre. The following day they lobbed forty thousand shells into the city, silencing its batteries and prompting the Egyptian commander to order an evacuation after nightfall. This activity caught the attention of British Captain Baldwin Walker (at the time, commander of the Turkish navy as "Rear Admiral Walker Bey"), who came aboard the *Guerriera* to propose to Frederick a landing that would take the citadel of Acre in a pre-dawn coup. The archduke hastened ashore with a small landing party but found only an equally modest British detachment waiting on the beach. Undeterred, he led the men through the rubble-strewn streets of the city, surprised what was left of the garrison, and at sunrise raised the British, Turkish, and Austrian flags above the citadel.[25]

Stopford was quick to reprimand Frederick for his recklessness, stressing "the absolute necessity of waiting for orders from the Commander-in-Chief before any partial enterprise should be undertaken, however worthy the motive or spirited the execution."[26] But no one could argue with success. The fall of Acre forced Mehemet Ali to open negotiations with the allies, and in late November he signed a convention pledging to evacuate both Syria and Lebanon and return the Turkish ships that had deserted to him in exchange for recognition as hereditary pasha of Egypt. The crisis among the powers of Europe, effectively ended by the fall of Thiers in late October, had as its dénouement the Straits Convention of July 1841 in which France joined the signatories of the Treaty of London in declaring the Dardanelles and Bosporus closed to all foreign warships as long as the Ottoman Empire remained at peace. The agreement represented a defeat for Russia, since it formally ended St. Petersburg's claim, dating from the Treaty of Unkiar-Skelessi, to the privileged position of sole protector of the Porte. This turn of events brought an international solution to the problem that Metternich had sought to contain in the Treaty of Münchengrätz. With Austria's diplomatic clout weakened by reductions in her military strength, it merely took longer for the chancellor to see his goals realized.

In February 1841 Frederick returned to Trieste with his frigate. A trip to Vienna the following month featured an emotional reception from Archduke Charles and Emperor Ferdinand, then a series of fêtes and ceremonies in which the young captain received numerous awards and decorations. Meanwhile, back in the Levant, Bandiera was ordered to detach the remaining Habsburg vessels from the British fleet and end the Anglo-Austrian cooperation. Admiral Stopford subsequently wrote to Metternich that he had been "satisfied with the zeal, tact, and bravery displayed on all occasions by the Rear Admiral [Bandiera], His Royal Imperial Highness the Archduke Frederick, and every officer and man" of the Austrian squadron.[27] Having proved its value in action, the navy was allowed to continue operations in the Eastern Mediterranean after the crisis ended.

Britain's praise for the Levant squadron reinforced Metternich's overall satisfaction with the navy. Paulucci likewise could only be content with the acclaim his fleet had earned after so many years of trial and uncertainty. Little did they know that the service was about to face its greatest test, this time from an internal threat. Just as the active leadership of the navy (with the exception of Frederick) was now in the hands of Bandiera's generation, the junior membership of the officer corps had passed for the most part to Italians born during or after the Napoleonic era. Coming of age in the wake of the revolutions of 1830, the new subalterns proved receptive to the ideals of nationalism. By 1840 the writings of Giuseppe Mazzini, founder of the Young Italy movement in 1831, enjoyed a special popularity among the junior officers of the Austrian navy. A number of factors combined to facilitate the spread of Mazzinian ideas within the corps: the tradition of deferrence to the empire's Italian population and the influence of Venice itself; the special social character of the naval officer corps; the atmosphere at the naval academy in Venice; and, most important, Paulucci's personal attitudes and their effect on the navy as a whole.

After 1814 Vienna had accepted the fact that Italians populated much of the littoral, dominated all of it, and were by nature the monarchy's chief seafaring people. In subsequent years the absence of Carbonari activity among Italians serving in the fleet reinforced the notion that there was no particular danger in Austria having an "Italian" navy. Venice seemed to have such a magical effect on newcomers that it made no difference that during the Paulucci era the percentage of non-Italians in the navy grew at a steady rate: they had to come to Venice and learn Italian in order to enter the service and invariably were assimilated.[28]

As for the corps itself, Austrian naval officers, like most military officer corps, constituted a close-knit social elite. The navy was the traditional profession of some of the leading aristocratic families of Venice, and many of the same surnames from among the Venetian commanders at the Battle of Lepanto (1571) also appear on rosters of Austrian naval officers before 1848. An inadequate number of scholarships made it difficult for the sons of lesser families to gain admission to the naval academy, and the high cost of a proper social life in Venice guaranteed a clientele from a wealthy, if not always aristocratic background. Dandolo and his Venetian peers treated all non-Venetians as outsiders but Bandiera's generation was far more tolerant, and as a result the corps grew even more cohesive through frequent marriages between non-Venetian (even non-Italian) officers and the daughters or sisters of their Venetian counterparts. The small size of the corps (between 100 and 150 sea officers) increased the effectiveness of social control through peer pressure and ensured that when a crisis did erupt, the primary loyalty of the officers would be to one another, not to Austria.

The naval academy at Venice was taken over intact from the Napoleonic kingdom of Italy and initially languished because of Vienna's lack of interest. It had only five students in 1820 when a series of reforms expanded the curriculum and ushered in better times. A standard five-year program was introduced, adding German, religion, and history to the traditional courses of mathematics and navigation. The quality of instruction improved markedly, and by the 1830s the enrollment averaged fifty students per year. Since only those on scholarships were obligated to enter the navy upon graduation, the academy educated a number of young men who went on to pursue other careers; the future world-renowned railroad builder Karl Anton von Ghega, son of a naval officer, was among its most famous civilian alumni. One graduate later characterized the course of study as the most liberal available at the time anywhere in Italy. The language of instruction was Italian; even German was taught in Italian, and history classes presented a version of the French Revolution and Napoleonic Wars that openly glorified both Napoleon and the ideals of nationalism. In the mid-1830s the staff of the academy took no action when Mazzinian literature began to circulate among their young charges.[29]

All of this was possible, of course, because of the manner in which the navy was run. Paulucci was a man of great tact, always careful to avoid clashes with higher authorities, but when it came to matters of internal policy he was in complete control and would brook no interference from Vienna or local Austrian military officials. He never cooperated with the state police and did so with the army only when it was absolutely necessary. Never a disciplinarian, he did not subscribe to Dandolo's traditional views on upholding the integrity of the corps. Instead, the marquis preferred to settle problems by sweeping them under the rug, delaying hearings sometimes for years, and never inflicting punishments to the degree prescribed by the navy's codes. His attitude toward regulations in general was far removed from that of the typical Austrian army commander. The decrees implemented by Conninck, introducing German as the administrative language of the navy and requiring its use in official dispatches, were ignored in the Paulucci era. The admiral himself did not like to use German and consequently did not require it of his subordinates. As a result, in practice Italian remained the written as well as the spoken language of the navy.[30]

It was under these circumstances that Mazzini began to win disciples among the younger officers of the corps. It helped tremendously that Francesco Bandiera's sons, Attilio and Emilio, were early converts to the Italian cause. Given their father's esteemed position, they were above reproach regardless of how indiscreetly they aired their nationalist views. Attilio, a 1828 graduate of the naval college, sailed to America in 1835 aboard the corvette *Adria* in one of the deportations of Polish exiles. While in New York he met an Italian nationalist émigré named Pietro Maroncelli, and their subsequent correspondence provided the first opportunity for him to articulate his revolutionary ideas.[31] His younger brother appears to have adopted Mazzinian views around the same time. Emilio, a 1836 graduate of the academy, was providing Young Italy literature to his classmates during his last year or two there.[32]

Toward the end of 1839 the Bandiera brothers began to conspire actively against the Austrian government, and in 1840 they founded the secret society Esperia with several of their fellow officers. During the campaign in the Levant, Attilio served as personal adjutant to his father, Rear Admiral Bandiera, aboard the flagship *Medea,* and Emilio was on the staff of Frederick's *Guerriera.* They did not distinguish themselves during the campaign (or at any other time during their careers), although Attilio was cited for his performance during the bombardment of Acre. Other initiates of the sect displayed a valor in action during 1840 that no doubt helped to shield them from suspicion in subsequent years. Cadet Domenico Chinca, one of the charter members of Esperia, was Frederick's standard-bearer for the landing at Sidon and led the storming of the citadel with cries of "Guerriera avanti!" He was decorated for bravery, as was Domenico Moro of the *Lipsia,* another early convert of the Bandieras.[33]

After the end of the Near Eastern crisis, Admiral Bandiera's squadron patrolled the Eastern Mediterranean in defense of Austrian political and commercial interests. Attilio continued to serve as adjutant to his father while proselytizing for the cause of Italian revolution. Because of its isolation from the centers of Italian émigré activity (the ships were based at Smyrna when not at sea), Esperia in its first years developed few connections with other Young Italy sects. This changed in 1842, when the requirements of Frederick's advancing career facilitated the group's first contact with Mazzini.

In March 1841, during Frederick's visit to Vienna, Archduke Charles suggested to the emperor that the position of *Marine-Ober-Kommandant* would be a suitable reward for his son's recent acts of heroism at Sidon and Acre. True, he had yet to see his twentieth birthday, but his older brothers had already been given regimental commands in the army, and they had never even been under fire. By Charles's reasoning, it was time for Frederick to receive a promotion. Within days plans were set in motion to groom the young archduke as Paulucci's successor. The marquis was nearing seventy and would have to be relieved within a few years anyway. In the meantime, *Hofkriegsrat* president Count Hardegg stressed to the emperor that Frederick would have to familiarize himself with the administrative duties of the commander and, to avoid offending the sensibilities of the existing naval hierarchy, must command at least one independent mission overseas.[34]

It was decided that the voyage should be to Britain. The archduke was to tour the bases and shipyards of the Royal Navy, meet with Stopford and other acquaintances from the Levantine campaign, and receive the Order of the Bath from Queen Victoria. In the spring of 1842 the new frigate *Bellona* was launched in the Arsenal at Venice and shortly thereafter assigned to Frederick for his voyage. As the first visit to Britain ever undertaken by a Habsburg warship, the cruise was intended to show off Austria's finest. The officers and crew were hand-picked and included a number of veterans from the campaign of 1840, among them Ensign Domenico Moro. In late June the vessel left port amid great fanfare; Charles and his sons Albrecht and Charles Ferdinand made the trip to Venice for the occasion. Few were aware that Moro was carrying a letter written in Smyrna by Attilio Bandiera and intended for Mazzini, who was living in exile in London.[35]

The mission went off smoothly for both Frederick and Moro. After stops at Algiers, Gibraltar, and Lisbon, the

Bellona reached England in September. A stay of three and a half months gave the archduke plenty of time to carry out his itinerary, the highlight of which was a visit with Victoria and Albert at Windsor Castle. The ensign, meanwhile, was able to find Mazzini in London and deliver the letter, in which Attilio introduced himself and the group he had formed, gave a broad sketch of his revolutionary philosophy, and pointed out his principal value to the cause: "I am an Italian and a man of war," he wrote, "not an exile." In Esperia, Mazzini had a devoted cell of followers unlike any other. They were operating within the armed forces of one of the governments that he sought to overthrow.[36]

The *Bellona* set sail from Spithead on New Year's Day, 1843 and reached Trieste three weeks later. In early February Frederick was promoted to rear admiral and brigadier of the naval infantry, his first major assignment on land. The *Bellona* was sent on to the Levant where it became the new flagship of Admiral Bandiera. During 1843, correspondence intensified between the Bandiera brothers and Mazzini, and Esperia began to work with other Young Italy sects in the Mediterranean. Their most important collaborator was Nicolo Fabrizi, a Modenese émigré living on Malta. After meeting Attilio during 1842, he became Esperia's chief connection with the rest of the Italian revolutionary movement and attempted to coordinate the activities of his own group, the Legione Italica, with those of the Bandieras. The brothers laid plans for a general mutiny of the Levant squadron to be led by Attilio aboard the *Bellona*, Emilio aboard the corvette *Clemenza*, Moro on the corvette *Adria*, and Ensign Ippolito Mazzuchelli on the brig *Tritone*. In late August 1843 Emilio wrote Fabrizi that Esperia could count on "120 men of the most firm resolution" to take over the four ships and place them at the disposal of the Italian cause.[37]

Fabrizi encouraged the Bandieras to act without delay. Working under the assumption that the ships could be seized, the Bandieras laid out several options for their future use, including a descent on Genoa or one of the Papal coasts, or operations off Naples or Sicily in support of landings by the Legione Italica. But Mazzini ultimately ordered a postponement of the plans on the grounds that an asset as valuable as a naval squadron should only be used in support of a revolution that had some chance of success; the mutiny would have to wait until such an uprising could be organized. In the meantime, he sent to the Levant a fellow exile, Tito Vespasiano Micciarelli, as his personal envoy to Esperia.

The brothers passed the last months of 1843 in idle plotting at the squadron's winter anchorage in Smyrna. There is some question about how much Admiral Bandiera knew of his sons' activity, but if later testimony of fellow officers is to be believed, Attilio and his cohorts regularly aired their nationalist views in his presence. Nevertheless, evidence of a plot by Attilio during the winter of 1843–44—to desert to Constantinople, seize an armed steamship and attack the *Bellona* in order to force his father to turn the frigate over to him—indicates that while probably aware of his sons' political leanings, the admiral did not sympathize with them or have any knowledge of their revolutionary schemes.[38] In not reporting Attilio or Emilio to the authorities, he merely behaved as any father would under similar circumstances. His past record left his own loyalty to the empire beyond question, but by 1843 his enthusiasm for the Habsburg service may have weakened a bit. Not yet sixty, Admiral Bandiera ranked behind only the aging Paulucci and Dandolo in seniority and was the man most hurt by the decision to designate Frederick as the next *Marine-Ober-Kommandant*. As a career officer so close to the top of the *Rangliste*, he must have aspired to command the navy himself and could not have been pleased to see an imperial prince less than half his age suddenly emerge to rob him of the honor.

The mutiny plans laid in the summer of 1843 were dashed toward the end of the year by the reassignment of two of Esperia's leaders; first Mazzuchelli was given a teaching position at the naval academy, then Emilio Bandiera was transferred to Venice and the post of personal adjutant to Paulucci. Emilio arrived in Venice in late December and according to the later recollection of the marquis, assumed his new duties with no indication of dissatisfaction at the transfer. In February 1844 the ensign asked Paulucci for a two-day leave to attend a Carnival ball in Trieste. The old commander, true to his traditional lenient standards, approved the request and on 17 February Emilio left Venice. Three days later he sent word via a Lloyd steamer that illness had detained him in Trieste, and on 23 February he disappeared. In early March, word reached Venice that Attilio Bandiera had left the *Bellona* on 28 February and had failed to return. The brothers had embarked on a fatal quixotic adventure, plunging the navy into the greatest crisis of its history.[39]

By 1844 Austria had begun to assign the navy more significant tasks than chasing pirates or simply showing the flag. The Levantine operations of 1840 marked the Habsburg Empire's first use of sea power as an instrument of foreign policy in a conflict involving the other powers of Europe. The activity of the navy during the Near Eastern war was based on Metternich's desire to have the "moral authority" of Austria demonstrated in a diplomatic crisis somewhat removed from her own borders, but the outcome of which was nevertheless vital to her interests. By showing its usefulness in the campaign against the Egyptians, the fleet rescued itself from the penury imposed by the general cuts in military spending that followed the death of Francis.

In the meantime, the founding of the Austrian Lloyd enabled the empire at last to break into the ranks of the commercial powers of the Mediterranean. Vienna's decision to extend financial assistance to the company marked a historic step away from the northward, inland orientation of the previous century of Habsburg grand strategy. But the modern vessels of the growing steamship line stood in sharp contrast to those of the navy, which still relied almost exclusively on ships inherited from the French at Venice over two decades earlier. While the Lloyd kept pace with the latest technological developments in ship design, the fleet charged with protecting it grew increasingly antiquated. The lack of funds for modernization and Paulucci's disdain for innovation raised fears that in the long run the navy would be unable to fulfill its duties. The crisis touched off by the desertion of the Bandiera brothers withered the fleet's newly won laurels and, albeit for a different reason, made the doubts about its effectiveness universal.

NOTES

1. Dandolo to Gyulai (HKR president), Vienna, 24 November 1830, KA, HKR Akten, Präs. 1830/1575, fol. 365–367.

2. Assignment to Vienna would have been disastrous for Dandolo, who could neither speak German nor ride a horse. Later in the 1830s Paulucci requested that the *Hofkriegsrat* retire him, but instead Dandolo was promoted to vice admiral in 1836 and official second-in-command of the navy in 1838.

3. The diplomatic context and preparation for the missions are discussed at length in Francis to Gen. Ignaz von Hardegg (HKR president), Schönbrunn, 22 July 1833, KA, HKR Akten, Präs. 1833/1201, fol. 3; HKR to Paulucci, Vienna, 7 August 1833, ibid., Präs. 1833/1275, fol. 1–6; HKR to Marine-Ober-Kommando, Vienna, 15 August 1833, ibid., Präs. 1833/1311, fol. 1–6; HKR circular, Vienna, 17 August 1833, ibid., Präs. 1833/1317–1318–1355, fol. 1–41; HKR to Hofkammer, Vienna, 26 August 1833, ibid., Präs. 1833/1379–1381, fol. 1–7; HKR circular, Vienna, 5 September 1833, ibid., Präs. 1833/1444, fol. 1–6. See also Khuepach and Bayer, *1814–1847*, pp. 228–38 passim.

4. HKR to Polizeihofstelle, Vienna, 13 December 1833, KA, HKR Akten, Präs. 1833/1898–1902, fol. 1–80; HKR to Polizeihofstelle, Vienna, 20 December 1833, ibid., Präs. 1833/1905–1942, fol. 1, 12.

5. The *Ussaro*'s crew numbered only ninety-two men, making the desertion of five seamen a great loss. Khuepach and Bayer, *1814–1847*, pp. 235–36, discuss the brig's mission without even men-

tioning that Confalonieri was aboard. Italian sources also fail to credit the Austrian navy with deporting him; however, the dates and description of the voyage confirm that he was among its passengers.

6. Hardegg to Ferdinand, Vienna, 8 March 1837, KA, HKR Akten, Präs. 1837/325, fol. 1–12; Ferdinand to Hardegg, Vienna, 19 April 1837, ibid., Präs. 1837/615, fol. 2–3; peacetime standard referred to in Baron Carl Friedrich Kübeck to Hardegg, Vienna, 27 October 1842, ibid., Präs. 1842/1849, fol. 3–4. In 1835 the military was budgeted 64.4 million florins, in 1837 only fifty million; annual military expenditure remained under sixty million through 1847. See figures in Brandt, *Neoabsolutismus*, 2:1098.

7. Joseph Bergmann, *Erzherzog Friedrich von Oesterreich und sein Antheil am Kriegszuge in Syrien im Jahre 1840* (Vienna: Tendler & Co., 1857), pp. 5–10. From 1831 to 1837, Bergmann tutored Frederick and his brothers in history, logic, Latin, and "psychologie."

8. Khuepach and Bayer, *1814–1847*, pp. 86–87, 90–94; Wilhelm Schutze (Dalmatian coal broker) to Metternich, Rijeka, 12 July 1841, HHSA, StK., Notenwechsel HKR, Carton 293, a.d. HKR, Marine 1800–52/2.

9. Radetzky, "Uebersicht des Küstengebietes von Triest über Venedig bis gegen Ravenna," n.d. [late 1830s], KA, Nachlass Radetzky, B/1151: A.27.

10. Adamić to Hudelist, Rijeka, 10 May 1814, HHSA, StK., Prov., Küstenland, Carton 5: Fiume 1761–1846, fol. 11–12; Khuepach and Bayer, *1814–1847*, p. 111.

11. Radetzky, "Militärischer Überblick Mittel-Italiens," Milan, [spring] 1839, KA, Nachlass Radetzky, B/1151: A.33, fol. 42–77.

12. HKR circular, Vienna, 5 August 1839, KA, HKR Akten, Präs. 1839/1239, fol. 1–5; Bergmann, *Erzherzog Friedrich*, p. 10.

13. Unless otherwise noted, the paragraphs below are based upon Coons, *Steamships, Statesmen, and Bureaucrats;* Stefani and Astori, *Il Lloyd Triestino;* and *Fünfundsiebzig Jahre österreichischer Lloyd* (Trieste: Verlag des österreichischen Lloyd, 1911), passim.

14. The Panfilli firm, founded in 1780, was the oldest and largest shipbuilding company in Trieste.

15. On Bruck's early life and career see Richard Charmatz, *Minister Freiherr von Bruck: Der Vorkämpfer Mitteleuropas* (Leipzig: S. Hirzel, 1916), pp. 5–28.

16. Khuepach and Bayer, *1814–1847*, p. 192. The sources listed in note 13 above make few references to relations between the Lloyd

and the navy. Coons mentions the fleet only in passing and does not comment on the possibility of military use for Lloyd steamers.

17. The Neapolitan shipping line was formed in 1836.

18. Stadion to Kübeck, Trieste, 19 October 1842, quoted in Coons, p. 99.

19. The D.D.S.G. continued to dominate riparian commerce in the Habsburg Empire. A complementary steamship line on the Sava River in Croatia failed in the fall of 1845 after only one year in operation. See Karaman, *Privreda i društvo,* pp. 29–32.

20. Archduke Charles to Hardegg, Vienna, 10 April 1837, KA, HKR Akten, Präs. 1837/514, fol. 2, discusses the selection of Marinovich as Frederick's naval tutor. Charles calls him an "excellent choice" and notes that he "has already earned the trust of my son."

21. Albrecht-Carrié, *Diplomatic History,* p. 54.

22. Khuepach and Bayer, *1814–1847,* p. 246. Radetzky, "Pro desideria in Bezug auf die Vertheidigung Italiens 1840," KA, Nachlass Radetzky, B/1151: A.31, echoes his earlier views on sea power.

23. Bergmann, *Erzherzog Friedrich,* pp. 29–30.

24. Ibid., pp. 31–33, 36.

25. Ibid., pp. 37–41.

26. Stopford to Bandiera, Beirut, 11 November 1840, text in Bergmann, p. 44.

27. Stopford to Metternich, Malta, 5 April 1841, text in Khuepach and Bayer, *1814–1847,* p. 263.

28. For the influence of Venice on future admirals Wilhelm von Tegetthoff and Maximilian von Sterneck see Franco Micali Baratelli, *La marina militare italiana nella vita nazionale (1860–1914)* (Mursia: U. Mursia editore S.p.A., 1983), pp. 96, 152, and Maximilian Daublebsky von Sterneck zu Ehrenstein, *Admiral Max Freiherr von Sterneck: Erinnerungen aus den Jahren 1847 bis 1897,* ed. Jerolim Benko von Boinik (Vienna: A. Hartleben, 1901), pp. 36–50 passim.

29. Salcher, *Marine-Akademie,* pp. 14–15, 15n, 34, 38–39, 45; Carlo Alberto Radaelli, *Storia dello Assedio di Venezia negli anni 1848–1849* (Venice: Tipografia Antonelli, 1875), pp. 1–3. Radaelli was a classmate of Emilio Bandiera (1836) and founding member of Esperia. In 1844 FMLt. Count Ferdinand Zichy, army commandant of Venice, complained to Metternich of the way that Napoleonic-era history was taught at the academy; Zichy notes on conversation with Metternich, Trieste, August 1844, KA, Nachlass Zichy, B/184:2, fol. 83–86.

30. Khuepach and Bayer, *1814–1847*, p. 99, notes Paulucci's differences with Dandolo over discipline; KA, Marineakten (hereafter cited as KA, MA), A/j 7 (1840), no. 5, and "Comissions-Vortrag sammt Gutachten," Venice, 27 July 1841, ibid., no. 5–a, give indications of Paulucci's attitude toward the police in a case involving one of his own sons, artillery captain Antonio Paulucci; Zichy notes on conversation with Metternich (Trieste, August 1844), KA, Nachlass Zichy, B/184:2, fol. 83–86, criticizes the admiral's refusal to cooperate with army officials in Venice and his attitude toward the German language.

31. Maroncelli had once been held at the famous Spielberg prison, where Confalonieri also served time, and according to Mazzini was brutally tortured by the Austrians; see Giuseppe Mazzini, "Italy, Austria and the Pope: A Letter to Sir James Graham" (1845), in *Scritti editi ed inediti di Giuseppe Mazzini* (Edizione Nazionale), 95 vols. (Imola: Cooperativa Tipografico Editrice Paolo Galeati, 1921), 31:303.

32. Mazzini, "Ricordi dei fratelli Bandiera" (1845), *Scritti editi ed inediti*, 31:62; Paulucci to HKR, Venice, 30 April 1844, KA, HKR Akten, Präs. 1844/684, fol. 1–15, 34, refers to Emilio's involvement in questionable political activity as early as 1834 when he was a fifteen-year-old student at the naval college.

33. Khuepach and Bayer, *1814–1847*, pp. 250–53, 261–62. Ernesto Simion and Mario Nani Mocenigo, *La campagna navale di Siria del 1840* (Rome: Tip. Ufficio del Capo di Stato Maggiore, 1933), p. 104, contend that Frederick's heroism has been overrated and that Chinca was the "true hero" of Sidon.

34. Ferdinand to Hardegg, Vienna, 22 March 1841, KA, HKR Akten, Präs. 1841/555, fol. 4; Hardegg to Ferdinand, Vienna, 26 March 1841, ibid., Präs. 1841/623, fol. 2–3, 6; HKR circular (to Charles and Paulucci), Vienna, 3 April 1841, ibid., Präs. 1841/609, fol. 1–2; Archduke Charles to Hardegg, Vienna, 5 April 1841, ibid., Präs. 1841/623, fol. 1.

35. See Bergmann, *Erzherzog Friedrich*, pp. 49–54; Khuepach and Bayer, *1814–1847*, p. 239; Mazzini, "Ricordi dei fratelli Bandiera," *Scritti editi ed inediti*, 31:24–25. Bergmann (writing in 1857) omits the names of Moro and other Esperia members from his list of Frederick's staff on the *Bellona* cruise, and neither he nor Khuepach and Bayer mention Moro's role as a messenger to Mazzini. Italian historians, on the other hand, never mention Frederick in their account of Moro's mission and usually refer to the ship as the *Adria,* a vessel Moro later served on.

36. Bergmann, *Erzherzog Friedrich,* pp. 54–67; Attilio Bandiera to Mazzini, Smyrna, 15 August 1842 [*sic*], quoted in Mazzini, "Ricordi dei fratelli Bandiera," *Scrittt editi ed inediti,* 31:23. August 15 could not have been the date on the letter Moro gave Mazzini unless Attilio Bandiera postdated it.

37. Emilio Bandiera to Fabrizi, n.p., 30 August 1843, quoted in Franco Della Peruta, "Attilio Bandiera," *Dizionario Biografico degli Italiani,* vol. 5 (Rome: Istituto della Enciclopedia Italiana, 1963), 683.

38. Zichy notes on conversation with Metternich, Trieste, August 1844, KA, Nachlass Zichy, B/184:2, fol. 83–86, refers to revolutionary talk "bey der Tafel des Contre-Admiral Bandiera zu Smirna." Zichy to Hardegg, Venice, 1 June 1844, KA, HKR Akten, Präs. 1844/973, fol. 2–7 reviews evidence including Attilio's "steamer plot."

39. Paulucci to HKR, Venice, 8 March 1844, KA, HKR Akten, Präs. 1844/532, fol. 7–8 (first official report of Emilio's disappearance); Capt. Alexander Bujacovich to Paulucci, Smyrna, 10 March 1844, ibid., fol. 15–20 (first report of Attilio's desertion from the *Bellona*).

CHAPTER

5

The Catastrophe

The crisis that crippled the navy in 1844 exposed all of the oversights of the past three decades and foreshadowed the disaster that was to occur in 1848. The admiral in command during the great upheaval of March 1848 later referred to the Venetian Revolution as "the catastrophe" because of the debilitating effect it had on the Habsburg fleet. Yet it is more accurate to apply this label to the entire period from the desertion of the Bandieras to the outbreak of the revolution. In the wake of the events of 1844, few believed that the navy would do its duty if called upon, and when revolution finally came to Venice, the disloyalty of the officers and men stationed there surprised no one. In the intervening years Vienna charged the youthful Archduke Frederick with the task of leading the navy out of the crisis, but even he could not escape the fact that a peaceful "de-italianization" of the fleet was impossible.

Deserters, Patriots, Martyrs: The Bandiera Brothers (1844)

The immediate motivation behind the desertion of the Bandieras remains a mystery. Italian authors, working from the brothers' correspondence with Mazzini and Fabrizi in the weeks following their flight, cast Field Marshal Radetzky and Mazzini's own envoy Micciarelli as the villains. According to their accounts, Micciarelli made contact with Attilio Bandiera in Smyrna during the winter of 1843–44, then in January 1844 betrayed him by informing the Austrian ambassador in Constantinople of his revolutionary activities. Shortly thereafter, when Attilio learned that he was to be transferred to Venice, he deserted to avoid arrest by Austrian authorities upon his return home. At the same time Emilio, in his capacity as personal adjutant to Paulucci, saw a letter to the commander from Radetzky in which the field marshal named him as the leader of a conspiracy within the navy. The younger Bandiera likewise deserted before being arrested.[1]

Archival materials not consulted in these reconstructions of the Bandiera desertions reveal that the Austrian envoy to the Porte, Count Bartholomäus von Stürmer, did not write to Vienna about Attilio until three weeks after he left the *Bellona*.[2] If Micciarelli indeed told Stürmer about his plots, the information could not have prompted an Austrian order for his arrest or transfer home. Attilio in fact was not ordered to Venice prior to his desertion, even though he himself had filed a request for reassignment there.[3] As for Radetzky, there is no evidence that he had prior knowledge of Emilio's seditious activity. His first dispatch concerning the Bandieras came one month after Emilio was confirmed as missing from Trieste, and in it the field marshal discusses the desertion of the brothers as he would any other news item.[4] Metternich's intelligence connections indicated that a major Italian uprising was being planned for the spring of 1844,[5] but he had no warning that Mazzinian cells within the navy were involved in the plotting. The Bandieras may have deserted to take part in this revolution or simply in reaction to their separation; the latter would also explain Attilio's requests for a transfer to Venice. As for their timing, February 1844—a mere two months after Emilio's reassignment—probably was the earliest date that they could arrange their respective escapes. It is clear that the Bandieras did not view their desertion as an abdication of their leadership of Esperia or an abandonment of the goal of revolutionizing the fleet. They were confident of the support of scores of fellow officers and seamen and assumed that others would follow their example. If anything, they felt that their personal break with Austria enhanced their positions as revolutionary leaders.

In his flight from Trieste, Emilio Bandiera was assisted by Giulio Canal, a native of the city and member of Esperia who had recently left naval service. Canal gave him a false passport, money, and civilian clothes, after which Emilio boarded the Lloyd steamer *Imperatore* for Corfu. The captain of the vessel, Tommaso Gelcich, was a veteran of the Levantine trade who knew Emilio; as a sympathizer with the Italian cause, Gelcich ensured that the fugitive's travel papers were not questioned. Emilio reached Corfu on 27 February, ten days after he left Venice.[6] The following day in Smyrna harbor, Attilio Bandiera left the *Bellona* with Paolo Mariani, a gunnery mate who had also been acting as his personal servant. One report had him going ashore in the afternoon to "settle an affair of honor," while another witness testified that he went into Smyrna that evening in the company of several officers to attend "a Jewish wedding" and did not return to the ship. In any event, Attilio spent several days in Smyrna before finally departing for Greece aboard a Greek merchant ship.[7]

Austrian attempts to have the brothers returned were complicated by Britain's policy of granting asylum to revolutionaries (which also applied to possessions such as Corfu and the Ionian Islands), the absence of an Austro-Greek extradition treaty, and above all the painful fact that the navy was of little use in the quest to track them down. Attilio wrote to Admiral Bandiera from Smyrna the day after his desertion, revealing his intentions; the elder Bandiera did not inform the authorities but subsequently removed himself from active command. It mattered little that he stepped aside since a search for Attilio conducted by the navy in Greek waters was half-hearted at best. Eleven days passed before a subordinate, Captain Alexander Bujacovich, sent first word of the desertion to Paulucci. Just as the news reached Venice, the commander also received confirmation of Emilio's whereabouts and revolutionary intentions. Captain Leone Graziani, Attilio's father-in-law, sadly but dutifully turned in two letters from Emilio, dated 13 and 14 March. Addressed to his daughter and to Baroness Bandiera, the mother of the two rebels, they proclaimed the brothers' desire for a "holy war" to unite Italy and revealed that their desertions had been coordinated, with a rendezvous slated for Corfu or Malta.[8]

Among Austrian military and civil leaders, opinions on how to deal with the Bandiera brothers were as varied and inconsistent as the reports of the events themselves. From Constantinople, Count Stürmer warned that the spectacle of Austrian warships combing Levantine waters in search of the deserters "probably would only compromise the imperial and royal flag."[9] Since disloyalty within the navy was a sensitive problem that could undermine Austria's strategic posture in the Adriatic and Eastern Mediterranean, the ambassador advised Metternich to take a low-key approach and keep the affair from attracting international attention. Military leaders tended to favor a zealous pursuit of the case. *Feldmarshalleutnant* Count Ferdinand Zichy, Metternich's brother-in-law and fortress commander of Venice since 1842, already had a healthy dislike for Paulucci and cautioned against allowing the navy to conduct its own inquiry. Nevertheless, in late March the *Hofkriegsrat* gave Paulucci full authority to investigate the desertions and determine the extent of revolutionary activity in the fleet. A circular letter did observe, however, that the desertion of "the sons of a man so highly placed as Rear Admiral Bandiera" naturally cast suspicion over the entire officer corps.[10]

Paulucci took offense at this suggestion, which he apparently attributed to Radetzky, and hastened to inform Vienna that in the event of a revolutionary landing or other action in Venice the navy would do its duty. *Hofkriegsrat* president Count Hardegg conveyed Paulucci's assurances to Metternich but noted that he personally agreed with the view that the navy could not be considered completely reliable; should the Bandieras organize an attack on the city, it would indeed be in danger.[11] By entrusting the investigation to Paulucci, Vienna ensured that nothing would be uncovered. From the start the marquis sought to contain the crisis rather than get to the bottom of it. He preferred to think of the Bandieras not as traitors or revolutionaries, but as a pair of misguided youths. In late April he supported an initiative by Archduke Rainer, the viceroy of Lombardy-Venetia, to send Baroness Bandiera to Corfu with offers of official pardons for her sons in exchange for their surrender.[12] The imperial government did not formally charge the brothers with desertion and high treason until after this plan had failed.

By the time the charges were promulgated on 4 May, Attilio Bandiera had finally arrived in Corfu after two months of wandering in the Greek islands, and Emilio had returned there from a trip to Malta to plot strategy with Fabrizi. Austrian officials tracked the younger brother on his journey to Malta and back and filed protests with the British for allowing a revolutionary figure obviously planning an insurrection to move so freely between their possessions. They received no satisfaction or cooperation, but their intelligence was good enough to ascertain that Fabrizi had provided Emilio with 20,000 francs to purchase a boat for an expedition from Corfu to the Italian peninsula.[13] Since Vienna could not count on London for help, the corvettes *Adria* and *Veloce* were diverted from a mission to Tunis and ordered to Malta to observe and report on the activities of the Italian émigré community there.

Far from fulfilling its purpose, the redeployment merely facilitated the desertion of another Esperia leader, Domenico Moro. On 7 May, shortly after the ships docked at Malta, Moro left the *Adria*. In a letter to his captain, Antonio Morari, he announced his intention to join the Bandieras, whom he referred to as "honorable patriots and comrades." Four days later the captain of the *Veloce,* veteran seaman Giorgio Bua, wrote to Paulucci confirming the desertion, but the distraught marquis did not bother to pass the news on to Vienna.[14] The commander's "investigation" of the Bandiera affair had taken the form of a circular dispatch to all of the captains of the fleet asking them to report any revolutionary activity among their subordinates; it had, of course, produced no further evidence of the Esperia conspiracy. Paulucci believed this information would satisfy Vienna that the Bandieras had acted alone and dispel the general suspicions of the navy's loyalty. Word of the desertion of Moro, an officer decorated for heroism in 1840, dashed Paulucci's hope that the crisis could be contained.[15]

Details of the latest desertion reached the imperial capital in a roundabout way. In the wake of Moro's departure, Morari and the *Adria* left Malta to rejoin the Levant squadron; upon his arrival in Smyrna the captain confided to Admiral Bandiera that he had received correspondence from Moro following the desertion. In a sudden burst of activity, the admiral (perhaps relieved that the affair no longer involved only his sons) promptly passed the information on to Vienna via Venice. It arrived on the heels of the first formal report of Moro's action, a dispatch from the army's Count Zichy dated 26 May. The delays infuriated Metternich, who was quick to contrast them with the speed of his own foreign intelligence connections. The latter produced the embarrassing news that a letter from Mazzini confirming the defection of Moro had reached Paris from London on 24 May. The incident was common knowledge in the French capital before anybody knew of it in Vienna.[16]

Moro's desertion and the manner in which the naval hierarchy responded to it convinced imperial authorities that the fleet was rotten from stem to stern. Even before word of it had reached Vienna, plans had been made to replace Paulucci and purge the service of its disloyal elements. On 17 May Emperor Ferdinand authorized Count Hardegg to investigate the navy and submit a report on "the true condition of this branch," something Vienna obviously had not gotten from the marquis. In his response a week later, the *Hofkriegsrat* president admitted that the navy's problems could be traced all the way back to Campoformio, or at least to the Napoleonic era. After 1814 Austria had failed to integrate the fleet with the remainder of the armed forces and instead allowed it to retain an Italian character. Now she was paying the price for this grave error, but Hardegg did not believe that all was lost. He suggested administrative changes to prevent future commanders from operating as independently as Paulucci had and stressed above all the need to replace the marquis himself.[17]

The options for a successor were limited. The next two officers on the seniority list were Dandolo and Bandiera; the latter, of course, could not be considered, and Hardegg characterized the former, now seventy-eight, as a "vegetating old man." He raised the possibility of bringing in a foreign commander, perhaps from Britain, but cited the language problems and the time that would be lost in finding the right man. He also feared that importing a commander from abroad would offend "the national feelings—of Italians as well as Austrians" within the service. This left Archduke Frederick as the "natural" choice for commander. Even though he had just turned twenty-three and was not slated to take over the navy until some time in the more distant future, Hardegg felt that he could handle the job, especially if his able teacher and confidant, Captain Marinovich, were to serve as his personal aide.[18]

Because any changes undertaken while the Bandieras and Moro were still at large would involve some risk, Hardegg's proposals were tabled for the moment. In mid-June, however, Ferdinand authorized the removal of Admiral Bandiera from command of the Levant squadron and ordered the frigate *Bellona* home from Smyrna. Their places were to be taken by Captain Bua and his corvette *Veloce*.[19] The transfers, intended to secure the fleet against a mutiny or further desertions, were made without the knowledge that the Bandieras and Moro had already assembled a band of revolutionaries at Corfu and set sail for Italy.

The group, twenty men in all, was led by the Bandiera brothers and Nicola Ricciotti, an aide of Mazzini's sent to Corfu from London to help coordinate the expedition. Aside from the brothers and Moro, the only Austrian deserter among them was Attilio's servant Mariani, the gunnery mate who had been with him ever since he left the *Bellona*. The rebels chose Calabria as their destination, motivated by word of an abortive uprising there in March 1844 and by its location—at the southern tip of Italy—which made it accessible from Corfu aboard the old fishing boat that the Bandieras had purchased for the passage. They left Corfu on the night of 12–13 June and, on the sixteenth, landed at Crotone on the Calabrian coast.[20]

The venture was doomed from the start. The Austrian consul at Corfu learned of the boat's departure and ordered a Lloyd steamer to carry the news across the mouth of the Adriatic to Otranto; from there a warning was telegraphed to Naples. The rebels encountered no resistance at their landing site but also won no support and were left with no choice but to wander inland. On 18 June the Corsican Pietro Boccheciampe deserted the band and turned himself in to the Neapolitan authorities. Later the same day a bungled attempt to revolutionize the village of Belvedere-Spinelli left two civic guards and one gendarme dead. The authorities quickly located the rebels and on the nineteenth killed two of them in a shootout at a nearby village. The wounded included Emilio Bandiera and Moro; the latter was captured on the spot, and the rest of the band were taken later in the day. After inspiring so much fear in Vienna and at the Italian courts, the Bandiera brothers proved to be dismal failures as revolutionaries.[21]

On 23 June the seventeen survivors of the mission were arraigned by a military court at Cosenza, the provincial capital of Calabria. The imperial government quickly waived its right to extradite the four Habsburg subjects to Austria in spite of the opposition of police director Count Joseph Sedlnitzky, Count Zichy, and other military leaders, all of whom saw an Austrian trial of the deserters as a necessary prelude to a broader purge of their co-conspirators from the navy. But cooler heads prevailed, Metternich no doubt realizing that Habsburg nooses around the necks of the young rebels would only enhance their status as Italian martyrs. The Neapolitans acceded to Vienna's wishes and on 25 July nine of the rebels, including the Bandieras, Moro, and Mazzini's deputy Ricciotti, were executed at Cosenza by a firing squad. Mariani and the others received prison terms.[22]

The conviction and execution of the Bandieras and Moro no doubt brought sighs of relief from some circles in Austria, but for the navy the real trial was just beginning. The zealous Count Zichy, in his capacity as the ranking military officer in Venice, had assumed the leading role in the investigation of the fleet and by August 1844 identified scores of suspects within the officer corps. The proceedings at Cosenza only raised more questions about the navy. Most unsettling was the testimony of the Corsican Boccheciampe, who revealed that the Bandieras had corresponded from Corfu with several of their old *Esperia* comrades and attempted to get more of them to desert. According to the articles of war, the bulk of the naval officer corps was guilty of high treason, some for their direct participation in revolutionary plotting and even more for failing to report or prevent treasonous activity. In early August the *Hofkriegsrat* finally learned that Admiral Bandiera had received correspondence from Attilio following his desertion; this meant that he, too, was guilty according to the letter of the law. Meanwhile, Paulucci avoided disgrace only by doing nothing to obstruct an investigation of his own son.[23]

The news from Cosenza brought a brief calm before the storm that was expected to come at the end of August with the arrival of Admiral Bandiera and the *Bellona* from the Levant. Taking advantage of the respite, the imperial government on 21 August retired Paulucci and promoted Archduke Frederick to vice admiral and *Marine-Ober-Kommandant*. Captain Marinovich, his aide, was to perform most of the duties of the second-in-command. Dandolo, meanwhile, was reconfirmed as official second-in-command and received the additional salve of the prestigious Order of the Golden Fleece. In his initial instructions to the archduke, Count Hardegg stressed the need to restore the spirit and honor of the navy. Having already given the emperor a frank account of its serious, fundamental problems, the *Hofkriegsrat* president was well aware of the tremendous burden being placed on Frederick's shoulders.[24]

The Navy under Archduke Frederick (1844–1847)

Just over seven years had passed since Frederick's entry into naval service, but despite his youth he was not unqualified for the post of commander. By all accounts a bright young man, he had demonstrated his bravery in battle and commanded an overseas mission. While away from the sea over the past year and a half, he had served as brigadier of the naval infantry and familiarized himself with administrative matters. His recent absence from the fleet also left him untouched by the Bandiera affair, and as a Habsburg prince his status could only help the navy in the difficult times that lay ahead. On the other hand, he depended too much on the advice of his personal aide Colonel Lebzeltern, who in 1840 had encouraged him to take the risks that made him the hero of Sidon and Acre, and on Captain Marinovich, an unpopular man considered by some to be the *de facto* head of the navy under the new arrangement. He continued to have a naive faith and trust in the officers he had served with in the Levant despite the questionable behavior of many of them during the recent crisis. And perhaps most significant of all (although certainly known to very few) the archduke, like any other young non-Italian who came to Venice to enter the navy, had succumbed to the attractions of the city. By the time of his appointment he had a Venetian mistress and at least one illegitimate child.[25]

The archduke had just assumed his new duties when the *Bellona* arrived from Smyrna. True to the unwritten code of the corps, few of its officers had anything to say about Attilio Bandiera or Esperia. Most of the testimony came from two army officers who had accompanied the ship to the Levant while on temporary assignment with the fleet: Captain Adolf

Kübeck, son of the *Hofkammer* president, and Count Ladislaus Karolyi, from a leading Hungarian family. They verified that Admiral Bandiera had known of Attilio's desertion from the beginning, as had his second-in-command, Captain Luigi Matticola. Karolyi, whose cabin had been next door to that of Ensign Francesco Baldiserotto, a founding member of Esperia, was especially eager to testify and quickly became the star witness for the prosecution. Unfortunately, he was more offended by Baldiserotto's homosexuality than by his revolutionary plotting. Zichy, determined that heads should roll, had the ensign put on trial for sodomy. After a long and acrimonious process, Baldiserotto was acquitted and Karolyi reassigned to Britain (out of reach of attempted reprisals) to serve as an attaché to the Royal Navy. The trial was the only one of an Esperia member ever conducted by an Austrian military court; it accomplished little other than to confirm that Admiral Bandiera had lost all control over his ship. All things considered, the navy was fortunate that it had not lost its newest frigate to a mutiny.[26]

In October 1844 an imperial decree brought the inevitable forced retirement of Admiral Bandiera. Captain Morari of the *Adria* also lost his commission for failing to report his receipt of Moro's correspondence. So many other officers were tainted by the scandal that the *Hofkriegsrat* soon realized it could not fire all of them and still keep the navy afloat. Most of the men under suspicion remained with the service, but efforts were made to place them in less sensitive jobs, if possible on land. Captain Bua, already in the Levant as Bandiera's replacement, had to be reassigned to a "safer" post in Trieste after revealing that while at Malta the previous May, he too had seen Moro's initial letter and advised Morari to burn it. Bua was relieved as head of the Levant squadron by Giuseppe Marsich, a trusted captain who also happened to be Admiral Bandiera's brother-in-law. Meanwhile, an investigation of the naval college (a result of the revelations of Emilio Bandiera's revolutionary activity there) led to the transfer of its director, Captain Andrea Bordini, to a post in Dalmatia.

Captain Kudriaffsky, the daring hero of the Moroccan mission years earlier, was to become head of the academy as soon as he returned from a temporary civilian assignment with the Austrian Lloyd.[27]

Forced for the present to rely on naval officers of dubious loyalty, the imperial government took decisive steps to ensure that the future corps would be more dependable. At the naval academy numerous dismissals of professors and students helped change the atmosphere almost overnight, and a series of reforms promised that in the years to come no single nationality would dominate the school. A conscious effort was made to cut through the ties of family and social class that reinforced the Italian character of the service. More scholarship positions were created, and sons of officers (whose admission had always been automatic) were required to meet the same entrance requirements as other students. Italian remained the language of the academy, but German instruction was improved and German literature added to the curriculum. At the same time, the course of study was reduced from five years to four. But, unfortunately, the academy lacked a competent and dedicated director to see the reforms through. Frederick unwisely named the disgraced Captain Matticola interim head for the 1844–45 term, and Kudriaffsky subsequently stayed for only two years before taking another civilian job, this time with the D.D.S.G.[28]

The reforms achieved their purpose at least in making the academy less appealing to Italians. By early 1848 the results began to show in the national composition of the cadet corps: 38 percent German, 34 percent Italian, and 10 percent South Slav, compared to the 1844 figures of 68 percent Italian, 14 percent German, and 11 percent South Slav. In contrast, the corps of sea officers changed little during Frederick's tenure: it was 59 percent Italian, 17 percent German, and 15 percent South Slav in 1844, and 60 percent Italian, 15 percent German, and 17 percent South Slav four years later, figures reflecting Vienna's decision not to conduct a purge. The official "end" of the Bandiera affair came early in 1845 when the *Hofkriegsrat* dropped plans to try Admiral Bandiera for treason and allowed junior officers under suspicion to return to active duty.[29]

In the months that followed, Frederick tried to lay to rest the events of 1844, but the shortage of reliable officers and strong fears for the loyalty of the fleet strengthened the case of those advocating a reduction in the number of active warships. In Vienna, Kübeck's support for the Lloyd was not accompanied by a strong sympathy for the navy. Ever since the resolution of the Near Eastern crisis of 1840, the *Hofkammer* president had called for the abolition of the Levant squadron and a return to the navy's peacetime standard of eight warships. In March 1845 at least part of his wish was fulfilled when, mostly for want of a trusted commander, the Levant squadron was merged with the Adriatic division. Only two "station" ships, one at Constantinople and one at Piraeus near Athens, were left to support Austria's growing Levantine interests.[30]

The archduke also encountered opposition when he attempted to modernize the navy. The Austrian fleet had only two small paddle steamers, compared to the scores of steam-powered warships in the other navies of Europe. Even the Sardinian fleet, languishing because of Charles Albert's disinterest, could boast of four steamers by 1845; the navy of Naples, under the patronage of Ferdinand II, had over a dozen. Shortly after taking command, Frederick sought to remedy the situation with the purchase of a "fully armed large war-steamer" from Britain, to be used as a prototype for the construction of steamships at the Venice Arsenal. The idea was rejected on financial grounds even though Hardegg and the *Hofkriegsrat* favored it. Metternich was no help to the archduke. Though an articulate supporter of the Lloyd and a firm believer in the strategic importance of steamships, the chancellor had woefully unsophisticated views when it came to steam-powered warships. Navy men no doubt bristled at his suggestion that their steamers should operate as armed merchantmen in peacetime rather than merely replace sailing warships.[31] After failing to win more steamships for the navy, Frederick had to acquiesce in a reduction of its sail-powered strength. In 1845 the frigate *Ebe* was ordered scrapped even though its replacement, the *Minerva,* was still under construction in the Arsenal. This left the fleet with only three frigates, its lowest number in two decades.[32]

Frederick's greatest success as commander came in the development of the naval base at Pola. During the course of an imperial visit to Trieste in September 1844, the archduke took Ferdinand and his entourage on a tour of the Istrian port; shortly thereafter, the work Paulucci had obstructed for a decade finally got underway. The abolition of the Levant squadron in 1845 made the Adriatic once again the focal point of the navy's activities, and Pola, as close to Ancona as to Venice, was an excellent base from which to control at least the northern half of the sea. An insurrection that fall in the Romagna necessitated a close surveillance of the Papal coast, and after the election of Pius IX the following summer the navy again was put on alert. Pola demonstrated its value on both occasions, so convincingly that starting in 1846 the navy kept one of its frigates stationed there on a regular basis. Late that year Metternich himself ordered that the port be made the center of operations for the active squadron.[33]

From the beginning of his tenure Frederick dutifully worked within the financial and strategic limits set by Vienna in the hope that eventually the navy would secure a larger budget and expand the scope of its duties. He was permitted only one major cruise outside the Adriatic, a state visit to Naples in the fall of 1846. The archduke took the frigate *Bellona,* a corvette, and a steamer on the mission, which allowed him to pay his respects to his sister the queen while he symbolically sealed a rapprochement recently engineered by Austria's new ambassador to the Neapolitan court, Prince Felix zu Schwarzenberg.[34] Denied more ships, Frederick habitually protested to Metternich about official abuse of the vessels currently in service. On one occasion he noted that the Austrian ambassador to Greece was using the station-ship *Vulcano,* the navy's newest steamer, as a "pleasure boat," a practice detrimental to its true purpose, which was "to bring to bear a moral influence through its station in Piraeus." This argument struck a responsive chord with the chancellor, but it did not bring an end to the civilian use of Austrian warships. For the years 1846–47 the archduke had to acquiesce in the loaning of his other steamer, the *Marianna*, to the Lloyd.[35]

In the years prior to the revolutions of 1848, the growth and activity of the Lloyd once again stood in sharp contrast to the stagnation of the Habsburg navy. Emilio Bandiera's escape to Corfu aboard one of its steamers underscored the fact that the company was operated by Italians, but by and large the loyalty of Trieste Italians was above question. They recognized the benefits that their city reaped from its privileged position as the main port of the Austrian Empire and did not wish to see a change in the political status quo. The Lloyd prospered along with Trieste. Bolstered by the million-florin government loan of 1845 and its acquisition of the overseas lines of the D.D.S.G., its profits more than doubled and it was never in serious financial trouble again. Vienna's demonstration of confidence in the Lloyd made its stock more attractive, and capital from new investors enabled it to repay its debt to the state in only eighteen months. In 1847, when the company sought money to expand its fleet, it turned not to the government but to a public sale of bonds that easily raised the 1.5 million florins needed. By the end of that year the Lloyd had twenty steamships in service and another five under construction. Its lines connected Trieste with all of the major ports of the Levant and, via the Turkish straits, with points as distant as Trebizond on the eastern coast of the Black Sea.[36]

The news was not all good for the Lloyd, however, since by 1847 it was clear that the company had lost its bid for the British–East Indian mail contract. Even though a series of trials conducted between August 1846 and February 1847 brought the Bombay post to London faster via Trieste than via Marseilles five out of six times, the British continued to send their mail through France, mainly because Trieste had no rail connections to the interior and the only projected line led to Vienna, not the northwest and Germany. But Lloyd officials and the diplomats supporting them were slow to give up on the project. As late as March 1848, when news of the February Revolution in Paris raised doubts about the security of the French mail route, the Austrians still hoped to gain the coveted contract.[37]

Austrian interest in India extended far beyond the British mail concession. Ever since the early 1840s Habsburg leaders had been fascinated with the project for a canal across the isthmus of Suez that would enable Lloyd steamers and other Austrian merchantmen to participate directly in trade with India and the Orient without rounding the Cape of Good Hope. Austria joined Britain and France in founding the *Société d'études pour le Canal de Suez* at Paris in 1846, but Metternich subsequently disappointed Kübeck, Stadion, and the merchants of Trieste by rejecting a direct Austrian role in the project, which he felt should be brought to fruition by private entrepreneurs.[38]

But while the officials of the Lloyd and the city of Trieste looked forward to the advantages that a Suez canal would bring them, their success and prosperity was causing considerable bitterness in Venice. In 1830 Austria had finally granted the city the status of a free port, but Habsburg policy continued to favor Trieste and the subsidies given to the Lloyd only made matters worse. The economic slump that struck Italy (and indeed, most of Europe) in the mid-1840s left Trieste virtually untouched; at the same time, the bankruptcies and hardship in Venice inspired protests over the long record of discrimination against the city. In March 1847 lawyer Daniele Manin led a group of young Venetian progressives in a petition to Vienna calling for an end to the favored status of Trieste and for Venice to become the chief entrepot of Austrian Levantine trade. Meanwhile, the nationalist tide that swept all of Italy after the election of Pius IX affected Venice as well. Liberal scholar Niccolò Tommaseo, returning to the city after years of exile, assumed leadership of its neo-Guelf party and promoted the new pontiff as the hope for a united Italy.[39]

In their quest to maintain order in Venice, the Austrian authorities were helped by the fact that it was essentially a conservative city. The radical Young Italy movement had never gained much of a following there, the society Esperia won few (if any) civilian converts, and the death of the Bandieras damaged what little popularity Mazzini enjoyed with the Venetian public.[40] Ever since his arrival in Venice, Zichy had felt confident that an uprising "would find little support" among the populace. His defensive strategy for the city was designed to ward off a seaborne French invasion or, after 1844, a landing by Italian revolutionaries, and paid little attention to internal security. He got along much better with Frederick than he had with Paulucci and no doubt was impressed by the archduke's efforts to improve discipline within the navy. Frederick contributed to the public order of Venice by increasing security at the Arsenal, where convicts supplied much of the labor; he also reduced the number of idle seamen at the base there by keeping the reserve ships in a higher state of readiness.[41]

After adding these reforms to his list of accomplishments, Frederick tackled the problem of the fleet's traditional dependence on Venice and the Veneto for its crews. He instituted an aggressive recruiting policy in Dalmatia that met with such success that by August 1847 he was able to assure Hardegg that "a number of volunteers" from the eastern littoral had increased his pool of manpower and put the navy in good shape for the future. Ironically, however, a further reduction in the active strength of the fleet sent many of these recruits home almost immediately, leaving the ships to be manned by veteran Venetians of questionable loyalty. By the end of the same month Austria had only two ships outside the Adriatic: a schooner at Constantinople and a corvette at Piraeus.[42]

Meanwhile, Radetzky's occupation of the Papal fortress of Ferrara in July 1847 further escalated tensions in Italy. Austria had the right by treaty to garrison Ferrara, but Pius IX protested the move and was quickly supported by Sardinia-

Piedmont and, to a lesser degree, Britain and France. Anti-Austrian sentiment reached new heights throughout Italy, and Radetzky soon requested a dramatic increase in the strength of his army. The imperial government started sending reinforcements but also sent Metternich's heir apparent, Count Karl Ludwig Ficquelmont, to army headquarters in Milan to keep the field marshal out of political trouble.[43] In this highly charged atmosphere, Frederick in mid-September shrewdly requested a rotation of Austrian warships away from Venice for reasons of "morale." The key to the redeployment was the transfer of the frigate *Guerriera* from Pola to Gravosa in southern Dalmatia and its replacement at Pola by the reserve frigate *Venere*, previously docked in the Venice Arsenal. The *Bellona*, flagship of the active squadron, was to continue to cruise the Adriatic in the company of several brigs with Pola as its home base.[44] It would cost the navy more to maintain all the frigates outside of Venice, but the archduke wanted to make certain that in the event of trouble in the city, none of his three largest ships would be stationed there.

Because Frederick feared a rejection on financial grounds, he closed his proposal with the observation that in three years as *Marine-Ober-Kommandant* he had never resisted a budget reduction or made an extravagant request. As for the necessity of the new deployment, Vienna would have to trust his judgment. The imperial government could hardly turn down such a convincing appeal for prudence since it already had troops on the way to Radetzky for much the same reason. Metternich subsequently modified the plan to ensure that the navy's two steamships were constantly at the disposal of the local governors in the littoral. The plan went into effect in mid-October, but to the great misfortune of the navy it was a posthumous victory for the archduke. On the first of October he informed the *Hofkriegsrat* that an attack of "jaundice" had forced him to turn over his duties temporarily to Dandolo and Marinovich. Five days later he died, most likely from a recurrence of the typhus that had almost killed him in his first months of naval service.[45]

Frederick remains an enigmatic figure. The traditional Austrian naval literature gives no critical evaluation of his performance as commander but takes for granted that had he lived another year, he somehow would have been able to prevent the navy's near collapse during the Venetian revolution of 1848.[46] One chronicler has pointed out that death spared the archduke the agony and calamity of the following year that cost many men of greater skill their reputations, rank, and honor.[47] As head of the navy, Frederick certainly was no maverick. He was a "good soldier," an obedient servant who never tested his limits. But even though he labored under the cloud of the events of 1844 and was handicapped by youth and inexperience, he still managed to implement some changes of great importance to the future of the service.

Because he was a Habsburg, it is difficult to ascertain how Frederick's contemporaries viewed him. Shortly after his death, the ranking members of the officer corps asked for a monument in his honor to be placed alongside those of the great Venetian admirals in the Arsenal chapel of San Biagio in recognition of his role in revitalizing the Austrian navy, "successor to the Venetian."[48] The officers were effusive in their praise for the late archduke. We may of course only speculate about their sincerity, but Frederick's reluctance to punish fellow officers who had been compromised by the Bandiera affair certainly did no harm to his popularity within the corps. Half of the officers who signed the letter of mourning were Italians; after the revolution of the following spring, only a third were still with the Austrian navy.

Toward Revolution (1847–1848)

Upon Frederick's death the naval command passed by default to Dandolo, the only admiral left on active duty. At eighty-one he returned to a post he had held, albeit briefly, over forty years earlier when L'Espine was recalled to Vienna during the war of 1805. His tenure was even shorter the second time around, since he followed the archduke to the grave in November 1847. For Dandolo, death was without question merciful; he certainly would have been unable to cope with the events of 1848. For Vienna, the problem was to find a man who could.

A look at the seniority list revealed that each of the four highest-ranking candidates—all captains—had some serious handicap. Andrea Bordini had been dispatched to Dalmatia in 1844 for his mishandling of the naval academy during the past decade. Leone Graziani, currently brigadier of the naval infantry, had a good record but family ties to the late Attilio Bandiera. Johann von Buratovich, currently head of the active squadron, had once been characterized by Hardegg as "a good practical seaman . . . but without higher independent usefulness."[49] The fourth captain, Marinovich, had had three years' experience as Frederick's right-hand man; he was widely disliked within the navy, however, and owed his high rank to the influence of the late archduke.

The only alternative was to bring in an outsider. Since the volatile international situation ruled out a search abroad, Hardegg turned to the army and *Feldmarschalleutnant* Anton von Martini. Widely recognized as the most intelligent Austrian general, Martini had served since 1843 as director of the Wiener Neustadt Military Academy. He had no experience with maritime matters but had excellent credentials as a soldier and diplomat, especially with regard to Italian affairs. He had served as an aide to Prince Karl zu Schwarzenberg at the Congress of Vienna and in the suite of Tsar Alexander at the Congress of Verona. In the early 1830s he had negotiated a military convention with Charles Albert of Sardinia-Piedmont and thereafter served for a decade under Radetzky in northern Italy, first as his chief of staff, then as a brigadier. His Italian surname was almost coincidental; he was born in Transylvania in 1792, the son of a Habsburg general and fortress commander of Lombard descent. Though fluent in the language, he never considered himself to be an Italian.[50]

At fifty-five, Martini was comfortable in Wiener Neustadt and somewhat shocked at the sudden reassignment. An old cavalryman, his main concern was that he would not be able to take his horses with him. The reluctant admiral did not report to Venice until late December, six weeks after his appointment.[51] In the meantime, Marinovich served as interim *Marine-Ober-Kommandant* and singlehandedly destroyed the delicate web of goodwill within the officer corps that was one legacy of the late archduke. In league with Zichy he resurrected the cases of Matticola, Baldiserotto, and others whose past conduct Frederick had considered a dead issue. Already disliked, Marinovich was soon despised by all quarters in the navy, not just the Italians. In late November cadet Max von Sterneck, a future navy commander, noted that while "Martini is awaited with great tension," the replacement of Marinovich would be "for the good of the navy and for us all."[52] When Martini assumed his post, the hated captain became his adjutant and commander of the Arsenal.

Thereafter, the deterioration of conditions within the navy at Venice mirrored the decline of public order in the city as a whole. In Milan, anti-Austrian sentiment had had its first major eruption at the funeral of Federico Confalonieri in December 1846. Tensions grew steadily through the Tobacco Riots of January 1848 when Radetzky's troops fired on unarmed mobs in the streets of the Lombard capital. In Venice the road to revolution lacked similar dramatic signposts, but Austrian authorities themselves provided the catalyst in mid-January 1848 by arresting Manin and Tommaseo, the former for encouraging anti-Austrian protests, the latter for his criticism of the censorship laws. The following month the government lost the support of the conservative elements of the city when two ancient rival clans, the Nicolotti and the Castellani, effected a public rapprochement and appealed to the populace to resist the Austrians. Public assaults on naval officers caught walking alone or in small groups subsequently led to an order that they dress in civilian clothes while off duty.[53] At the same time, renewed concerns for the loyalty of the navy (initiated by Radetzky in a letter to Metternich the previous December) led in February to the publication of warnings to the officer corps, naval administration, and the students at the naval academy that disloyal or suspicious behavior would be punished "with all force of the law."[54]

While the navy certainly was a subject of concern in Vienna, the loyalty of Radetzky's army caused even more worry. As a result of budget cuts, the imperial government after 1835 had reassigned an increasing number of regiments to their home districts and reduced the overall strength of the forces in northern Italy. After 1844 almost two-thirds of the Italian units in the Austrian army (twenty-one of thirty-one infantry battalions) were stationed in Lombardy or Venetia. In early 1847 these troops made up over half of Radetzky's infantry; by January 1848 ten additional battalions of non-Italians had diluted the figure somewhat, and ten units of Croatians en route from the Military Border were expected to shore up the situation even more. The garrison of Venice reflected the composition of the army as a whole: Zichy had five battalions, three Italian, two Styrian (Germans and Slovenes), with one Croatian on the way.[55]

In the meantime, the Venetian public followed the trials of Manin and Tommaseo with great interest and reacted to news from elsewhere in Italy and Europe, especially news of the revolutions in Naples in late January and in Paris a month later. In early March Manin and Tommaseo were acquitted of all charges but kept in prison in the interest of public order; their detention only inflamed the populace all the more. When put to the test, Zichy failed to back up his rhetoric with action. He ignored Radetzky's advice to declare a state of siege in the city and did not ask for reinforcements from the *terra firma*. The Austrians lost control of Venice on 17 March when word arrived of the revolution in Vienna four days earlier. The civil governor, Count Alois Palffy, appeased the mob by freeing Manin and Tommaseo and, on the eighteenth, permitting the formation of a civic guard. Shortly after his release Manin established contact with Major Antonio Paulucci, son of the former commander and head of the naval artillery. The guard soon had its own cannons.[56]

The unrest eased after Palffy promulgated the official news from Vienna of Ferdinand's promise of a constitution. But on 20 March things took a turn for the worse when the Styrian battalions, which had fired upon the mob in a brief clash two days earlier, were confined to their barracks by the civic guard. Martini, whose inexperience limited his usefulness to Zichy and Palffy, decided to send for two brigs from Pola to strengthen their hand. He had to rescind the order, however, after an uprising in the Arsenal the following day made him fear that the ships would arrive only after the entire city was in rebel hands. On the twenty-second he went to the Arsenal to try to restore calm; against all advice, Marinovich chose to accompany him. The sight of the hated captain provoked the workers to riot, and they hacked him to pieces with their tools before anyone could intervene. The naval infantry was called to the scene but deserted upon arrival. Their shouts of "Viva l'Italia! Viva la Repubblica! Viva San Marco!" were echoed by the naval artillery corps, which also deserted.[57]

The Italians of the army garrison likewise mutinied, and the civic guard occupied the Arsenal; Manin then arrived and declared Martini his prisoner. A proclamation later in the day announced the restoration of the Venetian Republic. Manin became president and foreign minister of a provisional government that included Tommaseo and Antonio Paulucci, the latter as navy minister. Captain Graziani, the ranking Italian naval officer in Venice, was named commander of the Venetian navy, which the government assumed would inherit all ships and personnel of the Austrian. He was ordered to send word to Pola of the restoration of the republic and to recall all of the warships to Venice.[58]

Meanwhile, Palffy and Zichy struck a deal with the new regime that allowed them and the non-Italians on their respective staffs to leave the city immediately. The three battalions of Styrians and Croatians were to be sent to Trieste as soon as their transportation could be arranged.[59] Martini and a handful of loyal naval officers were excluded from the bargain and left behind as hostages of the rebel government. The Austrian officials left Venice on the night of 22 March aboard a Lloyd steamer; Graziani instructed its captain, Massimiliano Maffei, to go first to Pola with his orders for the fleet before proceeding to Trieste. But once at sea, Maffei showed Palffy the packet of Graziani's instructions. In addition to the commands for the active squadron at Pola, it included orders recalling to Venice the Austrian warships stationed in Dalmatian waters and at Piraeus and Constantinople. Palffy directed Maffei to steam straight for Trieste, where he turned the information over to *Feldmarschalleutnant* Count Franz Gyulai, the military commander of the Küstenland. Gyulai promptly sent a warning to the head of the squadron, Captain Buratovich, and ordered him to keep his ships at Pola.[60] The Austrian navy was saved.

In the four years between the desertion of the Bandiera brothers and the Venetian revolution of 1848, questions about the loyalty and reliability of the navy brought a sharp curtailment of its operations. Partly because of a shortage of trustworthy captains, the Levant squadron was abolished and cruises to show the flag in the Mediterranean were eliminated. Restricted almost exclusively to duty in the Adriatic and watched closely by the authorities, the fleet subsequently showed little sign of being the same mutinous force that would have raised the Italian tricolor on Mazzini's orders during 1843. Still, Austria had to face the bitter fact that the Italian majority in her navy—whether of Admiral Bandiera's generation, apprenticed in the navy of the Napoleonic kingdom of Italy, or the generation of his sons, imbued with the new spirit of Italian nationalism—were professionals with no special loyalty to the empire. They happened to be from the Adriatic littoral, with aspirations for a career at sea, and the Austrian navy was their only option.

Revolutionary sentiment no doubt persisted within the navy after 1844, but it remained quiescent until ignited by the revolution in Venice. Archduke Frederick accomplished little in the way of fundamental changes during his three years as commander, but the ship relocations he ordered just weeks before his death were to prove decisive in the survival of the navy the following year. In the wake of the revolution the Venetians had an ample supply of officers and seamen but not enough ships; the loyal portion of the fleet at Trieste and Pola had plenty of ships but not enough personnel. This standoff marked the start of the most crucial years in the history of the Austrian navy, years in which its future role and character were more clearly defined.

NOTES

1. Mazzini, "Ricordi dei fratelli Bandiera," *Scritti editi ed inediti*, 31:37. See also Riccardo Pierantoni, *Storia dei fratelli Bandiera e loro compagni in Calabria* (Milan: Casa Editrice L. F. Cogliati, 1909), pp. 129–38, which remains the best secondary work on the brothers. Most of the literature on the Bandieras has been written by Italians using only Italian sources; most of it is hagiographic in nature. Aside from Pierantoni, the most useful is Filippo Nani Mocenigo, *La Marina Veneta e i fratelli Bandiera* (Venice: Tip. Orfanotrofia di A. Pellizzato, 1907), a pamphlet that provides an overview of the history of the "Venetian" Austrian navy from 1797–1866, with the Bandieras cast as its greatest heroes. A number of more general works on the Risorgimento manage to discuss the Bandieras without even mentioning that they were Austrian naval officers.

2. Stürmer to Metternich, Constantinople, 20 March 1844, HHSA, Die Akten des k.u.k. Ministeriums des Äussern 1848–1918, Administrative Registratur (hereafter cited as HHSA, Adm. Reg.), F 52—Sicherheitswesen, Carton 1: Politische Flüchtlinge 1835–45, fol. 257–70.

3. Paulucci to HKR, Venice, 30 April 1844, KA, HKR Akten, Präs. 1844/684, fol. 1–15, 34, and Zichy to Hardegg, Venice, 1 June

1844, ibid., Präs. 1844/973, fol. 2–7 confirm Attilio's desire to be transferred to Venice.
 4. Radetzky to Hardegg, Verona, 23 March 1844, ibid., Präs. 1844/436, fol. 1, 4.
 5. See Emiliana P. Noether, " 'Morally Wrong' or 'Politically Right'? Espionage in Her Majesty's Post Office, 1844–45," *Canadian Journal of History* 22 (1987): 53–54.
 6. Paulucci to MKdo. Küstenland, Venice, 15 March 1844, KA, HKR Akten, Präs. 1844/532, fol. 49; Luigi Carci, *La spedizione e il processo dei fratelli Bandiera* (Modena: Società tipografica modenese, 1939), p. 17. On Gelcich's role in Emilio's escape, see Stefani and Astori, *Il Lloyd Triestino*, pp. 260–70.
 7. Bujacovich to Paulucci, Smyrna, 10 March 1844, KA, HKR Akten, Präs. 1844/532, fol. 15–20; Zichy to Hardegg, Venice, 1 June 1844, ibid., Präs. 1844/973, fol. 2–7.
 8. Bujacovich to Paulucci, Smyrna, 10 March 1844, KA, HKR Akten, Präs. 1844/532, fol. 15–20; Emilio Bandiera to Marietta Graziani Bandiera and Baroness Anna Marsich Bandiera, Corfu, 13 and 14 March 1844 (copies), ibid., fol. 39–43; Paulucci to General-Polizei-Direktion, Venice, 20 March 1844, ibid., Präs. 1844/436, fol. 2–3; Zichy to Hardegg, Venice, 7 September 1844, ibid., Präs. 1844/1598, fol. 2–3. Austrian works give scant (and somewhat inaccurate) coverage to the desertions and are very charitable toward Admiral Bandiera, viewing his fall in the wake of the affair as a tragic end to the distinguished career of a loyal seaman; e.g., Khuepach and Bayer, *1814–1847*, p. 267, and Fleischer, *1802–1848 MS*, p. 115, neither of which mention that the admiral received correspondence from Attilio after his desertion.
 9. Stürmer to Metternich, Constantinople, 20 March 1844, HHSA, Adm. Reg., F 52, Carton 1, fol. 257–70.
 10. HKR circular, Vienna, 28 March 1844, KA, HKR Akten, Präs. 1844/432–433, fol. 1–6.
 11. Paulucci to HKR, Venice, 1 April 1844, KA, HKR Akten, Präs. 1844/485, fol. 1–2; Hardegg to Metternich, Vienna, 8 April 1844, ibid., Präs. 1844/499, fol. 1–4.
 12. Hardegg to Metternich, Vienna, 20 April 1844, KA, HKR Akten, Präs. 1844/584, fol. 1; Emilio Bandiera to Mazzini, Corfu, 22 April 1844, in Mazzini, "Ricordi dei fratelli Bandiera," *Scritti editi ed inediti*, 31:38–40; Carci, *La spedizione*, pp. 16–17.
 13. Mayersbach (Austrian consul) to Metternich, Corfu, 23

March 1844, HHSA, Adm. Reg., F 52, Carton 1, fol. 271–75; HKR circular, Vienna, 26 April 1844, KA, HKR Akten, Präs. 1844/594–595–612, fol. 1–2. Attilio later testified that he reached Corfu on 28 April. Though British officials there and at Malta gave the Austrians no help in tracking down the Bandieras, Mazzini later alleged that the British government, which was opening his mail at the time, had provided information on the brothers to Austria and to Naples, their ultimate destination; his accusations helped touch off a political crisis in England. See Noether, "Espionage in Her Majesty's Post Office," 47–49.

14. Moro to Morari, Malta, n.d. (copy), KA, HKR Akten, Präs. 1844/913–918, fol. 5; Bua to Paulucci, Malta, 11 May 1844, ibid., fol. 6–7. Moro joined the Bandieras at Corfu on 31 May.

15. Paulucci to Bua, Venice, 28 June 1844, KA, HKR Akten, Präs. 1844/1071, fol. 2 confirms that the commander felt he had contained the crisis prior to the Moro desertion.

16. Adm. Bandiera to Paulucci, Smyrna, 26 May 1844, KA, HKR Akten, Präs. 1844/984, fol. 4–11; Zichy to Hardegg, Venice, 26 May 1844, ibid., Präs. 1844/865–866, fol. 2–4; Metternich to Hardegg, Vienna, 7 June 1844, ibid., Präs. 1844/913–918, fol. 2–3. Zichy's source of information was a revolutionary tract by Moro published on 15 May in the Maltese newspaper *Il Mediterraneo;* in it, Moro prematurely declared that "the son of . . . Commandant Paulucci . . . has followed the example of the sons of Bandiera." Paulucci had three sons in the navy: artillery captain Antonio and sea officers Giuseppe (a lieutenant) and Guglielmo (an ensign). All were suspected of revolutionary activity at one time or another, but none of them left the navy prior to the Venetian revolution of 1848. Pierantoni, *Storia dei fratelli Bandiera,* p. 121, contends that Antonio and Giuseppe Paulucci were friends of the Bandieras and members of Esperia, but Emilio Bandiera to Fabrizi, Corfu, 7 June 1844, quoted in Mazzini, *Scritti editi ed inediti,* 26:199n, comments that Paulucci's sons "are all either cowards or egoists" and not true friends of the Italian cause.

17. Ferdinand to Hardegg, Vienna, 17 May 1844, KA, HKR Akten, Präs. 1844/776, fol. 1; Hardegg to Ferdinand, Vienna, 24 May 1844, ibid., Präs. 1844/1458, fol. 4–19.

18. Hardegg to Ferdinand, Vienna, 24 May 1844, KA, HKR Akten, Präs. 1844/1458, fol. 4–19.

19. Hardegg to Ferdinand, Vienna, 31 May 1844, KA, HKR Akten, Präs. 1844/1096–1110, fol. 4–18. The transfers were approved on 17 June 1844.

20. Mazzini, "Ricordi dei fratelli Bandiera," *Scritti editi ed inediti,* 31:61–66; Carci, *La spedizione,* pp. 10–26; Pierantoni, *Storia dei fratelli Bandiera,* pp. 325–67. Ricciotti favored the Marches over Calabria as a landing site, but the distance from Corfu to the Papal coast was too great for their boat to cover.

21. Paulucci to HKR, Venice, 18 June 1844, KA, HKR Akten, Präs. 1844/1005–1016–1043, fol. 7–8; Carci, *La spedizione,* pp. 26–43; Pierantoni, *Storia dei fratelli Bandiera,* pp. 368–96. The first reports by the Austrian consul greatly exaggerated the size of the expedition, estimating it at forty men.

22. Ferdinand (Resolution), Schönbrunn, 10 July 1844, KA, HKR Akten, Präs. 1844/1174, fol. 3; Sedlnitzky to Hardegg, Vienna, 26 July 1844, ibid., Präs. 1844/1303, fol. 2–7; copy of Cosenza proceedings enclosed in Zichy to Hardegg, Venice, 22 August 1844, ibid., Präs. 1844/1512; Carci, *La spedizione,* pp. 44–57; Pierantoni, *Storia dei fratelli Bandiera,* pp. 397–417. Ferdinand II of Naples pardoned the eight survivors of the Cosenza trial in April 1846. Mariani returned to his native Lombardy and eventually applied to Emperor Francis Joseph for a pardon.

23. Carci, *La spedizione,* p. 77; Paulucci to HKR, Venice, 4 August 1844, KA, HKR Akten, Präs. 1844/1383, fol. 1–10; Zichy to Hardegg, Venice, 4 August 1844, ibid., Präs. 1844/1399, fol. 2–3.

24. Ferdinand, approval of Hardegg *Vortrag* of 24 May, Vienna, 21 August 1844, KA, HKR Akten, Präs. 1844/1458, fol. 17–19 (margin); Hardegg to Archduke Frederick, Vienna, 22 August 1844, ibid., fol. 1.

25. Lebzeltern all but orchestrated Frederick's actions at Sidon and Acre; Sir Baldwin Walker (Walker Bey) observed at the time that the colonel "has on all occasions shown the greatest zeal." See Bergmann, *Erzherzog Friedrich,* pp. 42–43; for a biographical sketch of Marinovich see ibid., pp. 82–83. Frederick's mistress, Adelaide Turchi, was thirteen years older than he and from a lower-class background; she and the archduke's daughter Giuseppina (born twelve days before he became commander) lived an impoverished existence after his death but received some support after an investigation confirmed "dass das Töchterchen ... eine überraschende Ähnlichkeit mit dem verstorbenen Erzherzog hat." *Hofrat* Ferdinand Walcher, quoted in Erwin Schatz, "Gedenkstätten an Vize-Admiral Erzherzog Friedrich in Venedig," *MGH* 10 (1983): 46.

26. Zichy to Hardegg, Venice, 1 June 1844, KA, HKR Akten, Präs. 1844/973, fol. 2–7; Zichy to Hardegg, Venice, 7 September 1844, ibid., Präs. 1844/1598, fol. 2–3; Dandolo to Archduke Frederick, Venice, 6 September 1844, KA, MA, A/j 7 (1844), no. 1. During the Baldiserotto trial, an Italian seaman named as a co-defendant alleged that Attilio Bandiera had once forced him into a homosexual liaison; notwithstanding Attilio's treason and the fact that he was no longer around to defend himself, other naval officers—non-Italian as well as Italian—refused to corroborate the charges. The final report of the court noted that it was "unlikely, but also not impossible (unwahrscheinlich, aber doch nicht unmöglich)" that the seaman's accusations were true. From the evidence given, it appears that the homosexual circle aboard the *Bellona* and the Esperia sect shared many of the same members. See Guido Poosch, Baldiserotto proceedings and verdict, Venice, 23 May 1845, KA, MA, A/j 7 (1845), no. 1–b.

27. Khuepach and Bayer, *1814–1847*, p. 103.

28. Ferdinand, approval of Hardegg *Vortrag* of 24 May, Vienna, 21 August 1844, KA, HKR Akten, Präs. 1844/1458, fol. 17–19 (margin); Salcher, *Marine-Akademie,* p. 16. The dismissed faculty included Esperia leader Mazzuchelli (a mathematics professor) and history professor Emilio Tipaldo, an internationally acclaimed scholar and the only Ph.D. on the staff. Matticola, one of the highest officers implicated in Attilio Bandiera's escape, was exonerated on the strength of Frederick's personal acquaintance with him and affirmation of his honor; Archduke Frederick to Hardegg, Venice, 22 January 1845, KA, HKR Akten, Präs. 1845/869, fol. 13–17.

29. Figures compiled from *Militär-Schematismus,* 1844 and 1848; HKR circular, Vienna, 10 January 1845, KA, HKR Akten, Präs. 1845/10, fol. 1–164. Adm. Bandiera's deteriorating health was cited in the decision not to prosecute him; he died in 1847 at the age of sixty-two.

30. Kübeck to Hardegg, Vienna, 27 October 1842, KA, HKR Akten, Präs. 1842/1849, fol. 2–3; Khuepach and Bayer, *1814–1847,* p. 267.

31. Archduke Frederick to Hardegg, Venice, 14 October 1844, KA, HKR Akten, Präs. 1844/1829, fol. 3–9; Metternich to Hardegg, Vienna, 10 April 1842, ibid., Präs. 1842/1583, fol. 4–7.

32. The *Bellona*, launched in 1842, replaced the frigate *Medea*. The *Minerva*, begun in 1843, was launched in 1850 as the *Novara*.
33. Khuepach and Bayer, *1814–1847*, pp. 111–12; Archduke Frederick to Hardegg, Venice, 28 September 1845, KA, HKR Akten, Präs. 1845/1788, fol. 2–5 reveals that Austrian warships continued to cruise the Eastern Mediterranean on an irregular basis following the formal dissolution of the Levant squadron; Archduke Frederick to Hardegg, *Bellona* (Naples), 5 October 1846, ibid., Präs. 1846/2598, fol. 2 indicates that several naval officers received Papal decorations for their services in 1846; Hardegg to Archduke Frederick, Venice, 26 December 1846, ibid., Präs. 1846/2762, fol. 1–3.
34. Bergmann, *Erzherzog Friedrich*, p. 69; Adolph Schwarzenberg, *Prince Felix zu Schwarzenberg, Prime Minister of Austria 1848–1852* (New York: Columbia University Press, 1946), pp. 16–17.
35. Archduke Frederick to Metternich, Venice, 7 December 1845, HHSA, StK., Prov., L–V, Carton 3: StK.–Erz. Rainer 1818–47, fol. 113–14; Coons, *Steamships, Statesmen, and Bureaucrats*, p. 120n.
36. Coons, *Steamships, Statesmen, and Bureaucrats*, pp. 124–25; *75 Jahre österreichischer Lloyd*, p. 23.
37. Coons, *Steamships, Statesmen, and Bureaucrats*, pp. 167–68.
38. See Giuseppe Lo Giudice, *Trieste, l'Austria ed il Canale di Suez* (Catania: Università degli studi, 1979), pp. 43–65.
39. Paul Ginsborg, *Daniele Manin and the Venetian Revolution of 1848–49* (Cambridge: Cambridge University Press, 1979), pp. 30, 64–67.
40. Ibid., pp. 50, 141.
41. Zichy to Radetzky, Venice, 3 August 1842, KA, Nachlass Zichy, B/184:1, fol. 2–15; Zichy to Radetzky, Venice, 18 October 1845, KA, Nachlass Radetzky, B/1151:A.33, fol. 8–12; Archduke Frederick to Hardegg, Venice, 8 June 1846, KA, HKR Akten, Präs. 1846/1441–1445, fol. 2, 9.
42. Archduke Frederick to Hardegg, Venice, 3 August 1847, KA, HKR Akten, Präs. 1847/1249, fol. 2, 9; HKR circular, Vienna, 8 August 1847, ibid., fol. 1, 10.
43. Alan Sked, *The Survival of the Habsburg Empire: Radetzky, The Imperial Army and the Class War, 1848* (London: Longman, 1979), pp. 96–97.
44. Archduke Frederick to Hardegg, Venice, 12 September 1847, KA, HKR Akten, Präs. 1847/1670, fol. 1–13.

45. Metternich to Hardegg, Vienna, 23 September 1847, KA, HKR Akten, Präs. 1847/1670, fol. 3, 7; Hardegg to Ferdinand, Vienna, 27 September 1847, ibid., fol. 2, 8–11; Metternich to HKR, Vienna, 21 October 1847, ibid., Präs. 1847/1712, fol. 3, 6; Hardegg to MOK, Vienna, 24 October 1847, ibid., fol. 1, 7. Frederick's death has been attributed variously to a liver ailment, gall bladder attack, blood poisoning, or any combination of the three, brought on by earlier bouts with typhus and/or malaria. See Schatz, "Gedenkstätten," p. 40; Bergmann, *Erzherzog Friedrich*, p. 71; Khuepach and Bayer, *1814–1847*, p. 114.

46. E.g., Jerolim Benko von Boinik, *Geschichte der k.k. Kriegsmarine*, part 3: *Die k.k. österreichische Kriegsmarine in dem Zeitraume von 1848 bis 1871*, vol. 1: *Geschichte der k.k. Kriegsmarine während der Jahre 1848 und 1849* (Vienna: Verlag des k.k. Reichs-Kriegs-Ministerium, Marine-Sektion, 1884), p. 44; Fleischer, *1802–1848 MS*, p. 123; and Salcher, *Marine-Akademie*, pp. 15–17.

47. Khuepach and Bayer, *1814–1847*, p. 114.

48. Officer corps to Dandolo, Venice, 24 October 1847, KA, HKR Akten, Präs. 1847/1907, fol. 4–5.

49. Critique of Buratovich's abilities in Hardegg to Ferdinand, Vienna, 31 May 1844, KA, HKR Akten, Präs. 1844/1096–1110, fol. 4–18.

50. For a biographical sketch of Martini see Benko von Boinik, *1848–1849*, pp. 59–61. He was named vice admiral and *Marine-Ober-Kommandant* on 10 November 1847, four days before Dandolo actually died.

51. Martini to Hardegg, Vienna, 12 November 1847, KA, HKR Akten, Präs. 1847/2010, fol. 6–9; Hardegg to Ferdinand, Vienna, 15 November 1847, ibid., fol. 1–5, 10.

52. Marinovich to Zichy, Venice, 22 November 1847, KA, Nachlass Zichy, B/184:2, fol. 94–95; Sterneck to mother, Venice, 28 November 1847, Sterneck, *Erinnerungen*, p. 50.

53. Ginsborg, *Daniele Manin*, pp. 74–75; Benko von Boinik, *1848–1849*, p. 51n. The civilian dress order was already in effect for Austrian army officers throughout Lombardy and Venetia.

54. Metternich to Hardegg, Vienna, 27 December 1847, KA, HKR Akten, Präs. 1847/2200, fol. 1 discusses Radetzky's concerns about the navy; Hardegg to Martini, Vienna, 5 February 1848, KA, MA, M/c 27 (1848), no. 278–a (Carton 46); Martini to Heinrich Berthold (*Feldkriegs-sekretär*), Venice, 12 February 1848, ibid., no.

278–b; MOK circular, Venice, 12 February 1848, ibid., no. 278. Sked, *The Survival of the Habsburg Empire*, p. 125f, uses Radetzky's preoccupation with his own problems in Milan during the weeks before the revolution to conclude (quite erroneously) that the field marshal never gave much thought to the loyalty of the navy or the security of Venice.

55. Figures compiled from *Militär-Schematismus*, 1844, 1847, and 1848, and Alphons von Wrede, *Geschichte der k. u. k. Wehrmacht: Die Regimenter, Corps, Branchen und Anstalten von 1618 bis Ende des XIX. Jahrhunderts*, 7 vols. (Vienna: L. W. Seidel & Sohn, 1893–1900), passim.

56. Ginsborg, *Daniele Manin*, pp. 94–96; Oberst Lt. Eduard Hügl to Zichy, Venice, 22 March 1848, KA, Nachlass Zichy, B/184:2, fol. 110. General Constantin D'Aspre offered to send a battalion of Hungarians from Padua, plus a rocket battery to intimidate the populace with fear of bombardment, but Zichy did not respond. D'Aspre to Zichy, Padua, 20 February 1848, ibid., fol. 96–97. For Antonio Paulucci's earlier ties to Esperia and the Bandieras, see note 16 above. His father did not live to see the upheaval of 1848, having died three years earlier.

57. Benko von Boinik, *1848–1849*, pp. 66–77; Giovanni Minotto, "Particolari sugli avvenimenti dei 22 Marzo 1848 nell'Arsenale di Venezia" (copy), KA, Nachlass Zichy, B/184:2, fol. 119–22. Zichy's long-standing complaints about the use of forced labor in the Arsenal led to a campaign to hire more civilian workers; it was implemented on 17 March, the day the revolution began. Maj. Jacopo Coccon (director of shipbuilding) to MOK, Venice, 17 March 1848, KA, MA, M/c 27 (1848), No. 273–a (Carton 46).

58. Benko von Boinik, *1848–1849*, pp. 78–81, Ginsborg, *Daniele Manin*, p. 112.

59. Text of Zichy's capitulation in Benko von Boinik, *1848–1849*, pp. 86–87. He was arrested upon arriving in Trieste for having surrendered Venice without a fight.

60. Robert van Nuffel, "Intorno alla perdita della flotta all'inizio della rivoluzione veneziana," *Rassegna Storica del Risorgimento* 44 (1957): 786–91; Benko von Boinik, *1848–1849*, pp. 120–21.

CHAPTER

6

Out of the Ashes

In the wake of the revolution, the Austrian navy had to reorganize as quickly as possible to meet the threat posed by the new Venetian Republic and by Sardinia-Piedmont, which declared war on the Habsburg Empire the day after Venice fell. Like Radetzky and his army, regrouping in Verona after losing Milan, the loyal naval officials in Pola and Trieste were handicapped from the start by chaos and indecision in Vienna. Many Austrian leaders considered Lombardy and Venetia lost and favored a negotiated settlement in Italy, but in any event it was clear that sea power would be needed to save Trieste and the rest of the Adriatic littoral for the Habsburgs. The navy required strong leadership to make the transition to a non-Italian future; unfortunately, the lack of a competent commander made a quick recovery impossible. On a more ominous note, the Frankfurt Parliament's creation of a German navy threatened to lure young German Austrian officers away from the Habsburg fleet and deprive it of the only possible catalyst for a recovery.[1]

Picking up the Pieces (1848)

When notified of the events in Venice and Martini's status as a prisoner of the republican government, Count Gyulai, the ranking military official in the littoral, unilaterally took command of the Austrian navy. After ordering Buratovich to keep the squadron in Pola, he secured control over the navy's small contingent at Trieste by arresting its Venetian-born commander. In late March he gave all Lombard and Venetian naval personnel the option of a discharge on three months' pay. Through this generous offer, he hoped to keep Italian captains and crews from seizing warships merely in order to return home. The repatriation began the following day with Buratovich evaluating the cases at Pola and Lieutenant Anton Bourguignon, Gyulai's able assistant, supervising the process at Trieste. In ten days about 600 officers and men were disarmed and sent to Venice aboard rented merchant ships without incident and without the loss of a single naval vessel.[2]

The repatriated officers and those opting to stay in Venice after the revolution accounted for two-thirds of the entire corps. The majority of them were Italians but more than a quarter were not, evidence of the effective assimilation and "Italianization" of officers of other nationalities. The division of the officers between the Venetian and Austrian navies also cut across all lines of rank, size of ship, or location of assignment; the year of graduation from the naval academy seems to have made more difference than most other factors. By early April Germans were the largest group among the officers remaining with the Habsburg navy (36 percent), followed by a substantial Italian faction (35 percent), with South Slavs a distant third. The corps was hit hardest by defections in the higher ranks. Aside from Martini, who was not a seaman anyway, there were no admirals, and of sixteen captains on the active list at the time of the revolution, nine declared for Venice right away and one later; another (Marinovich) was killed, and after two Italians who turned down the offer of a discharge were forced to retire, the navy could count on only three men above the rank of lieutenant.[3]

Once the fleet had been purged of its disloyal elements, attention turned toward securing Trieste and Pola against a Venetian or Sardinian attack. Trieste had also had its share of unrest in March 1848, but unlike their counterparts in Venice the civilian and military leaders of the city did not lose their nerve. They were forced to concede a civic guard, but after respected city leaders such as Lloyd director Carl von Bruck donned its uniform there was no danger of the guard becoming a tool of the radicals. As a further precaution, a predominantly Slavic territorial militia was raised on the outskirts of Trieste. Pola, meanwhile, was guarded by the Twenty-second Infantry Regiment, a mixture of Trieste Italians and Slavs from the Küstenland province. Because of the shortage of manpower in the squadron there, many of these soldiers (a number of whom had some maritime experience) were pressed into service aboard ships.[4]

The days and weeks that followed were a time of uneasiness for the Austrian fleet. Much of the confusion stemmed from the absence of any clear direction from Vienna. Correspondence from Trieste in late March refers to the navy, hitherto the "kaiserliche königliche Kriegsmarine" ("Imperiale Regia Marina"), as the "Marina di Seiner Majestät Costituzionale."[5] With the dismissal of so many officers and seamen, the retention of its best warships was the only encouraging development. The fleet still had all three of its frigates, two of six corvettes, six of eleven brigs, and one of two steamers. But here, too, the navy had to endure a great deal of anxiety, for while the repatriations to Venice defused a potentially dramatic confrontation over the ships at Pola, the safe return of warships from stations outside the Adriatic was not achieved so easily. The recall of the frigate *Guerriera* and steamer *Vulcano*, sent out in late January 1848 to safeguard Austrian interests in the wake of the Neapolitan revolution, generated the most excitement.

The two ships initially cruised in Sicilian waters and did not reach Naples until 25 March, long after the rebels had gained control of the city. Ambassador Schwarzenberg urged the captain of the *Guerriera*, Alexander Bujacovich, to isolate his men from the calamity ashore, but small craft from the harbor soon swamped the frigate. Their passengers proclaimed the news of the revolutions in Vienna, Milan, and Venice, and encouraged the *Guerriera*'s Italian crew to mutiny; by the following day the ship was flying the Italian tricolor. But just as all seemed lost, Bujacovich, pushed by his non-Italian junior officers, ordered the vessel to sail. Once at sea he proclaimed an end to the foolishness, had the tricolor hauled down and the Austrian flag raised. His crew bowed to the show of strength, and the ship proceeded to Pola without further incident, arriving in mid-April. The *Vulcano* also made it home, with Schwarzenberg on board, but only after its crew attempted a mutiny that the prince barely managed to suppress.[6]

The safe return of the *Guerriera* demonstrated that even the most hopeless situation could be salvaged if officers kept their composure and acted in concert. Bujacovich was decorated for his accomplishment but not rewarded with a promotion. Though a more capable commander than Buratovich, he could not speak German and was not the sort of man to whom Gyulai wished to entrust the fleet once it returned to duty. The count instead called for Kudriaffsky to come out of retirement and take command of the squadron. The new war ministry (successor to the defunct *Hofkriegsrat*) quickly approved and in mid-April the captain left his job with the D.D.S.G. and reported to Pola.[7] At the same time, Vienna finally confirmed Gyulai as interim *Marine-Ober-Kommandant;* after Kudriaffsky took over at Pola, Buratovich became second-in-command in Trieste.[8]

Even though the navy could muster crews for only two frigates, two brigs, and the steamer *Vulcano,* Kudriaffsky at the end of April implemented a naval blockade of Venice. Left with the lesser warships of the old Habsburg navy, many of which would require weeks of fitting out before putting to sea, the Venetians did not attempt to mount a challenge but awaited the arrival of the Sardinian fleet and a squadron from Naples, which had also entered the war. Meanwhile, three steamships rented from the Lloyd helped Austria sustain the blockade. The vessels were armed as warships and commanded by naval officers, but owing to the shortage of naval personnel, they continued to be manned by their old crews. The entire makeshift operation crumbled with the appearance of the first serious threat. In mid-May, when a Neapolitan squadron of two frigates, five steamers, and one brig appeared off Venice, Kudriaffsky withdrew to Trieste.[9]

A week later a Sardinian squadron consisting of three frigates, one brig, and a schooner arrived in Venetian waters and joined forces with the Neapolitans. After Venice contributed an additional corvette and two brigs, the combined Italian fleet enforced a blockade on Trieste. Outnumbered at least two to one, the Austrian squadron was forced to stay in port. But confusion in the Neapolitan squadron and diplomatic warnings from the Frankfurt Parliament soon combined to save the city and the navy from destruction. Like his predecessor Correale in 1821, Neapolitan admiral Raffaele de Cosa had two sets of orders, one from the revolutionary government authorizing offensive operations, the other from his king cautioning against them. Meanwhile, the Frankfurt Parliament delivered a timely reminder that because Trieste was in the part of Austria belonging to the German Confederation, an Italian attack on the port would be treated as an attack against all of Germany. The peak of the tension passed in early June when De Cosa received word from Naples that a counter-revolution had restored Ferdinand II to full power. His squadron was recalled, leaving the Venetians and Sardinians to maintain the blockade on their own.[10]

On 13 June, the day of De Cosa's departure, Sardinian Vice Admiral Giuseppe Albini and Venetian Rear Admiral (former Austrian captain) Giorgio Bua gave the authorities in Trieste a formal declaration of their blockade. They lamented the need to disrupt peaceful trade but noted that the city was now a military stronghold and that Lloyd steamers and personnel had been used for the Austrian war effort. An appeal from Trieste to the Frankfurt Parliament, whose representatives included the city's own Carl von Bruck, brought a condemnation of the blockade and a formal declaration that an attack on the port would be considered a *casus belli* for all of Germany.[11] The Sardinian portion of the Italian fleet was reinforced to a strength of four frigates, two corvettes, two brigs, and eight steamers, but the new vessels failed to compensate for the departure of the Neapolitan squadron and the likelihood of a battle grew increasingly remote. The rumblings from Frankfurt finally prompted Turin to order Albini to confine his activities to a mere observation of Trieste; in the meantime, Bua's contingent was distracted by the arrival of Austrian troops on the shores of the lagoon to enforce a land blockade of Venice. The spectacular success of Radetzky's counter-offensive against the Sardinians and their Italian auxiliaries, beginning on 6 May at Santa Lucia and culminating on 25 July in the decisive victory at Custoza, ultimately freed the navy from its captive state. By 6 August Milan was again in Austrian hands; three days later Turin concluded an armistice, and on the eleventh the Italian fleet broke off its blockade of Trieste.[12]

The following day Rear Admiral Graziani announced that Venice would continue to resist without Sardinian help. The city, however, was divided politically and deeply demoralized by the recent events. In early July the Venetian assembly had voted in favor of annexation to Sardinia-Piedmont, a decision that ousted Manin and Tommaseo and brought to power a caretaker government. In the wake of the Austro-Sardinian armistice a Mazzinian group attempted a coup in Venice; Manin intervened to restore order and subsequently took power for himself, appointing Graziani and Colonel Giambattista Cavedalis (formerly with the Napoleonic and Habsburg armies) to serve with him in an executive triumvirate. Left to fight alone, the Venetian leaders suffered the consequences of their own decisions of the previous spring to provide only for the defense of Venice while waiting for the Sardinians or other allies to send armies and fleets for the war against Austria. Months after the revolution, the Venetian navy still had a surplus of idle seamen while former Habsburg ships sat in the Arsenal still not ready for sea duty. Bua, already under fire for his performance off Trieste, was to draw even more criticism in the future for his failure to engage the Austrian navy.[13]

Once Habsburg troops reconquered Venetia and laid siege to Venice by land, an exchange of prisoners gave Bua's squadron even more officers and sailors. Austria had discontinued the lenient repatriation policy in early April after it became clear that the Venetians would continue to hold Vice Admiral Martini and the rest of their hostages. From the late arrivals to Pola (such as the *Guerriera*), officers and cadets wanting to leave the navy were interned at Ljubljana pending the commander's release. By the time Venice finally agreed to a deal, Austria had accumulated some two dozen hostages of her own, all of whom were traded for Martini and the five officers held with him. Once freed, the vice admiral went to Trieste, formally resuming his role as head of the navy in early September.[14]

Martini tried to put the best face on the events of the past six months and stressed the fact that the Venetian revolution had purged the navy of its disloyal elements. As of the first of August, all of the ships had been manned, and on the surface the fleet appeared to have made a remarkable recovery from its miserable state of earlier months. But the admiral soon learned of the considerable weaknesses: the navy was commanded largely by non-Italian former junior officers now holding ranks a level or two higher than in March; the current junior officers were mere cadets and students from the naval academy who had received emergency promotions; the hiring of auxiliary officers from the Adriatic merchant marine had lowered the quality of leadership still more; and the crews, while replenished with a number of recruits from the Dalmatian islands, had retained such a strong Italian character that there could be no question of changing the language of command. Yet little more could be done under the prevailing circumstances. When Martini complained to Vienna about the shortage of qualified officers, war minister Count Baillet de Latour offered to send him a group of volunteers from the radical Academic Legion. Latour noted that they were German-speaking, enthusiastic and educated, many of them with technical backgrounds that would be useful in operating steamships. But the admiral was not about to replace the departed Italians with German revolutionaries from the Habsburg capital. He hastened to inform the minister that things were not as bad as they had initially seemed and that at present "the utilization of new individuals cannot be considered."[15]

Despite the problems, Kudriaffsky tried to reimpose the blockade of Venice; his attempt was foiled, however, by the arrival in September of a French squadron in the upper Adriatic. It was only a gesture by Paris, which by this time had decided not to intervene in Italy, but it caused the captain a great deal of anxiety. He remained on the station only until October, when he gave up his command on grounds of illness.[16] By then a second revolution in Vienna had emboldened the Sardinians once again, and in late October Albini's squadron (at Corfu since the armistice of August 1848) reappeared off Venice to join the French in a passive obstruction of the Austrian blockade. Over the winter of 1848–49, though, harsh weather forced Albini to withdraw most of his ships at Ancona, leaving little chance for a clash with the Habsburg squadron.[17]

The winter conditions also limited the operations of Kudriaffsky's successor, Baron August von Sourdeau. Born in the Austrian Netherlands of Walloon stock, Sourdeau had risen to captain's rank before leaving the navy in 1843, ostensibly after an argument with Paulucci. Calls for his reactivation began within days of the Venetian revolution; in the fall he finally came out of retirement to be given command of the squadron with the rank of rear admiral. Martini was deeply offended by his surly disposition, disheveled appearance, and preference for the French language. The two men got along miserably, and their failure to cooperate ultimately led the government to decide that both should be replaced.[18]

On 21 November 1848 Prince Felix zu Schwarzenberg became foreign minister of the Austrian Empire and president of a new ministry that finally brought an end to the political chaos of the preceding eight months. He hastened to confront as many of the empire's problems as possible; having survived a harrowing return from Naples aboard the mutinous *Vulcano,* he recognized the need for a loyal and capable fleet and gave the navy a high priority. The prince concluded that neither Martini nor Sourdeau would be of much use in the long run and resolved to look abroad for an officer to serve both as *Marine-Ober-Kommandant* and squadron commander. He entrusted the search to Count Ladislaus Karolyi, in exile with the Royal Navy since the Baldiserotto trial. The count left Britain and in December went to Holland, his first stop on a tour of northern Europe.[19]

While engineering the abdication of Emperor Ferdinand and succession of young Francis Joseph, Schwarzenberg continued his campaign to strengthen the fleet. He abandoned an attempt to recruit British officers for Austrian service (which Karolyi had initiated while still in England) but redoubled efforts to purchase British steamships and even sent a mission to Turkey and Egypt in search of warships for the fleet.[20] Yet as the year drew to a close, the goal of a stronger navy was jeopardized by an unexpected rival: the Frankfurt Parliament and its proposed German fleet. Austria found herself in competition with "Germany" for the same foreign officers and warships, while at home the most promising young German Austrian officers were tempted to abandon Habsburg service for careers in the new German navy. The challenge from Frankfurt drove Martini to fear for the future of "an independent imperial Austrian navy."[21] The navy had been broken by revolution; Austria was making an effort to pick up the pieces, but its future remained in doubt.

The Navy under Dahlerup (1849–1851)

As Count Karolyi embarked on his tour of northern Europe in search of a new commander for the fleet, his mission had the support of a wide range of Habsburg leaders. Even Radetzky agreed that the navy should look northward for its new admiral and voiced a preference for a man of good conservative political views, ideally one of the "well disposed Tories" of the British fleet.[22] But Karolyi's earlier efforts in Britain had been fruitless, and his trip to Holland likewise met with no success. He was given a lukewarm reception and learned that even the purchase of a warship from the Dutch navy would require parliamentary approval. At the end of January 1849 the count left The Hague for Copenhagen, where he found the Danish officials far more accommodating than the Dutch had been. Within a week of his arrival the Danes offered Karolyi the services of Commodore Hans Birch von Dahlerup.[23]

Denmark had ample motivation to seek friendship with Austria. In the spring of 1848 the Danes had gone to war with the German states over the status of their predominantly German duchies of Schleswig and Holstein, which they wanted to bring into a closer union with the rest of the kingdom. The Frankfurt Parliament subsequently deputized Prussia to fight Denmark on behalf of "Germany," but the Danes countered Prussian successes on land with a naval blockade of the north German ports. This blockade inspired the Frankfurt assembly to create its German navy, which in turn caused considerable concern for Martini and Austrian naval officials.

The blockade also brought a stalemate in the German-Danish war, and by the beginning of 1849 Denmark was eager to end the conflict and bring about a return to the *status quo ante* in the two duchies. With the offer to give up Dahlerup, one of their best seamen, they hoped to lay the groundwork for a rapprochement with Austria and in the process break the solid common front of the German states on the Schleswig-Holstein question. At least that was the way the Danish naval minister, Vice Admiral Christian Zahrtmann, presented it to the commodore after his initial talks with Karolyi. Dahlerup had no desire to leave Denmark but agreed to enter Austrian service after the admiral appealed to his sense of patriotic duty. On 22 February the deal was concluded; two weeks later he left for Vienna.[24]

To clear the way for the new commander, Martini was relieved of his post and appointed ambassador to Naples. Sourdeau, meanwhile, was to retire as soon as Dahlerup arrived to take active command of the squadron. On 16 March Schwarzenberg officially proclaimed Dahlerup's appointment as vice admiral and *Marine-Ober-Kommandant*. Carl von Bruck, since November 1848 trade minister in the new government, assisted in the orientation process and impressed Dahlerup with his "bold and practical" views of Austrian maritime affairs. The admiral no doubt left Vienna with an exaggerated sense of the Schwarzenberg ministry's commitment to the Adriatic.[25]

En route to the littoral Dahlerup received word that Turin had denounced the Austro-Sardinian armistice of the previous August. He reached Pola on 22 March, two days after the resumption of hostilities. Since Albini's squadron was still in its winter anchorage at Ancona, the new commander was spared the need to put to sea immediately; he did not have to act at all after Radetzky's decisive victory at Novara (23 March) brought a quick end to the fighting. A new armistice stipulated that the Sardinian squadron "with all its sail and steamships" must leave the Adriatic within fifteen days.[26]

With the Sardinian navy out of the way, Dahlerup resumed the blockade against Venice in mid-April. Demoralized by the second defeat of Piedmont and by the failure of their own army to break the Austrian siege on land, the Venetians resolved nevertheless to fight on and voted Manin dictatorial powers. The new Austrian vigilance at sea brought protests from Britain and France, yet at the same time both advised Manin to make peace with Vienna on any terms. The French retained their squadron in the northern Adriatic, but after April Paris was preoccupied with its own campaign against the Mazzinian Roman Republic and did nothing to jeopardize Austria's efforts at Venice. Dahlerup also commenced operations against the rebels of the Papal State and extended his blockade to Ancona, which Habsburg troops finally occupied in mid-June.[27]

Austro-Venetian peace talks held throughout May and June accomplished nothing, mainly because Bruck, acting as the Austrian negotiator, offered the city little more than the opportunity to surrender unconditionally. Manin then concluded an alliance with envoys of Louis Kossuth, promising to equip a Hungarian navy in the Adriatic in return for financial support. The agreement was implausible from the start, and the Russian invasion of Hungary rendered it meaningless.[28] Venice seemed on the verge of capitulation, but as the summer wore on, Dahlerup found it increasingly difficult to maintain his blockade with the antiquated vessels at hand. While Karolyi's mission had succeeded in hiring the admiral, it brought the navy no new warships. Over the winter of 1848–49 attempts to buy vessels from Britain, Russia, Naples, Turkey, and Egypt had all ended in failure.[29] The navy subsequently purchased two Lloyd steamers and rented four others but still lacked the means to sustain its efforts. Dahlerup even resorted to gimmicks such as launching balloons from his ships to drop bombs on Venetian forts, but the shelling of the city and its defenses did not begin in earnest until the end of July when the army wheeled its heavy siege guns into place for the final assault.

The daily rain of a thousand shells soon increased public pressure on the Venetian navy for a last-ditch sortie to break the blockade. The task fell to Captain Achille Bucchia, a zealous Esperia alumnus promoted to squadron commander ahead of several senior officers. He first tried to even the odds through sabotage, but an attempt to burn one of the Austrian frigates failed to put it out of action. Manin quickly lost his patience and ordered Bucchia to put to sea and stay there until he had engaged the Habsburg squadron. During the ensuing week of skirmishes the numerical inferiority of the Venetian fleet kept it from accomplishing anything; its four corvettes, three brigs, and one steamer were simply no match for the three frigates, one corvette, two brigs, and three steamers under Dahlerup's command. On 18 August Manin permitted Bucchia to dock, but only after receiving word that the cholera already ravaging the city had spread to the ships as well. During the following day the news of Hungary's capitulation reached Venice, confirming that it was the last outpost of revolution in Europe. On the twenty-second, after seventeen months of resistance, Manin finally agreed to surrender. He was permitted to leave aboard a French warship with Tommaseo and a number of other rebel leaders, including Admiral Graziani and Antonio Paulucci of the navy. Austrian troops then occupied the city.[30]

As Dahlerup set about the task of rebuilding the navy for the future, the shortage of ships ranked second on his list of problems behind the dearth of competent personnel. Most of the officers who had remained loyal after March 1848 received two promotions during 1848–49, some even rising three ranks. At the same time, many auxiliary officers not really suitable for full-time service had to be granted regular commissions. The government maintained a firm policy against rehiring any of the officers released in 1848, regardless of their talents or excuses, but even without them the service retained a strong Italian character. Italians still made up the bulk of the crews and at the start of 1850 accounted for 18 percent of the officers, second only to the Germans; Dahlerup's poor command of their language made his job much harder. The admiral could count on the naval academy eventually to turn out more German and German-speaking officers, but the revolution had disrupted naval education and to fill the gap foreign officers (especially Scandinavians) were commissioned. Ironically, the navy had to be internationalized before it could be truly "germanized."[31]

The material needs of the fleet also had to be satisfied with help from abroad. Since all of the navy's shipbuilders had gone over to the Venetians in 1848, Austria brought in Dutch engineer Karl Scheffer and other foreigners to design new warships. Dahlerup was hesitant to use the Venice Arsenal for new construction projects even though the facilities were undamaged by the recent Austrian bombardment; instead, he had Scheffer turn to the private shipyards of Trieste. In the fall of 1849 the Tonello brothers' firm (Stabilimento Navale Adriatico) was contracted to build two large paddle steamers for the fleet with engines imported from

Britain.³² In the meantime, the ships already under construction in the Arsenal were completed, among them the frigate *Minerva*, renamed *Italia* by the Venetian rebels but launched in 1850 as the *Novara*. Other new vessels built during Dahlerup's tenure were also named after Radetzky's recent victories. To confirm the official "de-italianization" of the navy, the older warships all lost their Italian names: the *Lipsia* became the *Leipzig*, *Venere* was changed to *Venus*, and *Vulcano* to *Vulkan*.

Because neither Austria nor Venice had lost a warship in the recent campaigns, the Habsburg navy in late 1849 had all of the vessels of the prerevolutionary fleet. But Dahlerup had a low opinion of the ships, condemning as worthless one of the four frigates, four of the six corvettes, and all twelve brigs. He appealed to Vienna for a formal commitment to a larger fleet and in March 1850 was called to the imperial capital to serve on a committee charged with determining the future of the navy. The group included Bruck and three field marshals, among them Count August von Degenfeld; Captain Bernhard von Wüllerstorf of the navy served as secretary. After five sessions it produced a plan for a sailing fleet of six ships of the line, six large and four small frigates, six corvettes, six brigs, and six schooners, to be supplemented by twelve large and six small paddle steamers and six auxiliary steamers for transport or courier service. Reflecting the chief concerns of the field marshals, the committee's final protocol noted that the steamers would be able to transport 12–15,000 troops in a single trip "from one coast [of the Adriatic] to the other without difficulty." Including the construction of new installations at Trieste and Pola, the program would cost eighteen million florins.³³

On 12 April Francis Joseph approved the fleet plan in its entirety, including recommendations that Trieste be made the headquarters of the navy and chief building site, Pola the main base, and Venice the arsenal only until facilities at the other two ports were ready. The interior ministry was ordered to limit the export of ship timber, and a ship of the line and frigate were to be laid down in Trieste as soon as the shipyards there were ready. The navy's ordinary budget was to continue at the "customary" pre-1848 level of 1.5 million florins per year but would be enhanced by extraordinary grants totalling 17.8 million over the next eleven fiscal years, through 1860. To avoid a repetition of the humbling blockades of 1848, the Austrian fleet was to be maintained at a level equal to the combined naval might of the Italian states, even if this entailed additional expenditure.[34]

Schwarzenberg appears to have had little direct involvement in the formulation or approval of the Navy Law of 1850, but the young emperor must have been influenced by his mentor's appreciation of the need for an effective fleet. The commitment to a much larger navy—one trailing only the British, French, and Russian in size and strength—seemed to reflect an Austrian desire never again to suffer humiliation in the Adriatic at the hands of hostile naval forces. Although Radetzky, like Scharzenberg, was not immediately involved in drafting the new program, his views on the importance of sea power clearly were reflected in the committee's proposal. A fleet of the recommended strength would secure the rear of an Austrian army in northern Italy against the threat of a French landing at Venice or elsewhere on the Adriatic coast. The inclusion of two dozen steamships, as noted in the final protocol, would enable the navy to transport large numbers of troops from Croatia to northern Italy, a capability Radetzky always considered vital.

While approving the building program, Francis Joseph also decreed the introduction of German as the language of "service and correspondence" for the navy. In this regard there was little that Dahlerup could do; his own second-in-command, Rear Admiral Bujacovich, not to mention the bulk of the personnel in the fleet, could not speak German. As the new commander sought to get the navy into shape, problems of nationality went hand in hand with those of discipline. After returning early in 1850 from a training cruise to Lisbon aboard the frigate *Venus*, Captain Louis Fautz observed that his crew had performed miserably and that many of them were recruits from the mountains of the Dalmatian hinterland who could speak "neither Italian nor German."[35] On the cruise to St. Petersburg of the corvette *Carolina* in 1850–51, discipline was more of a problem than the language barrier; Captain Karolyi (transferred from the army) gave his crew hundreds of lashes during the nine-month voyage and even had problems with newly recruited Scandinavian officers.[36] But the reports were not universally dismal. The corvette *Diana*, the first Austrian warship to visit Smyrna since 1848, made a trim and disciplined showing and inspired one observer to note that "a better era has begun" for the navy.[37]

If indeed a new era had begun, Austria's Danish admiral did not remain on the Adriatic long enough to see it unfold. Though free from the haunting presence of former admirals or commanders (by late 1849 Martini was in Naples, Sourdeau in retirement, Gyulai in Vienna as war minister, and Buratovich dead), Dahlerup from the start was obsessed with his own job security. In the spring of 1851 Francis Joseph finally gave him good reason to feel threatened, approving the entry into naval service of his own brother, the nineteen-year-old Archduke Ferdinand Max. Only one year after his ambitious fleet plan won approval, Dahlerup was forced to conclude that his "star had set with the Kaiser." At sixty-one he was not prepared to become a mere caretaker while the young prince was groomed for his job; he chose instead to retire to Denmark. In August 1851 the new army commander in Trieste, *Feldmarschalleutnant* Count Franz von Wimpffen, was named interim *Marine-Ober-Kommandant*.[38]

In his two and a half years at the helm, Dahlerup oversaw the navy's first steps away from its Italian past. In addition to obtaining an unprecedented commitment from the emperor for a dramatic expansion of the fleet, he authored its first complete set of German-language service regulations, reorganized the coastal defense of the littoral, and implemented an extensive program of training cruises. But his fleet plan, essentially for a sailing navy, included steamships only as auxiliaries and did not take into account recent technological developments. It was perhaps also too ambitious since as of 1850 Trieste lacked the facilities to construct the ships it required. Problems with personnel improved little under his command and in some ways worsened. The importation of foreign officers and the retention of former auxiliaries on a permanent basis caused considerable discontent, especially when the newcomers were given seniority over younger officers with pre-1848 Austrian service.[39] In the area of language reform, Dahlerup initiated the process but several years were still to pass before the Austrian navy became "German." On a positive note, the liquidation early in 1852 of the Frankfurt Parliament's fleet removed a potential competitor for German-Austrian seamen; instead of taking away badly needed talent, the German navy suddenly became a potential source of German-speaking officers for Austria. Nevertheless, the overall outlook was far from bright. While Ferdinand Max trained to take over the fleet, Count Wimpffen was to have his hands full.

In the wake of the revolution in Venice, embarrassment and uncertainty plagued the Austrian navy's attempt to make a decisive break with the past. The upheaval of 1848 left the fleet undermanned and impotent, unable to challenge the Sardinian navy at sea or prevent it from blockading Trieste. Seeking a way out of its humiliating straits, the navy hired a foreign commander and fell back on the resources of the Austrian Lloyd, which leased or sold one quarter of its vessels to the imperial government for conversion into warships. Under Dahlerup the fleet became trusted once again but was too weak to be an effective instrument of Austrian strategy or foreign policy after the return to peace. Its materiel remained antiquated by the standards of the day, and the Danish admiral himself did not answer the serious need for a talented and reliable leader. The Navy Law of 1850 and Archduke Ferdinand Max's entry into naval service appeared to provide long-range solutions for these deficiencies; nevertheless, it remained to be seen if Austria would implement the ambitious program or if the new archduke could accomplish any more than Frederick had. For Austria to continue to develop her overseas interests, the future commander needed to build a navy capable of defending them. Unlike his Habsburg predecessor, Ferdinand Max would have to be more than just a faithful servant of Vienna.

NOTES

1. See Lawrence Sondhaus, "*Mitteleuropa zur See?* Austria and the German Navy Question, 1848–1852," *Central European History* 20 (1987): 125–44.
2. Benko von Boinik, *1848–1849*, pp. 127, 134–39.
3. The ethnic division of the officer corps came as follows:

	Before Mar. 1848	% of Whole	Released Mar./Apr.	% of Natl.	Corps in Apr. 1848	% of Whole
Italians	94	60	75	80	19	35
Germans	23	15	3	13	20	36
South Slavs	26	17	19	73	7	13
Other*	13		4	31	9	
Totals	156		101	65	55	

(*-also unidentified). Figures compiled from *Militär-Schematismus*, 1848; Benko von Boinik, *1848–1849*, appendix pp. 7–67; Randaccio, *Le marinerie militari*, pp. 133–40. Figures on rank, station and academy class from Buratovich, Pola, 14 March 1848, KA, MA, M/c 27 (1848), no. 249 (Carton 46) and A. Milonopulo, Venice, 7 March 1848, ibid., no. 293. All of the active officers who had been classmates of Emilio Bandiera (1836) or Domenico Moro (1838) left the navy in March 1848.
4. Gustav Hubka von Czerczitz, *Geschichte des k. u. k. Infanterie-Regiments Graf von Lacy Nr. 22* (Zadar: Verlag des Regiments, 1902), pp. 269–73.

5. E.g., Lt. Anton Bourguignon (General Order), Trieste, 29 March 1848, KA, MA, M/c 27 (1848), no. 27 (Carton 44).
6. Benko von Boinik, *1848–1849,* pp. 171–90; Schwarzenberg, *Prince Felix zu Schwarzenberg,* pp. 144–47.
7. Benko von Boinik, *1848–1849,* pp. 144–47. On Bujacovich's language skills see Heinrich Bayer von Bayersburg, *Österreichs Admirale 1719–1866* (Vienna: Bergland Verlag, 1960), p. 23.
8. Gyulai to Peter von Zanini (war minister), Trieste, 19 April 1848, KA, MA, M/c 27 (1848), no. 33–c (Carton 44); Zanini to Gyulai, Vienna, 21 April 1848, ibid., no. 33–d.
9. Benko von Boinik, *1848–1849,* pp. 206–26.
10. Ibid., pp. 226–80; Radogna, *Storia della Marina,* pp. 120–22; Randaccio, *Le marinerie militari,* pp. 42, 95–97.
11. Benko von Boinik, *1848–1849,* pp. 281–303; Charmatz, *Freiherr von Bruck,* pp. 30–31; Resolution of the Frankfurt Parliament, 21 June 1848, Franz Wigard, ed., *Stenographischer Bericht über die Verhandlungen der deutschen constituirenden Nationalversammlung zu Frankfurt am Main,* 9 vols. (Frankfurt: Johann David Sauerlander, 1848), 1:391.
12. Marquis Pallavicini (Sardinia-Piedmont ambassador to Bavaria) to Frankfurt Parliament, Munich, 1 July 1848, text in Benko von Boinik, *1848–1849,* pp. 322–23, expresses Turin's non-violent intentions toward the German Confederation. See also ibid., p. 303, and Randaccio, *Le marinerie militari,* pp. 43–47. FMLt. Baron Welden, commander of an Austrian relief army, severed Venice's last links to the *terra firma* on 17 June.
13. Randaccio, *Le marinerie militari,* p. 51; Ginsborg, *Daniele Manin,* pp. 254–69.
14. Benko von Boinik, *1848–1849,* pp. 307–15, 380.
15. Latour to Martini, Vienna, 26 August 1848, KA, MA, M/c 27 (1848), no. 268 (Carton 46); Martini to Latour, Trieste, 30 August 1848, ibid., no. 268–a. Kudriaffsky to MOK, Trieste, 6 September 1848, ibid., no. 250 complains about the quality of auxiliary officers.
16. Over the winter of 1848–49, Kudriaffsky served as an Austrian representative on the Frankfurt Parliament's naval committee; see Sondhaus, "Austria and the German Navy Question," 130–32. In 1849 he turned down a commission in the new German navy and transferred to the Austrian army at the rank of *Feldmarschalleutnant.*
17. Randaccio, *Le marinerie militari,* pp. 52–53.

18. Benko von Boinik, *1848–1849*, pp. 510–23 passim.

19. Ibid., p. 492; Schwarzenberg to Count Moritz Esterhazy (ambassador at The Hague), Ölmutz, 18 December 1848, HHSA, Politisches Archiv 1848–1918 (hereafter cited as HHSA, PA), XL. Interna, Carton 80, fol. 521.

20. Latour to Gyulai, Vienna, 28 July 1848, KA, MA, M/c 27 (1848), no. 207–a (Carton 46) indicates that the search abroad for steamships was first authorized by an imperial decree on 7 July. Baron Koller (chargé) to Wessenberg [sic], London, 27 November 1848, HHSA, PA, XL. Interna, Carton 80, fol. 203–4 conveys British opposition to Austria hiring officers there. Schwarzenberg to Martini, Ölmutz, 23 November 1848, ibid., fol. 121–22 authorizes a mission to Alexandria to buy ships.

21. Martini to Baron Franz Cordon (war minister), Trieste, 9 December 1848, KA, MA, M/c 27 (1848), no. 254 (Carton 46).

22. Radetzky, "Entwurf über die numerische Stärke der Armee im Jahre 1848," KA, Nachlass Radetzky, B/1151:A.35, fol. 16–17.

23. Karolyi to Schwarzenberg, The Hague, 27 January 1849, HHSA, PA, XL. Interna, Carton 80, fol. 548–54; Baron Vrints (ambassador to Denmark) to Schwarzenberg, Copenhagen, 23 February 1849, ibid., fol. 567–70.

24. Hans Birch von Dahlerup, *In österreichischen Diensten*, 2 vols. (Berlin: Meyer & Jessen, 1911–12), 1:1–6; Vrints to Schwarzenberg, Copenhagen, 26 February 1849, HHSA, PA, XL. Interna, Carton 80, fol. 575–78.

25. Dahlerup, *In österreichischen Diensten*, 1:14; Schwarzenberg *Vortrag*, Vienna, 16 March 1849, HHSA, PA, XL. Interna, Carton 80, fol. 601–5.

26. Benko von Boinik, *1848–1849*, p. 553; Randaccio, *Le marinerie militari*, pp. 53–55; text of armistice in *Der Feldzug der österreichischen Armee in Italien im Jahre 1849*, 2 vols. (Vienna: Verlag von Karl Hölzl, 1854), 1:42–45.

27. Benko von Boinik, *1848–1849*, pp. 560–76, 607–19; Ginsborg, *Daniele Manin*, pp. 332, 336–37. HHSA, PA, XL. Interna, Carton 81, fol. 817–974 includes French protests and scores of reports of encounters with the French squadron between April and October 1849 (two months after the blockade ended); ibid., fol. 975–98 includes a smaller correspondence on British protests.

28. Ginsborg, *Daniele Manin*, pp. 345–47. On the Venetian-

Hungarian alliance of 3 June 1849 see Istvan Deak, *The Lawful Revolution: Louis Kossuth and the Hungarians, 1848–1849* (New York: Columbia University Press, 1979), p. 299.

29. Austria was interested in the British steamer *Caledonia*, which the Frankfurt Parliament also wanted to buy, and in five steamers Russia was having built in British shipyards. In Turkey and Egypt interest focused on the frigate *Reschid* (formerly the *Egiziana*, built for Mehemet Ali in Venice in 1826–27), while in Naples a deal to rent three steamers was concluded early in 1849 but cancelled when the ships were needed against Sicilian rebels. Koller to Wessenberg [*sic*], London, 27 November 1848, HHSA, PA, XL. Interna, Carton 80, fol. 195–202; Koller to Schwarzenberg, London, 17 January 1849, ibid., fol. 244; Cordon to Schwarzenberg, Vienna, 28 February 1849, ibid., fol. 59–60; Gen. Felice Sabatelli to Schwarzenberg, Naples, 15 February 1849, ibid., fol. 635.

30. Randaccio, *Le marinerie militari*, pp. 130–32; Benko von Boinik, *1848–1849*, pp. 634–42; Ginsborg, *Daniele Manin*, pp. 355–62; Ferdinand Boyer, "Les derniers jours de la République de Venise (août 1849)," *Rassegna Storica del Risorgimento* 56 (1969): 580. The Venetian navy respected seniority earned in the Habsburg navy while promoting everyone at least one rank. As a result, older ex-Austrian captains such as Graziani and Bua, armed with admirals' rank, dominated the fleet right up to the final crisis. Cf. *Militär-Schematismus*, 1848, and Randaccio, ibid., pp. 133–40.

31. Peter Handel-Mazzetti, *Geschichte der k.u.k. Kriegsmarine*, part 3, vol. 2: *1850–1866*, in 3 sections (MS, n.d.), KA, Ms/Ma 19, 1:9; statistics compiled from *Militär-Schematismus*, 1850. Seven Venetian officers applied for readmission to the corps (see Benko von Boinik, *1848–1849*, pp. 646–47n) and many others appealed to Francis Joseph for pardons or clemency.

32. Benko von Boinik, *1848–1849*, pp. 657–58. The Tonello firm, founded in 1840, built the ships on slips rented from the Panfilli yard, the oldest and largest shipbuilder in Trieste.

33. Handel-Mazzetti, *1850–1866 MS*, 1:5; Final Protocol of Committee, Vienna, 28 March 1850, copy in KA, Centralkanzleiakten (hereafter cited as KA, CK), Präs. 1862/562, fol. 31–42; Karl Netrval, "Feldzeugmeister August Graf Degenfeld-Schönburg: Offizier und Staatsmann" (Ph.D. diss., Vienna, 1971), p. 35.

34. Protocol of 28 March 1850 (with Francis Joseph's approval, Vienna, 12 April 1850), KA, CK, Präs. 1862/562, fol. 31–42; Handel-

Mazzetti, *1850–1866 MS*, 1:3. Even with the added wartime expenses, the navy spent less than 1.6 million florins in 1848 and just under 1.8 million in 1849. Under the Navy Law of April 1850 it was budgeted 2.3 million for 1850, 3.5 million per year for 1851–54, three million for 1855–60, and two million thereafter.

35. Fautz quoted in Benko von Boinik, *1848–1849*, p. 721.

36. Peter Handel-Mazzetti, "Eine Reise an der Zeitwende: Die Fahrt der Korvette *Carolina* in die Nordsee," *MGH* 7 (1980): 50–53; "Befehls-Buch, k.k. Corvette Carolina, II. Theil," in HHSA, Archiv Kaiser Maximilians von Mexiko (hereafter cited as HHSA, Archiv Max von Mexiko), Carton 183. Karolyi, considered a rising star within the corps, died in 1852 at age twenty-seven.

37. Cischini (consul) to FMLt. Count Franz Wimpffen (Mkdo. Trieste), Smyrna, 7 January 1850, HHSA, StK., Prov., Küstenland, Carton 4: Korr. Triester Guberniums 1848–64, fol. 164–65.

38. Dahlerup, *In österreichischen Diensten*, 2:206–12, 264.

39. Handel-Mazzetti, *1850–1866 MS*, 1:105–6. This practice came in spite of earlier promises that seniority would be respected. See Sterneck to mother, n.d. (1849), Sterneck, *Erinnerungen*, p. 68.

CHAPTER

7

The Frustrating 1850s

Austria and the Revolution in Naval Technology

The technological backwardness of the Austrian navy had been painfully evident during the naval campaign of 1848–49. The Venetian regime, though politically isolated, might never have been subdued militarily without the availability of Lloyd steamers. Prior to 1848 the vessels of the Habsburg fleet did not reflect the latest innovations in ship design or steam propulsion; even when Paulucci's efforts brought a modest expansion of the fleet, the commander's own distrust of innovations precluded any attempts at modernization. As a country with limited financial and industrial resources whose leaders traditionally did not give a high priority to the development of sea power, nineteenth-century Austria was in no position to engage in experimental shipbuilding. During the first half of the century, as the revolution in naval technology swept the navies of the world into the steam age, the Habsburg Empire resigned itself to a spectator's role.

The British blockade of American ports during the War of 1812 inspired the first project for a steam-powered warship.[1] The paddle steamer *Demologos* (later renamed the *Fulton*) was completed in 1814 and commissioned by the United States navy to defend New York harbor. The British fleet added its first steamship in 1822. The French followed suit in 1829 and used several steamers in their amphibious invasion of Algeria the following year. Over the next decade the lesser naval powers of Europe gradually added the ships to their fleets. In 1833 Naples commissioned its first steamer; the following year Sardinia purchased a pair from Britain, and in 1836 the Austrian navy launched its *Marianna*. In all countries naval leaders found the new technology not easily adaptable to traditional warship design or tactics of combat. The side-paddles eliminated one-fourth to one-third of the broadside of guns and were highly vulnerable to enemy fire. Furthermore, the cumbersome paddles made the ships slow and hard to maneuver under sail, a serious drawback since most naval engineers viewed steam power only as an auxiliary to the wind. There was no question of the paddle steamer replacing the sail-powered ship of the line as the foundation of the great battle fleets. Instead, the new vessels were assigned to traditional frigate duties, such as showing the flag, and used for the lesser roles of tugboats and transports.

The Habsburg navy, launching only its second steamer in 1843, lagged far behind its contemporaries in embracing the new technology. The fleets of Naples and Sardinia-Piedmont each had more steamships than the Austrian, while by 1845 the British navy had over a hundred, although only three dozen were armed as warships. Austria had yet to adjust to this first round of technological change when the introduction of the screw propeller pushed the competition onto a new plane. First used in merchant ships around 1840, the propeller was far more compatible with the needs of naval warfare than the paddle. The machinery rested entirely below the water line, was immune to hostile cannon fire, and did not break up the standard broadside arrangement of a ship's guns. Unlike side-paddles, the propeller did not affect the sailing qualities of a vessel. Naval architects also were able to incorporate propellers into ships of the line, frigates, and other warships of traditional design and even install them in vessels originally built as sailing ships.

The invention of the propeller has been attributed to or claimed by dozens of inventors, from Michelangelo down to a number of men in the 1830s. Austria too has her candidate, although in his time his work went completely unrecognized.

Josef Ressel, a Bohemian-born member of the Austrian navy's auxiliary forest service, designed an underwater propeller in the 1820s. In 1829, after overcoming financial difficulties and official opposition, he tested his invention in Trieste harbor aboard a vessel crowded with dignitaries. Unfortunately, five minutes into the voyage a steam pipe burst and even though the accident had nothing to do with the propeller, Austrian authorities forbade Ressel to conduct further experiments. He took his ideas to Britain and was soon forgotten by his countrymen. During the 1830s Swedish engineer John Ericsson also went to Britain after his idea for a propeller aroused no interest in his home country. He later emigrated to the United States, leaving Englishman Francis Smith to acquire the British patent for the screw propeller in 1837. Once the new technology gained acceptance, Ericsson and Smith were hailed as its discoverers. An Austrian account of the invention of the propeller written in 1844 does not even mention Ressel or his experiment at Trieste.[2]

Austria thus missed the opportunity to become a pioneer in naval technology, but in the years that followed she at least kept informed of further developments. To circumvent Paulucci and the naval hierarchy, the *Hofkriegsrat* in the early 1840s sent army engineer Karl Möring to the United States to investigate the latest innovations in warship technology and coastal fortifications. His visit coincided with the launching in 1847 of the American navy's first screw-powered warship, the *Princeton*. Upon his return to Austria he reported his findings to Archduke Frederick, but the new method of propulsion was considered too expensive and experimental to be applied to the Habsburg fleet.[3] Working within a tight budget and handicapped by the questionable loyalty of its personnel, the Austrian navy continued to watch the technological revolution from the sidelines. The British built a screw-schooner around the same time that the United States commissioned the *Princeton,* and in 1845–46 the Royal Navy ordered the experimental installation of propellers on several larger vessels. In the spring of 1847 the French ordered the construction of a new screw-powered ship of the line; the British responded in kind, touching off the first international naval competition since the Napoleonic era.

It was in this atmosphere that Dahlerup and the Austrian field marshals convened in March 1850 to draft the fleet plan that Francis Joseph subsequently signed into law. The admiral was the only navy man with voting powers on the committee, and his conservatism and suspicion of steam power were reflected in the Navy Law. Its ships of the line and frigates were all to be sail-powered and its steamships were all paddle steamers, intended only for auxiliary roles. The fleet Austria was committed to build was already obsolete while still on the drawing board; it is perhaps with good reason that some have viewed the early retirement of Dahlerup as a blessing in disguise for the Habsburg navy.[4]

In defense of the admiral it must be noted that the new technology was not greeted with universal enthusiasm. Even in Britain, the conservative Admiralty Board ordered the construction of new sailing ships of the line as late as 1848. Dahlerup was also at the helm when the Austrian navy acquired its first screw-powered vessel, the British yacht *Waterlily* (renamed *Seemöve*), in 1849. But when two large steamers were laid down in Trieste and three smaller ones in Venice in the same year, all were designed with paddle wheels, not propellers. As soon as the admiral resigned, the imperial government finally acted on a suggestion made by Archduke Frederick back in 1844 and ordered a modern warship to be built in Britain for use as a prototype in future domestic construction. Shortly after Wimpffen took over as commander a British shipyard started work on the screw-frigate *Radetzky*.

Following the departure of Dahlerup, Wimpffen and his superior in Vienna, war minister Baron Anton von Csorich, prudently kept the navy from wasting its money on more paddle steamers. In 1851, faced with the possibility of acquiring steamships from the defunct German navy, Csorich observed that "the purchase of used warships remains a risky business" and suggested the money would be better spent in building new vessels in Austrian shipyards, both to stimulate the growth of strategic domestic industries and help stem the flow of Austrian capital to foreign lands. A year later, while Habsburg officials in Frankfurt continued to pursue the purchase of German steamers, Wimpffen noted that the acquisition of the ships would strengthen the navy only for the present. In light of the new propeller technology, any money spent on paddle steamers could not be considered an investment.[5]

Taking note of the British example, Wimpffen in the summer of 1852 proposed the conversion of Austrian sailing warships to screw-powered steamers.[6] Unfortunately, Habsburg shipyards still lacked the capacity to do this sort of work; nor could they handle the volume of business promised by the Navy Law of 1850. As a result, little progress was made in strengthening the material state of the fleet in the early 1850s. Luckily for Austria, her regional rivals—Sardinia-Piedmont and Naples—were no better off. The Sardinians ordered their first screw-powered warship, the frigate *Carlo Alberto*, from a British shipyard at the same time that Austria was having the *Radetzky* built. Meanwhile, the Neapolitans continued to spend huge sums for obsolete warships. These included a new sailing ship of the line launched in 1850, and new paddle steamers purchased abroad during the following decade.[7]

In the 1830s and 1840s the Habsburg Empire commonly took note of developments in naval technology and implemented them modestly, if at all, after several years of delay. But after the impotent showing of the fleet in 1848–49 inspired the Navy Law of 1850, Austria found herself committed to build a respectable seagoing navy in a time of intensifying technological change. Dahlerup's fleet plan, obsolete at its birth, needed to be revised to include screw-powered steamers, and Austria's shipbuilding capabilities had to be modernized and mobilized to meet the requirements of modern warship construction. Wimpffen, in his capacity as temporary commander, was in no position to bring about such changes. Progress could come only after Ferdinand Max was prepared to take his place.

The Navy under Wimpffen (1851–1854)

Wimpffen was the third field marshal to be assigned command of the navy in the four years following the death of Archduke Frederick. Unlike Martini, his charge was strictly provisional, and in contrast to both Martini and Gyulai, he had the luxury of holding the post in a quieter time. But he was no more of a seaman than either of them and depended heavily on the advice and counsel of his junior officers. For his personal aide he chose one of the brightest men in the corps, Captain Bernhard von Wüllerstorf. Noted more as a mathematician and astronomer than a seaman, Wüllerstorf's comfortable life as a professor at the naval academy and head of the Austrian naval observatory had come to an abrupt end in 1848. The departure of two-thirds of the officer corps in the spring of that year catapulted him toward the top of the *Rangliste;* he subsequently served under Dahlerup on the blockade of Venice and on the committee that drafted the Navy Law of 1850. Before retiring, the admiral gave him his first seagoing command, but Wimpffen's call brought him back to Trieste after only a few months of duty in the Eastern Mediterranean.[8]

An eager administrator, Wüllerstorf helped Wimpffen complete the reorganization of the navy along the lines laid down by Dahlerup. With the shipbuilding program temporarily on hold, attention was focused on improving the training and quality of personnel. Under Dahlerup the desperate need for officers had combined with a shortage of qualified teachers to reduce naval education to a series of irregular courses from which aspirants were graduated and commissioned as quickly as possible. But with the 1852–53 term came the reestablishment of a regular four-year course of study, in the German language and at an academy housed in new permanent quarters in Trieste.[9] Unlike the old naval college at Venice where students not on scholarships were under no obligation to enter naval service, the new academy was in every respect a true military school. Austria also fell back on the resources of the other German states to speed the "Germanization" of the officer corps. During the second half of 1852, one-sixth of the officers and cadets of the defunct German fleet were granted Habsburg commissions, and in future years the Austrian navy recruited actively throughout Germany.[10] Yet despite the progress, the general quality of leadership remained poor. At the end of 1852 the corps still included a number of auxiliary officers taken in from the Adriatic merchant marine, among them several whom Kudriaffsky had branded as worthless four years earlier.[11]

As we have seen, on their first postwar cruises the crews of Austrian warships received mixed reviews, with more bad reports than good. Having resolved never again to depend primarily on Venetian personnel, the navy recruited heavily in Istria and Dalmatia from 1848 onward. When voluntary enlistments failed to fill out the crews, the fleet resorted to conscription. With an eye toward the needs of its future shipbuilding program, the naval command in July 1851 declared a service liability in Dalmatia not only for all able-bodied seamen, but also for carpenters and all other craftsmen with skills useful to the navy.[12] At the same time, Wimpffen and Wüllerstorf continued Dahlerup's practice of turning to the interior provinces of the Habsburg Empire in search of new manpower. Slovene and German recruits from Carinthia, Carniola, and Styria helped make up for the loss of Italian seamen, and as the decade progressed these provinces came to produce the bulk of the navy's non-commissioned (petty) officers.[13]

Wimpffen's greatest achievements resulted from the vigorous manner in which he implemented policies that already existed on paper when he took command. Under his direction the language regulations were enforced to the letter, and a number of South Slavs and loyal Italians lost their posts in the corps or naval administration because of their inability to speak German.[14] As an outsider, the field marshal was able to order the discharges with little remorse. Only Rear Admiral Bujacovich, nominally his second-in-command, was spared from the purge, and after commanding the active squadron in the Adriatic in 1851–52, he never again held a meaningful assignment. Since Italian was still the native language of most of the sailors, the "Germanization" campaign pointed the navy toward an uneasy future in which an officer corps dominated by one nationality commanded a fleet manned largely by another, a situation common to most regiments of the Habsburg army but which had never been the case in the navy. The commissioning of new officers who spoke no Italian at all, such as those brought in from the German navy, only compounded the problem. Wimpffen also brought the navy its first taste of genuine military discipline, but at the time this discipline was of dubious value; combined with the changes in the national composition of the personnel, it created new strains the service could have done without. Nevertheless, by the end of his tenure he could claim to have effected a fundamental change in the character of the navy.[15]

While Wimpffen's three years at the helm were placid compared with the previous three, they were not entirely uneventful. The material strength of the fleet did not increase, but it was kept from declining by the launching of the five paddle steamers laid down by Dahlerup and the completion of Austria's last sailing frigate, the *Schwarzenberg*, in 1853. The navy did not maintain a squadron outside of the Adriatic, but in 1853 the frigates *Novara* and *Venus* were sent with two corvettes, three brigs, and four steamers to the southern Dalmatian coast to demonstrate Austrian displeasure over the Turkish invasion of Montenegro.[16] Later the same year the onset of hostilities between Russia and Turkey brought the relocation of most of the active squadron to the Eastern Mediterranean where it showed the Austrian flag in greater force than at any time in the past decade.[17]

As head of a caretaker administration, Wimpffen's main purpose was to provide Ferdinand Max with enough time to develop the skills he needed to command the navy. In 1851 the archduke entered active service as a lieutenant, a lower rank than Frederick had been given at a much younger age. Since everyone realized that the future of the navy depended upon "the circle of Archduke Max," the younger officers of the corps clamored to be assigned to his personal entourage, no doubt mindful of the heights Marinovich had reached on the coattails of Frederick.[18] The emperor selected Lieutenant Count Carlo Michieli to serve as his brother's "Marinovich," a puzzling choice not only because of his nationality but also his past record. In addition to being an Italian in a navy striving to rid itself of Italians, Michieli also had been tainted by the Bandiera affair. He was known to have been a friend of the brothers, and after 1844 his name appeared frequently on lists of suspected revolutionaries. But in March 1848 he remained with the navy and demonstrated his loyalty when given the sensitive task of courier between Buratovich at Pola and Gyulai at Trieste. Following Michieli's death, an old classmate of Emilio Bandiera identified him as one of the founders of Esperia but also as the only member to fight against *Italia* in 1848.[19]

The motives behind Michieli's selection remain a mystery. We also know little about the nature or extent of his influence on Ferdinand Max. We do know that the count introduced him to the naval profession and supervised his whirlwind course of study; he did not shield the archduke from his fellow officers, as Marinovich had with Frederick, and those who met Ferdinand Max were "surprised by his friendliness." The young prince was promoted quickly to captain and given the corvette *Minerva*, which under his command won recognition as a "model ship." Two years after he entered the service, one officer noted that "it is inconceivable to all of us, how he has acquired so much maritime knowledge . . . in such a short time."[20] Though a source of wonder to those around him, his orientation came none too soon for the emperor. In September 1854 Francis Joseph promoted his brother to rear admiral and *Marine-Ober-Kommandant*.

The Era of Ferdinand Max: The Early Years

At twenty-two, Ferdinand Max was a year younger than Frederick had been when named commander a decade earlier. His three years of training were also less than half what his Habsburg cousin had received, and he had neither seen action in battle nor commanded an overseas mission. But he was the most gifted leader the navy had ever had, or ever would have. Since childhood he had often overshadowed Francis Joseph, causing observers to remark that the older brother appeared duller and less talented than the younger. In sending Ferdinand Max to the littoral, the emperor gave him a task that needed to be done and a challenge great enough to test his abilities. Perhaps more important, the navy command kept him occupied far away from the imperial capital and domestic politics, making it impossible for opponents of Francis Joseph to use him as the catalyst for a circle at court.

Upon taking command, the archduke assured Radetzky that the navy's postwar recovery would continue. "In the future the navy, like the army, shall have as its foundation a strict discipline," he promised, and would "develop into a useful corps, dependable in times of crisis and animated with a good spirit."[21] His tactful reference to the army's good example did not reflect his true feelings, however. It soon became clear to all that Ferdinand Max, in sharp contrast to Frederick, had a personality that would prevent him from being merely a "good soldier" and obedient servant of the crown. He sought to assert both his own independence and that of the navy, and he was helped by the muddled state of the Habsburg military administration. Following the Sylvester Patent of 31 December 1851, Francis Joseph ruled the Austrian Empire as an absolute monarch. In 1853 he subordinated the war ministry to the *Armee-Ober-Kommando* under Archduke William, a son of Archduke Charles; thereafter, the emperor in effect let the army administer itself while he personally represented it in the conference of ministers. His general-adjutant, *Feldmarschalleutnant* Count Carl Grünne, subsequently exercised the greatest influence over military affairs. Following the demise of the war ministry, the navy technically came under the jurisdiction of the *Armee-Ober-Kommando,* but under Wimpffen the *Marine-Ober-Kommando* began to push for separate financing. Though it was to take a couple of years for the navy to gain formal independence from the army command, Ferdinand Max never recognized its authority and went directly to the emperor with all proposals and requests for additional funds. Francis Joseph responded by giving him *carte blanche,* especially when it came to the shipbuilding program.

In November 1854, only weeks after the archduke took command, the screw-frigate *Radetzky* was delivered from Britain. Fears that the British would seize the ship for use in their own war effort against Russia proved unfounded, but the threat of such action served to underscore the dangers of dependence on foreign yards to build warships. The emperor promptly ordered the construction of a new drydock for Pola and the expropriation of the Tonello brothers' Navale Adriatico shipyard in Trieste, then authorized a screw-powered ship of the line to be built at Pola and a pair of screw-frigates, on the design of the *Radetzky,* at Trieste. Eager to modernize the fleet as quickly as possible, Ferdinand Max did not hesitate to build ships in Venice as well. By the end of 1854 he had two screw-corvettes under construction in the old Arsenal.[22]

While the navy had to import engines from Britain for its new screw-steamers, the program still depended heavily on domestic facilities and involved the greatest mobilization of resources in the littoral since Napoleon's shipbuilding efforts at Venice a half-century earlier. But the naval buildup also called attention to the lack of depth of these resources. Coinciding with the collapse of the old Panfilli firm, the government takeover of the Tonello wharves limited the options of civilian customers and jeopardized the modernization of the merchant marine. The Lloyd, foreseeing the seizure of the private yards for warship construction, started to build its own arsenal in 1853. Pending the completion of this new shipyard, the company shifted its orders to other builders and was not forced to curtail its own expansion program.[23]

The Lloyd recovered quickly from the warfare and blockades of 1848–49 and in 1851 became the largest steamship line in the Mediterranean. By 1856 it had sixty-one steamers in service, three times as many as in 1847. The company also had more foreign competitors, but an annual imperial subsidy of one million florins granted by Francis Joseph in 1855 guaranteed its future good health. The city of Trieste continued to grow along with the Lloyd; in 1853 the total value of its trade reached the 200 million–florin mark for the first time, and the new level of prosperity was maintained until the war of 1859. Optimism reigned after French engineer Ferdinand de Lesseps was awarded the concession to build the Suez Canal in 1854. Though Austria's foreign minister, Count Buol-Schauenstein, was not pleased to see a French consortium undertake the construction of the waterway, the businessmen of Trieste applauded the development, aware that their city would benefit from the canal regardless of who built it. An ensuing round of over-speculation caused the merchants of Trieste to suffer considerable losses in the worldwide panic of 1857, but the completion of the Vienna-Trieste railroad (the Südbahn) in the same year created even more business for the Lloyd and spurred the city to a rapid recovery.[24]

After putting ships at government disposal for the campaign against Venice, the Lloyd again demonstrated its strategic value in the Crimean War, leasing the navy six more paddle steamers during the years 1853–55. The vessels were not converted for active military use, but their service in home waters freed regular warships for duty in the Levant where the Austrian navy maintained a considerable presence. In May 1854, before the Habsburg army even occupied the Danubian Principalities, Buol ordered Austrian vessels in the war zone to cooperate with the fleets of Britain, France, and Turkey against Russia. By the spring of 1855 Ferdinand Max had four frigates, four corvettes, and two paddle steamers on patrol in the Mediterranean, giving special attention to the eastern basin.[25]

Not since the days of Charles VI had Austria put so many larger warships to sea, but her achievement paled in comparison to the forces of Britain and France, or even Sardinia-Piedmont. For the campaign of 1855 the British deployed a fleet consisting entirely of screw-powered warships, not just in the Black Sea but in the Baltic as well. During the same year the Sardinians, in support of their expeditionary corps in the Crimea, had an all-steam squadron in the theater, although with the exception of the new screw-frigate *Carlo Alberto* the vessels were all paddle steamers. Austria, in contrast, still relied almost entirely on sailing ships to show her flag in the region, supplemented by a handful of paddle steamers. Until the new propeller ships were completed, she had little alternative. The navy was still catching up with the last round of technological advances when the French successfully used armor-plated floating batteries to bombard Russia's Black Sea forts in October 1855. It soon became clear that another great breakthrough in naval technology lay just over the horizon, one that would involve unprecedented expenditure for all European powers.[26]

But for the moment, Ferdinand Max was concerned with the immediate rather than the more distant future. In the summer of 1855 he personally took command of the Austrian squadron. After going ashore to tour Egypt and the Holy Land, the archduke left the Levant with half of the warships to show the flag in the Western Mediterranean. He called at Toulon, Livorno, and Naples before returning to Trieste in the fall. As a training exercise, the cruise left the commander encouraged by the improved seamanship and discipline of his personnel. At the same time it gave him a first-hand knowledge of new lands, about which he soon aired his views to the emperor. Ferdinand Max recognized the importance to Trieste of the proposed canal across the isthmus of Suez and recommended that Austria take advantage of British and French involvement in the Crimean War to expand her own influence in Egypt. The archduke also gave a damning report of the domestic policies of Ferdinand II in Naples and questioned the fitness of Martini, the former *Marine-Ober-Kommandant*, to serve as Habsburg ambassador there.[27] Francis Joseph, true to form, ignored his brother's political advice. Austria subsequently made no effort to increase her stake in Egypt, and Martini kept on sending Vienna inaccurate reports from Naples right up to 1860.

Nevertheless, when it came to the navy itself, the emperor continued to give Ferdinand Max a free hand. In early 1856 he authorized the construction of three screw-schooners and the sale of a trio of sailing brigs they were to replace. But the disposal of the old ships covered only a fraction of the cost of the new ones; it also proved impossible for the navy to complete the larger screw-powered vessels within the limits prescribed by the Navy Law of 1850. Because the funds approved by Francis Joseph had been based upon Dahlerup's calculations of the prices of sailing ships, naval spending exceeded the legal limit in every year after 1850. In 1856 the service received more than double the authorized sum, prompting Count Grünne to protest on the army's behalf. But the finance ministry did not complain about the additional burden even though the recent mobilization during the Crimean War had made a shambles of the imperial finances. Baron Bruck, after serving as trade minister under Schwarzenberg, returned to the ministry in 1855 to take the finance portfolio. As an old proponent of Austrian maritime interests, he did not object to the archduke's activities and acquiesced in the dramatic increases in naval spending. The independence that Ferdinand Max had exercised since taking command of the fleet finally became official in August 1856 when Francis Joseph formally decreed the separation of the navy from the army effective at the start of the 1857 fiscal year.[28]

Shipbuilding was not the only area in which Ferdinand Max spent unprecedented amounts of money. He spared no expense on the training of personnel and from 1855 onward kept as many ships as possible on active duty to improve the general level of seamanship. After the naval academy had to evacuate its quarters in Trieste to make way for a waterfront railway yard, he had a new school built in Rijeka.[29] The archduke also spent freely on other land installations, especially at Pola. After being obstructed by Dahlerup, who like Paulucci before him did not approve of the site, the work at Pola had finally begun in earnest under Wimpffen. In 1856 Ferdinand Max laid the cornerstone of the new Pola arsenal (designed by Karl Möring) and commissioned the American firm of John Gilbert to build its drydock, the latter to be constructed not from readily available Croatian oak but of expensive imported Georgia pine and higher quality American oak timber.[30] The archduke's policies provided the fleet with better personnel and facilities, but the high costs ultimately were to cause a backlash against the navy.

As long as Ferdinand Max had the absolute authority of the emperor behind his plans, however, the opponents of naval spending could do nothing to stop him. Over the winter of 1856–57 he implemented the administrative reforms that accompanied the new status of the navy and at the same time laid plans for an ambitious world cruise by the frigate *Novara*. No Austrian vessel had ever circumnavigated the globe, and the archduke was determined that one would, in the interest of science. Of all the navy's captains, Wüllerstorf alone had the scientific background necessary to lead the mission. Ferdinand Max recalled him from a frigate command in the Mediterranean where he had served since losing his post in Trieste after the resignation of Wimpffen. As he began to prepare for the voyage, the foreign ministry in Vienna secured international recognition of the *Novara*'s neutrality in order to protect it "from all possible eventualities."[31] The ship was to be escorted on the first leg of its journey by the corvette *Carolina*, which would then cruise in South American and African waters on a mission of its own.

In March 1857, a month before the ships left Trieste, Francis Joseph appointed Ferdinand Max governor-general of Lombardy and Venetia, a new post created in the wake of the retirement of Field Marshal Radetzky. The archduke did not give up command of the navy and continued to run it from his new quarters in Milan, aided by a second-in-commnd in Trieste. Bujacovich, for years the titular assistant, finally had to be retired in favor of an officer capable of doing the job. The honors fell to Captain Anton Bourguignon, an old adversary of Wüllerstorf who had languished since his brief moment in the sun as Gyulai's assistant in 1848, orchestrating the peaceful repatriation of the Venetians from Trieste. His promotion to rear admiral and second-in-command, combined with the departure of Wüllerstorf and his protégés aboard the *Novara*, appeased all of the various cliques within the officer corps.[32]

Ferdinand Max's move to Milan had negative repercussions for both the navy and his personal relationship with the emperor and did nothing to improve the situation in northern Italy. He received a cold reception from the subjects of Lombardy and Venetia, and in spite of his efforts their feelings for him never warmed. Only months after taking office he angered the *Armee-Ober-Kommando* by calling for a moratorium on conscription. He also had trouble getting along with Count Gyulai, the heir to Radetzky's military functions. At the end of his first year in office the archduke appealed to Vienna for sweeping reforms and liberal political institutions for Lombardy and Venetia as the only way to defuse tensions and foil the ambitions of Count Cavour and Sardinia-Piedmont. But his foreign policy advice only offended Count Buol, and the call for liberal change stirred the hostility of the rest of the ministry, which believed firmly in absolutism and bureaucratic centralism. After failing to gain concessions for his subjects, Ferdinand Max in the summer of 1858 threatened to resign as governor-general, then spent several months on leave before finally returning to his post in November. Doomed to accomplish nothing, he was to welcome with great relief his return to naval duty the following spring.

During the archduke's tenure in Milan the strength of the Austrian navy increased markedly, but only because of the completion of ships laid down in previous years. Between the fall of 1856 and the beginning of 1859 the screw-frigates *Donau* and *Adria* (sister ships of the *Radetzky*) were launched at Trieste, the screw-corvettes *Dandolo* and *Erzherzog Friedrich* and a schooner at Venice, and the propeller ship of the line *Kaiser* at Pola. All were put into service except for the latter, which still awaited its engines from Britain. In July 1858 Francis Joseph finally conceded a revision of the Navy Law of 1850 to account for the introduction of propeller warships. The six ships of the line in the original plan were to be completed as screw-powered vessels, the ten sailing frigates were increased to twelve screw-frigates, and the six corvettes were to be built with propellers as well. The brigs and schooners were scratched from the program, as were Dahlerup's two dozen sailing gunboats. Twelve screw-powered schooners and gunboats were to provide for coastal defense, and the existing sailing ships and paddle steamers were to be reduced to auxiliary roles.[33] Francis Joseph made no attempt to revise the budget projections of the 1850 law, however, preferring instead to continue his policy of granting money on an ad hoc basis. For the 1859 fiscal year the emperor ordered construction to begin on a second ship of the line and another schooner.

The navy was forced to curtail its operations after the end of the Crimean War but remained active while Ferdinand Max served as governor-general. To keep up with the continuing revolution in naval technology, in 1857 the archduke sent an Austrian captain to Toulon to engage in industrial espionage. The spy was eventually uncovered, but conservative French naval officials were not angered by the incident. Instead they expressed a willingness to help and obtained permission from Paris for one of their own engineers to go to Trieste in the service of Austria. Thus a Frenchman, Eugène Sandfort, followed the Dutchman Scheffer and a Swede, August Ljungstedt, as head of the Habsburg navy's corps of engineers. At the same time, to lessen the dependence on foreign expertise in future years, the navy sent young Austrian engineering cadets to study shipbuilding in Copenhagen.[34]

In addition to the overseas missions of the *Novara* and *Carolina*, the Austrian navy in the summer of 1857 sent the frigates *Radetzky* and *Adria* and the corvette *Friedrich* on a training cruise to the North Sea and Baltic. It was the first mission ever undertaken by a squadron of screw-powered Austrian warships and the first single cruise to involve so many of the navy's larger vessels outside of the Mediterranean. Their itinerary, however, betrayed the political isolation of the Habsburg Empire in the wake of the Crimean War: the ships called at Hamburg, Danzig, Copenhagen, and Karlskrona in Sweden, but not at St. Petersburg or in any British or French port en route to northern waters. The following summer a renewal of the Turco-Montenegrin war brought a number of Turkish warships to the lower Adriatic as well as international naval "observation" by Britain, France, and Russia. Austria had to respond with a strong showing of her own and kept the bulk of the fleet on duty in home waters. The French presence—which included a pair of new screw-powered ships of the line—was by far the strongest but had nothing to do with Montenegro. In May 1858 Napoleon III, soon to conclude the secret treaty of Plombières with Cavour, promised Turin that he would "send a fleet to the Adriatic under pretext of the Montenegrin difficulties" as a sign of his sympathy with Sardinia-Piedmont's Italian ambitions.[35]

Though not as strong as a fleet, the French showing at the mouth of the Adriatic certainly caught Vienna's attention. Nevertheless, it was not until after the French emperor's famous New Years' Day quip about the poor state of Franco-Austrian relations that a war scare started in earnest.[36] The navy had planned to maintain a half-dozen warships in the Mediterranean during 1859, but in early February Buol ordered the fleet to start concentrating its forces in the Adriatic against an attack by the Sardinian navy. Little did he know that Paris had already concluded a military alliance with Turin in late January. As the crisis reached its climax, it became clear that the foreign minister had led the empire to war without allies, but to the end Buol optimistically counted on

France not to enter the conflict and on Prussian aid if she did. On 19 April the conference of ministers in Vienna voted to send an ultimatum to Sardinia-Piedmont; it was delivered on the twenty-third and rejected by Cavour on the twenty-sixth. Two days later, Ferdinand Max embarked on the fleet flagship as active commander of the Austrian navy.[37]

"A Long and Painful Summer": The War of 1859

The months prior to the outbreak of war were an active time for the Austrian navy. Starting in January, its paddle steamers were employed to ferry thousands of troops from Trieste to Venice. The task proved to be too great for the fleet alone and before the month was over Lloyd steamers had to be rented as auxiliary transports. Forced to man the leased ships and meet the army's needs first, the navy had to postpone its own preparation until the eve of war. While still in Milan, Ferdinand Max laid plans for the defense of the Adriatic and ordered the Venice Arsenal stripped of all useable naval stores. The fleet was to be concentrated at Pola or some point on the Dalmatian coast, and if the Sardinian navy alone came to challenge it, the archduke proposed to seek battle immediately. But if France entered the war and sent ships into the Adriatic, the Austrians would concentrate on defending the coast.[38]

Although Ferdinand Max did not hesitate to take on the Sardinians alone, no one felt confident of a victory against them. It was difficult to compare the material strength of the two navies since both included a variety of newer warships as well as a number of obsolete sailing and paddle-driven vessels. The Austrian fleet went into the war with three screw and three sailing frigates, two screw and five sailing corvettes, nine old brigs, and a dozen paddle steamers, plus the vessels just rented from the Lloyd. The ship of the line *Kaiser* could not be used because the British firm building its engines had yet to deliver them; the frigate *Novara*, still on its world cruise, was unavailable for the campaign. For their part, the Sardinians had two screw and four sailing frigates, two sailing corvettes, a half-dozen old brigs, and eight paddle steamers. The size of the screw-frigates (54-gun, compared to the Austrian 31-gun models) helped balance the ledger, and the impending completion of their two sister ships, under construction at Genoa, threatened to give Sardinia the advantage. The archduke had no doubts about his personnel, even though many of the seamen were Italian, and his training cruises in recent years more than made up for the experience the Sardinian navy had gained during the Crimean War. As far as officers were concerned, the younger Sardinian commanders were imbued with a sense of duty to *Italia*, the consequence of Cavour's insistence that a nationalist spirit prevail at the naval academy in Genoa. The corps had also been strengthened during the 1850s by a number of veterans of the Venetian navy of 1848–49, but the higher ranks were deeply divided between these newcomers and an older Genoese clique.[39]

Once the war began, the naval might of France rendered comparisons between Austria and Sardinia meaningless. The French battle fleet, with a core of thirty-one screw-powered ships of the line, was virtually equal in numbers to the British and many times larger than the navies of the other two belligerents.[40] On 3 May, only four days after Gyulai's army invaded Piedmont, France formally entered the war; within two weeks the first squadron of French and Sardinian warships arrived in the Adriatic. Ferdinand Max assumed a defensive posture, gathering the propeller ships at Pola with the best of the sailing vessels and paddle steamers and distributing the rest of the fleet among the islands and coastal ports of Dalmatia. Two old sailing ships and three of the steamers leased from the Lloyd were sunk to block the entrances to Venice and other strategic harbors. On 2 June the French declared a blockade of Venice, but the allied fleet did not reach full strength until weeks later. In early July the allies occupied the island of Lussin as a base for an amphibious assault on the mainland.[41] By then, however, the war had already been decided on land by the Austrian defeats at Magenta (4 June) and Solferino (24 June).

Magenta delivered Milan and most of Lombardy to the allies and forced the Austrians to retreat toward their Quadrilateral fortresses. After Gyulai resigned his post, Francis Joseph took personal command of the army and called Ferdinand Max to his field headquarters. The archduke left Rear Admiral Johann Scopinich in charge of the active squadron with orders to guard against a rumored Franco-Sardinian landing between Venice and Trieste.[42] Within days an Austrian counterattack ended at Solferino in the biggest and bloodiest battle since the Napoleonic wars. The victorious Napoleon III was no less sickened by the spectacle than Francis Joseph, and the added pressure of a Prussian mobilization led him to open peace talks. On 11 July the emperors signed the armistice of Villafranca, leaving Austria in control of Venetia and the Sardinians, despite the promises of Plombières, with just Lombardy.

The French navy sent only six ships of the line into the Adriatic, but along with three armored batteries and a number of frigates and smaller vessels they more than sufficed to keep the Habsburg fleet at bay. The Austrians made good use of the broken Dalmatian coastline and despite the odds were able to move freely in coastal waters. The navy even preyed on French commerce in the Adriatic, and its capture of one merchant bark led to the only sea encounter of the war. When the ship was interned at Zara, a French screw-frigate followed to demand its release. After the request was denied, the warship was driven off by fire from shore batteries and a pair of Austrian paddle steamers.[43] The navy hailed the incident as evidence of its success in defending the coastal ports against the enemy fleet. The French later admitted as much and credited the Habsburg navy with a good showing under the circumstances.[44] But the praise was not echoed at home. The main propeller squadron, expensive ships built within the past five years, saw no action at all during the war, and to many domestic observers the performance of the fleet did not measure up to the unprecedented sums of money it had consumed over the past decade. On the contrary, it was all too reminiscent of the humiliations of 1821, 1832, and 1848.

The end of the war came none too soon for the navy. When word of Villafranca reached the littoral, the army was already disarming the ships and confiscating all naval artillery for use on land in the defense of Venetia. Fearful of an attack on Pola, Ferdinand Max had made emergency plans to scuttle the ship of the line *Kaiser* to keep it from falling into enemy hands.[45] After the armistice the archduke's efforts to deflect criticism from the navy were aided by a fortunate coincidence: in early July the *Novara* reached Gibraltar, having taken two years and three months to circle the globe. Ferdinand Max dispatched a pair of warships to escort the frigate the rest of the way home and laid plans for its gala arrival at Trieste. When the ship reached Pola, the entire fleet turned out to accompany it, and the vessels, in fighting trim, sailed into Trieste in two columns behind the archduke's flagship and Wüllerstorf in the *Novara*.[46] The impressive spectacle served its purpose and boosted the morale of a service frustrated by the recent course of events. But the impotence of the wartime months could not be masked by a single showy review of the fleet. As Ferdinand Max himself admitted, it had been "a long and painful summer."[47]

During his first five years as commander, Ferdinand Max accomplished more than any of his predecessors had, giving the empire a better-trained navy with new warships and modern land facilities. Perhaps of greatest importance, the archduke used his influence to free the navy from army control, the ultimate triumph in a battle for administrative independence that had started when the navy was a mere flotilla run by the authorities in Trieste. Having the emperor's brother at the helm naturally drew more public attention to the fleet, and publicity from cruises such as the *Novara* mission ensured that the navy would have no shortage of recruits in future years. By the end of the 1850s all nationalities of the monarchy, even those far removed from the sea, were represented in the ranks of the navy, a dramatic improvement over the situation of a decade earlier.

While the navy became more important to the empire as a whole, its traditional coastal base reaped special benefits from the expansion of Habsburg sea power. The demand for modern warships stimulated the development of the industries of the littoral, in particular the shipyards of Trieste. The empire's leading port benefited as well from the continuing growth and prosperity of the Austrian Lloyd. After leasing a half-dozen steamers to the fleet during the Crimean War, the Lloyd again demonstrated its strategic value in 1859 when it provided a total of eighteen of its vessels for conversion to auxiliary warships or use as troop transports. The war, however, was a humbling blow to the cause of Austrian sea power in general and provided grist for the mill of every opponent of Ferdinand Max and the fleet. To make matters worse, the political changes wrought by the defeat of 1859 were soon to cast a new pall of uncertainty over the future of the Austrian navy. The archduke would have to muster all of his talents and energies to turn the experience into the impetus for an even greater future.

NOTES

1. The general information on naval technology in this and the following paragraphs has been compiled from a number of works. The best monograph on the subject (though somewhat Anglocentric in focus) is Andrew Lambert, *Battleships in Transition: The Creation of the Steam Battlefleet, 1815–1860* (Annapolis, Md.: U.S. Naval Institute Press, 1984).

2. Karl Möring, "Armee und Flotte der Vereins-Staaten" (1844), KA, Nachlass Möring, B/209: no. 5. The Republic of Austria has recognized Ressel's accomplishment by featuring his likeness and a screw-powered steamship on its 500-Schilling bank notes.

3. Möring, frustrated by the lack of action, published "Armee und Flotte" as a pamphlet, to which he appended his own liberal *grossdeutsch* political views.

4. E.g., Ulrich Schöndorfer, "Der österreichische Kriegsschiffbau von 1848 bis 1914," *Schriften des Heeresgeschichtlichen Museums (Militärwissenschaftliches Institut) in Wien*, vol. 8: *Österreich zur See* (Vienna: Österreichischer Bundesverlag, 1980), p. 25.

5. Csorich to Schwarzenberg, Vienna, 16 September 1851, HHSA, PA, II. Deutscher Bund, Carton 87: Deutsche Flotte, 1851/fol. 583–94; Wimpffen to Grünne, Venice, 14 August 1852, ibid., Carton 89: Deutsche Flotte, 1852/fol. 1024–29.

6. Handel-Mazzetti, *1850–1866 MS*, 1:12.

7. Radogna, *Storia della Marina*, pp. 130–33.

8. Friedrich Wallisch, *Sein Schiff Hiess Novara: Bernhard von Wüllerstorf, Admiral und Minister* (Vienna: Verlag Herold, 1966), pp. 55–63. After starting his military career as a cadet in the army engineers, Wüllerstorf transferred to the navy in 1833. He started teaching at the academy in 1839 (at the age of twenty-three) and became head of the naval observatory upon its creation in 1840.

9. Salcher, *Marine-Akademie*, pp. 17–22.

10. Austria eventually gave commissions to fifteen of the ninety officers and cadets of the German navy. Cf. "Liste der Offiziere, Fähnriche und Seejunker . . . nach dem Stande vom 1. Mai 1850," in Hubatsch, ed., *Die Erste Deutsche Flotte 1848–1853*, pp. 104–9 and *Militär-Schematismus*, 1853.

11. Cf. Kudriaffsky to MOKdo., Trieste, 6 September 1848, KA, MA, M/c 27 (1848), no. 250 (Carton 46) and *Militär-Schematismus*, 1853.

12. Handel-Mazzetti, *1850–1866 MS*, 1:75–76.

13. Miroslav Pahor, *Slovenski mornarji Austrije v obrambi Dalmacije in Istre 1849–1917* (Piran: Pomorski muzej Sergej Mašera, 1978), p. 4.

14. Handel-Mazzetti, *1850–1866 MS*, 1:109–10. Strict enforcement of the language policy purged the higher ranks of most of the remaining Italians and South Slavs; of the half-dozen holding captain's rank in 1853, only two survived. Cf. *Militär-Schematismus*, 1853 and 1856.

15. Handel-Mazzetti, *1850–1866 MS*, 1:12.

16. Ibid., 1:206–12; see also Kenneth W. Rock, "Loyalty and Legality: Austria and the Western Balkans, 1848–1853," in *Nation* *and Ideology: Essays in honor of Wayne S. Vucinich,* ed. Ivo Banac, John G. Ackerman, and Roman Szporluk (Boulder, Colo.: Eastern European Monographs, 1981), pp. 138–39.

17. Austria's naval activity in the Levant during the summer of 1853 included a rare clash with the United States in the Turkish port of Smyrna. At issue was the capture and internment aboard an Austrian warship of a Hungarian, Martin Koszta, who had once fought for Kossuth. Koszta claimed American citizenship and later was allowed to emigrate to the United States. See Lawrence Sondhaus, "Die Koszta-Affaire: Eine österreichisch-amerikanische Konfrontation in Smyrna 1853," *MGH* 13 (1986): 153–57.

18. Sterneck to mother, Trieste, 17 April 1851, Sterneck, *Erinnerungen,* pp. 76–77.

19. Zichy to Hardegg, Venice, 1 December 1844, enclosure to KA, HKR Akten, Präs. 1845/869, and Marinovich to Zichy, Venice, 22 November 1847, KA, Nachlass Zichy, B/184:2, fol. 94–95 are two of the reports in which Michieli's name appears most prominently. See also Radaelli, *Storia dello Assedio di Venezia,* pp. 7–8.

20. Sterneck to mother, Trieste, 4 April 1853, Sterneck, *Erinnerungen,* p. 80; Sterneck to mother, Pola, 31 October 1853, ibid., p. 91. Unlike Marinovich, Michieli did not become an important figure within the navy after his young charge took command. He reached captain's rank before dying in 1860, most likely from the effects of syphillis. See ibid., editor's note, p. 76n.

21. Ferdinand Max to Radetzky, Trieste, 26 October 1854, in Bernhard Duhr, ed., *Briefe des Feldmarschalls Radetzky an seine Tochter Friederike, 1847–1857* (Vienna: Josef Roller & Comp. 1892), p. 140.

22. Handel-Mazzetti, *1850–1866 MS,* 1:14–15, 217–19; Stefani and Astori, *Il Lloyd Triestino,* pp. 216–17; Schöndorfer, "Kriegsschiffbau," pp. 25–26. The Austrians first solicited bids from British firms and an American yard in New York before finally deciding to build the ship of the line at Pola; see Lambert, *Battleships in Transition,* p. 114.

23. Giuseppe Gerolami, *Trieste e il Mare* (Trieste: Borsatti, 1955), pp. 56–57. The failure of the Panfilli (founded in 1780) left the Tonello firm as the largest shipbuilder in Trieste.

24. *75 Jahre österreichischer Lloyd,* pp. 26–35; Lo Giudice, *Canale di Suez,* pp. 106–7, 138. In 1858 Trieste's trade reached its prewar peak with a value of 213 million florins for the year.

25. Handel-Mazzetti, *1850–1866 MS*, 1:215.
26. Lambert, *Battleships in Transition*, pp. 44–45; Baratelli, *La marina militare italiana*, p. 41; James P. Baxter, *The Introduction of the Ironclad Warship* (Cambridge, Mass.: Harvard University Press, 1933; reprint, Archon Books, 1968), pp. 83–84.
27. Ferdinand Max to Francis Joseph, aboard the *Schwarzenberg*, 23 July 1855, HHSA, Hausarchiv, Familienkorrespondenz A, Carton 52: Briefe Erzhs. Ferdinand Max an S.M.K. Franz Josef I., fol. 28–38; Ferdinand Max to Francis Joseph, aboard the *Schwarzenberg*, 12 August 1855, ibid., fol. 40–43; Ferdinand Max to Francis Joseph, Trieste, ibid., fol. 45–48; Ferdinand Stepanek, "Marine-Amtsgeschichte, 1854 bis 10. April 1864," p. 34, MS in HHSA, Archiv Max von Mexiko, Carton 113.
28. Cf. figures in Francis Joseph (decree), Vienna, 12 April 1850, copy in KA, CK, Präs. 1862/562, fol. 31–42, and Ferdinand Max to Ignaz von Plener, n.d. (June 1860), HHSA, Archiv Max von Mexiko, Carton 113, I: fol. 27–44; Schmidt-Brentano, "Österreichs Weg zur Seemacht," p. 125; Wagner, "Die obersten Behörden," pp. 3–4.
29. Handel-Mazzetti, *1850–1866 MS*, 1:17–18; Salcher, *Marine-Akademie*, pp. 22–23.
30. Handel-Mazzetti, *1850–1866 MS*, 1:61–62. Dahlerup considered Pola too dirty and malaria-ridden to be the site for a base. See Pahor, *Slovenski mornarji Austrije*, pp. 4–5.
31. Wallisch, *Sein Schiff Hiess Novara*, p. 67; Ferdinand Max to Ministerium des Äussern, Milan, 20 January 1857, HHSA, StK., Notenwechsel HKR, Carton 294, fol. 201–2; Ministerium des Äussern to Ferdinand Max, Vienna, 23 March 1857, ibid., fol. 35–40. The neutrality of the *Novara* (which carried a reduced battery of cannon) was recognized by the European powers as well as by Brazil and New Granada (Colombia). Only the United States refused to acknowledge its special status (see ibid., 4 May 1857, fol. 59–60). On the scientific aspects of the voyage see Gunther Hamann, "Die österreichische Kriegsmarine im Dienste der Wissenschaften," *Schriften des Heeresgeschichtlichen Museums (Militärwissenschaftliches Institut) in Wien*, vol. 8: *Österreich zur See* (Vienna: Österreichischer Bundesverlag, 1980): 64–68.
32. Wagner, "Die obersten Behörden," pp. 10–15. Bourguignon retired from the navy when Wüllerstorf returned from the mis-

sion only to be reactivated after his nemesis left the service in 1864. Though he never commanded the navy, in 1875 he became the first man in its history to reach the rank of full admiral.

33. Francis Joseph to Ferdinand Max, Laxenburg, 6 July 1858 (copy), KA, CK, Präs. 1862/562, fol. 8.

34. Capt. Eugen von Preu to Ferdinand Max, Toulon, 31 January 1857 (copy), HHSA, StK., Notenwechsel HKR, Carton 294, fol. 217–18; Bujacovich to Ministerium des Äussern, Trieste, 11 February 1857, ibid., fol. 215–16, 219; Ministerium des Äussern to MOK, Vienna, 10 April 1857, ibid., Carton 294, 1855–60, fol. 43; Handel-Mazzetti, *1850–1866 MS*, 1:116–17.

35. Dr. Conneau to Cavour, Paris, 15 May 1858, text in Mack Walker, ed. *Plombières: Secret Diplomacy and the Rebirth of Italy* (London: Oxford University Press, 1968), p. 215. Conneau, Napoleon III's personal physician, was a friend of Cavour and acted as an unofficial agent between the two men.

36. Made to the Austrian ambassador, Count Joseph von Hübner, at a reception in the Tuileries.

37. Fautz to Ministerium des Äussern, Milan, 13 December 1858, HHSA, PA, XL. Interna, Carton 93; Buol to MOK, Vienna, 4 February 1859, ibid., Carton 97; Wagner, "Die obersten Behörden," p. 18.

38. Handel-Mazzetti, *1850–1866 MS*, 1:343–58.

39. As early as 1850 the Austrian ambassador in Turin noted that a "great number" of former Venetian naval officers had applied for entry into Sardinian service and that their petitions were being accepted despite the "animosity" caused by the resulting delay in "the advancement of indigenous officers." Count Rudolph Apponyi to Schwarzenberg, Turin, 28 February 1850, HHSA, PA, XI. Italienische Staaten, Carton 44: Sardinien, Berichte 1850, fol. 84–85. On the "national mission" and the Sardinian naval academy see Sante Romiti, "La politica navale del Piemonte nel decennio 1849–1859," *Rassegna Storica del Risorgimento* 39 (1952): 781.

40. Lambert, *Battleships in Transition*, pp. 140–43.

41. Baratelli, *La marina militare italiana*, pp. 41–45; Handel-Mazzetti, *1850–1866 MS*, 1:358–409 passim.

42. Wagner, "Die obersten Behörden," p. 18; Handel-Mazzetti, *1850–1866 MS*, 1:386. Rechberg to Prince Richard Metternich, Vienna, 9 June 1859, HHSA, PA, XL. Interna, Carton 98 (Metternich

mission to Verona, 1859) indicates that the Austrians received intelligence reports warning of a landing by 15,000 French troops.

43. Handel-Mazzetti, *1850–1866 MS*, 1:404. The encounter, between the 56-gun French frigate *Impetieuse* and the Austrian paddle steamers *Prinz Eugen* and *Curtatone*, occurred on 7 July.

44. Mariano Gabriele, *La politica navale italiana dall'unita alla viglia di Lissa* (Milan: A. Giuffrè Editore, 1958), p. 77.

45. Handel-Mazzetti, *1850–1866 MS*, 1:410.

46. See Wallisch, *Sein Schiff Hiess Novara*, p. 45; Handel-Mazzetti, *1850–1866 MS*, 1:333.

47. Ferdinand Max, *Aus meinem Leben: Reiseskizzen, Aphorismen, Gedichte*, 7 vols. (Leipzig: Verlag von Duncker und Humblot, 1867), 5:3 (entry for 10 November 1859).

CHAPTER

8

The Italian Challenge

In the fall of 1859 Ferdinand Max concluded that the best way to defend the navy would be to launch an offensive of his own. Without waiting for the critics to assemble, he proposed to the emperor a fleet large and strong enough to show the flag and defend commerce worldwide. As one of the great powers, Austria should have a navy worthy of a great power; anything less would be a meaningless drain on the imperial budget. But the end of absolute government made the archduke's campaign more difficult at the same time that the introduction of ironclad warships made it far more expensive. His greatest ally in the coming battle was also the greatest foe of Austrian sea power: the threat of a new united Italy on the other side of the Adriatic.

The Adriatic and the Unification of Italy (1859–1861)

The war of 1859 signalled the beginning of the end for an Italian state system that had survived virtually intact since the Congress of Vienna. In late April 1859, only days after the fighting began, a revolution toppled the Habsburg grand duke of Tuscany; by the middle of June the monarchs of Parma and Modena were likewise overthrown and their states occupied by Sardinian troops. Naples and the Papal State sought to remain neutral, but Austria ignored the wishes of the latter and maintained garrisons at Bologna and Ancona until the French naval buildup in the Adriatic made their positions untenable. The withdrawal of Habsburg troops from Papal territory in June occasioned a revolt in the Romagna that freed the area from the control of Rome.

After the armistice of Villafranca, Napoleon III encouraged the new Habsburg foreign minister, Count Johann von Rechberg, with signs of willingness to agree to a conservative restructuring of Italy. The Peace of Zurich, concluded on 10 November, gave only Lombardy to Sardinia-Piedmont and left the fate of the central Italian duchies, as well as the question of a future Italian confederation, to a European congress. Cavour considered Napoleon's armistice with Francis Joseph a betrayal of the Franco-Sardinian alliance and resigned his posts as minister-president and foreign minister as soon as it was concluded. But while the moderates despaired over France's magnanimity toward Austria, Giuseppe Garibaldi and other radicals welcomed it since it freed the Italian cause from the moral constraints of treaties and alliances.[1]

The rapid progress of events doomed the Zurich treaty before it was even signed. In August and September 1859 constitutent assemblies in Modena, Parma, and the Romagna convened and voted for union with Sardinia-Piedmont; Turin responded by sending Garibaldi and other émigré generals in Sardinian service to organize a central Italian army. Faced with a fait accompli in the central Italian duchies, Rechberg refused to attend an international congress that would only ratify the new order. In January 1860 the congress project collapsed, the agreements of Villafranca and Zurich officially died, and Cavour returned to office in Turin. In March, after plebiscites confirmed the annexation of Tuscany, Modena, Parma, and Romagna, the Sardinian army was swollen by the addition of the central Italian regiments. Later the same month Cavour personally assumed the portfolio of naval minister and began to lay the groundwork for the future Italian fleet. In April he incorporated the tiny Tuscan navy into the Sardinian, then ordered two armored corvettes from a French shipyard in Toulon.[2]

The rapid expansion of Sardinia-Piedmont and her army caused considerable alarm in Vienna and prompted Francis Joseph to keep Habsburg forces on a war footing. At the same time, Cavour's first steps toward building an Italian navy went virtually unnoticed and caused no special concern about the security of the Adriatic. During the summer, when a crisis over Lebanon attracted a number of warships to Levantine waters, Austria felt confident enough to send a small contingent of her own under Captain Wilhelm von Tegetthoff, a young firebrand who had wanted to challenge the French blockade in 1859. But Tegetthoff had barely arrived in the Levant when the news of Garibaldi's conquest of Sicily forced his quick return home.[3]

In May 1860 Garibaldi and his "Thousand" landed on the coast of Sicily to aid a local rebellion that had begun the previous month. Cavour had serious misgivings about Garibaldi's republican principles, but as volunteers flocked to the island and it became clear that he would succeed in taking it, Sardinia-Piedmont acquiesced in the operation. Wüllerstorf, recently promoted to rear admiral and squadron commander, responded to the landing by sending Austrian warships to Neapolitan waters. The Habsburg vessels joined those of the other powers in observing as Garibaldi, from a modest start of two paddle steamers, collected a navy of over a dozen steamships to support his impending invasion of Naples. In July 1860 a mutiny in the Neapolitan fleet gave the rebels their first true warship along with scores of officers and seamen. The following month Garibaldi completed his conquest of Sicily and crossed over to the mainland. Naples fell in a matter of weeks, and the Austrian ships on hand could do little more than help transport the young King Francis II and his suite to their refuge at Gaeta.[4] Garibaldi delivered the Neapolitan navy to Count Carlo Pellion di Persano, the commander of the Sardinian squadron that had monitored his activities, and subsequently turned over his conquests to Victor Emmanuel II.

The fall of Naples touched off a panic in Vienna over the security of the Adriatic coastline. With the general international acceptance of Garibaldi's deeds, Cavour lost his inhibitions about invading the Papal State and sent a squadron into the Adriatic to blockade Ancona in support of a Sardinian campaign in the Marches. The warships raised concerns for Austria, but the greatest fear was that Garibaldi or his followers would attempt to repeat their recent successes with a revolutionary landing in Istria or Dalmatia. Habsburg leaders were well aware that most Italian nationalists considered these lands part of *Italia irredenta* because of their historical ties to Venice. It also did not escape Vienna's notice that Garibaldi had employed hundreds of Hungarian revolutionaries in his invasions of Sicily and Naples. These same men no doubt would join in any campaign to ignite the western Balkans and ultimately free their own homeland from Habsburg rule.[5]

In mid-September Francis Joseph addressed the dangers by declaring that Sardinian ships were to be "denied entry into all [Austrian] harbors and, in cases of resistance, impeded with armed force" and that all vessels carrying "Garibaldini or volunteers" were to be "treated as pirates, regardless of their flag."[6] The latter pronouncement was particularly bold since in the recent campaign Garibaldi's transports had sailed under the American, British, and French flags, as well as the Sardinian. In the fall of 1860 Wüllerstorf backed up the emperor's decree by deploying most of the navy on regular patrols between the mouth of the Po and the southern tip of Dalmatia. But the Austrians did not interfere when Admiral Persano's Sardinian squadron blockaded Ancona and shelled the city into submission. The Sardinians reciprocated by prudently leaving the Adriatic in early October as soon as the Papal garrison surrendered.[7]

The fall of Ancona gave the Sardinians their first major port on the Adriatic and drove the Austrian Lloyd to seek an accommodation with the new order on the Italian peninsula. The company had recently lost its lucrative Trieste-Venice passenger trade to a new rail line and could not afford a further drop in business; furthermore, new Lloyd routes in the Western Mediterranean to Marseilles and Barcelona stood exposed and vulnerable to a hostile Italy. In their quest to maintain their position in spite of the recent political changes, the Lloyd's directors first contacted Cavour's special commissioner in the Papal Marches, Lorenzo Valerio, on the matter of the company's future access to Ancona. Valerio confirmed their right to trade in the port but interpreted the conciliatory tone of their letter as an indication of sympathy with the Italian cause. He promptly issued a statement referring to Trieste as part of *Italia irredenta* and called for Italians to gain control over the Lloyd through investment.[8]

The resulting scandal embarrassed the Lloyd and forced its directors to be more discreet in future overtures to the new government. But since Vienna refused to recognize the political changes of 1859–60, further contacts by the company could do little to improve the conditions under which Austrian merchants had to work. The transformation of the Italian peninsula disrupted commercial patterns that dated from the eighteenth century. A major share of Trieste's exports traditionally consisted of the transshipment of goods to northern Italy, and Naples and the Papal State had always been among Austria's leading maritime trading partners. Thus, with Turin in control of the entire Italian Adriatic coast south of the Po and the long-term fate of Venetia (and of Trieste itself) in doubt, the port was not able to recover immediately from the war of 1859. The total annual value of its trade dipped under the 200 million–florin mark and was not to return to prewar levels until after 1866, when conditions again stabilized.[9]

Meanwhile, Austria's hopes for French diplomatic cooperation against Italian unity were dashed during 1860 by Napoleon III's puzzling inconsistency. The French emperor wanted an orderly transition in Italy but recognized that only close Anglo-French cooperation could keep the unification process from running its course. Unfortunately, he was locked into a nasty naval arms race with Britain and further handicapped by British disinterest in an international solution to the Italian question. Lord Palmerston and the Whigs wrapped themselves in the cloak of "non-intervention" and quietly cheered for the incorporation of Rome and the Austrian cession of Venetia from the sidelines.

Yet toward the end of 1860 Palmerston did the Habsburg Empire a great service by making it clear to the radical irredentists that Britain would not recognize the Italian claim to Istria and Dalmatia. The threat of concerted international opposition blocked the Italian bid for the eastern coast of the Adriatic, but it did not deter Garibaldi and his lieutenants from plotting a landing on behalf of the Hungarians. This was not a new idea. Vienna had been receiving reports of plots involving Kossuth, Györgi Klapka, and Stefan Türr ever since June 1859 and, with good reason, took all of them seriously.[10] In December 1860 Klapka actually met with Garibaldi's aide Nino Bixio; the following month they completed plans for a landing in Istria by two divisions of volunteers, one Hungarian and one international, under Garibaldi's command. In late February 1861 Bixio met with Cavour to sound out the official Italian attitude toward the operation, but by then Turin was preoccupied with the impending proclamation of the kingdom of Italy, and Kossuth, whose support Bixio considered essential, was disillusioned by the degree to which constitutional reform had defused tensions within the Habsburg Empire. The scheme was dropped for the present, as were wider negotiations involving Croatian radicals and the princes of Serbia and Montenegro. By the spring of 1861 the invasion scare subsided. The Austrian navy reduced its patrols of the Adriatic but still kept at sea its propeller squadron of one ship of the line, three frigates, and two corvettes.[11]

In January 1861 a French squadron withdrew from the waters off Gaeta where it had blocked Persano's Sardinian warships from shelling the citadel. The following month Francis II of Naples went into exile, ending the last organized Bourbon resistance. On 17 March 1861 Victor Emmanuel was declared king of Italy, a title which the conservative powers of Europe, thanks to Rechberg's diplomatic efforts, refused to recognize.[12] Two weeks later the Italian navy was officially founded, and Cavour made a dramatic appeal to the Chamber of Deputies in Turin for an extraordinary grant of twenty million lire (around eight million florins) for naval construction and the establishment of an Adriatic base at Ancona.[13] Austria, a mere spectator to these events, continued to withhold acknowledgment of the unification of Italy but could not long ignore the threat it posed to her only window to the sea.

Expansion and Ironclads: The Great Naval Debate (1860–1862)

The defeat of 1859 discredited Austria's absolute system of government and gave rise to widespread sentiment for political reform. Ferdinand Max was among the advocates of constructive change, but the introduction of constitutional rule and the attitudes of Francis Joseph's new ministers were to be the greatest impediments to his bid to meet the Italian challenge. In July 1859, only days after Villafranca, the emperor withdrew to his estate south of Vienna and issued the so-called "Laxenburg Manifesto," promising political reform. At first the only change was the dismissal of most of the men associated with the absolutism of the 1850s, but in March 1860 Francis Joseph took a small step toward representative government by expanding the imperial council (*Reichsrat*) to include over three dozen envoys from the provincial assemblies.

For Ferdinand Max the months following the war were a time of frustration and disappointment. In the fall of 1859 the emperor first ignored his arguments for a larger navy, then acquiesced in the cancellation of construction orders for the second ship of the line, originally promised in 1858.[14] The archduke was also forced to accept the promotion of Wüllerstorf. Though a logical consequence of his own fanfare over the return of the *Novara*, it nevertheless made a man he personally disliked the second most powerful figure in the service. At the same time Ferdinand Max was deeply dismayed by the political disarray in Vienna and by Francis Joseph's attempts to answer the need for change with piecemeal concessions rather than true reforms. Over the winter of 1859–60 he sought refuge at sea and captained the paddle steamer *Kaiserin Elisabeth* on a cruise to Brazil. But in the spring of 1860, within weeks of returning home, the archduke was forced to endure yet another discouraging development—the dismissal and death of finance minister Carl von Bruck.

The loss of Bruck, easily the greatest blow to the navy during the first phase of reform, came at the climax of a long scandal. In October 1859 the former Lloyd director had admitted responsibility for a series of irregularities in earlier state loans. Over the months that followed the indictment of several of his former Trieste business associates on charges of war profiteering caused him further embarrassment. Then in the spring of 1860 he suffered a great personal defeat when a new state loan failed despite the support of the Rothschilds. Realizing that Bruck had outlived his usefulness as finance minister, Francis Joseph in late April replaced him with his long-time liberal adversary, Ignaz von Plener.[15]

Bruck committed suicide the day after his dismissal, and within weeks the new finance minister was wielding an equally lethal knife at the navy's budget. In Plener, Ferdinand Max faced the most tenacious opponent to naval expenditure since Stadion forty years earlier. His first correspondence with the archduke in early June 1860 served notice that the sympathetic policies of Bruck were a thing of the past. Plener noted that the fleet was still legally bound by the spending limits of the Navy Law of 1850 but had consumed three times its authorized allotment in the fiscal year of 1859 and was on course to spend a similar sum in 1860. Citing the "interests of financial order," he proposed to give the navy only five million florins in 1861, a reduction of almost 50 percent. To meet the new figure he called for furloughs for personnel of all ranks, the disarmament of all but a bare minimum of warships, tight control over cruises outside of the Adriatic, and a ban on operations outside of the Mediterranean that were not justified by "special interests of state."[16]

When presented with the budget proposal, Ferdinand Max offered no private response but instead published his views in a pamphlet. The tract criticized Plener's figure of five million florins, and while not proposing an alternative, it called for a "defensive navy, which in peacetime serves the defense of trade in the farthest seas." Using arguments similar to those Germany's Admiral Alfred von Tirpitz would employ decades later, the archduke contended that "a well-ordered propeller squadron" only "a few hours from Corfu and the Italian coast" would also make Austria a more attractive ally to Britain or France. He closed with an appeal to the *Reichsrat* for a "statesmanlike, patriotic judgement" on the naval budget.[17]

Following the collapse of Naples in September, the archduke had a publicist write a second pamphlet exploiting the issue of a united Italian fleet and the Adriatic invasion scare. In response to the navy's critics, it concluded that the war of 1859 had demonstrated the need for an even stronger fleet. The Adriatic coast, the natural "Achilles' heel" of Austria's defenses, was in all the more danger now that the Italians had "the fourth navy in Europe" behind only Britain, France, and Russia. To meet this challenge, and the threat from the likes of Garibaldi, Klapka, and Türr, the Habsburg fleet would need "money, money, and more money," some sixty million florins over the next several years. If Austria proved incapable of building the ships necessary for her own defense, she should turn to the resources of Britain and the United States. The pamphlet likened the Italian threat to that of the Prussians a century earlier but observed that "the clever spirit of Cavour" made Italy a greater menace to contemporary Austria than Frederick the Great had been in Maria Theresa's time.[18]

Over the fall and winter of 1860–61 the continuing constitutional crisis overshadowed the campaign for a larger navy. Once the expanded *Reichsrat* convened in May 1860, it became clear that its powers were too limited to satisfy the proponents of reform. The body failed to hold a plenary session during the summer, and on 20 October Francis Joseph decreed the creation of a federal empire along conservative lines, restoring the pre-1848 constitutions of Hungary and other crown lands. But since the October Diploma only provided for a weak *Reichsrat* grafted onto the restored prerevolutionary provincial institutions, it satisfied no one. In December the emperor started to build a new liberal ministry around Frankfurt Parliament veteran Anton von Schmerling, and on 26 February 1861 he issued a new decree establishing a bicameral parliament with a lower house elected by the provincial assemblies.

Until the February Patent created a functioning assembly, Ferdinand Max and the navy were free from parliamentary restrictions; however, the archduke still had to deal with Plener. He finally responded to the finance minister's proposal for a budget of five million florins for 1861 with one of his own for 14.8 million; the bluff succeeded and the navy got half of his request, or 7.4 million. During the winter of 1860–61 work finally resumed on the fleet program. In late October Francis Joseph approved the construction of nine screw-powered gunboats, and at the end of the year Ferdinand Max made the most controversial move of his career to date, personally ordering two armored screw-frigates to be built in Trieste.[19]

The pair of ironclads were a direct response to the two armored corvettes that Cavour had ordered in Toulon. Even though the armoring of warships was a new and controversial technological development, the onset of construction on the Italian warships (in June and December of 1860) compelled the archduke to move without further delay. The ironclad revolution had begun when Britain and France both built armored floating batteries for use in the Crimean War. Only the French batteries saw action, however, and France subsequently led the way in developing seagoing armored warships. In March 1858 the French government authorized construction of the frigate *Gloire,* a wooden ship covered with iron plates. The British responded in April 1859 by ordering the *Warrior,* an armored frigate with an iron hull rather than a wooden one. As early as December 1858 a British shipbuilder offered to construct ironclads for the Austrian navy, but Rear Admiral Fautz, Ferdinand Max's aide in Milan, observed that such ships "would absorb uncommonly large sums" of money. He noted that Austria could not even afford to import plates from Britain to armor domestically built vessels and lacked the fully developed iron industry necessary to build her own armored warships.[20] The archduke also considered it unrealistic for Austria to think of having such ships and held firm even after the launching of the *Gloire* in November 1859 demonstrated the feasibility of seagoing ironclads. He finally acted only after Cavour forced his hand.[21]

The difficulties Ferdinand Max faced at the end of 1860 were the same ones Fautz had noted two years earlier: armored ships were expensive, and Austria lacked both money and the industrial means to construct them. To complicate matters further, Austria had lost her French director of shipbuilding, Sandfort, as a result of the recent war and had no seasoned naval architects to fill the void. But with the florin trading at its lowest rate ever, the archduke could not think of turning to a foreign shipyard as Cavour had done. Instead, he was forced to see just how far the empire's capabilities would take him. The government still owned the Navale Adriatico shipyards in Trieste, and the littoral had two machine shops that had recently developed the ability to build large engines for propeller ships: Wilhelm Strudthoff's Stabilimento Tecnico Triestino, and Englishman Robert Whitehead's Stabilimento Tecnico Fiume in Rijeka. The provinces of Inner Austria also had mines and ironworks adjacent to the Südbahn, the railway to Trieste. And to design the ships the navy had its own Danish-trained engineers, led by the bright but inexperienced Joseph Romako. It was a tremendous gamble, but Ferdinand Max believed that he could build ironclad warships entirely from domestic resources.[22]

In mid-December 1860 the archduke ordered two large engines from Stabilimento Tecnico Triestino and had the wooden hulls of the two frigates laid down at Navale Adriatico. Two months later, after Francis Joseph formally authorized the work, he sold the shipyard back to Giuseppe Tonello, thereby increasing the stake of the private sector in his ironclad program.[23] The armor was ordered from the Henkel von Donnersmark works in Zeltweg, Styria, but it became clear almost immediately that the firm could not produce the iron plates fast enough to meet the needs of the project. Ferdinand Max turned to the foundries of the Loire Valley in France for additional plates, a tricky business since Napoleon III had banned armor exports in the interest of his own ironclad program. The French armor was contracted and paid for by Austrian agents based in Geneva, then exported from Marseilles aboard foreign merchant ships whose captains were not told of their destination until the eve of their departure. The secrecy of the operation drew the attention of French officials, who detained the first shipment at Marseilles because they thought it consisted of arms for the Garibaldini. Naval officials had to inform Rechberg that the French, "erroneously thinking to favor" Austria, were in fact blocking the delivery of materials vital to her defense. An overture through a third party, "without naming the Austrian government," finally secured the release of the cargo, and there were no problems with subsequent deliveries.[24]

The imported plates only drove the cost of the ships higher, however, a distressing development since they were already the most expensive vessels Austria had ever built. By the time they were completed and launched in 1862—as the *Salamander* and *Drache*—the first two Habsburg ironclads had cost 2.3 million florins apiece, six times the amount spent on the *Donau* and *Adria,* domestically built unarmored screw-frigates of comparable size. Ferdinand Max realized that for ironclad construction to continue, future navy budgets would have to be much greater. Since the newly elected *Reichsrat* was to determine the allotment for 1862, he made an early start in the campaign for an increase in funding. In April 1861, before the parliament convened, the archduke withdrew to his new palace at Miramar, near Trieste, and composed his first appeal for an armored battle fleet.

Delivered in the form of a *Vortrag* to the emperor, the proposal argued that the introduction of ironclad warships had created a "tabula rasa" in the international naval balance that Austria could use to her advantage. The construction of seven more ironclads by the fall of 1863 would make the Habsburg navy roughly one-third the strength of the French, a fact that would surely make Austria an appealing ally for Britain and thus help her to break out of her current diplomatic isolation. The archduke did not offer an estimate of the cost of the program but noted that Italy was authorizing enormous sums of money for her navy and that Austria could not afford to fall behind.[25] While he did not dismiss the possibility of constructing new unarmored warships, he effectively abandoned plans to build the half-dozen wooden ships of the line that had been the core of the fleet plans of 1850 and 1858.

The *Reichsrat* assembled in late April, substantially smaller than planned because of boycotts by Hungarian, Croatian, and Venetian deputies. Barely 200 of the 343 seats were filled, and the littoral's only voice came from the heavily Italian delegations of Trieste, Dalmatia, and Istria.[26] Since Ferdinand Max, as a Habsburg prince, could not represent the navy before parliament, he appointed Wüllerstorf to take his place. The hero of the *Novara* mission was a good "political" admiral with connections in German Austrian liberal circles, but he could work no miracles. The representatives conceded only six million florins for 1862, a figure Plener had proposed.

The archduke's first encounter with the Austrian parliament ended in failure, but by the end of the summer of 1861 the growing threat from the Italian navy gave his campaign new life. Late in 1860 New York shipbuilder William Webb visited Turin and secured a deal from Cavour for two large armored frigates to be laid down by the end of 1861. The agreement was kept from the Italian parliament and was still unofficial when Cavour died in June 1861. Sardinian general Luigi Menabrea subsequently assumed the naval portfolio and in early August signed the contracts with Webb.[27] A month later Ferdinand Max took the news to the council of ministers in Vienna and requested an additional 9.1 million florins for naval construction in 1862.

The latest Italian transaction left her navy with four ironclads and an unarmored propeller fleet of one ship of the line, nine frigates, and four corvettes, counting vessels still under construction or conversion from sailing ships. Austria, by comparison, had only the two armored frigates under construction, with a wooden propeller squadron of one ship of the line, three frigates, and two corvettes. The archduke proposed to use the 9.1 million for the construction of three new ironclads and the conversion to screw of the sailing frigates *Schwarzenberg* and *Novara*. The slight advantage in armored warships (five to four) was to compensate for the Habsburg navy's continuing inferiority in unarmored propeller ships and make it strong enough to take on the Italian fleet by the middle of 1862. Plener naturally rejected the appeal, as did minister of state Schmerling and foreign minister Rechberg, but in early October the emperor authorized the work anyway.[28]

Francis Joseph's use of the imperial prerogative infuriated the opponents of naval spending, but it came as a great relief to Ferdinand Max, who hastened to place orders for the new warships. Like the *Drache* and *Salamander* they were laid down at Tonello's Navale Adriatico with engines constructed by Stabilimento Tecnico Triestino.[29] To supplement the capacity of the Zeltweg works and improve the chances of future navy bills, the archduke ordered some of the armor from the rolling mill of *Reichsrat* member Johann von Putzer near Celje in southern Styria. The French foundries were contracted to supply the ram bows for the ships as well as plates to cover the more vulnerable areas of the hull. The Loire valley armor still had to be exported covertly, but the onset of the American Civil War brought such a boom in undercover arms dealing that the Austrians operating out of Geneva were in less danger of detection than before: they merely pretended to be

American agents.³⁰ The conversion of the two sailing frigates was a far simpler operation. The *Novara* had a Stabilimento Tecnico Triestino engine installed in Strudthoff's own shipyard, and the *Schwarzenberg* received one of Whitehead's Fiume engines in the naval arsenal at Pola.³¹

Though the extraparliamentary authorization got the work underway, it caused a tremendous backlash against the navy and Ferdinand Max himself. As head of both the fleet and the naval administration, the archduke was an anomaly in the new constitutional empire since even the army was once again under a responsible war minister. After the end of 1860 there were increasing calls for him to give way to someone able and willing to operate within the new system of government.³² For his part, Ferdinand Max realized that his inability to go before the *Reichsrat* handicapped the navy at budget time, and as early as May 1861 he raised the question of his own replacement. Wüllerstorf's subsequent failure to get more money for the fleet only confirmed the need for the navy to have a political head free to appear in the parliament. Yet at the same time, the archduke feared for the survival of the gains he had made and did not want to step aside unless a navy ministry was established to preserve them. In January 1862 Francis Joseph agreed and created a new ministry responsible for the fleet and the merchant marine over the opposition of both army and political leaders. The minister for trade, Count Matthias von Wickenburg, was given the post pending the appointment of a permanent navy minister. Ferdinand Max remained *Marine-Ober-Kommandant*, officially in control only of naval operations.³³

There remained the problem of reconciling the additional naval construction with the opposition of ministers Plener, Rechberg, and Schmerling, not to mention the matter of the *Reichsrat*'s right to pass judgment on the imperial budget. To clear the air, war minister Count Degenfeld proposed a special commission to review the purpose of the navy and determine its future course. In February the emperor appointed Rechberg to head the committee, which included

Wickenburg, Degenfeld, and Plener from among the ministers. Rear Admiral Alphons Wissiak (Wüllerstorf's successor as envoy to the *Reichsrat*) and old Vice Admiral Dahlerup, recently called back from Denmark, were the navy's spokesmen while five generals, including Schmerling's brother, represented the army. Of the eleven, only Dahlerup and Degenfeld were veterans of the previous naval commission of 1850. Francis Joseph asked the body to determine if the navy were essential to Austria's status as a great power, if it were necessary for it to dominate the Adriatic and be the equal of Italy's, and if it would be more practical to adopt a system of coastal defense in place of a seagoing navy.[34]

The weeks that followed found the supporters of an ironclad battle fleet locked in a heated debate with the proponents of a coastal defense navy. The latter were mostly German liberals from the interior provinces of Austria or traditionalists who refused to accept the fact that the Habsburg Empire had substantial interests at sea. Karl Möring, for two decades a self-styled naval expert, emerged as the elder statesman of the anti-ironclad movement. Long enamored of coastal fortifications and a gunboat defense, Möring authored a pamphlet in early 1862 expounding these ideas and criticizing the premises of Ferdinand Max's arguments for an armored or seagoing battle fleet. He contended that an offensive navy would be of no strategic value against the Italians; if Austria went to war with them alone, she would win the conflict on land, and if Italy had a naval ally, the result in the Adriatic would be no different from that of 1859. He pointed to the futility of France's many naval challenges to Britain and argued that a state should pursue an active policy at sea only if it had the resources to confront and defeat its potential enemies. Möring concluded that Austria could never build a navy with such capabilities and therefore should concentrate only on defending her coastline. For this purpose armored warships were completely unnecessary. As an old army engineer fascinated with heavy artillery, he questioned the efficacy of armor and argued that if a large navy had to be built, the four unarmored screw-frigates that could be constructed for the price of one armored one could easily subdue the ironclad in battle.[35]

But the general argument that it would be futile for Austria to become a legitimate sea power was no longer so convincing. In earlier years, opponents of the navy could point to the huge gap between the British, French, and Russian navies on one hand and the Austrian on the other, and argue quite persuasively that it would be impossible for Austria to attain a comparable level of naval strength. Now the question was one of catching up with the new Italian fleet, a force larger than the Austrian but certainly not out of reach. Furthermore, no one denied that the Italian navy endangered Austrian security; disagreement centered around the question of how best to deal with the threat. Dismissing the extreme anti-navy view, the issues confronting the commission were the size of the navy and the feasibility of armored ships.

When the commission finally met on 15 March, Degenfeld opened the proceedings by declaring flatly that Austria must have a battle fleet at least as strong as Italy's. Wickenburg added that the need for a navy to protect commerce had long been established and could not be open for further discussion. As for the basic purpose of the Habsburg fleet, Dahlerup observed that the difference between an "offensive" and "defensive" navy could not be clearly defined. In response, Rechberg attacked the strategic reasoning for naval expansion by reciting Möring's scenario of a war against Italy. He also argued that a battle fleet could not be counted upon to enhance Austria's stature as a potential ally because it would take several years to build and the "constellation" of powers could change in the meantime. The foreign minister concluded that "Austria is a land power, whose fate in case of war will be determined on land."[36]

The following day Rechberg opened the commission's second session by observing how far the navy had overstepped the spending limits of the Navy Law of 1850. Wickenburg countered with the observation that the law had been amended in 1858, and Wissiak cited the unforeseen costs caused by the tremendous technological changes of the past dozen years. The navy minister repeated Degenfeld's earlier call for parity at sea with Italy and characterized naval expenditure as a good investment in the future. In his rebuttal Plener painted a bleak picture of an Austria too weak to confront Italy both on land and at sea, but no one seconded his opinion. At the end of the session Rechberg took a preliminary poll, and by a vote of six to five the commission favored a fleet equal in size to the Italian. The majority was based around Dahlerup, Wissiak, and Wickenburg; Degenfeld concurred and carried two of the five generals with him. As a formality, the foreign minister also asked for a poll on a simple coastal defense navy; it lost by a margin of seven to four since Plener, who had already voted against the first measure, voted against the second on the grounds that even coastal defense was too expensive. Sensing a deadlock, Rechberg closed the session by ordering a one-month recess for further consultations with technical experts.[37]

In appointing the commission, Francis Joseph had hoped for the sort of unanimity that had led its predecessor to produce the Navy Law of 1850. But after the first two sessions it became clear that the group had polarized into two factions and any definitive verdict on the future of the fleet would come by a bare majority. After the adjournment one of Ferdinand Max's aides in Vienna, Captain Wilhelm von Breisach, attempted to break the stalemate via a letter to Möring, only to have the overture taken as a personal attack. Breisach then predicted to his chief that things could only get nastier when the commission resumed its meetings; "the old friends of Möring" in any event would prevent the body from giving the navy a strong vote of confidence. The archduke concluded that no good could come from the commission and appealed directly to Rechberg for an indefinite postponement of its proceedings. The foreign minister granted his wish and in a brief third session on 12 April adjourned the group until recent dramatic developments in armor and naval tactics could be thoroughly analyzed.[38]

In requesting the postponement, Ferdinand Max had given Rechberg the sensational news of the American Civil War battle of Hampton Roads. On 8 March 1862 the Confederate ironclad *Virginia* attacked the wooden vessels of the Union blockade fleet and easily destroyed two of them, then on the following day fought the Union turret ship *Monitor* in the first action ever between armored warships.[39] After examining accounts of the battle, naval experts everywhere agreed that the era of the wooden battleship had definitely ended. Rechberg did not bother to reconvene the commission and instead called upon the *Reichsrat* to ratify the recent naval expenditure.

By imperial fiat the navy had spent 7.2 million florins on the three new ironclads and the conversion of the two wooden frigates, bringing the total outlay for 1862 to 13.2 million. The representatives refused to approve the larger sum without a debate, but since few educated observers still believed that ironclads were unnecessary, the speeches made against the bill came mostly from deputies of the interior provinces who showed their ignorance in ridiculing the need for an Austrian navy. One *Reichsrat* member pointed out the irony that many of the same German liberals who had supported the creation of the German navy while serving in the Frankfurt Parliament years earlier were now among the most vocal critics of the Habsburg fleet. Rechberg, no doubt embarrassed by the unsophisticated lampooning of the issue, ended the debate with the observation that the navy was indeed necessary to Austria's security. On 23 June the *Reichsrat* ratified the budget but instructed the navy to cut administrative costs, arm as few ships as possible in peacetime, use more domestic coal, and send ships out of the Mediterranean only when absolutely necessary.[40]

The navy was granted only 8.9 million of the 10.9 million florins it requested for 1863, but Wickenburg subsequently went back to the *Reichsrat* for a supplementary grant of four million florins to be added to the outlay for 1862. In November the measure finally gained approval, bringing the navy's total budget for 1862 to a staggering 17.2 million florins, more than it was to receive in any year before 1900.[41] Ferdinand Max thus won the great debate over ironclads and naval expansion. As in earlier years, he owed his success to the intervention of his brother, whose decree in the fall of 1861 had sustained the program until the timely arrival of the news from Hampton Roads. Unfortunately for Austria, the same news had an equally profound effect in Italy, where the leaders of the navy were locked in a struggle to preserve their own ironclad program following the death of Cavour.

The Italian Ironclad Program (1861–1864)

Throughout the unification of Italy and into the spring of 1861, Cavour put the full weight of his personality behind naval expansion and the acquisition of ironclad warships. His death came as a serious blow to the Italian navy at a time when it was having enough problems assimilating the maritime personnel and materiel it had inherited from the various states. His successor Menabrea concluded the contracts to build Italy's third and fourth ironclads in New York, but at heart he did not believe in an armored navy and in subsequent months took steps to alter the course Cavour had staked out. Nino Bixio, a respectable member of the chamber of deputies when not plotting revolution, became Menabrea's greatest ally in the fight against an ironclad fleet. Like his mentor Garibaldi, Bixio as a young man had served in the Sardinian navy and was widely respected in parliament as an expert on naval matters. Against them stood Vice Admiral Persano, a veteran officer from the Sardinian fleet who had salvaged a checkered career in the recent campaigns against Ancona and Gaeta, emerging as the most prominent Italian commander.[42]

In the fall of 1861 Menabrea assembled a special navy commission that quickly determined that Italy needed a fleet equal to the combined strengths of the Austrian and Spanish navies. Vienna and Madrid at no time contemplated joint operations against the new kingdom, but the Italian naval leadership took note of the fact that Bourbon Spain had been second only to Austria in denouncing the unification of the peninsula and had joined her in refusing to recognize Victor Emmanuel's title as king of Italy. To the admirals meeting in Turin, the threat of an Austro-Spanish naval alliance seemed very real indeed.[43]

Since Menabrea stacked the commission with older admirals, it came as no surprise when they concluded that the future battle fleet should be based around unarmored screwships of the line rather than armored frigates. The navy minister was only too happy to promulgate their findings, which he used to justify the construction of four ships of the line as the core of a new fleet plan for the years 1862–65. The rest of his program, however, represented a comical attempt to satisfy all parties in the chamber: it included two ironclads from British shipyards for the proponents of armor, a dozen screw-gunboats for advocates of coastal defense, and a number of transports to appease the hotheads who called for immediate invasions of Venetia, Istria, and Dalmatia. The plan satisfied no one and was under fire from all sides when the head of the cabinet, minister-president Bettino Ricasoli, fell from power in February 1862. Urbano Rattazzi was chosen to head a new government in which Persano received the naval portfolio.[44]

Pro-ironclad forces rejoiced at the fall of Menabrea and encouraged Persano to dismantle the current naval program in favor of one with more armored ships. The new government was presented to the Senate and Chamber of Deputies on 7 March, the day before the Battle of Hampton Roads. In the weeks that followed, the admiral used the news of the *Monitor* and *Virginia* as justification for the deletion of the four ships of the line from the fleet plan. In their place he proposed to order four ironclads from France, and to appease advocates of domestic construction, three more were to be laid down in Italian yards. In early June, Persano formally presented the revised program to the chamber; including the two ships Menabrea had proposed to build in Britain, the program would give Italy nine new armored ships over the next four years. For his supporters the simple figures on ironclads currently under construction (five Austrian and two Spanish, to only four for Italy) spoke for themselves, and the goal of thirteen by the end of 1865 was not unreasonable. Opponents of the revisions had yet to formulate their rebuttal when a week after the presentation the cabinet let Persano sign contracts for the four armored frigates from France.[45]

Over the protests of Menabrea and other politicians of the opposition, the navy minister continued to implement his ironclad program in the months that followed. After spreading his business around in France (two of the ships were laid down in Toulon, one in Bordeaux, and one in Nantes), in October 1862 he turned to Britain, where he chose to have one very expensive twin-turreted ram (along the lines of the American *Monitor,* only much larger) laid down instead of the two armored frigates proposed by his predecessor. Before the end of the year he ordered his domestic ironclads—two in Genoa, one in Naples—and supplemented the program even more by authorizing the conversion to armored frigates of two screw-frigates currently on the stocks in Livorno and Genoa. Thanks to the efforts of Persano, by the spring of 1863 Italy could boast of fourteen ironclads although only Cavour's original pair were ready for sea.[46]

By that time the admiral was out of office, toppled with the rest of the Rattazzi cabinet in the wake of Garibaldi's attempt to take Rome. After a brief interlude Marco Minghetti formed a stable government in which General Efusio Cugia served as navy minister. Cugia took office at the peak of pro-navy sentiment with the public applauding an appeal by a new commission of admirals for a huge fleet of forty armored warships. His job was made easier by Bixio's conversion to the ironclad cause; in the months and years to come, the veteran revolutionary was to be among the strongest supporters of an armored fleet. During his tenure Minghetti sought to inflate the Venetian question in order to divert attention from the stalemate over Rome, and as part of his program Cugia ordered transports and the type of shallow-draft gunboats and batteries essential for a naval assault on Venice. The new ships included two more ironclads, which brought the Italian total to sixteen.[47]

The flurry of activity in the Italian camp stood in sharp contrast to the ordeal Ferdinand Max had to endure to gain armored ships for the Habsburg navy. But Italy was no more able to pay her bills than Austria, and the tremendous cost of the naval buildup—forced even higher by the dependence on foreign shipyards—soon took its toll. In each of the years from 1861 to 1865 the Italian navy was budgeted more money than the Austrian, and each year it exceeded its allotment by millions of lire.[48] After Minghetti's agreement with France on the Roman question (the September Convention of 1864) brought his fall from power, a new government under General Alfonso La Marmora finally addressed the problem and undertook to limit naval expenditure.

Citing Spain's recent decision to recognize the kingdom of Italy, the proponents of economy argued that the navy was already large enough to handle the Austrian fleet alone. Over the vehement protests of Bixio and other supporters of the fleet, La Marmora and his navy minister, General Diego Angioletti, turned their focus away from new warship construction and succeeded in reducing the navy's budget. Certain that Italy would be strong enough to crush any Habsburg challenge at sea, they concentrated on the development of land installations and the completion of ships already laid down.[49] Despite the smug confidence of the new ministry, it remained to be seen whether Italy's investment in an ironclad battle fleet would pay off in the Adriatic.

The Era of Ferdinand Max: The Final Act (1862–1864)

The huge naval budget of 1862 represented the high-water mark of Ferdinand Max's tenure as *Marine-Ober-Kommandant*. It ensured that Austria would have an ironclad core for her fleet, but the bitter debate and the smaller appropriation for 1863 made the archduke aware of the limits of his power and forced him to scale down his plans for the future. The budget for 1863 included money for two more armored frigates but not for a third that he had wanted. When a project to convert the ship of the line *Kaiser* into an ironclad received no funding, he had to accept the fact that he would get only seven of the nine armored warships he had called for in April 1861.[50]

To repair the navy's relations with Vienna, Ferdinand Max cut expenses in every area but construction. He curtailed patrols of the Adriatic, and aside from a small squadron under Tegetthoff sent to monitor the Greek crisis of 1862–63, few Habsburg warships ventured far from home waters. At the same time the archduke actively sought to broaden the base of domestic support for the fleet. In the summer of 1863, when Croatian officials complained that Rijeka was not getting its share of naval contracts, he won them over by having Whitehead's firm build the engines for one of the new armored frigates.[51] Even though the ironclad program did not always rely entirely on domestic resources, it spurred the development of key industries and gave more of them a stake in the navy's future.

The home construction of all of Austria's ironclads helped keep her shipbuilding expenses below those of Italy, but the modest capacity of the Trieste shipyards and the financial constraints imposed by Vienna made it impossible for the fleet to keep pace with the Italian buildup. Ferdinand Max had to turn down foreign offers to supplement the Austrian program, including one from American John Ericsson for one or more "Monitors" and another from the Arman firm of Bordeaux (which was already building two ironclads for Italy) for an armored frigate.[52] To reduce the Italian advantage the archduke resorted to a personal diplomatic offensive to try to sabotage their foreign ironclad projects. His main targets were the two armored frigates Cavour had ordered in the United States. Corresponding directly with Carl Loosey, the Austrian consul in New York, he tried to get the Union to exercise its rights as a belligerent and expropriate the vessels for its own war effort. The bid failed, however, and in 1864 the *Re d'Italia* and *Re di Portogallo* were delivered to the Italian navy.⁵³

In his initial proposal for an armored fleet, Ferdinand Max indicated that he did not wish to put all of the navy's eggs in the ironclad basket; there was still a place for unarmored screw-powered vessels, and even the old paddle steamers and sailing ships could be used for auxiliary functions. But a desire to raise additional income for the construction of more ironclads drove him to consider the sale of the bulk of the unarmored ships of the fleet when the opportunity arose. In November 1862 Vienna gave a cordial welcome to Englishman Louis Merton, an arms dealer for the Confederacy in search of steamships for use against the Union blockade of the southern United States. The following February Ferdinand Max responded to the overture by sending the new navy minister, Friedrich von Burger, a long list of vessels he considered to be for sale.⁵⁴

The ships included the propeller frigate *Radetzky* and the corvettes *Dandolo* and *Friedrich,* nine screw-powered gunboats and schooners, nine paddle steamers, and five Danube river gunboats. He proposed to sell the lot for just over six million florins, a sum that he calculated would cover one new armored frigate of the largest type. Aside from the paddle steamers, all of the vessels were less than ten years old; the *Dandolo* had entered service as recently as 1859. In further discussions the archduke's assistant, Rear Admiral Wissiak, raised the possibility of including the *Radetzky*'s two Austrian-built sister ships on the list as well. Against the argument that the sale would weaken auxiliary support for the ironclad fleet, Wissiak noted that in case of war the navy could always rent Lloyd steamers to fill the void in unarmored ships.⁵⁵

Merton subsequently became distracted by a proposal to build Confederate ironclads in Trieste. The plan infuriated Ferdinand Max, who criticized its sponsor, the Putzer ironworks of Styria, for putting "personal motives" in the way of a transaction that was potentially of great importance to the navy. But Merton's mandate to buy only shallow-draft ships capable of negotiating the shoals and sandbars of Southern harbors while running the Union blockade was probably the primary reason behind his loss of interest in the navy's offer. After the archduke refused to support the plan to build armored ships for him in Trieste, Merton tried to enlist the Turkish government to act as a surrogate buyer for Putzer's iron plates, which would then be shipped via Constantinople to a country willing to build the ironclads. In early 1864 the navy ministry in Vienna ordered an end to all negotiations with him.[56]

Over the winter of 1863–64 the deteriorating fortunes of the Southern states gave Austria the opportunity to buy three ironclads that had been under construction for the Confederacy in British yards. Ferdinand Max was enthusiastic about the offer and dispatched chief engineer Romako to inspect the ships, but the deal collapsed when the price proved too high for the navy budget to handle.[57] The appropriation for 1864, passed by the *Reichsrat* in December 1863, was increased to 12.1 million florins but included no money for new ironclads or for the acceleration of work on the two currently under construction in Trieste. Still, it guaranteed that the ships would be completed by 1865. In light of Austria's financial straits, it was the best the archduke could have hoped for.[58]

The introduction of parliamentary institutions made Ferdinand Max's work far more difficult, but his problems paled in comparison to those of the emperor. One of the most vexing consequences of the move toward a constitutional Habsburg Empire (and one largely ignored by historians) was that it left Francis Joseph with far fewer options for the employment of the archdukes, including his brother. In the early 1860s a number of imperial relatives had to be removed from positions of responsibility, among them the emperor's cousins Albrecht (demoted from military governor of Hungary to a corps command) and William (from *Armee-Ober-Kommandant* to the meaningless post of general inspector of artillery).[59] As for Ferdinand Max, he himself noted that since the navy had to have its funding approved by a parliament, it would be impossible for him to stay on indefinitely as *Marine-Ober-Kommandant*. After the creation of the navy ministry he found it hard to command a fleet that was no longer his personal fief, and while he got along well enough with Wickenburg and Burger, he certainly cast a long shadow over their office. At the same time his expensive ironclad program had made him the central figure in one of the first great domestic controversies debated by the new parliament and underscored the fact that his assignment to the naval command—made in the first place to get him out of Vienna and out of the internal politics of the empire—was no longer serving its primary purpose.

The empire's financial problems only added to Ferdinand Max's dilemma since the fiscal retrenchment made a further expansion of the fleet out of the question. In view of the political realities and his past relationship with Francis Joseph, it was equally impossible for him to receive a new position of importance elsewhere within the empire. For the archduke, now thirty-two, the only alternatives lay abroad. Since October 1861 negotiations had been underway to place him on the throne of a Mexican empire. During the Greek crisis of 1862 he fancied himself as the successor to the Bavarian-born King Otto, but Francis Joseph rejected the idea and the archduke himself lost interest after Tegetthoff sent him detailed reports of Greece's domestic problems.[60] In October 1863 a delegation from Mexico formally offered him their crown, and in January 1864 he resigned his post as *Marine-Ober-Kommandant* in order to accept it. The emperor-elect then went to Paris for talks with Napoleon III, whose armed intervention in Mexico had created the opportunity in the first place. On 10 April their agreements were confirmed in the Convention of Miramar, which formally gave him the Mexican throne and defined France's obligation to support his regime in future years. Four days later he left for the New World aboard the well-travelled frigate *Novara*.[61]

History remembers Archduke Ferdinand Max as the ill-fated Emperor Maximilian of Mexico, a quixotic figure lured to America by his own foolishness and vanity. Studies of his life invariably concentrate on the Mexican adventure and fail to mention that he ever commanded the Austrian navy. The literature, much of it heavily romanticized, depicts him as a weak and feeble-minded man, a characterization irreconcilable with that of the strong-willed, tenacious *Marine-Ober-Kommandant*.[62] In light of what we know about his decade as naval commander, Ferdinand Max appears not as a pathetic figure but rather as a talented man with a dynamic personality, desperate for a challenging occupation and, by the end of 1863, without options at home. The throne of Mexico, a position entailing great responsibilities, was the only alternative commensurate with the dignity of a Habsburg prince. As for his work with the fleet, the founding of the navy ministry appeared to ensure its future independence from the army, and the guaranteed completion of the armored ships already under construction promised to bring the ironclad program to fruition. Thus when the Mexican offer materialized, the archduke finally felt free to step down as *Marine-Ober-Kommandant,* assured that the gains of his years at the helm would not be lost.

In his last days at Miramar the archduke wrote a personal farewell to old Vice Admiral Dahlerup in which he observed with pride that the Habsburg fleet had become the envy of all other naval powers of the second rank.[63] His feelings were justified since the navy owed its present position almost exclusively to his efforts. When he assumed command of the fleet it was little more than a motley collection of old sailing ships—some of Napoleonic vintage—and small paddle steamers. Ten years later it had a core of seven ironclads and eight large screw-powered wooden ships and for the first time ever was in a position to offer a credible defense of the empire's overseas interests. By the time the *Novara* set sail for

Veracruz, the navy had weathered another stormy period of its history and was well on the way to becoming a modern force befitting a great power. Skeptics, however, could still point to the fact that the fleet had yet to vindicate itself in action or erase the embarrassing memories of 1859 and earlier wars. Moreover, by 1864 it became clear that when the showdown over the Adriatic finally did come, the Austrian navy would be vastly outnumbered by its Italian rival. But within weeks of Ferdinand Max's departure the Habsburg fleet was given the opportunity to improve its record, not against Italy but in the distant waters of the North Sea, where it went into battle against the Danish navy.

NOTES

1. See Franco Valsecchi, "La paix de Zurich (1859)," *Revue d'histoire moderne et contemporaine* 7 (1960): 110–20; Wilhelm Deutsch, *Habsburgs Rückzug aus Italien: Die Verhandlungen von Villafranca und Zürich 1859* (Vienna: Adolf Luser Verlag, 1940), pp. 53–62. Sardinia acceded to the treaty as a third party.

2. Gabriele, *La politica navale italiana*, pp. 12–15, 89.

3. AOK to Degenfeld, Vienna, 14 March 1860, KA, CK, Präs. 1860/1334, fol. 1–35; Handel-Mazzetti, *1850–1866 MS*, 2:33–40.

4. See Wallisch, *Sein Schiff Hiess Novara*, p. 68; Handel-Mazzetti, *1850–1866 MS*, 2:41–43.

5. Angelo Tamborra, "Balcani, Italia ed Europa nel problema della Venezia (1859–1861)," *Rassegna Storica del Risorgimento* 44 (1957): 813–14.

6. Francis Joseph (decree), Vienna, 16 September 1860, KA, Militär-Kanzlei Seiner Majestät, 1860/3696, fol. 1.

7. Handel-Mazzetti, *1850–1866 MS*, 2:45–47; Baratelli, *La marina militare italiana*, pp. 48–50.

8. Giuseppe Stefani, *Il problema dell'Adriatico nelle guerre del Risorgimento* (Udine: Del Bianco, 1965), pp. 20–22; Tamborra, "Balcani, Italia ed Europa," p. 815; *75 Jahre österreichischer Lloyd*, pp. 54–55.

9. Lo Giudice, *Canale di Suez*, p. 138.

10. Tamborra, "Balcani, Italia ed Europa," p. 815; Rechberg to Metternich, Vienna, 7 June 1859, HHSA, PA, XL. Interna, Carton 98 (Metternich mission to Verona, 1859); Rechberg to FMLt. Lazarus Mamula (military governor of Dalmatia), Vienna, 30 September 1860, ibid., Carton 105: Korr, mit der Statthalterei in Zara 1860, fol. 161; Mamula to Rechberg, Zara, 6 November 1860, ibid., fol. 182.

11. See Stefani, *Il problema dell'Adriatico*, pp. 18–19; Angelo Tamborra, *Cavour e i Balcani* (Turin: I.L.T.E., 1958), pp. 154–92 passim.

12. Baratelli, *La marina militare italiana*, p. 53; Friedrich Engel-Janosi, "Österreich und der Untergang des Königreichs Neapel," *Historische Zeitschrift* 194 (1962): 82–83; Richard Blaas, "L'Austria e la proclamazione del Regno d'Italia," *Archivio Storico Italiano* 119 (1961): 331–61.

13. Gabriele, *La politica navale italiana*, pp. 117–18, 123–24; Italy, Ministero della Marina, *Ordinamento della Marina Militare dello Stato per Regio Decreto 1 Aprile 1861* (Turin: Ministero della Marina, 1861).

14. Already named the *Österreich*, it was to have been a 101-gun screw-powered ship of the line. As late as November 1859 Ferdinand Max sought to save the project by having the vessel laid down in the United States where it would cost less to build. See Handel-Mazzetti, *1850-1866 MS*, 1:422.

15. See Charmatz, *Freiherr von Bruck*, pp. 128–42.

16. Plener to Ferdinand Max, Vienna, 2 June 1860, HHSA, Archiv Max von Mexiko, Carton 113, I: fol. 163–73. According to Brandt, *Neoabsolutismus*, 2:921, Plener favored the temporary removal of Austria from the ranks of the great powers while she restored her finances and recovered from the war of 1859.

17. Ferdinand Max, *Erlauternde Bemerkungen zum Budget der kais. Kriegs-Marine* (Trieste: Buchdruckerei des Oesterreichischen Lloyd, 1860), dated 15 June 1860.

18. [Johann Perthaler], *Die österreichische Marine. Von einem österreichischen Seemanne* (Vienna: Typographisch-Literarisch-Artistische Anstalt, 1860). The anonymous original edition was widely attributed to Ferdinand Max himself, and continues to be to this day. See Friedrich Jahn, "Bibliographie der k.k./k.u.k. Marine," *Schriften des Heeresgeschichtlichen Museums (Militärwissenschaftliches Institut) in Wien*, vol. 8: *Österreich zur See* (Vienna: Österreichischer Bundesverlag, 1980): 144–45.

19. Cf. Philipp von Ziemssen (chief of administrative section, MOKdo.), sketch of budget for 1861, HHSA, Archiv Max von Mexiko, Carton 113, I: fol. 24–26, and "Staats-Voranschlag des österreichischen Kaiserstaates für das Verwaltungs-Jahr 1862. Erforderniss B. II. Marine-Ober-Commando," ibid., fol. 179–97.

20. Gabriele, *La politica navale italiana*, p. 89; Fautz to Ministerium des Äussern, Milan, 11 February 1859, HHSA, StK., Notenwechsel HKR, Carton 294, fol. 406–7. On the ordering and launching of the *Gloire* and the *Warrior*, see Baxter, *The Ironclad Warship*, pp. 99, 109, 131, 159. Since the armored warships referred to here and below all were equipped with screw propellers, they will be referred to simply as "armored frigates," "armored corvettes," etc., rather that "armored screw-frigates," etc.

21. As recently as his *Erlauternde Bemerkungen* of June 1860, Ferdinand Max called for another screw-powered ship of the line and more screw-frigates, not the construction of ironclads.

22. In 1847 Strudthoff and his brother Eduard founded the Fabbrica Macchine di Sant'Andrea, which in 1857 became the Stabilimento Tecnico Triestino (STT); the company opened its own shipyard in Trieste in 1860. See Gerolami, *Trieste e il Mare*, p. 56, and Stefani and Astori, *Il Lloyd Triestino*, p. 217. After importing British engines for the *Kaiser*, the screw-frigates, and the screw-corvettes, the Austrian navy had the engines for its screw-powered schooners and gunboats built by STT, the Stabilimento Tecnico Fiume (STF), and the Sigl firm of Vienna. Dependence on domestic firms became essential with the dramatic fall in value of the Austrian florin; by December 1860 it had slipped to an all-time low on international money markets and stood at almost 15:1 against the British pound, down a third from the normal exchange rate of 10:1. See tables in *The Economist* (London), 26 December 1860.

23. Edmund Bauer (STT) to MOK, Trieste, 17 January 1861, KA, MA, T/c 5 (1861), no. 5, fol. 1–2; Bourguignon to k.k. Bau-Commission, Trieste, 14 February 1861, KA, MA, A/c 14 (1861), no. 19 a–f, fol. 1–15. The government put Navale Adriatico up for sale in July 1858 after the completion of the screw-frigates *Donau* and *Adria*. Tonello bought the yard on 15 February 1861, ten days after Francis Joseph authorized the two armored frigates and guaranteed him the contracts.

24. MOK to Joseph Engerth (*Maschinen-Meister*), Trieste, 12 April 1861, KA, MA, T/c 6 (1861), no. 22 a–e, fol. 1–55 relates the problems with the Zeltweg works, noting that the same firm was used earlier, in 1860, to provide armor for the *Feuerspeier,* a floating battery in the lagoon at Venice. The French armor came from the foundries of Russery, Lacombe et Compagnie and Marrel Frères, both of Rive-de-Gier on the Loire. MOK to Marine Kanzlei, Trieste, 13 April 1861, KA, MA, M/c 15 (1861), no. 10 a–k recounts the detention of the *Grossfürstin Katharina,* a merchant brig from Mecklenburg contracted to carry the shipment of plates from Marseilles. Austria later used British merchantmen for the secret deliveries, and eventually Lloyd steamers.

25. Ferdinand Max. "Vortrag über das Extraordinarium für S.M. Kriegsmarine," Miramar, April 1861, HHSA, Archiv Max von Mexiko, Carton 113, I: fol. 109–15.

26. After the provincial election of 1860–61, Italians held twenty-five of twenty-seven seats in the Istrian assembly and twenty-nine of forty-two in the Dalmatian, despite the fact that a great majority of the population of both provinces were South Slavs. Istria initially joined in the boycott of the *Reichsrat,* then sent representatives in the fall of 1861. See Mijo Mirković, "O smislu u sadržaju narodnog preporoda u Istri," in Jakša Ravlić, ed., *Hrvatski narodni preporod u Dalmaciji i Istri* (Zagreb: Matica Hrvatska, 1969): 284; Božo Milanović, "Biskup Dobrila i njegovo doba (1861–1882)," in ibid., 363, 373–74; Giovanni Paladin, "La questione dalmatica vista da Niccolò Tommaseo e da Antonio Baiamonti," *Rassegna Storica del Risorgimento* 38 (1951): 540–41.

27. Robin Higham, "William H. Webb: Foreign Warship Construction and the Civil War," *Journal of the American Society of Naval Engineers* (February 1961): 181; Gabriele, *La politica navale italiana,* p. 129. Capt. Stephan Herzfeld, "Ausweis über die in Bau befindlichen und projektirten italienischen Kriegsschiffe," Trieste, 12 March 1861, HHSA, Archiv Max von Mexiko, Carton 113, I: fol. 79 indicates that Austria knew Italy would lay down another pair of ironclads in 1861 but assumed that, like the first two, they would be built in Toulon.

28. Schmidt-Brentano, "Österreichs Weg zur Seemacht," pp. 135–36. Commissions-Protocol, Trieste, 2 September 1861, KA, MA, T/c 6 (1861), no. 85, fol. 1–3 reveals that Ferdinand Max initially was thinking in terms of five new armored frigates rather than three.

29. Tonello contract, Trieste, October 1861, KA, MA, T/c 6

(1862), no. 40 t–3, fol. 178–207; STT contract, Trieste, 6 October 1861, KA, MA, T/c 5 (1862), no. 20 a–s, fol. 19–46.

30. Plener balked at Putzer's demand for an advance grant of 100,000 florins, but it was paid anyway. Plener to Ferdinand Max, Vienna, 8 November 1861, KA, MA, T/c 6 (1862), no. 68 a–t, fol. 281–84; Rear Adm. Alphons Wissiak to Station Kdo., Trieste, 9 February 1862, ibid., fol. 24–25; Eduard von Rüti (*k.k. Maschine-Inspector*), Promemoria, Geneva, 22 December 1861, KA, MA, T/c 6 (1862), no. 89 a–t, fol. 121–2; Rüti to MOK, Trieste, 11 February 1862, ibid., fol. 114–15.

31. STF contract, Rijeka, 9 October 1861, KA, MA, T/c 5 (1862), no. 10–u, fol. 78–101. STT contract referred to in KA, MA, T/c (1862), no. 15 a–v passim.

32. Archduke William, head of the *Armee-Ober-Kommando* in the 1850s, wanted to stay on as war minister but was passed over in favor of FZM. Count Degenfeld. FMLt. Ludwig Benedek, the only Austrian field general to emerge from the war of 1859 with his reputation intact, was among those calling for Max to step aside. See Gunther E. Rothenberg, *The Army of Francis Joseph* (West Lafayette, Ind.: Purdue University Press, 1976), p. 59; Benedek to Degenfeld, Verona, 29 December 1860, KA, CK, Präs. 1861/868, fol. 1–8.

33. Wagner, "Die obersten Behörden," pp. 29, 32. The navy ministry was discussed in the council of ministers on 4 January; Francis Joseph conveyed his decision to the same body ten days later. See *Die Protokolle des österreichischen Ministerrates 1848–1867,* part 5: *Die Ministerien Erzherzog Rainer und Mensdorff,* vol. 3 (Vienna: Österreichischer Bundesverlag, 1985), no. 177 (4 January 1862) and no. 183 (14 January 1862).

34. Netrval, "Degenfeld," pp. 169–71.

35. Karl Möring, *Zur Marine-Frage* (Vienna: Carl Gerold's Sohn, 1862). The navy's Captain Tegetthoff issued a rebuttal to Möring's remarks in an article in the Austrian military journal; the general responded to his arguments in a later issue. Wilhelm von Tegetthoff, "Zur Würdigung des Aufsatzes 'Zur Marine-Frage'," *Österreichische Militärische Zeitschrift* 3 (1862), vol. 1: 418–26, 104–12, 179–92; Karl Möring, "Besprechung des Aufsatzes: 'Zur Polemik über die Marine-Frage'," ibid., pp. 409–17.

36. Commission protocol (first session), Vienna, 15 March 1862, KA, CK, Präs. 1862/562, fol. 10–17. Degenfeld had been in charge of the land defense of the littoral during the war of 1859 and

had come to the conclusion that a seaborne deterrent was the best defense against amphibious invasions. Degenfeld to AOK, Trieste, 19 June 1859, KA, Kriegsministerium, Präs. 1859/2631, fol. 2–9.

37. Commission protocol (second session), Vienna, 16 March 1862, KA, CK, Präs. 1862/562, fol. 18–27.

38. Breisach to Ferdinand Max, Vienna, 7 April 1862, HHSA, Archiv Max von Mexiko, Carton 113, I: fol. 193–208; Commission protocol (third session), Vienna, 12 April 1862, KA, CK, Präs. 1862/562. fol. 28–29.

39. See Baxter, *The Ironclad Warship*, pp. 291–301.

40. 132d, 133d, and 134th Sessions of Reichsrat, Vienna, 18, 20, 23 June 1862, Austria, Reichsrat, *Stenographische Protokolle des Abgeordnetenhauses des Reichsrathes*, 22 vols. (Vienna: k.k. Hof- und Staatsdruckerei, 1862–1918), 1:3104–27, 3130–61, and 3169. The remark about the German liberals was delivered by one Dr. von Muhlfeld of Niederösterreich in the session of 20 June (see ibid., 1:3131–32).

41. Stepanek, "Marine-Amtsgeschichte," p. 162; 183d Session of Reichsrat, Vienna, 10 November 1862, *Stenographische Protokolle*, 1:4456–60.

42. Gabriele, *La politica navale italiana*, pp. 127–30. The darkest episode of Persano's career came in 1853 when he wrecked one of the Sardinian navy's newest steamers while taking the royal family on an excursion. His subsequent attempt to portray himself as their rescuer failed to conceal the fact that he had been responsible for the accident, and he did not hold another command until 1859. For the best biographical sketch of Persano see Angelo Iachino, *La campagna navale di Lissa 1866* (Milan: Casa editrice Il Saggiatore, 1966), pp. 44–62.

43. Gabriele, *La politica navale italiana*, pp. 134–39.

44. Ibid., pp. 139–40.

45. Ibid., pp. 154–63; Baxter, *The Ironclad Warship*, p. 199.

46. Franco Bargoni, *Le prime navi di linea della marina italiana (1861–1880)* (Rome: Edizioni Bizzarri, 1976), passim; Gabriele, *La politica navale italiana*, p. 161.

47. Gabriele, *La politica navale italiana*, pp. 165–66, 193–236.

48. There is considerable uncertainty over the amount of money spent by the Italian navy between 1861 and 1865; Gabriele alone gives four different sets of figures (*La politica navale italiana*, pp. 268–69) and admits his own confusion. Converted into florins (at the nominal exchange rate of 2.5 lire = 1 florin) the sums of money actually authorized by the Italian parliament compare with the Austrian outlays as follows (rounded off, in millions):

	Italy	Austria
1861	11	7.4
1862	19	17.2
1863	12	8.9
1864	12.5	12.1
1865	9	7.1
	63.5	52.7

The Italian navy appears to have exceeded its budget by some thirty million florins during this period, raising its figure to ninety-three or ninety-four million. The Austrian navy was never permitted to overspend by more than a few hundred thousand florins in any given year.

49. Gabriele, *La politica navale italiana*, pp. 241–58.

50. Schmidt-Brentano, "Österreichs Weg zur Seemacht," p. 143. Ferdinand Max, "Vorlage des Marine-Ober-Commandanten für den hohen Reichsrath," Miramar, 3 December 1861, HHSA, Archiv Max von Mexiko, Carton 113, I: fol. 125–36 includes the initial proposal for armoring the *Kaiser*.

51. Baron Josip Šokčevič (Ban of Croatia) to Burger, Zagreb, 3 June 1863, KA, MA, T/c 5 (1863), no. 12 a–w, fol. 17–18; Ivan Mažuranić (Croatian Court Chancellor) to Burger, Vienna, 9 June 1863, ibid., fol. 21–22; Burger to Mažuranić, Vienna, 25 June 1863, ibid., fol. 19; Mažuranić to Burger, Vienna, 27 June 1863, ibid., fol. 23. Peter Handel-Mazzetti and Hans Hugo Sokol, *Wilhelm von Tegetthoff: Ein Grosser Österreicher* (Linz: Oberösterreichischer Landesverlag, 1952), pp. 153–62 gives a detailed account of Tegetthoff's mission in Greek waters.

52. Loosey to MOK, New York, 15 May 1862, KA, MA, T/c (1862), no. 45, fol. 2–7; Jean-Lucien Arman to Ferdinand Max, ibid., no. 83–a, fol. 2–5.

53. Stepanek, "Marine-Amtsgeschichte," p. 162; Higham, "Foreign Warship Construction," pp. 185–86.

54. Merton to Marineministerium, Vienna, 25 November 1862, KA, MA, T/c 3 (1863), no. 4–a, fol. 2–3; Wickenburg to Ferdinand

Max, Vienna, 26 November 1862, ibid., no. 4–b, fol. 4–5; Ferdinand Max to Burger, Miramar, 22 February 1863, ibid., no. 4 g–h, fol. 15–20. See also Lawrence Sondhaus, "Die österreichische Kriegsmarine und der amerikanische Sezessionskrieg 1861–1865," *MGH* 14 (1987): 81–84.

55. Wissiak, "Commissions-Protocoll," Vienna, 25 March 1863, KA, MA, T/c 3 (1863), no. 4–q, fol. 33–36.

56. Johann von Putzer to Burger, Vienna, 26 January 1863, KA, MA, T/c 3 (1863), no. 4–e, fol. 12–13; Ferdinand Max to Burger, Miramar, ibid., no. 4–g, fol. 15; Capt. Baron Eduard Hohenbruck to MOK, Constantinople, 11 December 1863, KA, MA, M/c 22 (1863), no. 141; Stepanek, "Marine-Amtsgeschichte," pp. 173–74. Hohenbruck to Ferdinand Max, Vienna, 26 November 1862, KA, MA, T/c 3 (1863), no. 4–c, fol. 6–8 gives first mention of the shallow draft problem which came up repeatedly in subsequent correspondence.

57. Burger to Ferdinand Max, Vienna, 9 November 1863, KA, MA, T/c 3 (1863), no. 14, fol. 1; Ferdinand Max to Burger, Lacroma (telegram, n.d.), ibid., fol. 5; Romako to Ferdinand Max, London, 24 December 1863, HHSA, Adm. Reg., F 44—Marinewesen, Carton 3: Generalia 1860–70, Lieferungen; and Burger to Romako, Vienna, 28 December 1863, ibid., all refer to two Confederate turret ships seized from Laird of Liverpool by the government. Metternich to Burger, Paris, 14 December 1863, KA, MA, T/c 3 (1863), no. 18 a–d, fol. 4–5; Ferdinand Max to Burger, Miramar, 29 December 1863, ibid., fol. 6–7; and Burger to Romako, Vienna, 31 December 1863, ibid., fol. 8–9 discuss an armored frigate, presumably Confederate, under construction in Britain but owned by a French banking house.

58. Fifty-third Session of Reichsrat, Vienna, 2 December 1863, *Stenographische Protokolle*, 2:1153–86; Schmidt-Brentano, "Österreichs Weg zur Seemacht," pp. 148–49. The sum of 12.1 million covered the period from November 1863 through December 1864, the result of a reform making the fiscal year conform to the calendar year.

59. Under the new system only cousins safely distant from the throne were assigned roles of even symbolic importance, such as Archduke Rainer (son of the late viceroy of Lombardy-Venetia) to the post of titular minister-president of Austria during the liberal Schmerling ministry (1861–65).

60. Wilhelm von Tegetthoff, *Aus Wilhelm von Tegetthoff's Nach-*

lass, ed. Adolf Beer (Vienna: Druck und Verlag von Carl Gerold's Sohn, 1882), pp. 222–334 includes most of Tegetthoff's correspondence from Greek waters.

61. Arnold Blumberg, *The Diplomacy of the Mexican Empire, 1863–1867* (reprint edition, Malabar, Fla.: Robert E. Krieger Publishing Co., 1987), pp. 8–22 recounts in detail the months of machinations leading up to the Convention of Miramar. In addition to taking the famous round-the-world cruise in 1857–59, the *Novara* had also had the honor of carrying Ferdinand Max on his first sea voyage in the summer of 1851.

62. Egon Caesar Corti, *Maximilian and Charlotte of Mexico,* 2 vols., trans. Catherine Allison Phillips (New York: Alfred A. Knopf, 1928) remains the classic work on the archduke and Mexico. In lieu of a proper scholarly biography, it is also the best work on his life in general. Corti was the first historian to gain access to the Archiv Kaiser Maximilians von Mexiko in Vienna, but he gives no evidence of having examined its naval material and consequently mentions Ferdinand Max's naval service only in passing. Blumberg's *Diplomacy of the Mexican Empire,* otherwise an excellent work, gives a similar treatment to the matter and relies on Corti for information about the archduke's personality.

63. Handel-Mazzetti, *1850–1866 MS,* 2:230. HHSA, Archiv Max von Mexiko, Carton 113 contains a number of touching personal farewell letters from Ferdinand Max to various higher-ranking officers.

CHAPTER

9

The Adriatic Secured

It would have been difficult to find a man able or willing to replace Ferdinand Max as *Marine-Ober-Kommandant,* and for the moment no attempt was made to do so. After his formal resignation from the navy in January 1864, the post of commander was simply left vacant. The void was soon filled, at least in part, by the rise of Baron Wilhelm von Tegetthoff to the unofficial position of first seaman of the empire. By leading the navy to victory in battle, Tegetthoff was to bring Habsburg sea power the international respect that the archduke, despite his efforts, was never able to win. Though the war of 1866 was a disaster on other fronts, Austria's success at sea blunted Italian ambitions in the Adriatic and established an undisputed Habsburg hegemony over the region, providing the basis for the empire's entry into the ranks of the world's major maritime trading powers.

Baptism of Fire: The Danish War (1864)

The Schleswig-Holstein question had been left unresolved after the German-Danish war of 1848–49 when a simple restoration of the *status quo ante* had been used to end hostilities. In 1863 Denmark reopened the controversy by once again attempting an outright annexation of Schleswig. A wave of national indignation quickly swept through Germany, and Rechberg, fearful that Prussia's Count Otto von Bismarck would exploit the situation to Austria's disadvantage, agreed to a joint Austro-Prussian military intervention against the Danes. In February 1864 Austrian troops joined Prussian units in an invasion of the disputed duchies and soon forced the outnumbered Danish army to retreat. Denmark responded as it had in 1848, with a naval blockade of the north German ports.

The Prussian fleet, built largely around ships and personnel inherited from the German navy of 1848–52, had no ironclads or large unarmored ships and was too weak to take on the Danes alone. Talk of a German federal navy, or at least a coast guard, had surfaced once again in 1861 under Prussian sponsorship; Rechberg, however, had refused to support the idea, arguing that the states of northern Germany, like Austria herself, should be responsible for their own coastal defense.[1] But by blocking the formation of a north German naval force, the foreign minister only increased Vienna's moral obligation in the matter. When war came, Austria, as the leading naval power of Germany, had to shoulder the burden of the war at sea.

Unfortunately, the recent general inactivity of the Habsburg fleet had left it in no shape to go to war. Over the past two years Ferdinand Max had sacrificed all other aspects of preparedness to free more funds for ship construction. The extensive training cruises of the 1850s had been abandoned, and the navy no longer kept as many ships ready for sea. As a consequence, the overall level of seamanship declined and the process of mobilizing for war became more complicated. The naval academy had been closed prior to the war of 1859 when the older students were pressed into service; after the return of peace, classes were held aboard the old frigate *Venus*, anchored as a school-ship in Trieste harbor, and the standards of naval education deteriorated. But perhaps the most serious problem of all in the postwar navy was its declining morale, a direct result of the frustrating experience of 1859. Some of the younger officers were so discouraged by the fleet's relative inactivity in the war that they transferred to the Habsburg army. In the postwar years Ferdinand Max occasionally scolded his officers for their "malaise" of spirit and petty bickering, but to no avail.²

Without the archduke's unifying influence the problems of morale and leadership only worsened. At the beginning of 1864 the navy had no unquestioned leader, and to make matters worse the remaining admirals had little experience in battle. Old Vice Admiral Dahlerup, forced by the Danish war to postpone his second retirement, had not been to sea in years, and none of the three rear admirals, Fautz, Wissiak and Wüllerstorf, had ever held a significant wartime command. The former two had been "armchair" admirals for quite a while, occupied with administrative posts in Trieste or Vienna. Wüllerstorf at least had the *Novara* cruise to his credit, and the acclaim resulting from it obscured the fact that by training he was more of a mathematician and scientist than a fighting seaman. In February 1864, after the Austrian and Prussian armies invaded Denmark, he was put in charge of the fleet bound for the North Sea.

As Wüllerstorf set about the task of preparing his warships for the campaign, Captain Tegetthoff was sent ahead with the screw-frigates *Schwarzenberg* and *Radetzky* and the gunboat *Seehund,* all of which had been at sea as the Austrian contingent in Greek waters. In late 1863, after the abdication of King Otto ended the crisis over Greece, they were assigned general cruising duties in the Levant, only to receive their new orders just weeks later. Tegetthoff was supposed to rendezvous with Wüllerstorf en route to the North Sea, but when the preparations at Pola took longer than expected, he was instructed to proceed alone and try to break the blockade of Hamburg.³

The decision to send the fleet to war against Denmark was made with little regard for Austria's security in the Adriatic. The Italian navy had maintained a much larger squadron in Greek waters than the Austrian and had kept its ships at sea after that crisis had passed. Yet despite its larger numbers, the Italian fleet had only two ironclads on active duty (to Austria's five) and inspired far less fear in Vienna than the threat that revolutionaries would take advantage of the navy's absence to attempt a landing in Dalmatia.[4] Still more ominous were the rumblings from Britain, where Palmerston's Liberal government was openly pro-Danish despite formally limiting itself to the policy of non-intervention. In February, after it became known that Austria would send ships to the North Sea, foreign secretary Lord John Russell raised the possibility of deploying a British squadron in the Adriatic.[5] Rechberg considered it a bluff, however, and proved to be right. Nevertheless, the British attitude toward the war was to cause the Habsburg navy its share of headaches.

In late April Tegetthoff arrived off the English coast. His ships were permitted to take on coal, but afterward a mysterious "mistake" by an English harbor pilot caused the *Seehund* to run aground. The gunboat incurred so much damage that it had to be left behind, and Tegetthoff proceeded to Cuxhaven with just the two frigates. To his relief the Danes had kept the bulk of their navy (including their lone ironclad) in the Baltic Sea and were blockading Hamburg with a propeller squadron of only two frigates and one corvette. The Prussians, however, also kept most of their modest fleet in the Baltic and could offer the Austrians just three small vessels (one paddle steamer and two screw-gunboats), which joined Tegetthoff's squadron on 4 May. Five days later the flagship *Schwarzenberg* led the allied warships out to break the blockade.[6]

Tegetthoff found the Danish squadron off the island of Helgoland, which commanded the approaches to the Elbe estuary and Hamburg. Because the Prussian gunboats were so small, his overall strength in guns was less than that of the three enemy ships, which also had more modern artillery. The rival squadrons dueled for several hours, both commanders content to exchange shots at a distance. The Austrian frigates suffered significant damage but remained in action, their predominantly Italian crews bolstered by appeals for "coraggio" and answering with enthusiastic shouts of "Evviva Imperatore!" The battle ended in late afternoon before either side lost a ship. Both squadrons withdrew, the allies to Cuxhaven and the Danes to the north, eventually all the way to the Skagerrak. Tegetthoff refused to call the draw a victory, but the Danes did not attempt to reestablish the blockade and for the remainder of the war confined their naval operations to the Baltic.[7]

Meanwhile, in April Wüllerstorf had finally left the Adriatic with the ship of the line *Kaiser*, the screw-corvette *Friedrich*, the paddle steamer *Elisabeth*, and one gunboat. He also took one of the navy's newest ironclads, the *Juan d'Austria*. A second armored frigate, the *Kaiser Max*, followed later, while their sister ship *Prinz Eugen* remained on guard in home waters with the older ironclads *Drache* and *Salamander*.[8] Beset the entire way by bad weather and mechanical problems, Wüllerstorf lamented the poor quality of his crews and complained bitterly of having to conduct a training cruise while en route to the war zone. To make matters worse he was shadowed much of the way by superior British naval forces demonstrating London's disapproval of the operation. The fleet was anchored in the French port of Cherbourg when word arrived of the battle off Helgoland, and by the time it finally reached the North Sea, the enemy had withdrawn and the war was nearing an end. The ships joined Tegetthoff's squadron in operations against the islands along the western coast of Jutland before an armistice in July brought the fighting to a close.[9]

For Wüllerstorf the results of the campaign were less than pleasant. The authorities in Vienna held him responsible for the time lost in arming the fleet at Pola and, discounting the seriousness of the problems he had faced along the way, attributed his late arrival to a reluctance to push his men and ships to the limit. Upon returning home in the fall of 1864, he was stripped of his command and removed from the active list. Though a hard personal blow (he was only forty-eight), the forced retirement of Wüllerstorf was no great loss to the navy. A controversial figure since his days as Wimpffen's adjutant, he always got along better with the army than most other navy leaders and was even friendly with Karl Möring, whom most sea officers detested. He had strong connections with German liberal circles in Austria, but his friendships with a number of implacable political foes of the fleet did not help the navy's cause and only weakened his own position within the service. After his departure the admiral hastened to use these same ties to his own advantage, embarking upon a career in politics.[10]

Tegetthoff, on the other hand, emerged from the war as the navy's new hero. Even though the encounter off Helgoland was neither glorious nor decisive, it was hailed as the baptism of fire of the "new" Austrian navy: German officers had commanded Dalmatian and Venetian seamen in action, and it had worked. On the day after the battle Francis Joseph promoted Tegetthoff to rear admiral despite the fact that he was tenth in seniority among captains. The extraordinary advancement topped a rapid rise through the ranks that had taken him from cadet to admiral in just sixteen years. At thirty-six, he was the youngest man in the history of the service (aside from the archdukes Frederick and Ferdinand Max) ever to reach such heights. But for the moment there was no question of giving him a position of greater authority within the navy. Tegetthoff received command of the active squadron for 1865; the post of *Marine-Ober-Kommandant* remained vacant.[11]

Intermezzo (1864–1866)

Under the terms of the Treaty of Vienna of October 1864, Denmark surrendered the duchies of Schleswig and Holstein to the joint custody of the victorious powers. Rechberg's policy of cooperation with Prussia was considered a failure, and after the peace was signed he was replaced as Habsburg foreign minister by General Count Alexander Mensdorff-Pouilly. But Mensdorff merely broadened his predecessor's course of seeking an accommodation with Berlin, offering Bismarck control over both duchies in return for a Prussian guarantee of Venetia. This initiative, an effort to find a "German" solution for the security needs of the littoral, ended in failure. In August 1865 the Convention of Gastein provided for the Prussians to administer Schleswig and the Austrians Holstein, but the issue of the long-term fate of the duchies soon provided the pretext for the final showdown over the future of Germany.

Austro-Prussian naval cooperation continued even after the political relationship began to deteriorate. The bulk of the Austrian fleet returned to the Adriatic once the Danes were defeated, but the armored frigate *Kaiser Max* remained on guard in the North Sea until the summer of 1865 and the screw-corvette *Friedrich* until the spring of 1866. Austria tried to help the Prussian navy acquire ironclad warships of its own and forwarded a bid by Tonello's Navale Adriatico to construct armored frigates for Prussia at Trieste. General Albrecht von Roon, Prussian war and navy minister, ultimately rejected the proposal because the Austrian shipyard could build only armor-plated wooden ships and not the more desirable all-iron models.[12] While Prussia did not avail herself of Austria's shipbuilding resources, the Habsburg navy hastened to accept an offer from the Prussian firm of Krupp to produce guns for its two newest ironclads. Krupp's modern naval artillery was vastly superior to the guns manufactured by the *k.k. Eisengusswerk* in Mariazell, Styria, which had provided the armament for the navy's first five armored frigates. After the two ships (named *Ferdinand Max* and *Habsburg*) were launched in 1865, they remained unarmed pending the delivery of the Prussian ordnance.[13]

As Austria's political relations with Prussia worsened, the rise to power of La Marmora made Italy easier to deal with. The new minister-president and foreign minister was a conservative at heart and refused to go along with Victor Emmanuel's schemes to ignite the Balkans or destabilize Austria by fomenting revolts in Hungary and Galicia. Following the September Convention with France (the backlash of which had swept the general to power), Italy turned her attention away from Rome and toward Venice. La Marmora, however, disappointed the radical irredentists by making it clear that Venetia alone was on the agenda of his ministry. He rejected as unrealistic any further Italian aggrandizement in the Adriatic and went so far as to concede that on commercial grounds, Austria had a legitimate right to Trieste. In answer to the ensuing criticism he argued that Prussia and the other German states would never agree to an Italian annexation of Trieste anyway. Claims to the city could only hurt the campaign for Venetia, which he hoped to acquire by peaceful diplomacy.[14]

La Marmora stemmed the tide of Italian naval spending, but in 1865 he acquiesced in construction orders for two new armored frigates to be built in Italian shipyards.[15] He made up for the added expenditure by having his navy minister, General Angioletti, reduce the number of ships on active duty. Italy continued to amass a state debt no less staggering than Austria's, but the united kingdom inherited Sardinia-Piedmont's good credit rating and never had any trouble floating loans on the money markets of London and Paris. The Habsburg Empire, with the Venetian question still unresolved and half of the nationalities boycotting its fledgling parliamentary system, was not considered as good a risk. Throughout the early 1860s Plener lamented that even in an emergency Austria would be unable to borrow more than a nominal sum of money abroad.[16]

Notwithstanding Ferdinand Max's confidence that the accomplishments of his tenure would be preserved, moves were afoot shortly after his departure for Mexico to return the navy to its status of earlier years. On 17 April 1864, only three days after the archduke left Miramar, Burger himself proposed the dissolution of the navy ministry. The minister, a former governor of Trieste well acquainted with maritime affairs, questioned the propriety of giving a civilian politician authority over purely military matters, such as granting promotions within the officer corps. The dual nature of the ministry, which also had jurisdiction over the merchant marine, made the post a difficult one to fill: either a civilian such as Burger would have to be in charge of the navy, or a higher naval officer would have control over seaborne commerce. The emperor came to the conclusion that the merchant marine should once again fall under the ministry of trade and the navy under the war ministry. He decreed the dissolution of the navy ministry effective in January 1865.[17]

Burger still submitted the navy's budget for 1865 to the *Reichsrat*, which allocated the service a mere 7.1 million florins and, again, no money for new warships. To stay within the new limits the navy kept even fewer ships at sea in 1865 than it had in the last years of Ferdinand Max's command. The emperor of Mexico was responsible, however, for the extension of naval operations into one new area: the *Novara* remained in Mexican waters for a year after delivering him to his adopted country and in May 1865 was replaced as station-ship off Veracruz by the screw-corvette *Dandolo*. Until his brother's throne appeared more secure, Francis Joseph wanted to keep an Austrian warship at his disposal to facilitate a quick exit.[18]

Burger in fact held office long after the January deadline, and the navy ministry was not formally abolished until July 1865 when the Schmerling ministry gave way to a new one under Count Richard Belcredi. Count Johann von Larisch replaced Plener as finance minister; Mensdorff was the only major figure to survive the turnover. The new leadership was for the most part conservative but did include a minority of liberals, among them Wüllerstorf as minister for trade. The emperor at the same time dissolved the *Reichsrat*, suspended the February Patent, and opened negotiations with the Hungarians, who had never accepted the reforms of 1860–61.[19]

After its loss of independence the navy was administered by a newly-created *Marinesektion* of the war ministry headed by the highest-ranking active officer, Vice Admiral Fautz. Francis Joseph still refused to fill the vacant post of naval commander, instead creating the new office of *Marine Truppen-und Flotteninspektor* for his cousin Archduke Leopold. A son of Archduke Rainer, the late viceroy of Lombardy-Venetia, Leopold in the spring of 1864 had mediated Ferdinand Max's renunciation of his rights to the Habsburg throne and family fortune. This issue, arising at the last minute, almost kept the former *Marine-Ober-Kommandant* from going to Mexico. Leopold had provided a valuable service to the family and the new post most likely was the emperor's way of rewarding him.[20]

There certainly was no other justification for the appointment. A soldier by training, Leopold had no knowledge of naval affairs and little idea of how to do the job, which was never properly defined. He depended heavily upon his subordinates and, by building his own network of favorites, only exacerbated the internal divisions of the officer corps. Tegetthoff was the principal victim of the new arrangement since he did not get along well with either Fautz or Leopold's adjutant and chief protégé, Captain Friedrich von Pöck. Tegetthoff's recent promotion, over the heads of so many officers of greater seniority, only served to arouse the jealousy of his peers. Leopold subsequently tried to reduce the power of the hero of Helgoland with a series of promotions of his own, including that of Pöck to rear admiral, back-dated to restore his seniority over Tegetthoff. The archduke's only positive contribution came in the area of naval education; he recognized the failure of the *Venus* school-ship and ordered the naval academy at Rijeka reopened for the 1866–67 school year. The navy also gained a modest increase in its budget for 1866, to 7.8 million florins, but Larisch was no greater fan of the fleet than Plener had been and for the third year in a row no money was allocated for new warships.[21]

In this generally gloomy atmosphere the only source of excitement for the navy was a proposed expedition to the Far East to begin in the summer of 1866. Fifteen years had passed since American commodore Matthew Perry had opened Japan to foreign trade, and in the recent Second Opium War both Britain and France had gained extensive commercial concessions from China. Ever since work had begun on the Suez Canal in 1859 there had been talk of a trade mission to the Far East to pave the way for future Austrian commerce, but the decision to send a naval squadron was not made until after Wüllerstorf took over as trade minister. It was assumed that Tegetthoff would head the expedition, but the winter of 1865–66 witnessed a fierce competition for other positions in the official entourage. By March of 1866, however, the growing likelihood of war with both Prussia and Italy put the mission in jeopardy. Should Austria have to take on the Italian navy in the Adriatic, she certainly would need every available ship; furthermore, the navy could hardly run the risk of going to war with Tegetthoff and the best captains in the Far East.[22]

After obtaining a pledge of French neutrality in a meeting with Napoleon III in the fall of 1865, Bismarck in March 1866 offered an alliance to Italy. La Marmora still hoped for a peaceful acquisition of Venetia and instructed his negotiators to avoid commitments that would preclude this possibility. To sweeten the bargain Bismarck hinted that Prussia might accept the Italian acquisition of the South Tyrol after the war, but for fear of an adverse reaction in the German states he stopped short of actually promising Italy any of Austria's German federal territory. By the terms of an alliance concluded on 8 April, Italy committed herself to intervene in an Austro-Prussian war provided that the conflict began within the next two months. Prussia did not pledge aid to Italy if Austria should attack her first, however, and the vague definition of the territorial spoils made many Italian leaders uneasy about the whole arrangement. Nevertheless, the experience of 1859–60 had demonstrated that a war against Austria undertaken with the support of a powerful ally could unleash forces that the great powers—even the ally herself—could not control. The precise terms of the alliance mattered little since the Italian cause had nothing to lose. On 30 April the Chamber of Deputies voted unanimously to authorize "measures necessary for the national defense," and the country began preparing for war.[23]

For the Habsburg leadership the impending conflict clearly was over Germany, not Venetia. A two-front war was the last thing Austria needed, and Mensdorff quickly reaffirmed the primacy of the German question among Habsburg strategic concerns by offering to cede Venetia to Italy in return for her neutrality.[24] La Marmora no doubt wanted to accept the proposal but could not since the prospect of acquiring even more land through the Prussian alliance had left few Italians content to take just Venetia. Austria subsequently sought to limit the damage by seeking a pledge of neutrality from France.

As the diplomatic situation worsened, Tegetthoff waited in Vienna for the decision either to arm the fleet for war or to proceed with plans for the Far Eastern expedition. The admiral confided to his good friend Captain Max von Sterneck that he was "on pins and needles" over the uncertainty. On 30 April, the same day that the Italian chamber authorized preparations for war, the order was finally given to put the navy on a war footing. Leopold, preoccupied with his own assignment to an army corps in Bohemia, did not push for Pöck to be given command of the fleet. Even if he had, he most likely would have been overruled since Tegetthoff's battle experience against the Danes made him the logical choice for the task. In early May Archduke Albrecht, supreme commander of Austrian forces in the south, confirmed that Tegetthoff would be in charge. Pöck was placated with the post of navy liason officer in Albrecht's Venetian field headquarters.[25]

Once appointed, Tegetthoff hurried to the littoral to supervise the arming of the fleet. Since Venice no longer serviced any ships other than the small gunboats of its own lagoon flotilla, the entire operation was carried out in the relative security of Pola. The admiral ordered a concentration of ships in the Adriatic and recalled the corvette *Friedrich* from its station in the North Sea. The corvette *Dandolo* in Mexican waters was the only one not summoned home since the worsening conditions in Mexico made it more important than ever for Emperor Maximilian to have a warship at his disposal.[26] Tegetthoff of course had greater worries than the absence of one ship (and an unarmored one at that). He had only seven ironclads while Italy, including those authorized in 1865, had a total of twenty built or under construction. Austria also had far fewer wooden warships than her rival, but the addition of five steamers rented from the Lloyd helped make up the difference. The worst news during the mobilization was the Prussian government's suspension of delivery of the guns the navy had ordered from Krupp, a move that left Tegetthoff with no artillery for his two newest ironclads.[27]

Austria's negotiations with France were no more encouraging. Mensdorff had hoped that Napoleon III would be of some help in the present crisis. The previous fall, when Larisch turned to the Paris money market in search of a loan to cover the Habsburg deficit, the French emperor had intervened on his behalf to get Austrian bonds listed at the Bourse. Vienna attached great political significance to the move, unaware that he had already assured Bismarck of France's neutrality in an Austro-Prussian war. Mensdorff, sold the same bill of goods as Bismarck, on 12 June settled for a cession of Venetia to Italy via France in return for Napoleon III's promise of neutrality in the coming war.[28]

Only days later Prussia commenced hostilities against Austria's German allies. Italy, guaranteed Venetia regardless of the outcome of the war, continued its preparations nonetheless. Since La Marmora feared both a breach with Prussia and a backlash from the enthusiastic war party in Italy, he did not openly associate his government with the Franco-Austrian agreement and maintained the fiction that Venetia was to be liberated by force. His stance also served the purpose of leaving Italy a free hand to take as much territory as it could from the Habsburg Empire. Italian war plans called for a two-pronged offensive, one up the Adige through the Tyrol to take Innsbruck and a second across Venetia and the Julian Alps to take Carinthia, Styria, and, eventually, Vienna. Bismarck urged a strong Italian effort at sea, including a landing by Garibaldi on the Dalmatian coast to coincide with a Hungarian revolution already planned in Prussian talks with Kossuth. Garibaldi himself favored the idea but La Marmora, a consistent opponent of revolutionary plotting and adventurism, rejected it. Prussian chief of staff Helmut von Moltke called for an Italian advance through Venetia to Trieste, arguing that the vital Habsburg seaport could be taken with the help of the fleet, but La Marmora had already written off Trieste and had no desire to arouse the hopes of the radical irredentists. Navy minister Angioletti went so far as to advise against an active war at sea; he was particularly opposed to the Dalmatian landing and refused to participate in any planning for it.[29]

Angioletti no doubt realized that the Italian fleet, despite its numerical superiority vis-à-vis the Austrian, was in a state of disarray and hardly able to make a positive contribution to the war effort. The common sailors were poorly trained and the navy lacked competent gunners, machinists, and petty officers. As for the officer corps, bitter regional differences made it less cohesive than its multinational Habsburg counterpart. The Neapolitans and Sardinians did not get along very well, and the Venetian émigrés, probably the best seamen of the lot, were contemptuous of the other groups and consequently despised by all. To make matters worse, Admiral Persano, the former navy minister, had used his connections to gain the post of commander of the fleet. A much better politician than seaman, he was widely hated by his fellow officers, some of whom even refused to serve under him.[30] But as he gathered his warships at Taranto in the heel of the Italian boot, his problems were not just with personnel. Only twelve of the navy's twenty ironclads had been commissioned for duty, and these included the eleven ordered from foreign shipyards in the years 1860–62. Of the nine armored warships under construction in Italy, only one was completed in time for the war; the unfinished vessels included one laid down in 1861 and three begun in 1863. Austria, on the other hand, was to have the services of both of the ironclads that she had started in the latter year. Still, Italy was guaranteed an advantage of almost two to one (twelve to seven) in armored ships and also had a larger unarmored fleet than her rival. Despite the problems, most observers expected great things from the navy. When Nino Bixio proclaimed it "incontestibly superior" to the Habsburg fleet, his views were echoed by scores of other politicians.[31]

On 17 June La Marmora relinquished the job of minister-president to Bettino Ricasoli in order to become chief of staff to Victor Emmanuel, and Angioletti surrendered the navy portfolio to Agostino Depretis in exchange for command of an army division. The changes took effect on the twentieth, the day Italy declared war on Austria. Because Ricasoli had none of his predecessor's doubts and inhibitions, Italian war aims quickly escalated from Venetia and perhaps the South Tyrol to encompass Istria and Dalmatia, including the main Habsburg ports of Trieste and Rijeka. Depretis, who shared none of Angioletti's concerns about the navy, sought nothing less than hegemony over the Adriatic. The new government clearly viewed the Prussian alliance as a license for Italy to take whatever she could get.

Italy deployed over 200,000 troops in three armies, one in eastern Lombardy under the king and La Marmora, one in the Romagna under General Enrico Cialdini, and a smaller volunteer force in the Alps under Garibaldi. Archduke Albrecht, meanwhile, defended Venetia with a field army of just over 75,000 men. On 20 June the king's army crossed the Mincio and invaded Venetia from the west. Garibaldi advanced against the Tyrol, and Cialdini was supposed to cross the Po and invade Venetia from the south. The Italians expected the archduke to stay on the defensive but instead he advanced toward the Mincio and on the morning of the twenty-fourth stumbled onto Victor Emmanuel and La Marmora on the field of Custoza, the site of Radetzky's great victory of 1848. The ensuing action was more a series of chance skirmishes than a planned battle. Both sides suffered similar casualties but while Albrecht's army remained intact, the Italians fell into a disorganized state of shock. La Marmora ordered a retreat back across the Mincio, and after Garibaldi and Cialdini heard the news, they too assumed defensive positions even though neither faced much opposition.

Because of its fragile psychological condition, the entire Italian army was paralyzed by the single defeat. As far as Venetia was concerned it mattered little since Austria was bound by treaty to cede the province regardless of the outcome of the war. But after the battle the pressure increased for a face-saving victory that would at least preserve the myth that the gains were being won by force of arms. Attention became focused on Persano and the Italian fleet, which arrived at Ancona on the day after Custoza. Ricasoli and Depretis began to press immediately for an active campaign in the Adriatic.[32]

"Hearts of Iron": The Lissa Campaign (1866)

As the war on land began, Tegetthoff completed his preparations at Pola. In lieu of their Krupp guns, the new armored frigates *Habsburg* and *Ferdinand Max* received makeshift batteries of older cannon. The admiral designated the latter as his flagship and chose Sterneck for his flag captain. Knowing that the Italians would have a great advantage in ironclads, he resolved to commit his wooden ships to battle, too, and had them draped in chains and scrap iron for added protection. No one seriously believed that this provisional armor would be effective; nevertheless, by the time Italy invaded Venetia, Tegetthoff exuded confidence and even assured an old Prussian friend that the Austrian fleet was "not as weak as you seem to believe." When questioned about the use of the wooden ships, he countered with expressions of faith in the superiority of his own officers and crews, remarking that "behind wooden walls beat hearts of iron."[33]

In the first days of the war Tegetthoff was instructed to stay close to Pola in order to cover Venice and Trieste in the event of an Italian breakthrough on land. After Custoza, however, Albrecht gave him free rein to engage the Italian fleet, advising him only to keep an eye on the mouths of the Po and the Venetian coast. As soon as the admiral learned of Persano's arrival at Ancona, he steamed across the Adriatic and challenged him to come out. The Italians refused to budge even though Tegetthoff made his demonstration with only six ironclads and an assortment of wooden steamers. The Austrians later learned that their cruise, on 27 June, had been based upon faulty intelligence. In fact, Persano's warships were still taking on coal and provisions after their voyage from Taranto and could not have given battle regardless of the odds.[34]

Tegetthoff's taunting sortie was far from useless because it demoralized the Italian fleet and stirred dissension among the younger officers against Persano's indecisive leadership. The news from Ancona also drove Ricasoli and Depretis to argue all the more vehemently for an active campaign in the Adriatic. Recovering from the shock of Custoza, they began to view the fleet as more than just the means to break even with Austria. Italy still had a clean record at sea, and given the clear numerical superiority over the Habsburg navy, there seemed little reason not to attack the Austrian coastline. After all, Bismarck himself had urged an invasion of Dalmatia and Moltke an assault on Trieste.[35]

La Marmora, still the king's chief of staff, warned as late as 4 July that an offensive in the Adriatic would be a mistake. On the following day, after receiving word of Prussia's decisive victory at Königgrätz (3 July) and a mediation attempt by Napoleon III, he urged Ricasoli to do nothing to compromise the prearranged cession of Venetia to Italy via France. But by then Persano's concern for his own job had driven him to write enthusiastic and bellicose letters to Depretis begging to put to sea. The admiral proposed to blockade Tegetthoff's fleet, then ravage the coasts of Istria and Dalmatia. High on his list of targets were the ships and docks of the Austrian Lloyd, which once again was contributing to a war effort against the Italian cause. On 5 July Depretis responded by ordering Persano to engage or blockade the enemy fleet. Once Tegetthoff was out of the way he was to land troops at Nabresina (Aurisina) on the coast north of Trieste to sever the city's rail and telegraph connections, occupy a number of strategic Dalmatian islands, and secure control over the mouth of the Adriatic.[36]

Persano, however, reverted to his characteristic disdain for action just as the French mediation effort raised fears of an early end to the war and made the need for an Italian victory all the more urgent. A week after Königgrätz, Albrecht was named commander-in-chief of the Habsburg armed forces, and put in charge of defending the line of the Danube against the southward advance of the Prussian armies. He withdrew three-quarters of his army from Venetia for duty in the north, and Cialdini, in command of the main Italian field army, started to occupy the province. Working from the assumption that the Austrian armies were crumbling, Ricasoli on 12 July advocated a series of bold strokes that would enable Italy to dictate the peace from a position of strength. In three letters to war minister Emilio Visconti Venosta he outlined plans for Garibaldi and 40,000 volunteers to invade the Croatian coast, a landing of regular forces to occupy Istria, and the occupation of the Tyrol by regulars in lieu of Garibaldi's men. To Persano he sent a direct appeal for "the destruction of the enemy fleet and the occupation of Istria" before an armistice precluded further territorial gains.[37]

On the following day the king met with his generals and ministers and approved a more conservative plan under which Cialdini would continue his advance across the Isonzo, lay siege to Trieste, and then possibly cross the Julian Alps for a march on Vienna. While he advanced, the navy was to gain mastery over the Adriatic, then blockade Trieste to ensure its fall. In the meantime Persano put to sea, but he steered clear of Pola and returned to Ancona after five days without having engaged the Austrian fleet. This timid sortie hardly satisfied Depretis, who went to Ancona and in person ordered Persano to venture out again without delay. This time he had the specific assignment to "take possession of an important station in the Adriatic," the island of Lissa. The operation would give Italy a base for operations against Dalmatia and complement the landing in Istria, which remained Ricasoli's top priority.[38]

On 16 July the admiral set sail, his American-built flagship *Re d'Italia* leading an armada of thirty-four vessels that included all twelve of the Italian ironclads plus transports with 3000 troops. Two days later Persano arrived off Lissa and began bombarding its fortifications in preparation for a landing. The Austrian forts could not be subdued by gunfire alone, however, and Persano lacked the troops to storm them. In any event, he did not want to start disembarking men for fear that Tegetthoff would appear in the middle of the operation. The shelling continued throughout the nineteenth, but the forts held out.[39]

On the morning of 19 July, Tegetthoff received word that Persano was at Lissa with the entire Italian battle fleet. He left Pola immediately with the twenty-seven warships at his disposal. Approaching Lissa from the northwest at midmorning on the twentieth, he formed his fleet into three V-shaped squadrons: the first consisted of the seven armored frigates, led by his flagship *Ferdinand Max;* the second, of the seven larger wooden screw-powered vessels, led by the ship of the line *Kaiser* under Commodore Anton von Petz; and the third, bringing up the rear, a mixture of thirteen screw-powered gunboats and paddle steamers. Persano formed a line between the approaching Austrians and the island of Lissa with his eleven "foreign" ironclads; the lone Italian-built armored frigate served as flagship for his unarmored vessels, which fell into line far to the rear. At the last minute Persano switched his flag from the *Re d'Italia* to the twin-turreted ram *Affondatore,* the newest and best of the Italian ironclads. His subordinate commanders were unaware of the change and throughout the battle looked in vain to the wrong ship for signals. It mattered little, for as soon as the *Ferdinand Max* broke through the Italian line, followed moments later by the *Kaiser* and the wave of unarmored ships, the battle deteriorated into a chaotic mêlée.[40]

As the two fleets wheeled and exchanged shots at close range, neither side was able to do much damage: the Austrian warships had inferior guns, the Italians incompetent gunners.

Persano's wooden ships continued to observe things from a distance rather than plunge into the fray. In contrast, Tegetthoff's unarmored vessels remained in the thick of the fight, and the *Kaiser*, the largest ship in the battle, became a prize target for the Italian ironclads. She incurred heavy damages, but when Persano's own *Affondatore* attempted to ram her, a timely broadside warded off the attacker and disabled one of its revolving turrets. Since Tegetthoff had planned to use ramming tactics to compensate for his inferior artillery, the general chaos was much to his liking; his flagship *Ferdinand Max* finally caught its prey, the *Re d'Italia*, and rammed a hole in her side just below the waterline. The ship went under in a matter of minutes, a demoralizing sight for the rest of the Italian fleet. In four hours of close combat Persano's vessels were unable to sink a single Austrian warship, not even a wooden one, but by the time the fleets disengaged, a second Italian ironclad, the *Palestro*, was on fire and in serious danger. She finally exploded as Persano signalled a retreat to Ancona. Since his own ships were too slow to give chase, Tegetthoff remained off Lissa temporarily and then returned to Pola.[41]

The Austrian commander, promoted to vice admiral by Francis Joseph on the day after the battle, was well aware of how lucky he had been. "The whole thing was chaos," he wrote his Prussian friend, "a *mêlée* in the fullest sense of the word.... It is a miracle that we did not lose a ship."[42] Italian leaders did not initially appreciate the magnitude of the defeat. Upon reaching Ancona on 21 July Persano even claimed victory, despite the loss of two of his ironclads. He could not maintain his lie for long, however, as word soon arrived that the Habsburg fleet had suffered no losses.[43] On the same day as the Battle of Lissa, an armistice ended fighting between Austria and Prussia, and the Habsburg army completed its withdrawal to the Isonzo, leaving Venetia in Italian hands. France and Prussia then pressured Italy to conclude an armistice of her own with Austria. Ricasoli, however, still refused to be content with just Venetia. On 22 July, even after learning that the Austrian navy had not lost a ship at Lissa, he insisted that Italy would negotiate only if her right to her "natural frontiers" was recognized. His terms included the direct cession of Venetia and the South Tyrol and a guarantee that Italian interests south of the Julian Alps (in Istria) would be respected. He did not mention Dalmatia and also dropped his claim to Trieste but proposed to make the latter a "free city with equal ties to Germany [sic] and Italy."[44]

The minister-president's agenda for peace talks ignored the fact that Austria had won control of the sea and that the Austro-Prussian armistice had strengthened the Habsburg hand. The Italian fleet was in no shape to venture out again, and Tegetthoff remained on patrol to ensure that it did not. Meanwhile, the Südbahn, which had transported tens of thousands of men from Trieste to Vienna less than two weeks before, was used to rush troops back to the Italian front from the Danube. After the preliminary Austro-Prussian peace of Nikolsburg (26 July), Albrecht sent every available unit to the Venetian frontier to back up an Austrian offer for armistice talks. Ricasoli reduced his demands to the cession of Venetia and the South Tyrol, after which Victor Emmanuel, on the twenty-ninth, dropped all territorial conditions other than the direct transfer of Venetia.[45]

The talks were slated to open on 5 August in the village of Cormons just west of the Isonzo. Francis Joseph appointed the navy's old nemesis, Karl Möring, to head the Austrian delegation, and the obstinate German liberal, now a major general, proved to be the perfect man for the job. At the start of the first meeting he informed the Italians that Austria would cede Venetia only under the terms of the Franco-Austrian treaty of 12 June, and that if Italy did not evacuate the non-Venetian Habsburg lands it held (in the Tyrol and around Gorizia), Austria would continue fighting.[46]

The Italians were stunned but quickly realized that they had little choice. By 5 August the troop trains of the Südbahn had raised the strength of the Austrian army on the Isonzo to 140,000 men—almost twice as many as Albrecht had had at Custoza—and Tegetthoff continued his show of force at sea.

At the same time international opinion favored an Italian acceptance of Venetia and an end to the war. On 12 August Italian general Agostino Petitti signed the Armistice of Cormons. The agreement even allowed Austrian troops back into Venetia to occupy key areas pending a formal peace treaty. Another six weeks of acrimonious negotiations finally produced the definitive Treaty of Vienna (3 October 1866), which confirmed Italy's acquisition of Venetia but nothing more.[47]

Tegetthoff conducted a naval review at Trieste on the day after the armistice was signed. Albrecht presided over the occasion and praised the fleet for its role in the war. The admiral accepted the accolades graciously, but at heart he was bitterly disappointed that Francis Joseph had declined to attend the fête himself. For the army, the disaster at Königgrätz more than overshadowed the victory at Custoza; the navy, however, emerged from the war with a spotless record that led Tegetthoff and his captains to expect better treatment in the future. But because the peace settlement excluded the Habsburg Empire from both Germany and Italy, it was not clear just what its strategic priorities were to be in the years to come or what role the navy would have. As Tegetthoff grew increasingly skeptical about the future, he could console himself with the knowledge that his mentor Ferdinand Max, the father of the modern Habsburg battle fleet, had learned of the victory. The beleaguered Mexican emperor sent his congratulations and awarded the admiral the Grand Cross of the Order of Guadalupe.

The Battle of Lissa attracted a great deal of attention from Tegetthoff's contemporaries.[48] As the first action ever fought between fleets of ironclad warships, it has been given its due by naval historians ever since. Yet political and diplomatic works (if they mention it at all) universally dismiss the Austrian victory at sea in 1866 as a meaningless dénouement to a war Austria had already lost. Since Bismarck and Napoleon III ultimately were against Italian aggrandizement other than in

Venetia, it has been assumed that regardless of the outcome of the conflict in the south and at sea Italy would have gained no other territory. This view ignores the precedent of 1860 when the process of Italian unification ran its course largely against the wishes of the great powers, precisely because no one was willing to intervene militarily to undo the fait accompli. There is no more reason to believe that had Italy won the Battle of Lissa and taken Dalmatia or even Istria, any of the powers would have gone to war with her to restore these lands to Habsburg control. Whereas Trieste or the South Tyrol could have been saved by the Austrian army alone, Dalmatia could not have been retaken without outside help once the Italian navy had gained control over the Adriatic.

During June and July of 1866 the expressed war aims of the Ricasoli government included the reduction of Austria to a landlocked country, or at least one with a nominal coastline no greater than her pre-1797 holdings. An Italian victory at sea, needless to say, would have been catastrophic for the Habsburg Empire's overseas interests. But the navy's success in the war of 1866 gave Austria an unprecedented, unquestioned hegemony over the Adriatic. Coming on the heels of the respectable showing against Denmark in 1864, the performance demonstrated to even the most skeptical opponents of the fleet that sea power could be useful to a traditional land power such as the Habsburg monarchy. Though some still questioned the huge sums of money spent on the ironclad battle fleet during the last years of Ferdinand Max's tenure, few would have traded it for a coastal defense flotilla during the war of 1866.

NOTES

1. Degenfeld to Rechberg, Vienna, 26 April 1861, HHSA, PA, II. Deutscher Bund, Carton 89: Deutsche Flotte, 1861/fol. 13–19; Rechberg to Degenfeld, Vienna, 27 February 1862, ibid., XL. Interna, Carton 114: Korr. mit Militärbehörden 1862, Kriegsministerium, fol. 55–62. See also Hans-Joachim Häußler, "Küstenschutz und deutsche Flotte, 1859–1864," *Forschungen zur brandenburgischen und preussischen Geschichte* 51 (1939): 311–43.

2. E.g., Ferdinand Max circular, Miramar, 3 February 1861, KA, MA, M/c 15 (1861), no. 2, fol. 2–3. Ironically, one of these young officers was killed in 1866 at Königgrätz just two weeks before the navy won its victory at Lissa. See Sterneck, *Erinnerungen*, p. 148n. The school-ship *Venus* followed the example of the British navy's school-ship *Britannia,* which opened in 1858.

3. Handel-Mazzetti, *1850–1866 MS,* 2:136, 150–72 passim; D. Paschen, "Der blutige Tag von Helgoland," *Marine Rundschau* 44 (1939): 470–71.

4. Ministerium des Äussern to Marineministerium, Vienna, 1 April 1864, HHSA, Adm. Reg., F 44—Marinewesen, Carton 3: Generalia 1860–70. On the Italian navy during the Greek crisis see Gabriele, *La politica navale italiana,* pp. 315–46.

5. Rechberg to Burger, Vienna, 23 February 1864, HHSA, PA, XL. Interna, Carton 118: Korr. mit dem Marineministerium 1864, fol. 15. Russell ultimately was satisfied by an Austrian pledge to send no warships into the Baltic. See W. E. Mosse, "Queen Victoria and her Ministers in the Schleswig-Holstein Crisis of 1863–1864," *English Historical Review* 78 (1963): 274–77.

6. Paschen, "Der blutige Tag," p. 471; Peter Handel-Mazzetti, "Das Seegefecht bei Helgoland am 9. Mai 1864," *Marine Rundschau* 39 (1934): 195. In 1863 Tegetthoff scoffed at the tiny gunboats Prussia sent to the Levant to show her flag during the Greek crisis, observing that they were "hardly larger than our Lake Garda boats." (Quoted in Handel-Mazzetti, *1850–1866 MS,* 2:133).

7. Handel-Mazzetti, *1850–1866 MS,* 2:173–82; Handel-Mazzetti, "Seegefecht bei Helgoland," pp. 195–97. The Austrians lost 138 men killed and wounded, the Danes roughly half as many, the Prussians none. Tegetthoff may not have claimed victory, but the Danes, despite their withdrawal from the North Sea, did not hesitate to do so. Helgoland was reported as a Danish victory in the British House of Commons, where the news drew cheers. To this day Danish history records the battle as a victory, and the commander's flagship *Jylland* remains docked at Copenhagen as a national historic monument and tourist attraction. See F. H. Kjølsen, "The Old Danish Frigate," *The Mariner's Mirror* 51 (1965): 27–33.

8. The armored frigates *Kaiser Max, Juan d'Austria,* and *Prinz Eugen,* laid down on Francis Joseph's order in October 1861, were completed by the summer of 1863.

9. Wallisch, *Sein Schiff Hiess Novara,* pp. 73–76; Handel-Mazzetti, *1850–1866 MS,* 2:182–200.

10. Wallisch, *Sein Schiff Hiess Novara,* pp. 76–77; Handel-Mazzetti, *1850–1866 MS,* 2:203; Antonio Schmidt-Brentano, *Die Armee in Österreich: Militär, Staat und Gesellschaft 1848–1867* (Boppard am Rhein: Harald Boldt Verlag, 1975), pp. 286, 327.

11. Ulrich Schöndorfer, *Wilhelm von Tegetthoff* (Vienna: Bergland Verlag, 1958), p. 33; Handel-Mazzetti, *1850–1866 MS,* 2:203; Handel-Mazzetti and Sokol, *Tegetthoff,* p. 221.

12. Ministerium des Äussern to Count B. Chotek (chargé, Berlin), Vienna, 20 October 1864, HHSA, Adm. Reg., F 44, Carton 3: Generalia 1860–70; Chotek to Mensdorff, Berlin, 2 November 1864, ibid.; Chotek to Mensdorff, Berlin, 6 January 1865, ibid. Prussia finally bought two small ironclads, one each from Britain and France, in time for the war of 1866.

13. See Josef Fleischer, *Geschichte der k.k. Kriegsmarine,* part 3: *Die k.k. österreichische Kriegsmarine in dem Zeitraume von 1848 bis 1871,* vol. 3: *Geschichte der k.k. Kriegsmarine während des Krieges im Jahre 1866* (Vienna: Verlag des k.u.k. Reichskriegsministeriums, Marinesektion, 1906), p. 27n.

14. Stefani, *Il problema dell'Adriatico,* pp. 35–37; Ivan Scott, "Italian Conspiracy on a Grand Scale: The Abortive Galician Project of 1864," *Eastern European Quarterly* 8 (1974–75): 45–53.

15. Gabriele, *La politica navale italiana,* p. 257.

16. Brandt, *Neoabsolutismus,* 2:976.

17. Wagner, "Die obersten Behörden," pp. 49–51, 54–55.

18. Handel-Mazzetti, *1850–1866 MS,* 2:227. Ferdinand Max took around a dozen naval officers with him in his personal entourage, and the Austrian corps of volunteers later recruited for service in Mexico included 300 seamen. He drafted plans and regulations for an imperial Mexican navy, but amid the tremendous problems he faced he was not able to implement them. Francis Joseph to Ferdinand Max, Vienna, 8 April 1864, KA, MA (1864), 8–3/10; Breisach to Marineministerium, Trieste, 4 November 1864, ibid.; Corti, *Maximilian and Charlotte,* 1:345.

19. Wagner, "Die obersten Behörden," p. 137; Wallisch, *Sein Schiff Hiess Novara,* p. 83.

20. On Leopold's role in the renunciation talks see Blumberg, *Diplomacy of the Mexican Empire*, p. 77, and Corti, *Maximilian and Charlotte*, 1:335–52 passim.

21. Schöndorfer, *Tegetthoff*, p. 35; Salcher, *Marine-Akademie*, p. 21. As finance minister Larisch made a special effort to limit military and naval spending.

22. Wallisch, *Sein Schiff Hiess Novara*, p. 84; Schöndorfer, *Tegetthoff*, pp. 38–39.

23. Stefani, *Il problema dell'Adriatico*, pp. 68–70, 76.

24. Eduardo Scala, *La guerra del 1866 ed altri scritti* (Rome: Tipografia Regionale, 1981), p. 19.

25. Tegetthoff to Sterneck, Vienna, 24 March 1866, Sterneck, *Erinnerungen*, pp. 140–41; Schöndorfer, *Tegetthoff*, p. 41. Mindful of the fact that a prewar panic in 1859 had caused the collapse of Austrian currency and bonds, Belcredi and Mensdorff postponed mobilization as long as possible in 1866. See Angelo Filipuzzi, "La mobilitazione austriaca alla vigilia della campagna del 1866," in *Atti del convegno storico di studi su: "Il Lombardo Veneto dal 1849 al 1866"* (Padua: Società Solferino e San Martino, 1977): 55.

26. Schöndorfer, *Tegetthoff*, pp. 42–49. In addition to keeping the *Dandolo* off Veracruz, Austria also continued to permit the recruitment of volunteers for Mexican service even after the mobilization began. Mensdorff finally suspended the recruiting in May 1866 under heavy pressure from the United States. See Blumberg, *Diplomacy of the Mexican Empire*, pp. 202–5.

27. Handel-Mazzetti and Sokol, *Tegetthoff*, p. 238.

28. See Lawrence D. Steefel, "The Rothschilds and the Austrian Loan of 1865," *Journal of Modern History* 8 (1936): 27–39; Heinrich von Srbik, "Der Geheimvertrag Österreichs und Frankreichs vom 12. Juni 1866," *Historisches Jahrbuch* 57 (1937): 454–507.

29. Stefani, *Il problema dell'Adriatico*, pp. 72, 77–81; Rinaldo Cruccu, "I piani operativi per la liberazione del Veneto," *Atti del convegno storico di studi su Lombardo Veneto*, p. 151. Moltke's idea for an attack on Trieste also went against Bismarck's preference for directing Italian energies away from German federal territory.

30. Iachino, *La campagna navale di Lissa*, pp. 32–42, 132.

31. Bargoni, *Le prime navi di linea*, passim. Bixio quoted in Mack Smith, *Victor Emmanuel, Cavour, and the Risorgimento* (London: Oxford University Press, 1971), p. 305.

32. Iachino, *La campagna navale di Lissa*, pp. 201–8; Stefani, *Il problema dell'Adriatico*, p. 81.

33. Tegetthoff to Baroness Emma Lutteroth (wife of Prussian consul, Trieste), Fasana, n.d. (June 1866), Sterneck, *Erinnerungen*, p. 143. Sterneck's memoirs contain some of Tegetthoff's most interesting letters, including those to Lutteroth.

34. Fleischer, *1866*, pp. 76–79; Baratelli, *La marina militare italiana*, pp. 110–12; Sterneck memoir, n.d. (July 1866?), Sterneck, *Erinnerungen*, pp. 146–47.

35. Iachino, *La campagna navale di Lissa*, pp. 215–47; Stefani, *Il problema dell'Adriatico*, pp. 81–82.

36. La Marmora to Ricasoli, Malamberti, 5 July 1866, in Sergio Camerani and Gaetano Arfè, eds., *Carteggi di Bettino Ricasoli*, vol. 22: *20 giugno–31 luglio 1866*, no. 81 of *Fonti per la storia d'Italia* (Rome: Istituto storico italiano per l'età moderna e contemporanea, 1967), p. 137, no. 191 (hereafter cited as *Carteggi Ricasoli*); Stefani, *Il problema dell'Adriatico*, pp. 82–84.

37. Ricasoli to Visconti Venosta, n.p., 12 July 1866 (two letters, one telegram), *Carteggi Ricasoli* 22:250–52, nos. 358–60; Ricasoli to Persano, Bologna, 12 July 1866, ibid., 22:240–41, no. 339.

38. Stefani, *Il problema dell'Adriatico*, pp. 89–90; Baratelli, *La marina militare italiana*, pp. 114–18. Instructions to Persano summarized in Depretis to Ricasoli, Florence, 17 July 1866, *Carteggi Ricasoli* 22:298, no. 421, which also confirms that the Lissa campaign was intended only as a prelude to a direct assault on Istria.

39. Both sides suffered over a hundred casualties during the artillery duel of 18–19 July. See Baratelli, *La marina militare italiana*, pp. 118–23; Fleischer, *1866*, pp. 145–181.

40. This and the following paragraph are based upon Iachino, *La campagna navale di Lissa*, pp. 379–488 and Fleischer, *1866*, pp. 185–299, both meticulously detailed accounts of the battle, as well as Baratelli, *La marina militare italiana*, pp. 123–28, and Handel-Mazzetti and Sokol, *Tegetthoff*, pp. 251–69.

41. The Austrian casualties were thirty-eight men killed and 138 wounded, while the Italians suffered losses of 612 killed and thirty-eight wounded with nineteen men taken prisoner.

42. Tegetthoff to Baroness Lutteroth, "at sea," 22 July 1866, Sterneck, *Erinnerungen*, pp. 149–50.

43. The king himself gave the minister-president confirmation of the Austrian victory. See Victor Emmanuel to Ricasoli, Ferrara, 22 July 1866, *Carteggi Ricasoli*, 22:336, no. 484; Baratelli, *La marina militare italiana*, pp. 129–31. After La Marmora and Cialdini evaded blame for the disaster at Custoza, Admiral Persano became the principal scapegoat for the miserable war effort. An Italian senator, he was tried in April 1867 by his political peers. The two weeks of hearings have been characterized by some as a "second Lissa" for the Italian navy; afterward Persano was forced to retire in disgrace, stripped of his rank and pension (the latter eventually restored by the king). See Baratelli, pp. 145–47; for detailed accounts of the proceedings see Fleischer, *1866*, pp. 339–404 and Iachino, *La campagna navale di Lissa*, pp. 538–638.

44. Ricasoli to Viscount Venosta, n.p., 22 July 1866, *Carteggi Ricasoli*, 22:337–38, no. 487.

45. Ricasoli to Celestino Bianchi, n.p., 26 July 1866, *Carteggi Ricasoli*, 22:381–82, no. 553; Giovanni Battista Falzari, "L'armistizio di Cormons del 1866," *Studi Goriziani* 21 (1957):7–10. In 1866 Austria became the first country ever to move troops by rail from one theatre of a war to another.

46. Falzari, "L'armistizio di Cormons," pp. 10–11. Möring, though firm at Cormons, had long favored an Austrian withdrawal from Italy. See Möring, *Politische Miscellen* (Vienna: Verlag von Tendler et comp., 1848), pp. 294–96.

47. Falzari, "L'armistizio di Cormons," pp. 12–21. Gen. Menabrea and Count Felix von Wimpffen were the plenipotentiaries at the final peace talks in Vienna.

48. Tegetthoff's ramming tactics were adopted by all of the major navies of the world, and the ram-bow remained a feature of battleship design until the 1920s.

EPILOGUE

The road to 1866 had not been an easy one for the fleet. The Habsburg Empire traditionally was not a maritime state, and the navy had few historical roots predating 1797 upon which to build. Ignored and underfinanced for much of the succeeding seven decades, it would not have developed into an effective institution without the timely intervention of interested outsiders. In this regard the political leaders of the empire were of little help. Thugut had no appreciation for maritime affairs, and Stadion also opposed expenditure on the navy. Metternich slowly came around to the view that a fleet could be useful but never had any strong convictions on the matter. Felix Schwarzenberg supported the navy in the first crucial years after 1848, but like his predecessors, he believed that Austria's primary strategic interests lay in Germany. In later years Rechberg and Schmerling were the most prominent of the many Austrian civil leaders critical of naval expansion. And while some proponents of the development of overseas commerce, such as Bruck, also favored a larger fleet, others, such as Kübeck, were enthusiastic about the merchant marine but not the navy.

Throughout its formative years, the most important support for the cause of sea power in Austria came from the traditional centers of Habsburg authority. The imperial house and the army, often criticized by historians for their lack of foresight and opposition to progress, repeatedly produced men whose appreciation for the navy to some extent helped override the general skepticism of the government's civilian ministers. Just after the turn of the century, Archduke Charles made the first attempts to capitalize on the materiel inherited from the old Venetian navy. Almost four decades later his son Frederick brought the service publicity and acclaim in its first major overseas campaign. And in the early 1860s Ferdinand Max was responsible for building the armored fleet. As for the army, Charles was only the first of many Habsburg military leaders sympathetic toward the navy.

Laval Nugent, Karl Schwarzenberg, Radetzky, and Degenfeld each in his own way aided its cause at crucial times. But Ferdinand Max's decision to pursue a naval career marked the turning point. Without the great advances of his decade as commander, the Austrian success in the Adriatic in 1866 would not have been possible.

Tegetthoff's victory at Lissa had a number of positive consequences for the Habsburg monarchy. The battle preserved as Austria's outlet to the sea the bulk of the coastal property that she had first acquired at Campoformio in 1797; this coastline, as much as Bismarck's postwar moderation, guaranteed that she would remain in the ranks of the great powers. Italy, after losing her bid for the Adriatic, in the 1870s turned to the Western Mediterranean and North Africa where she became embroiled in a naval and colonial rivalry with France. Meanwhile, Habsburg control over the Adriatic enabled the Austrian Lloyd and the merchants of Trieste to exploit the opening of the Suez Canal in 1869. In its first years of operation only the British and French ranked ahead of the Austrian merchant marine in their use of the waterway. Trieste in turn prospered anew, finally breaking out of the long recession ushered in by the War of 1859.[1] The foundation appeared to be in place for a bright future for the navy, the merchant marine, and the ports of the Austrian littoral.

Paradoxically, however, the heroes of Lissa soon found that their triumph had been too complete and that the navy would not be sharing the fruits of victory. For a number of reasons, 1866 marked the end rather than the beginning of a positive era of development for Habsburg sea power. Within Austria, Lissa compared too favorably to the army's debacle at Königgrätz. Whereas the land forces obviously required a major overhaul, the fleet certainly could not claim to need rebuilding. The constitutional changes of 1867 which transformed the Habsburg Empire into the dual monarchy of Austria-Hungary only made matters worse. Henceforth, all common expenses, including the naval budget, had to be approved by delegations from both the Austrian *Reichsrat* and the Hungarian Diet. Many Hungarians considered the navy a purely Austrian interest undeserving of common funds; their shrewder colleagues simply used the threat of a veto to give Hungary a voice in the way the service was run. For domestic political reasons Hungarians were granted commissions in sufficient numbers to displace the Italians as the second nationality of the officer corps,[2] and ultimately Rijeka (a "Hungarian" port) had to be given a share of the navy's shipbuilding contracts. For most of its life under the dual monarchy, the navy would not receive the sort of attention it had enjoyed in the heyday of Ferdinand Max's time at the helm.

The Italian navy emerged from the war in such disarray that it could not be portrayed even as a theoretical danger to Habsburg security. Still more significant was the new course in foreign policy, initiated in 1866 by Count Friedrich Ferdinand von Beust and continued by his successors, that made friendship with Italy one of the pillars of Habsburg diplomacy. By the time the Triple Alliance of 1882 sealed the Austro-Italian rapprochement, the armored battle fleet had been robbed of its raison d'être. Without a hostile power on the opposite shore of the Adriatic there was little justification for future naval expansion.

Combined with the domestic difficulties, the removal of the Italian threat dealt the navy a crippling blow. Tegetthoff, in a brief term as *Marine-Kommandant* from 1868 until his death in 1871, managed to stave off the decline and even secured funding for four new ironclad battleships, but subsequent commanders were unable to maintain a successful political defense for the service.[3] The Austrian navy once again became technologically backward and increasingly weaker in comparison to the other fleets of Europe. In an era of peace and retrenchment the needs of an expanding Habsburg merchant marine provided the navy with its only stimulus. Between 1866 and the beginning of the First World War, the fleet routinely undertook cruises to protect commerce and show the flag in distant waters. Some eighty-five overseas missions, thirty-four of them to the Far East, helped fill the void left by the elimination of the need for vigilance in the Adriatic.[4]

Thus the navy came full circle, from a protector of commerce earlier in the century to a battle fleet grouped in home waters in the 1860s, then back again to a protector of commerce during the last quarter of the century. The history of the navy under the dual monarchy of Austria-Hungary mirrors that of the period before 1866: years of neglect, followed by a slow recovery, culminating finally in the construction of another respectable battle fleet before the outbreak of World War I. By 1914 the Habsburg Empire had taken its place among the major maritime powers,[5] a status none of its successor states was able to maintain after 1918. At the end of the war Austria's experience with the sea drew to a close, and Italy, in possession of Trieste, Istria, and even Rijeka (Fiume), became undisputed mistress of the Adriatic.

NOTES

1. In 1871 the total trade of Trieste reached a new record value of 267 million florins. The economic growth levelled off later in the 1870s, but in the early 1880s another boom lifted the city's annual trade over the 300-million florin mark. See Lo Giudice, *Canale di Suez,* pp. 177–221 passim, and Babudieri, *Industrie, commerci e navigazione,* pp. 140–50.

2. From 1885 onward, Germans made up between 45 percent and 55 percent of the officer corps, Hungarians 10 percent to 15 percent. The *Jahresbericht der k.(u.)k. Kriegsmarine,* 1885 through 1913, provides figures on the national composition of the navy.

3. On Tegetthoff's tenure as commander see Schöndorfer, *Tegetthoff,* pp. 54–60. The admiral was rewarded with the top post in the service not after the victory at Lissa but after successfully negotiating the return from Mexico of the remains of Emperor Maximilian following his execution at Queretaro in June 1867.

4. Figures on missions 1868–1914 cited in Allmayer-Beck,

"Die Geschichte von Österreichs Seemacht als historiographisches Problem," p. 17.

5. On the eve of World War I Austria-Hungary had the tenth-largest merchant marine in the world, trailing (in order) Britain, Germany, the United States, Norway, France, Japan, Italy, the Netherlands, and Sweden. Of the countries with larger merchant fleets, three (Norway, the Netherlands, and Sweden) had navies that were much smaller than Austria's; only one country with a smaller merchant marine (Russia) had a larger navy. For figures on steamship tonnage see Babudieri, *Industrie, commerci e navigazione,* p. 194.

Europe and the Mediterranean

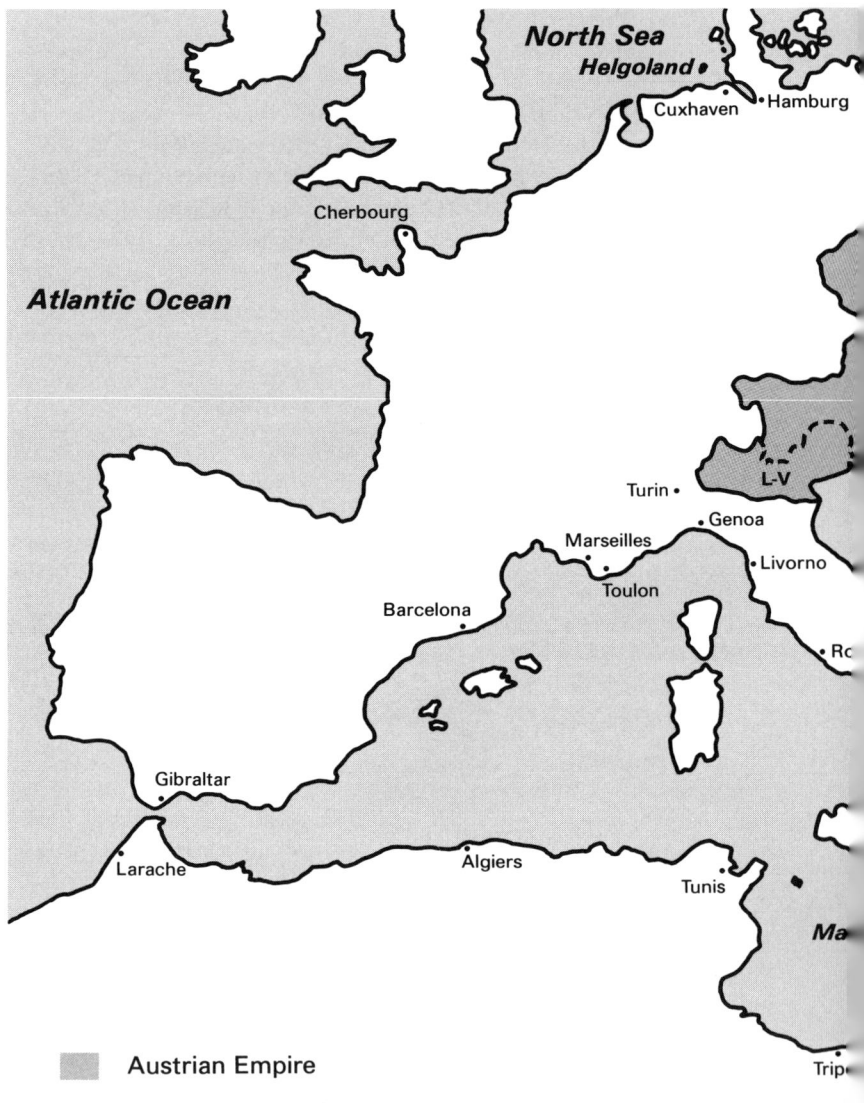

Austrian Empire

L-V = Lombardy-Venetia

Adapted from *Goode's World Atlas*, 13th ed. (Chicago: Rand McNally & Co., 1970)

The Adriatic

Adapted from *Goode's World Atlas*

Maps 273

The Lissa Campaign—1866

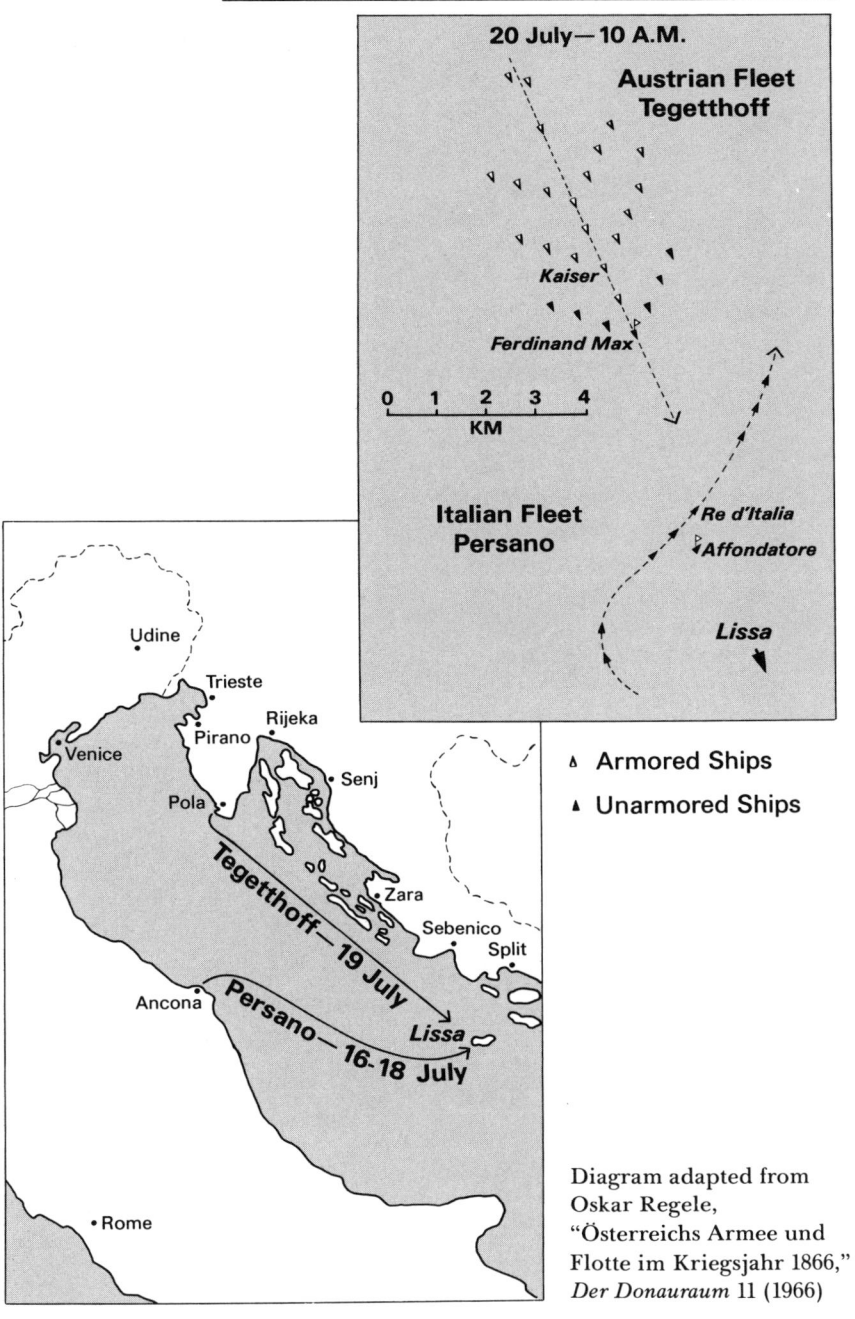

Diagram adapted from
Oskar Regele,
"Österreichs Armee und
Flotte im Kriegsjahr 1866,"
Der Donauraum 11 (1966)

APPENDIX A

SAILING SHIPS OF THE AUSTRIAN NAVY

Does not include smaller vessels (brigs, schooners, gunboats) or any in service before 1814. New ships taking the names of earlier vessels are marked with a roman numeral (II, III). Except for the frigate *Schwarzenberg* (built by Navale Adriatico, Trieste) all ships were constructed in the Venice Arsenal. Principal source: Franz F. Bilzer, "Die Schiffe und Fahrzeuge der k.(u.)k. Kriegsmarine," *Marine—Gestern, Heute* 12 (1985), no. 3 to 15 (1988), no. 2 (continuing series, in eleven parts). *NOTE:* most ships entered service within a year of being launched.

Ships of the Line	Laid down	Launched	Scrapped
Severo (ex-*Rigeneratore*) Rebuilt as frigate *Bellona* 1823–24	1806	1811	1831
Italiano (ex-*Reale Italiano*) Rebuilt as frigate 1827–29; school and harbor ship	1806	1812	1836

(Eight other former Napoleonic ships of the line were burned or scrapped between 1814 and 1830)

Frigates	Laid Down	Launched	Scrapped
Lipsia (ex-*Principessa di Bologna*)	1810	1811	1826
Austria (ex-*Piave*)	1810	1812	1826–27
Augusta (ex-*Anfitrite*)	1811	1815	1826
Ebe	1811	1821	1845–46
Guerriera (renamed *Juno* in 1849)	1811	1829	1851[1]
Medea (ex-*Moscava*)	1813	1827	1842–44
Venere (renamed *Venus* in 1849)	1813	1832	1860[2]
Bellona (II)	1840	1842	1868[3]
Novara	1843	1850	1861[4]
Schwarzenberg	1851	1853	1861[4]

APPENDIX A

Corvettes	Laid Down	Launched	Scrapped
Carolina/Adria/Carolina[5]	1807	1808	1832
Adria (II)	1825?	1826[6]	1852[7]
Lipsia (II) (renamed Leipzig 1849)	1825?	1826[8]	1859
Veloce	1812	1827[9]	1836[10]
Abbondanza	1828	1831	1833[11]
Cesarea (renamed Titania 1849)	1829	1833	1859[12]
Carolina (II)	1832	1833	1843
Veloce (II) (renamed Diana 1849)	1833	1834	1868[13]
Clemenza (renamed Minerva 1849)	1833	1838	1861[14]
Carolina (III)	1843	1847	1870

1. Out of service 1851; sold for scrap 1858
2. School ship 1860–66; sold for scrap 1872
3. Harbor watch and hulk in Pola 1868–1902; scrapped 1903
4. Converted to propeller frigate (see steamships chart)
5. Also referred to as frigate; sailed under name *Adria* 1815–19
6. Begun as brig *San Marco;* rebuilt as corvette; renamed 1827
7. Converted to coal hulk 1852; scrapped 1859
8. Begun as brig *Emo;* rebuilt as corvette; renamed 1827
9. Launched as brig 1818; converted to corvette 1827
10. Converted to coal hulk 1836; scrapped 1839
11. Lost in storm 1833
12. Scuttled to block entrance to Venice harbor in war of 1859
13. Out of service 1868; sold for scrap 1870
14. School ship 1861; scrapped 1893

APPENDIX B

STEAM-POWERED SHIPS OF THE AUSTRIAN NAVY (THROUGH 1866)

Does not include paddle steamers or smaller propeller steamers (i.e., schooners and gunboats). New ships taking the names of earlier vessels are marked with a roman numeral (II, III). Principal source: Franz F. Bilzer, "Die Schiffe und Fahrzeuge der k.(u.)k. Kriegsmarine," *Marine—Gestern, Heute* 12 (1985), no. 3 to 15 (1988), no. 2 (continuing series, in eleven parts). *NOTE:* most ships entered service within a year of being launched.

Ships of the Line	Builder	Laid down	Launched	Scrapped
Kaiser	Pola Arsenal	1855	1858	1869[2]

Frigates	Builder[1]	Laid Down	Launched	Scrapped
Radetzky	England	1852	1854	1869[3]
Donau	N.A. Trieste	1855	1856	1871–72
Adria (III)	N.A. Trieste	1855	1856	1868[4]
Novara (II)	S.T.T. Trieste	1861	1862	1876[5]
Schwarzenberg (II)	Pola Arsenal	1861	1862	1869[6]

Corvettes	Builder	Laid Down	Launched	Scrapped
Friedrich	Venice Arsenal	1854	1857	1897–99
Dandolo	Venice Arsenal	1854	1858	1879[7]

Armored Frigates	Builder[1]	Laid Down	Launched	Scrapped
Drache	N.A. Trieste	1860	1861	1875[8]
Salamander	N.A. Trieste	1860	1861	1883[9]
Kaiser Max	N.A. Trieste	1861	1862	1873
Juan d'Austria	N.A. Trieste	1861	1862	1874
Prinz Eugen	N.A. Trieste	1861	1862	1873

Armored Frigates	Builder[1]	Laid Down	Launched	Scrapped
Ferdinand Max	N.A. Trieste	1863	1865	1886[10]
Habsburg	N.A. Trieste	1863	1865	1886[11]

1. Builders: N.A. Trieste = Navale Adriatico (Tonello firm, San Marco wharves); S.T.T. Trieste = Stabilimento Tecnico Triestino (Strudthoff firm, San Rocco wharves); England = Money, Wigram & Sons
2. Converted to armored warship 1869–74
3. Sunk by munitions explosion
4. School ship 1868; hulk 1871
5. School ship 1876; scrapped 1898–99
6. School ship 1869; scrapped 1900
7. School ship 1879; scrapped 1900
8. Out of service 1875; scrapped 1883–84
9. Out of service 1883; scrapped 1895–96
10. School ship 1886; scrapped 1916–17
11. Harbor watch in Pola 1886; scrapped 1898–1900

APPENDIX C

COMPARATIVE STRENGTH OF THE AUSTRIAN AND ITALIAN FLEETS, 1866*

AUSTRIA				ITALY			
Armored Ships							
Ferdinand Max	FRG	16g.	4757t.	Re d'Italia	FRG	36g.	5700t.
Habsburg	FRG	16g.	4757t.	Re di Portogallo	FRG	28g.	5700t.
Kaiser Max	FRG	30g.	3330t.	Ancona	FRG	27g.	4250t.
Prinz Eugen	FRG	30g.	3330t.	Castelfidardo	FRG	27g.	4250t.
Juan d'Austria	FRG	28g.	3330t.	Maria Pia	FRG	26g.	4250t.
Drache	FRG	26g.	2824t.	San Martino	FRG	26g.	4250t.
Salamander	FRG	26g.	2824t.	Pr. di Carignano	FRG	22g.	4086t.
				Affondatore	RAM	2g.	4070t.
				Terribile	CORV	20g.	2700t.
				Formidabile	CORV	20g.	2700t.
				Palestro	GUNB	5g.	2000t.
				Varese	GUNB	5g.	2000t.
Unarmored Propeller-Ships							
Kaiser	SOL	92g.	5194t.	Re Galantuomo	SOL	43g.	3800t.
Novara	FRG	51g.	2497t.	Maria Adelaide	FRG	32g.	3459t.
Schwarzenberg	FRG	46g.	2514t.	Duca di Genova	FRG	50g.	3515t.
Radetzky	FRG	31g.	2198t.	Principe Umberto	FRG	50g.	3501t.
Adria	FRG	31g.	2198t.	Vitt. Emmanuele	FRG	50g.	3415t.
Donau	FRG	31g.	2198t.	Garibaldi	FRG	54g.	3680t.

APPENDIX C

AUSTRIA

Friedrich	CORV	22g.	1474t.
Dandolo	CORV	22g.	1474t.
2 schooners			
7 gunboats			

ITALY

Italia	FRG	54g.	3680t.
Gaeta	FRG	54g.	3980t.
Carlo Alberto	FRG	50g.	3200t.
Magenta	CORV	20g.	2552t.
Pr. Clotilde	CORV	20g.	2182t.
San Giovanni	CORV	20g.	1780t.
Etna	CORV	10g.	1524t.
3 gunboats			

Paddle Steamers

AUSTRIA:
12 seagoing steamers
4 auxiliary steamers

ITALY:
c. 24 seagoing and aux. steamers

Sailing Ships

AUSTRIA:
2 frigates
2 corvettes
8 brigs

ITALY:
3 frigates
4 corvettes
2 brigs

KEY: SOL—ship of the line, FRG—frigate, CORV—corvette, GUNB—gunboat, g.—guns, t.—tons

*From Josef Fleischer, *Geschichte der k.k. Kriegsmarine*, part 3: *Die k.k. österreichische Kriegsmarine in dem Zeitraume von 1848 bis 1871,* vol. 3: *Geschichte der k.k. Kriegsmarine während des Krieges im Jahre 1866* (Vienna: Verlag des k.u.k. Reichskriegsministeriums, Marinesektion, 1906), pp. 360–63.

APPENDIX D

COMMANDERS AND LEADING PERSONNEL OF THE AUSTRIAN NAVY, 1797–1866

Williams (November 1797–February 1798)

Querini (February 1798–January 1802)

    Commander of "Trieste Navy": Williams (1798–99)
    Marine Bureau in Vienna: Crenneville (1801–2)

L'Espine (January 1802–August 1805)

    Second-in-command (Arsenal director): Dandolo (1803–5)
    Marine Bureau in Vienna: Crenneville (1802–5)

Dandolo (provisional, August–December 1805)

    Second-in-command (Arsenal director): Pasqualigo (1805)
    Marine Bureau in Vienna: L'Espine (1805)

L'Espine (provisional, 1806; official, April 1807–January 1810; provisional, August 1813–July 1814)

    Second-in-command (various duties): Conninck (1806-10)

Conninck (July 1814–March 1824)

    Squadron commanders: Pasqualigo (1815–21)—Adriatic, special missions
        Paulucci (1821–23)—Neapolitan waters
        Dandolo (1823–24)—Neapolitan waters
        Armeni (1821–24)—Levant
        Accurti (1824)—Levant
    Special inspectors: Paulucci (1819–20)
        Crenneville (1822)

Paulucci (March 1824–August 1844)

>*Second-in-command (ad latus):* Flanegan (1824–38)
>   Dandolo (1838–44)
>*Squadron commanders:* Dandolo (1824–26)—Neapolitan waters
>   Accurti (1824–26)—Levant
>   Paulucci (1826)—Levant
>   Dandolo (1826–29)—Levant
>   Bandiera (1828–30)—Moroccan waters
>   Accurti (1829–30)—Levant
>   Bandiera (1831–39)—Adriatic, special missions
>   Bandiera (1839–44)—Levant

Archduke Frederick (August 1844–October 1847)

>*Second-in-command (ad latus):* Dandolo (1844–47)
>*Adjutant:* Marinovich (1844–47)
>*Squadron commanders:* Bua (1844–45)—Levant
>   Marsich (1845)—Levant
>   Marsich (1845–46)
>   Buratovich (1846–47)

Dandolo (provisional, October–November 1847)

>*Adjutant:* Marinovich (1847)
>*Squadron commander:* Buratovich (1847)

Martini (November 1847–March 1848)

>*Adjutant and Arsenal director:* Marinovich (1847–48)
>*Squadron commanders:* Buratovich (1847–48)
>   Bujacovich (1848)—Neapolitan waters

Gyulai (provisional, April–September 1848)

>*Second-in-command (ad latus):* Buratovich (1848)
>*Squadron commander:* Kudriaffsky (1848)

Martini (September 1848–February 1849)

>*Second-in-command (ad latus):* Buratovich (1848–49)
>*Squadron commanders:* Kudriaffsky (to October 1848)
>   Sourdeau (1848–49)

Gyulai (provisional, February–April 1849)

    Second-in-command (ad latus): Buratovich (1849)
    Squadron commander: Sourdeau (1849)

Dahlerup (April 1849–August 1851)

    Second-in-command (ad latus): Buratovich (died August 1849)
    Bujacovich (1849–51)
    Squadron commander: Dahlerup (1849–51)

Wimpffen (provisional, August 1851–September 1854)

    Second-in-command (ad latus): Bujacovich (1851–54)
    Adjutant: Wüllerstorf (1851–54)
    Squadron commanders: Bujacovich (1851–52)
                       Ivanossich (1852)
                       Fautz (1852–53)
                       Joseph Pöltl (1853–54)
                       Lewartowsky (1854)

Archduke Ferdinand Max (September 1854–January 1864)

    Second-in-command (ad latus): Bujacovich (September 1854–December 1856)
                               Gyuito (January–May 1857)
                               Bujacovich (May–August 1857)
    Second-in-command at Milan (Stellvertreter): Fautz (August 1857–April 1859)
    Second-in-command at Trieste (Marinekommandant): Bourguignon (August 1857–June 1859)
    Second-in-command (Stellvertreter): Bourguignon (June 1859–October 1860)
                               Alphons Wissiak (October 1860–March 1861)
                               Hadik (March–July 1861)
                               Alphons Wissiak (July 1861–August 1864)
    Squadron commanders: Ferdinand Max (1855)
                       Fautz (1855)
                       Alphons Wissiak (1857)
                       Scopinich (1858–59)
                       Ferdinand Max (1859)

Fautz (1859–60)
Wüllerstorf (1860)—Neapolitan waters
Bourguignon (1860–61)
Tegetthoff (1862–64)—Greek waters and Levant

(*Commander's post vacant, January 1864–March 1868*)

Minister of Marine *Stellvertreter:* Fautz (March 1864–July 1865)
Chief of *Marinesektion,* War Ministry: Fautz (July 1865–March 1868)
Truppen- und Flotteninspektor: Archduke Leopold (July 1865–March 1868)
Truppen- und Flotteninspektor Stellvertreter: Pöck (1866–68)
Squadron commanders; Wüllerstorf (1864)—against Denmark
Tegetthoff (1865–66)

NOTE: the lists of squadron commanders are incomplete and include some officers officially designated as division commanders. Unless otherwise noted, their sphere of operations was limited to the Adriatic or general patrols of the Mediterranean.

GLOSSARY

The types of ships referred to most frequently in the text, in descending order of size:

Ship of the Line: A ship large and strong enough to hold a place in the "line of battle." These vessels had three masts and at least two gun-decks. In the eighteenth century it was not uncommon for a ship of the line to have as few as sixty cannon, but by the Napoleonic era the 74-gun model was standard. The wooden equivalent of the modern battleship, the last vessels of this type (built in the 1850s by Britain and France) carried as many as 131 guns.

Frigate: A three-masted ship with one gun-deck, much faster than a ship of the line. Some eighteenth-century frigates had as few as two dozen cannon, but nineteenth-century models commonly carried between forty-four and sixty guns. Until the 1850s, Austria's largest warships were sailing frigates.

Corvette: The smallest three-masted warship, called a "sloop" by the British and American navies. Most corvettes had all of their guns (usually between twenty and twenty-four) mounted on the top deck, and had no gun-deck below. A popular ship type in the Austrian navy.

Brig: A stout, slow two-masted vessel, armed with up to eighteen guns. Built for cargo capacity rather than speed, the brig often carried troops or supplies. In the Adriatic, it was also a popular ship type for merchants.

Schooner: A small, fast vessel, usually with two masts, armed with up to twelve guns.

Gunboat: The smallest warship, armed with one to six cannon. In the age of sail, gunboats were usually one-masted vessels fit only for coastal duty.

Propeller or Screw: As a prefix to any of the above, describes a vessel of one of the traditional sailing designs equipped with steam engines and an underwater screw-propeller. All of the ship types listed above (except brigs) had screw-powered versions by the middle of the nineteenth century.

Paddle Steamer: A steamship of any size, propelled by large side-paddles. Vessels of this design saw only auxiliary duty after the introduction of the screw propeller.

Ironclad: Any armored warship. This term, properly applied, refers only to the first generation of armored vessels, ships of either wood or iron construction covered with thick iron plates rather than modern armor.

Ram: An armored warship equipped with a pointed bow below the waterline for use in ramming enemy vessels.

Turret Ship: An ironclad with guns in one or more revolving turrets; patterned after the American *Monitor*, turret ships were often referred to as "Monitors."

BIBLIOGRAPHY

Unpublished Documents

    Haus- Hof- und Staatsarchiv, Vienna
        Administrative Registratur
            F 44—Marinewesen
            F 52—Sicherheitswesen
        Archiv Kaiser Maximilians von Mexiko
        Hausarchiv
            Familienkorrespondenz A
        Politisches Archiv
            II. Deutscher Bund
            XI. Italienische Staaten
            XL. Interna
        Staatskanzlei
            Acta secreta
            Interiora
            Notenwechsel mit dem Hofkriegsrat
            Provinzen
                Illyrien
                Küstenland
                Lombardo-Venezien

    Hofkammerarchiv, Vienna
        Kommerz
            Litorale 1749–1813

    Kriegsarchiv, Vienna
        Centralkanzleiakten
        Feldakten 1813
            Feldzug in Istrien
        Hofkriegsrat Akten
            Präsidialreihe
        Kriegsministerium
            Präsidialreihe
        Manuskripte
        Marineakten
            Administrative Akten

Militärische Akten
Technisches Archiv
Militär-Kanzlei Seiner Majestät
Nachlässe
   Folliot de Crenneville
   Möring
   Radetzky
   Zichy

Princeton University Library, Princeton, N.J.
   The Papers of Prince Eugene de Beauharnais
   Boxes 34 and 35

Published documents, Letters, and Memoirs

Austria. *Die Protokolle des österreichischen Ministerrates 1848–1867*, part 5: *Die Ministerien Erzherzog Rainer und Mensdorff*, vol. 3. Vienna: Österreichischer Bundesverlag, 1985.

Austria. Reichsrat. *Stenographische Protokolle des Abgeordnetenhaus des Reichsrathes.* 22 vols. Vienna: k.k. Hof- und Staatsdruckerei, 1862–1918.

Camerani, Sergio, and Arfè, Gaetano, eds. *Carteggi di Bettino Ricasoli*, vol. 22: *20 giugno–31 luglio 1866. Fonti per la storia d'Italia*, no. 81. Rome: Istituto storico italiano per l'età moderna e contemporanea, 1967.

Dahlerup, Hans Birch von. *In österreichischen Diensten.* 2 vols. Berlin: Meyer & Jessen, 1911–12.

Duhr, Bernhard, ed. *Briefe des Feldmarschalls Radetzky an seine Tochter Friederike, 1847–1857.* Vienna: Josef Roller & Comp., 1892.

Ferdinand Max, Archduke (Maximilian I, Emperor of Mexico). *Aus meinem Leben: Reiseskizzen, Aphorismen, Gedichte.* 7 vols. Leipzig: Verlag von Duncker und Humblot, 1867.

Hoste, William. *Memoirs and Letters of Capt. Sir William Hoste.* 2 vols. London: Richard Bentley, 1833.

Italy. Ministero della Marina. *Ordinamento della Marina Militare dello Stato per Regio Decreto 1 Aprile 1861.* Turin: Ministero della Marina, 1861.

Jones, Pitcairn, ed. *Piracy in the Levant 1827–8. Publications of the Navy Records Society*, vol. 72. London: Spottiswoode, Ballantyne & Co., Ltd., 1934.

Mazzini, Giuseppe. *Scritti editi ed inediti di Giuseppe Mazzini*. Edizione Nazionale. 95 vols. Imola: Cooperativa Tipografico Editrice Paolo Galeati, 1921.

Metternich-Winneburg, Clemens Lothar Wenzel von. *Memoirs of Prince Metternich*, ed. Prince Richard Metternich, trans. Mrs. Alexander Napier. 5 vols. New York: Harper & Brothers, 1880–82.

Radaelli, Carlo Alberto. *Storio dello Assedio di Venezia negli anni 1848–1849*. Venice: Tipografia Antonelli, 1875.

Sterneck zu Ehrenstein, Maximilian Daublebsky von. *Admiral Max Freiherr von Sterneck: Erinnerungen aus den Jahren 1847 bis 1897*, ed. Jerolim Benko von Boinik. Vienna: A. Hartleben, 1901.

Tegetthoff, Wilhelm von. *Aus Wilhelm von Tegetthoff's Nachlass*, ed. Adolf Beer. Vienna: Druck und Verlag von Carl Gerold's Sohn, 1882.

Wigard, Franz, ed. *Stenographischer Bericht über die Verhandlungen der deutschen constituirenden National-versammlung zu Frankfurt am Main*. 9 vols. Frankfurt: Johann David Sauerlander, 1848.

Contemporary Periodicals, Tracts, and Reference Works

Ferdinand Max, Archduke (Maximilian I, Emperor of Mexico). *Erlauternde Bemerkungen zum Budget der kais. Kriegs-Marine*. Trieste: Buchdruckerei des Oesterreichischen Lloyd, 1860.

Jahresbericht der k. (u.) k. Kriegsmarine.

Militär-Schematismus des österreichischen Kaiserthums. (Annual. Title varies).

Möring, Karl. *Politische Miscellen*. Vienna: Verlag von Tendler et comp., 1848.

———. *Zur Marine-Frage*. Vienna: Carl Gerold's Sohn, 1862.

[Perthaler, Johann]. *Die österreichische Marine. Von einem österreichischen Seemanne*. Vienna: Typographisch-Literarisch-Artistische Anstalt, 1860.

[*Streffleur's*] *Österreichische Militärische Zeitschrift.*

Monographs and General Works

Albrecht-Carrié, René. *A Diplomatic History of Europe Since the Congress of Vienna*. Rev. ed. New York: Harper & Row, 1973.

Babudieri, Fulvio. *L'espansione mercantile austriaca nei territori d'oltremare nel XVIII secolo*. Milan: Dott. A. Giuffrè editore, 1978.

———. *Industrie, commerci e navigazione a Trieste e nella regione Giulia*. Milan: Dott. A. Giuffrè editore, 1982.

Baratelli, Franco Micali. *La marina militare italiana nella vita nazionale (1860–1914)*. Mursia: U. Mursia editore S.p.A., 1983.

Bargoni, Franco. *Le prime navi di linea della marina italiana (1861–1880)*. Rome: Edizioni Bizzarri, 1976.

Baxter, James P. *The Introduction of the Ironclad Warship*. Cambridge, Mass.: Harvard University Press, 1933.

Bayer von Bayersburg, Heinrich. *Österreichs Admirale 1719–1866*. Vienna: Bergland Verlag, 1960.

Benko von Boinik, Jerolim. *Geschichte der k.k. Kriegsmarine*, part 3: *Die k.k. österreichische Kriegsmarine in dem Zeitraume von 1848 bis 1871*, vol. 1: *Geschichte der k.k. Kriegsmarine während der Jahre 1848 und 1849*. Vienna: Verlag des k.k. Reichs-Kriegs-Ministerium, Marine-Sektion, 1884.

Bergmann, Joseph. *Erzherzog Friedrich von Oesterreich und sein Antheil am Kriegszuge in Syrien im Jahre 1840*. Vienna: Tendler & Co., 1857.

Blaas, Richard. "L'Austria e la proclamazione del Regno d'Italia." *Archivio Storico Italiano* 119 (1961): 331–61.

Blumberg, Arnold. *The Diplomacy of the Mexican Empire, 1863–1867*. Reprint ed. Malabar, Fla.: Robert E. Krieger Publishing Co., 1987.

Boyer, Ferdinand. "Les derniers jours de la République de Venise (août 1849)." *Rassegna Storica del Risorgimento* 56 (1969): 576–86.

Brandt, Harm-Hinrich. *Der österreichische Neoabsolutismus: Staatsfinanzen und Politik 1848–1860*. 2 vols. Göttingen: Vandenhoeck & Ruprecht, 1978.

Bratulić, Vjekoslav. "Političke stranke u Istri za vrijeme narodnog

preporod." *Hrvatski narodni preporod u Dalmaciji i Istri*, ed. Jakša Ravlić (Matica Hrvatska, 1969): 289–334.
Braudel, Fernand. *The Mediterranean and the Mediterranean World in the Age of Philip II*, trans. Sian Reynolds. 2 vols. New York: Harper & Row, 1972.
———. *Civilization and Capitalism, 15th–18th Century*, vol. 2: *The Wheels of Commerce*, trans. Sian Reynolds. New York: Harper & Row, 1982.
Carci, Luigi. *La spedizione e il processo dei fratelli Bandiera*. Modena: Società tipografica modenese, 1939.
Cessi, Roberto. *Campoformido*. Padua: Editrice Antenore, 1973.
———. *La repubblica di Venezia e il problema adriatico*. Padua: C.E.D.A.M., 1943.
Charmatz, Richard. *Minister Freiherr von Bruck: Der Vorkämpfer Mitteleuropas*. Leipzig: S. Hirzel, 1916.
Coons, Ronald E. *Steamships, Statesmen, and Bureaucrats: Austrian Policy Towards the Steam Navigation Company of the Austrian Lloyd, 1836–1848*. Wiesbaden: Franz Steiner Verlag, 1975.
Corti, Egon Caesar. *Maximilian and Charlotte of Mexico*, trans. Catherine Allison Phillips. 2 vols. New York: Alfred A. Knopf, 1928.
Cruccu, Rinaldo. "I piani operativi per la liberazione del Veneto." *Atti del convegno storico di studi su: "Il Lombardo Veneto dal 1849 al 1866"* (Padua: Società Solferino e San Martino, 1977): 150–69.
Czerczitz, Gustav Hubka von. *Geschichte des k.u.k. Infanterie-Regimentes Graf von Lacy Nr. 22*. Zadar: Verlag des Regimentes, 1902.
Deak, Istvan. *The Lawful Revolution: Louis Kossuth and the Hungarians, 1848–1849*. New York: Columbia University Press, 1979.
Deutsch, Wilhelm. *Habsburgs Rückzug aus Italien: Die Verhandlungen von Villafranca und Zürich 1859*. Vienna: Adolf Luser Verlag, 1940.
Engel-Janosi, Friedrich. *Die Jugendzeit des Grafen Prokesch von Osten*. Innsbruck: Universitäts-Verlag Wagner, 1938.
———. "Österreich und der Untergang des Königreichs Neapel." *Historische Zeitschrift* 194 (1962): 62–84.
Falzari, Giovanni Battista. "L'armistizio di Cormons del 1866." *Studi Goriziani* 21 (1957): 5–21.
Filipuzzi, Angelo. "La mobilitazione austriaca alla viglia della campagna del 1866." *Atti del convegno storico di studi su: "Il Lombardo*

Veneto dal 1849 al 1866" (Padua: Società Solferino e San Martino, 1977): 54–75.

Der Feldzug der österreichischen Armee in Italien im Jahre 1849. 2 vols. Vienna: Verlag von Karl Hölzl, 1854.

Fleischer, Josef. *Geschichte der k.k. Kriegsmarine,* part 3: *Die k.k. österreichische Kriegsmarine in dem Zeitraume von 1848 bis 1871,* vol. 3: *Geschichte der k.k. Kriegsmarine während des Krieges im Jahre 1866.* Vienna: Verlag des k.u.k. Reichskriegsministeriums, Marinesektion, 1906.

Fünfundsiebzig Jahre österreichischer Lloyd. Trieste: Verlag des österreichischen Lloyd, 1911.

Gerolami, Giuseppe. *Trieste e il Mare.* Trieste: E. Borsatti, 1955.

Ginsborg, Paul. *Daniele Manin and the Venetian Revolution of 1848–49.* Cambridge: Cambridge University Press, 1979.

Hamann, Günther. "Die österreichische Kriegsmarine im Dienste der Wissenschaften." *Schriften des Heeresgeschichtlichen Museums (Militärwissenschaftliches Institut) in Wien.* vol. 8: *Österreich zur See* (Vienna: Österreichischer Bundesverlag, 1980): 59–90.

Handel-Mazzetti, Peter. "Eine Reise an der Zeitwende: Die Fahrt der Korvette *Carolina* in die Nordsee." *Marine—Gestern, Heute* 7 (1980): 50–53.

———. "Das Seegefecht bei Helgoland am 9. Mai 1864." *Marine Rundschau* 39 (1934): 193–98.

———. "Vor 110 Jahren: El Araisch." *Marine Rundschau* 44 (1939): 746–54.

Handel-Mazzetti, Peter, and Sokol, Hans Hugo. *Wilhelm von Tegetthoff: Ein grosser Österreicher.* Linz: Oberösterreichischer Landesverlag, 1952.

Häußler, Hans-Joachim. "Küstenschutz und deutsche Flotte, 1859–1864." *Forschungen zur brandenburgischen und preussischen Geschichte* 51 (1939): 311–43.

Helfert, Joseph Alexander. *Kaiser Franz I. von Österreich und die Stiftung des lombardo-venetianischen Königreichs.* Innsbruck: Verlag der Wagner'shen Universitäts-Buchhandlung, 1901.

Helleiner, Karl. *The Imperial Loans: A Study in Financial and Diplomatic History.* London: Oxford University Press, 1965.

Herlihy, Patricia. "Russian Grain and Mediterranean Markets, 1774–1861." Ph.D. diss., University of Pennsylvania, 1963.

Higham, Robin. "William H. Webb: Foreign Warship Construction

and the Civil War." *Journal of the American Society of Naval Engineers* (February 1961): 177–90.
Höbelt, Lothar. "Die Marine." *Die Habsburgermonarchie 1848–1918*, vol. 5: *Die bewaffnete Macht* (Vienna: Österreichische Akademie der Wissenschaften, 1987): 687–763.
Iachino, Angelo. *La campagna navale di Lissa 1866*. Milan: Casa editrice Il Saggiatore, 1966.
Jahn, Friedrich. "Bibliographie der k.k./k.u.k. Marine." *Schriften des Heeresgeschichtlichen Museums (Militär-Wissenschaftliches Institut) in Wien*, vol. 8: *Österreich zur See:* 109–97. Vienna: Österreichischer Bundesverlag, 1980.
Karaman, Igor. *Privreda i društvo: Hrvatske u 19. stoljeću*. Zagreb: Školska knjiga, 1972.
Khuepach, Artur von. *Geschichte der k.u.k. Kriegsmarine*, part 2: *Die k.k. österreichische Kriegsmarine in dem Zeitraume von 1797 bis 1848*, vol. 2: *Geschichte der k.k. Kriegsmarine während der Jahre 1802 bis 1814*. Vienna: Staatsdruckerei Wien, 1942.
Khuepach, Artur von, and Bayer, Heinrich von. *Geschichte der k.u.k. Kriegsmarine*, part 3: *Die k.k. österreichische Kriegsmarine in dem Zeitraum von 1797 bis 1848*, vol. 3: *Geschichte der k.k. Kriegsmarine während der Jahre 1814–1847*. Graz: Verlag Hermann Böhlaus Nachfolger, 1966.
Kjølsen, F. H. "The Old Danish Frigate." *The Mariner's Mirror* 51 (1965): 27–33.
Körner, Karl Klaus. "Die *Carolina* 1808–1832: Schicksal und Rekonstruktion." *Marine—Gestern, Heute* 13 (1986): 1–11, 49–60, 105–13, 158–63.
Kraehe, Enno E. "Foreign Policy and the Nationality Problem in the Habsburg Monarchy, 1800–67." *Austrian History Yearbook* 3 (1967), pt. 3: 3–36.
———. *Metternich's German Policy*, vol. 1: *The Contest With Napoleon, 1799–1814*. Princeton, N.J.: Princeton University Press, 1963.
Kramer, Hans. *Österreich und das Risorgimento*. Vienna: Bergland Verlag, 1963.
Lambert, Andrew. *Battleships in Transition: The Creation of the Steam Battlefleet, 1815–1860*. Annapolis, Md.: U.S. Naval Institute Press, 1984.
Lehnert, Josef von. *Geschichte der k.u.k. Kriegsmarine*, part 2: *Die k.k.*

österreichische Kriegsmarine in dem Zeitraume von 1797 bis 1848, vol. 1: Geschichte der österreichisch-venetianischen Kriegsmarine während der Jahre 1797 bis 1802. Vienna: Gerold & comp., 1891.

Levy, Cesare Augusto. Navi da Guerra construite nell'Arsenale di Venezia dal 1664 al 1896. Venice: by the author, 1896.

Lo Guidice, Giuseppe. Trieste, L'Austria ed il Canale di Suez. Catania: Università degli studi, 1979.

Mack Smith, Denis, ed. The Making of Italy 1796–1870. New York: Walker & Co., 1968.

———. Victor Emmanuel, Cavour, and the Risorgimento. London: Oxford University Press, 1971.

Mackesy, Piers. The War in the Mediterranean, 1803–1810. Cambridge, Mass.: Harvard University Press, 1957.

Milanović, Božo. "Biskup Dobrila i njegovo dobo (1861–1882)." In Hrvatski narodni preporod u Dalmaciji i Istri, ed. Jakša Ravlić, 351–402. Zagreb: Matica Hrvatska, 1969.

Mirković, Mijo. "O smislu u sadržaju narodnog preporoda u Istri." In Harvatski narodni preporod u Dalmaciji i Istri, ed. Jakša Ravlići, 283–86. Zagreb: Matica Hrvatska, 1969.

Mosse, W. E. "Queen Victoria and her Ministers in the Schleswig-Holstein Crisis of 1863–64." English Historical Review 78 (1963): 217–85.

Nani Mocenigo, Filippo. La Marina Veneta e i fratelli Bandiera. Venice: Tip. Orfanotrofio di A. Pellizzato, 1907.

Netrval, Karl. "Feldzeugmeister August Graf Degenfeld-Schönburg: Offizier und Staatsmann." Ph.D. diss., University of Vienna, 1971.

Noether, Emiliana P. " 'Morally Wrong' or 'Politically Right'? Espionage in Her Majesty's Post Office, 1844–45." Canadian Journal of History 22 (1987): 41–57.

Nuffel, Robert van. "Intorno alla perdita della flotta all'inizio della rivoluzione veneziana." Rassegna Storica del Risorgimento 44 (1957): 784–91.

Pahor, Miroslav. Slovenski mornarji Austrije v obrambi Dalmacije in Istre 1849–1917. Piran: Pomorski muzej Sergej Mašera, 1978.

Paladin, Giovanni. "La questione dalmatica vista da Niccolò Tommaseo e da Antonio Baiamonti." Rassegna Storica del Risorgimento 38 (1951): 536–56.

Paschen, D. "Der blutige Tag von Helgoland." *Marine Rundschau* 44 (1939): 470–76.
Pierantoni, Riccardo. *Storia dei fratelli Bandiera e loro compagni in Calabria.* Milan: Casa Editrice L. F. Cogliati, 1909.
Radogna, Lamberto, *Storia della Marina Militare delle Due Sicilie (1734–1860).* Mursia: U. Mursia editore S.p.A., 1978.
Ragsdale, Hugh. *Détente in the Napoleonic Era: Bonaparte and the Russians.* Lawrence, Kans.: The Regents Press of Kansas, 1980.
Randaccio, C. *Le marinerie militari italiane nei tempi moderni (1750–1850).* Turin: Artero e comp., 1864.
Rechberger von Rechkron, Josef. *Geschichte der k.k. Kriegsmarine,* part 1: *Österreichs Seewesen in dem Zeitraume von 1500–1797.* Vienna: Verlag des k.k. Reichs-Kriegs-Ministeriums, Marine-Section, 1882.
Rock, Kenneth W. "Loyalty and Legality: Austria and the Western Balkans, 1848–1853." In *Nation and Ideology: Essays in honor of Wayne S. Vucinich,* ed. Ivo Banac, John G. Ackerman, and Roman Szporluk, 121–48. Boulder, Colo.: Eastern European Monographs, 1981.
Roider, Karl A., Jr. *Austria's Eastern Question 1700–1790.* Princeton, N.J.: Princeton University Press, 1982.
———. *Baron Thugut and Austria's Response to the French Revolution.* Princeton, N.J.: Princeton University Press, 1987.
Romiti, S. "La politica navale del Piemonte nel decennio 1849–1859." *Rassegna Storica del Risorgimento* 39 (1952): 780–808.
Rothenberg, Gunther E. *The Army of Francis Joseph.* West Lafayette, Ind.: Purdue University Press, 1976.
———. *Napoleon's Great Adversaries: The Archduke Charles and the Austrian Army, 1792–1814.* Bloomington: Indiana University Press, 1982.
Salcher, Peter. *Geschichte der k.u.k. Marine-Akademie.* Pola: Carl Gerold's Sohn, 1902.
Scala, Eduardo. *La guerra del 1866 ed altri scritti.* Rome: Tipografia Regionale, 1981.
Schatz, Erwin. "Gedenkstätten an Vize-Admiral Erzherzog Friedrich in Venedig." *Marine—Gestern, Heute* 10 (1983): 40–51.
Schmidt-Brentano, Antonio. *Die Armee in Österreich: Militär, Staat und Gesellschaft 1848–1867.* Boppard am Rhein: Harald Boldt Verlag, 1975.

Schmidt-Brentano, Antonio. "Österreichs Weg zur Seemacht: Die Marinepolitik Österreichs in der Ära Erzherzog Ferdinand Maximilian (1854–1864)." *Mitteilungen des österreichischen Staatsarchivs* 30 (1977): 119–52.

Schöndorfer, Ulrich. "Der österreichische Kriegsschiffbau von 1848 bis 1914." *Schriften des Heeresgeschichtlichen Museums (Militärwissenschaftliches Institut) in Wien*, vol. 8: *Österreich zur See:* 23–42. Vienna: Österreichischer Bundesverlag, 1980.

———. *Wilhelm von Tegetthoff*. Vienna: Bergland Verlag, 1958.

Schroeder, Paul. *Metternich's Diplomacy at its Zenith, 1820–1823*. Austin: University of Texas Press, 1962.

Schwarzenberg, Adolph. *Prince Felix zu Schwarzenberg, Prime Minister of Austria 1848–1852*. New York: Columbia University Press, 1946.

Scott, Ivan. "Italian Conspiracy on a Grand Scale: The Abortive Galician Project of 1864." *East European Quarterly* 8 (1974–75): 45–53.

Simion, Ernesto, and Nani Mocenigo, Mario. *La campagna navale di Siria del 1840*. Rome: Tip. Ufficio del Capo di Stato Maggiore, 1933.

Sked, Alan. *The Survival of the Habsburg Empire: Radetzky, the Imperial Army and the Class War, 1848*. London: Longman, 1979.

Sokol, Hans Hugo. *Geschichte der k.u.k. Kriegsmarine*, part 3: *Des Kaisers Seemacht: Die k.k. österreichische Kriegsmarine 1848 bis 1914. Abschlussband des Geschichtswerkes der k.u.k. Kriegsmarine*. Vienna: Almathea Verlag, 1980.

Sondhaus, Lawrence. "Die Koszta-Affaire: Eine österreichisch-amerikanische Konfrontation in Smyrna 1853." *Marine—Gestern, Heute* 13 (1986): 153–57.

———. "*Mitteleuropa zur See?* Austria and the German Navy Question, 1848–1852." *Central European History* 20 (1987): 125–44.

———. "Die österreichische Kriegsmarine und der amerikanische Sezessionskrieg 1861–1865." *Marine—Gestern, Heute* 14 (1987): 81–84.

Srbik, Heinrich von. "Der Geheimvertrag Österreichs und Frankreichs vom 12. Juni 1866." *Historisches Jahrbuch* 57 (1937): 454–507.

Steefel, Lawrence D. "The Rothschilds and the Austrian Loan of 1865." *Journal of Modern History* 8 (1936): 27–39.

Stefani, Giuseppe. *Il problema dell'Adriatico nelle guerre del Risorgimento.* Udine: Del Bianco, 1965.
Stefani, Giuseppe, and Astori, Bruno. *Il Lloyd Triestino (1836–1936).* Trieste: A. Mondadori, 1938.
Szabo, Franz. "Unwanted Navy: Habsburg Naval Armaments under Maria Theresa." *Austrian History Yearbook* 17–18 (1981–82): 29–53.
Tamaro, Attilio. *Storia di Trieste.* 2 vols. Rome, 1924. Reprint. Trieste: Edizioni Lint, 1976.
Tamborra, Angelo. "Balcani, Italia ed Europa nel problema della Venezia (1859–1861)." *Rassegna Storica del Risorgimento* 44 (1957): 813–18.
———. *Cavour e i Balcani.* Turin: I.L.T.E., 1958.
Valsecchi, Franco. "La paix de Zurich (1859)." *Revue d'histoire moderne et contemporaine* 7 (1960): 111–22.
Wagner, Walter. "Die obersten Behörden der k.u.k. Kriegsmarine 1856–1918." *Mitteilungen des österreichischen Staatsarchivs,* Ergänzungsband 6 (1961).
Walker, Mack, ed. *Plombières: Secret Diplomacy and the Rebirth of Italy.* London: Oxford University Press, 1968.
Wallisch, Friedrich. *Sein Schiff Hiess Novara: Bernhard von Wüllerstorf, Admiral und Minister.* Vienna: Verlag Herold, 1966.
White, D. Feodotoff. "The Russian Navy in Trieste During the Wars of the Revolution and the Empire." *American Slavic and East European Review* 6, no. 18–19 (1947): 25–41.
Wrede, Alphons von. *Geschichte der k.u.k. Wehrmacht: Die Regimenter, Corps, Branchen und Anstalten von 1618 bis Ende des XIX. Jahrhunderts.* 7 vols. Vienna: L. W. Seidel & Sohn, 1893–1900.

INDEX

Unless otherwise indicated, all institutions, titles, and ranks are Austrian. Individual ranks reflect the highest levels reached by 1866.

A

Aberdeen, George Hamilton Gordon, Earl of, British foreign secretary, 98
Academic Legion (Vienna), 156–57
Achmed Pasha, Turkish admiral, 94
Acre, 103–4, 108, 109
Adamić, A. L., Rijeka merchant, 33–34, 41–42, 45
Adige River, 32, 34, 249
Adrianople, Treaty of (1829), 72–73
Adriatic Sea: traditional domination of Venetian Republic in, 2; Italian as trading language of, 4; during Napoleonic wars, 4, 5, 7–10, 12, 14–21, 30–35, 46–47; and Revolutions of 1820–21, 58–60; during Revolutions of 1831–32, and French presence in, 77–79; in Radetzky's strategic planning, 92–93; Austrian navy concentrated in (1845), 130–31; and Revolutions of 1848–49, 153–57, 160–62; and War of 1859, 190–93; and Garibaldi invasion scare, 203, 205; British threat to enter, during War of 1864, 240; and War of 1866, 252–56. *See also* individual cities and provinces on Adriatic coastline

Aegean Sea, 63, 81
Albert, Prince Consort of England, 110
Albini, Giuseppe, Sardinian vice admiral, 154–55, 157, 160
Albrecht, Archduke, 90, 109, 225, 248, 251, 252, 254, 257–58
Alessandria, 60
Alexander I, Tsar of Russia, 19, 137
Alexandria, 95
Algeria and Algiers, 8, 41, 79, 89, 109, 172
Allen, John, British steamship entrepreneur, 94–95
American Civil War (1861–65), 213–14, 218
Amiens, Treaty of (1802), 12
Ancona: during Napoleonic wars, 4, 9–10, 11, 12, 17, 34, 47; and campaign against Naples (1821), 58–59; during Italian Revolution of 1831–32, 78; occupied by French, 78–79, 81, 88; in Radetzky's strategic planning, 93; during Revolution of 1848–49, 157, 160; during War of 1859, 200; taken by Sardinians (1860), 203; and Austrian Lloyd, 204; Italian naval base at, 206; during War of 1866, 252–54, 256
Angioletti, Diego, Italian general and navy minister, 222, 244, 250–51

300 INDEX

Arman, Jean-Lucien, French shipbuilder, 223
Armee-Ober-Kommando, 181–82, 187
Armeni, Antonio, Captain, 58
Armored warships, 184, 209–10. *See also* entries for individual navies; names of individual vessels under warships
Arsenal. *See* Venice Arsenal
Austerlitz, battle of (1805), 17
Austria: budget and financial problems of, 4, 29, 42, 62, 68, 80, 90, 130, 135, 139, 185, 207–19 *passim*, 225, 244, 245, 246, 266–67. *See also* entries for specific nationalities, provinces, cities, leaders, wars, etc.
Austrian army: in Napoleonic wars, 5, 7, 10, 16, 17, 20, 21, 31–32, 34–35, 47; and Revolutions of 1820–21, 58, 60; in occupation of Naples and Sardinia-Piedmont, 61–62; and Revolutions of 1831–32, 78–79; strength of, in northern Italy, 139; and Revolution of 1848–49, 150, 155, 160–62; and Crimean War, 183, 185; and War of 1859, 191–92; during unification of Italy, 201–2; and War of 1864, 238, 239; and War of 1866, 251–52, 256–58; postwar condition of, 258, 266; attitude of leaders of, toward navy, 265–66. *See also* Albrecht; Charles; Degenfeld; Nugent; Radetzky; Karl Schwarzenberg; entries for other generals and officers
Austrian East India Company, 3, 49

Austrian Lloyd, Steam Navigation Company of the: founding of, 86, 94–95; and Austrian postal contract, 95–96; strategic significance of, 96, 112–13, 114–15n.16; financial problems of, 96–97; and British-East Indian mail contract, 97–99, 132–33; and D.D.S.G., 99–100, 132; borrows navy steamers, 132; prosperity of, 100–101; 132, 183; and Revolution of 1848–49, 161, 166; builds own arsenal, 182–83; and Crimean War, 183; and War of 1859, 190, 191, 194; and unification of Italy, 203–4; and War of 1866, 253; and opening of Suez Canal (1869), 266
Austrian navy: as "Trieste navy," 3–6; incorporation of Venetian navy, and resulting problems, 6–17 *passim*; as "Second Trieste navy," 18–21; disbanded, 21–22; returns to sea, 32–33; inherits Napoleonic Italian navy, 36–43; size fixed by imperial decree (1817), 43, 44, 66; *Marine-Kommando* administered under army *Generalkommando* at Padua, 67; *Marine-Kommando* becomes *Marine-Ober-Kommando* (1824), 67; packet-boat service of, 50–51, 60, 77, 96; formal separation of, from army, 185; and industrial espionage, 188; navy ministry created (1862); navy ministry dissolved, 244–45; *Marinesektion* created (1865), 245; overseas

missions of, after 1866, 267–68. *See also* entries for individual commanders, officers, issues, missions, wars, etc.
Austrian Netherlands, 1, 3. *See also* Belgium

B

Baldiserotto, Francesco, Ensign, 128, 138
Balkans, 4, 63, 243
Baltic Sea, 19, 184, 189, 240, 241, 260n.5
Bandiera, Baroness Anna Marsich, 121, 122
Bandiera, Baron Attilio, Lieutenant, 89; Mazzinian plotting of, 107–12; desertion of, 112, 118–20; on Corfu, 122; and expedition to Calabria, 124–25; execution of, 126; alleged homosexuality of, 146n.26
Bandiera, Baron Emilio, Ensign: Mazzinian plotting of, 108–12, 116n.32; desertion of, 112, 119–20; on Malta and Corfu, 121–22; and expedition to Calabria, 124–25; execution of, 126
Bandiera, Baron Francesco, Rear Admiral: and expedition against Morocco, 74–75; captures Carlo Zucchi in Adriatic, 78; and deportation cruises of Poles, 88–89; as commander in Levant, 94, 101–5, 108, 110; and his sons' revolutionary sympathies, 111; and Attilio's desertion, 120, 126, 128; and Moro's desertion, 123; relieved of Levant command, 124; retirement of, 128; death of, 146n.29
Barbary pirates, 7–9, 41, 65, 75–76
Barcelona, 203
Bavaria, 31, 32
Beauharnais, Prince Eugene de, viceroy of Italy, 31, 32, 34, 35
Beirut, 95, 103
Belcredi, Count Richard, minister-president, 245
Belgium, 1, 5, 97–98. *See also* Austrian Netherlands
Bellegarde, Count Heinrich, Field Marshal, *Hofkriegsrat* president, 32, 34, 35, 57–58, 60, 65, 66
Belvedere-Spinelli, 125
Beust, Count Friedrich Ferdinand von, foreign minister, 267
Bismarck, Count Otto von, Prussian minister-president and foreign minister, 237–38, 242–43, 247, 249, 253, 258, 266
Bixio, Nino, Italian revolutionary and politician, 205, 219, 221–22, 250–51
Black Sea, 19, 72, 73, 95, 99, 100, 132, 184
Boccheciampe, Pietro, Italian revolutionary, 125, 126
Bohemia, 31, 58, 248
Bologna, 78, 79, 200
Bonaparte, Louis Napoleon. *See* Napoleon III
Bonaparte, Napoleon. *See* Napoleon I
Bordeaux, 221, 223
Bordini, Andrea, Captain, 128, 137

Bosporus, 73, 104
Boulogne, 98
Bourguignon, Anton von, Vice Admiral, 151, 187, 197n.32
Braudel, Fernand, historian, 2
Brazil, 48–49, 197n.31, 207
Breisach, Wilhelm von, Captain, 217
Brindisi, 10, 79
Britain: and Napoleonic wars, 7, 12, 14, 17, 18, 19; subsidizes Austria, 15–16; and Austria's return to the sea, 33–34, 35, 37, 41, 42; gains protectorate over Ionian Islands, 42; seen as guarantor of Austrian maritime interests, 42–43, 51–52; and sale of surplus Austrian warships, 44, 62; and Barbary pirates, 48; dumps goods on Adriatic market, 52; Austria re-evaluates ties with, 61, 66, 81; and Greek War for Independence, 70; imports Croatian ship timber, 73; accepts Polish exiles, 89; in Radetzky's strategic planning, 93; and Near Eastern crises of 1839–40, 94, 101–2; steam engines from, to Austrian shipyards, 95, 190; and East Indian mail contract, 97–99, 132–33; voyage of Archduke Frederick to, 109–10; and Bandiera desertions, 120, 122, 144n.13; Austrian plans to buy steamships in, 130, 158, 170n.29; and Suez Canal project, 133; protests Austrian occupation of Ferrara (1846), 135; protests Austrian blockade of Venice (1849), 160; sells steamers to Sardinia, 173, 176; builds *Radetzky* for Austria, 175, 182; naval arms race with France, 175, 204; and unification of Italy, 204–5; in Ferdinand Max's calculations, 208, 212; and armored warships, 209–10; builds ironclad for Italy, 220–21; Austria seeks ex-Confederate ironclads in, 225; and War of 1864, 240; and China trade, 246; use of Suez Canal by, 266

British East India Company, 68

British navy: in Mediterranean, during Napoleonic wars, 8; at Trafalgar, 16; in Adriatic, 1809, 20–21; and 1813–14, 31–33; and 1815, 47–48; Austrian officers on assignment with, 49, 128, 158; during Greek War for Independence, 71–72; during Near Eastern crisis (1840), 103–5; and steam technology, 172–75; during Crimean War, 183–84; during Montenegrin crisis (1858), 189; during War of 1864, 241

British officers: in "Trieste navy," 3; proposals to hire, 69, 158; proposals to hire commander from among, 124, 158–59

Bruck, Carl Ludwig von: and the Austrian Lloyd, 95; and Trieste Revolution of 1848, 152; at Frankfurt Parliament, 154; as trade minister, 160; negotiates with Venetian rebels, 160–61; on naval committee of

1850, 163; as finance minister, 185, 207; suicide of, 207; mentioned, 265
Bua, Giorgio, Captain, later Venetian rear admiral, 89, 122, 124, 128, 154–56, 170n.30
Bubna, Count Ferdinand, *Feldmarschalleutnant*, 61
Bucchia, Achille, Lieutenant, later Venetian captain, 161–62
Bujacovich, Alexander, Rear Admiral, 120, 152–53, 164, 179, 187
Buol-Schauenstein, Count Carl Ferdinand, foreign minister, 183, 187, 189–90
Buratovich, Johann von, Rear Admiral, 137, 141, 150–51, 153, 165
Burger, Friedrich von, navy minister, 224, 244–45

C

Calabria, 125
Campoformio, Treaty of (1797), 1, 4–5, 10, 17, 23, 35, 42, 123
Canal, Giulio, Ensign, 120
Canton, 49
Capetown, 49
Carbonari, 40, 51, 106
Carinthia, 21, 178, 249
Carniola, 21, 178
Castellani, Venetian clan, 138
Castlereagh, Robert Stewart, Viscount, British foreign secretary, 62
Cattaro (Kotor), 8, 18, 19, 37, 46–47, 59, 72, 93

Cavedalis, Giambattista, Venetian colonel, 155
Cavour, Camillo Benso di, Sardinian-Italian foreign minister and minister-president, 187, 189–90, 201, 205, 208; and Sardinian-Italian navy, 191, 201–2, 203, 206, 209–10, 212; death of, 212, 219
Celje, 213
Charles, Archduke: appointed minister of war and navy, 10; personnel changes of, 11, 13; complains about piracy, 14; decline of influence of, 15, 16; during War of 1805, 16, 17; during War of 1809, 20; exclusion of, from affairs of state, 30, 90; and son Frederick's naval career, 91, 101, 105, 109, 115n.20; mentioned, 18, 43, 64, 265
Charles VI, Holy Roman Emperor, 2, 22
Charles Albert, King of Sardinia-Piedmont, 76, 130, 137
Charles Felix, King of Sardinia-Piedmont, 60, 75, 76
Charles Ferdinand, Archduke, 90, 109
Cherbourg, 241
China, 49–50, 246
Chinca, Domenico, Cadet, 108, 116n.33
Cialdini, Enrico, Italian general, 251, 254
Cisalpine Republic, 1
Cobenzl, Count Johann Ludwig, foreign minister, 15, 17
Commerce, seagoing. *See* Merchant marine; Austrian Lloyd

Confalonieri, Federico, Italian patriot, 89–90, 113–14n.5, 138
Confederate States, 218, 224–25. *See also* American Civil War
Conninck, August de, Major General: favored by British, 33; named *Marine-Kommandant*, 37; problems in organizing navy, 37–40, 44; not considered for command against Naples (1821), 57–58; retirement of, 67; mentioned, 107
Constantinople, 18, 102, 111, 119, 130, 141
Copenhagen, 159, 188, 189
Corfu (Kérkira), 50–51, 120–21, 124–25, 126, 157, 208. *See also* Ionian Islands
Cormons, armistice of (1866), 257–58
Correale, Baron Matteo, Neapolitan admiral, 59–60, 154
Corsairs. *See* Piracy; Privateering
Cosenza, 125–26
Court War Council. *See Hofkriegsrat*
Crenneville, Count Louis Folliot de, *Feldmarschalleutnant*, 11, 13, 16, 64–66, 92
Crete, 102
Crimean War, 179, 183–85
Croatia: during Napoleonic wars, 3, 17, 21, 31, 32; visited by Francis, 44; caravan trade across, 73; logging industry in, 73–74; Sava steamship line in, 115n.19; radicals in, and ties to Italy, 205; and *Reichsrat* boycott (1861), 212; leaders of, and naval contracts, 223; in Italian war plans and aims (1866), 254

Croatian Military Border, 3, 93, 139
Croatians: in "Trieste navy," 3; in War of 1809, 20; in French navy, 36; reentering Austrian service (1814), 36–37. *See also* South Slavs
Crotone, 125
Csorich, Baron Anton von, *Feldmarschalleutnant,* war minister, 175–76
Cugia, Efusio, Italian general and navy minister, 221–22
Custoza, battle of (1848), 155
Custoza, battle of (1866), 251–52, 258
Cuxhaven, 240–41

D

Dahlerup, Hans Birch von, Vice Admiral: accepts position of *Marine-Ober-Kommandant,* 159; and war against Venice, 160–62; problems of, while rebuilding navy, 162–66; resigns, 165; and technological change, 165–66, 175; and base at Pola, 186, 197n.30; returns to Austrian service, 215, 217, 227, 239
Dalmatia: during Napoleonic wars, 1, 6, 7, 8, 17, 18, 20, 21, 23, 32, 33; communications with, 41; visited by Francis, 44; during campaign against Naples (1821), 60; and Revolution of 1848–49, 141; and War of 1859, 190, 191, 192; and Garibaldi invasion scare, 203, 205,

239–40; Italian claims to, 203, 205, 220; represented in *Reichsrat,* 212; in Italian war plans and aims (1866), 249–50, 251, 253–54, 257, 259; naval recruiting and conscription in, 134, 156, 165, 178

Dandolo, Count Sylvestro, Vice Admiral: named provisional *Marine-Kommandant,* 16; in Franco-Italian service, 39, 54n.18; seniority of, after Napoleonic wars, 39; personality and self-image of, 40, 87, 106; and Neapolitan campaign of 1821, 58; as commander in Greek waters, 68, 70–72; tensions with Paulucci, 87–88, 113n.2; under Archduke Frederick, 124, 126; as provisional *Marine-Ober-Kommandant* after Frederick's death, 135, 136–37; death of, 137

Dante Alighieri, 6

Danube River, 4, 21, 72, 73, 254, 257

Danube Steam Navigation Company (D.D.S.G.), 95, 99–100, 115n.19, 132

Danzig, 189

Dardanelles, 73, 104

D.D.S.G. *See* Danube Steam Navigation Company

De Cosa, Raffaele, Neapolitan admiral, 154

Degenfeld, Count August von, *Feldzeugmeister:* on naval committee of 1850, 163; as war minister, 214–17, 232nn.32,36, 266

De Lesseps, Ferdinand, Suez Canal builder, 183

Denmark: negotiates to buy surplus warships, 41, 44; offers Dahlerup's services, 159; and War of 1864, 237–42

Depretis, Agostino, Italian navy minister, 251–52, 253–54

Des Geneys, Giorgio, Sardinian admiral, 75

Dietrich, Baron Joseph von, Trieste merchant, 65, 68

Dom Pedro I, Emperor of Brazil, 48

Dubrovnik. *See* Ragusa

Duperré, Guy, French vice admiral, 35

E

Eastern Mediterranean. *See* Levant

Egypt, 10, 97; sale of Austrian warships to, 45, 69, 70, 72–73; at war with Turkey (1832–41), 80, 94, 98, 101–4; Austrian attempt to buy warships from, 158, 161, 170n.29; visited by Ferdinand Max, 184–85. *See also* Levant

El Araisch (Larache), 75

Elbe River, 240

English Channel, 97

"English Company," early Venice-Trieste steamship line, 95, 96

Ericsson, John, Swedish-American naval engineer, 174, 223

Esperia, 108, 110–11, 116n.35, 119, 123, 126–28, 134, 161, 180

Eugene de Beauharnais. *See* Beauharnais, Prince Eugene de

F

Fabrizi, Nicolo, Italian revolutionary, 110, 118, 122
Far East, 3, 246–47. *See also* China; Japan
Fautz, Louis, Vice Admiral, 164–65, 210, 239, 245, 246
February Patent (1861), 209, 245
Ferdinand I, King of Naples, 47, 51, 59, 76
Ferdinand I, Emperor of Austria, 90, 105, 123, 124, 131, 140, 158
Ferdinand II, King of Naples, 76, 91, 130, 145n.22, 154
Ferdinand Max, Archduke, Vice Admiral: enters naval service, 165, 166–67; early career, 179–80; appointed *Marine-Ober-Kommandant*, 180; relationship with Francis Joseph, 181; during Crimean War, 183–85; and Suez Canal project, 184; and naval budget, 182, 185, 207–8, 209, 212–13, 218–19, 223, 225; and expansion of wooden fleet, 182, 185, 187–88; and training of personnel, 185–86, 238; administrative reforms of, 186; and base at Pola, 186; and *Novara* cruise, 186, 193; as governor-general of Lombardy-Venetia, 186–87; and War of 1859, 190–94; and cruise to Brazil, 207; and constitutional changes, 206–7, 214, 225–26; and armored warships, 209–12, 213–14, 223–24, 225; and creation of navy ministry, 214, 227; and naval commission of 1862, 217–18; proposes sale of ships to Confederacy, 224–25; and Greek throne, 226; becomes Emperor of Mexico, 226–28; plans for a Mexican navy, 261n.18; and deteriorating conditions in Mexico, 248; and Battle of Lissa, 258; execution of, 268n.3; character and personality of, 181, 227; mentioned, 265–67
Ferrara, 134
Ficquelmont, Count Karl Ludwig, *General der Kavallerie*, 135
Fiume. *See* Rijeka
Flanegan, Matthew, Captain, 39, 58
France: and Napoleonic wars, 1, 4–5, 7–10, 12, 14–15, 17–21, 29–34; in Austrian strategic planning, 66, 93; and Greek War for Independence, 70; invades Algeria (1830), 79, 172; accepts Italian exiles, 88; accepts Polish exiles, 89; and Near Eastern crisis of 1839–40, 94, 104; creates Mediterranean steamship line, 95, 97; and Suez Canal project, 133, 183; and British-East India mail contract, 98, 132–33; protests Austrian occupation of Ferrara (1846), 135; protests Austrian blockade of Venice (1849), 160; and unification of Italy, 201, 204; in Ferdinand Max's

calculations, 208, 212; and armored warships, 209–10; builds ironclads for Italy, 201, 209, 220–21; Austrian armor imports from, 211, 213; and September Convention (1864) with Italy, 222, 243; and Mexican Empire, 226; and China trade, 246; neutrality of, in War of 1866, 247–49, 256; use of Suez Canal by, 266; naval and colonial rivalry with Italy, 266. *See also* French navy; Napoleon I; Napoleon III

Francis I, Emperor of Austria: favors coastal defense, 4; appoints Charles minister for war and navy, 11; proclaims Austrian Empire, 14; and War of 1805, 17; and War of 1809, 20; and liquidation of navy, 22; and War of Liberation, 31, 34; indecision over size and role of navy, 41–44, 48; and Neapolitan Revolution of 1820, 51, 60; and Crenneville's inspection tour of 1822, 64, 66; creates *Marine-Ober-Kommando* under Paulucci, 67; and Greek independence, 72; approves deportation of Poles by sea, 88; death of, 90

Francis I, King of Naples, 76

Francis II, Holy Roman Emperor. *See* Francis I, Emperor of Austria

Francis II, King of Naples, 202, 205

Francis Joseph I, Emperor of Austria: accession to throne, 158; approves Navy Law of 1850, 163–64, 175; and Ferdinand Max's naval career, 165, 180; and neoabsolutism, 181; and Austrian Lloyd, 183; relations with Ferdinand Max as *Marine-Ober-Kommandant*, 181–82, 185, 186, 213, 226; relations with Ferdinand Max as governor-general of Lombardy-Venetia, 186–87; decrees separation of navy from army, 185; concedes revision of Navy Law, 188; and War of 1859, 192, 201; and unification of Italy, 202, 203; and constitutional reform, 206–7, 209, 225, 245; creates navy ministry, 214; and naval commission of 1862, 214–15, 217; and Tegetthoff, 242, 256, 258; abolishes navy ministry, 245; relations with Ferdinand Max as Emperor of Mexico, 245; and War of 1866, 256–58

Franco-Austrian War. *See* War of 1859

Franco-Italian navy. *See* Italy, Napoleonic kingdom of, navy

Frankfurt Parliament, 150, 154, 158, 166, 169n.16, 170n.29, 218

Frederick, Archduke, Vice Admiral: enters naval service, 90–91; and Near Eastern Crisis of 1839–40, 94, 101–5; voyage of, to England, 109–10; as brigadier of naval infantry, 110; named *Marine-Ober-Kommandant*, 124, 126; and Bandiera desertions, 127, 136; and naval academy, 129; and strength of fleet, 130–32; and base at Pola, 131, 135; on cruise to Naples, 131; reforms of, in Venice, 134; and recruiting in Dalmatia, 134; redeploys frigates, 135; death of, 135–36, 148n.45; mentioned, 167, 174, 175, 180–81, 265

Frederick the Great, King of Prussia, 208

Fremantle, Thomas, British rear admiral, 31, 32, 33–34, 37

French émigrés: in Austrian naval officer corps, 11–13, 22, 37

French navy: privateers of, in Adriatic, 9, 12, 14–15, 17; at Trafalgar, 16; and surrender of Venice (1814), 34–35; South Slavs serving in, 36; during Greek War for Independence, 70–71; operates in Adriatic (1832), 78–79; during Near Eastern crisis (1840), 102; gives moral support to Venetians (1848–49), 157; and steam technology, 172; during Crimean War, 183–84; and Austrian naval espionage, 188; and Montenegrin crisis (1858), 189; during War of 1859, 191, 192; off Gaeta (1860–61), 205. *See also* Italy, Napoleonic kingdom of, navy

Frimont, Count Johann Maria von, Field Marshal, 58–60, 78

G

Gaeta, 202, 205
Galicia, 30, 37, 88, 243
Galileo Galilei, 6
Gallo, Duke of, Habsburg plenipotentiary at Campoformio, 5
Garibaldi, Giuseppe, Italian revolutionary leader, 201–3, 205, 208, 221, 249, 251, 254
Gastein, Convention of (1865), 243
Gelcich, Tommaso, Austrian Lloyd captain, 120
Geneva, 211, 213
Genoa, 65, 110; shipyards of, 191, 221; Sardinian naval academy in, 191
German. *See* Language of command, German
German navy of 1848–1852, 150, 158, 166, 175–76, 178, 179, 218, 238
Germans, ethnic: in Austrian naval officer corps, 13, 22, 37–38, 129, 151, 162, 195n.10, 242, 268n.2
Ghega, Karl Anton von, Austrian railroad builder, 107
Gibraltar, 109, 193
Gilbert, John, American engineer, 186
Goro, 32
Gospić, battle of (1809), 20
Graziani, Leone, Captain, later Venetian rear admiral, 120–21, 137, 140–41, 155, 162, 170n.30
Great Britain. *See* Britain
Greece: War for Independence, 63, 70–73; visited by Archduke Frederick, 91, 102; and Bandiera desertions, 120; crisis

of 1862–63 in, 223, 226, 239.
  See also Otto, King of Greece;
  Piraeus
Grünne, Count Carl,
  Feldmarshalleutnant, 182, 185
Gyulai, Count Franz,
  Feldzeugmeister, 141, 150–51,
  153, 165, 187, 191, 192

H

Haifa, 103
Hamburg, 189, 239, 240
Hampton Roads, battle of (1862),
  218, 219, 220
Hardegg, Count Ignaz von,
  Hofkriegsrat president: 97, 121,
  123–24, 126–27, 130, 134, 137
Hargood, William, British commodore, 20–21, 33
Helgoland, battle of (1864), 240–41, 260n.7
Henkel von Donnersmark
  ironworks, 211
Hiller, Baron Johann,
  Feldmarschalleutnant, 31, 32
Hofkammer ("Court Chamber" or
  treasury), 99. See also Stadion,
  Johann Philipp; Kübeck, Carl
  Friedrich von
Hofkriegsrat (Court War Council):
  11, 32, 57, 58; and Maria
  Theresa's navy, 3; and "Trieste
  navy," 4; fires L'Espine, 37;
  and size of navy after 1814,
  42–43; and ship sales, 45, 49;
  and packet-boat service, 50–51,
  60; drops emergency plans for
  naval expansion (1821), 61;
  and Crenneville mission
  (1822), 64–66; and Paulucci,
  67; and Near Eastern crisis
  (1840), 102–3; and Bandiera
  brothers (1844), 121, 126, 130;
  and Frederick's plan to buy
  British steamer, 130. See also
  Bellegarde; Hardegg
Holland, 44, 159
Holy Roman Empire, 3, 14
Hoste, William, British captain, 21
Hungary: grain trade of, 73; during Revolution of 1848–49,
  161, 162; subsequent revolutionary schemes with Italy, 203,
  205, 208, 243; and constitutional reform, 209, 212, 245;
  and War of 1866, 249; and
  Habsburg navy, after 1867,
  267, 268n.2

I

Illyrian provinces, 21, 30, 31
India, 98, 133
Inner Austria, 31, 210. See also
  Carinthia, Carniola, Styria
Innsbruck, 249
Inzaghy, Count Carlo d', governor
  of Venice, 51
Ionian Islands: during Napoleonic
  wars, 5, 9, 10, 15, 17, 19; postwar British protectorate over,
  42
Ironclads. See Armored warships
Isonzo River, 16, 254, 256, 257
Istria: coveted by Austria, 1; under
  Napoleonic kingdom of Italy,
  17; under Illyrian Provinces,

21; naval recruiting in, 178; and Garibaldi invasion scare, 203, 205; Italian claims to, 203, 205, 220; represented in *Reichsrat*, 212, 231n.26; in Italian war plans and aims (1866), 251, 253, 254, 257, 259; Italian annexation of (1918), 268

Italian. *See* Language of command, Italian

Italian navy: Cavour lays groundwork for, 201–2; official creation of (1861), 205–6; fear of, exploited by Ferdinand Max, 208; has ironclads built in foreign yards, 209, 210, 212–13, 220–21, 224; strength of, vis-à-vis Austrian navy, 213, 216, 217; general expansion of, 219–22; budget of, 222, 233–34n.48, 244; during Greek crisis of 1862–63, 239; during War of 1866, 252–56; postwar condition of, 267. *See also* Sardinian navy

Italians: in "Trieste navy," 3; in Austrian naval officer corps, pre-1848, 13, 22, 38, 40, 66, 105–13 *passim*, 127–29, 141; and post-1848, 151, 162, 178–79, 195n.14, 267; among common sailors, 36, 66, 152–53, 162, 179; and Bandiera desertions, 120–24; living in Trieste, 132, 151–52; in Austrian army, 139, 140. *See also* Venetians

Italy, kingdom of: formation proclaimed (1861), 205; fears Austro-Spanish alliance, 219–20; September Convention (1864) with France, 222, 243; concludes alliance with Prussia (1866), 247; rejects Austrian offer of Venetia, 248; war plans and aims of, 249–59 *passim;* army of, during War of 1866, 251–52, 254, 256–58; naval and colonial rivalry with France, 266; and Triple Alliance (1882), 267; annexes Trieste, Istria, and Rijeka (1918), 268. *See also* Sardinia-Piedmont; individual states and provinces

Italy, Napoleonic kingdom of, 17, 31, 34–35; navy of, 18, 29, 31, 34–35, 40, 50

J

Japan, 246
John, Archduke, 20, 30
Joseph II, Holy Roman Emperor, 3–4
Julian Alps, 31, 249, 254, 257
Jutland, 241

K

K.k. Eisengusswerk, 243
Karlskrona, 189
Karolyi, Count Ladislaus, Captain, 128, 158–59, 161, 165, 171n.36
Klapka, Györgi, Hungarian revolutionary, 205, 208
Kolowrat, Count Franz Anton, interior minister, 80, 86, 90, 96, 100

Königgrätz, battle of (1866), 253, 254, 258, 266
Kossuth, Louis, Hungarian revolutionary leader, 161, 196n.17, 205, 249
Koszta, Martin, Hungarian revolutionary, 196n.17
Kotor. *See* Cattaro
Kraljevica. *See* Porto Ré
Krupp guns, for Austrian ironclads, 243, 249, 252
Kübeck, Baron Adolf, army captain, 127–28
Kübeck, Baron Carl Friedrich, *Hofkammer* president, 99–100, 130, 133, 265
Kudriaffsky, Ludwig, Captain, 75, 129, 153–54, 157, 169n.16, 178
Küstenland, province, 4, 78–79, 91, 152. *See also* Istria

L

Laibach. *See* Ljubljana
Lake Constance, 6
Lake Garda, 34
La Marmora, Alfonso, Italian general and politician, 222, 243–44, 247–48, 249–51, 253
Language of command, German: becomes official language of naval correspondence, 38; not used under Paulucci, 107; use decreed by Francis Joseph, 164; enforced, 178–79, 195n.14; new service regulations in, 165
Language of command, Italian: in "Trieste navy," 4; in Austrian navy, 13, 38, 106, 107
Larache. *See* El Araisch
Larisch, Count Johann von, finance minister, 245, 246, 249
Latour, Count Theodor Baillet de, war minister, 156–57
Lattermann, Baron Christian, *Feldmarschalleutnant*, 33, 36
Laxenburg Manifesto (1859), 206
Lebanon, 102–4, 202
Lebzeltern, Wilhelm, Colonel, tutor of Archduke Frederick, 102, 103, 127, 145n.25
Legione Italica, 110–11
Leipzig, battle of (1813), 32
Leoben, Armistice of (1797), 4
Leopold, Archduke, *Marine Truppen- und Flotteninspektor*, 245–46, 248
Leopold II, Holy Roman Emperor, 4
Leopoldine, Archduchess, Empress of Brazil, 48
Lepanto, battle of (1571), 106
L'Espine, Chevalier Joseph, *Feldmarschalleutnant:* and piracy, 9; and "Flag Affair" at Ancona, 9; named *Marine-Kommandant*, 11; expands navy, 12; and budget cuts, 13; favors French émigrés, 13; named head of Marine Bureau, 16; and evacuation of Venice in 1805, 17; commands "Second Trieste Navy," 18–21; receives army commission, 22; returns to littoral as provisional *Marine-Kommandant*, 32; rebuilds navy, 33, 35, 36; poor relations of,

with British, 21, 33–34; reassignment to army, 37; mentioned, 38, 58, 136
Levant, 5, 63, 65, 90, 94, 95, 105, 108, 110–11, 132, 183–84, 239. *See also* Egypt; Greece; Lebanon; Ottoman Empire; Syria
Linz, 99
Lisbon, 19, 109, 165
Lissa (Vis): as British base during Napoleonic wars, 48; blockaded by Neapolitans (1821), 59–60; in Radetzky's strategic planning, 93; in Italian war plans and aims, 254; battle of (1866), 255–56, 258–59, 263nn.39,41, 266
Livorno, 184, 221
Ljubljana (Laibach): Congress of (1821), 57–58, 60; Italians interned in (1848), 156
Ljungstedt, August, naval engineer, 188
Lloyd. *See* Austrian Lloyd
Loire Valley, ironworks of, 211, 213–14, 230–31n.24
Lombardy: ceded to Cisalpine Republic (1797), 1; retaken by Austrians (1814), 34–35; and annexed, 42; shifts Austrian focus away from Adriatic, 51; strength of army in, 139; and War of 1859, 192; ceded to Sardinia-Piedmont, 201; and War of 1866, 251. *See also* Milan
Lombardy-Venetia, 92; under Ferdinand Max, 186–87. *See also* Lombardy; Venetia
London Protocols (1829, 1830), 72–73

London, Treaty of (1827), 70
London, Treaty of (1840), 102–3, 104
Loosey, Carl, Austrian consul in New York, 223
Louis Philippe, King of France, 78, 88
Ludwig, Archduke, 90
Lunéville, Treaty of (1801), 10, 12
Lussin (Lošinj), 191

M

Mack von Leiberich, Baron Karl, *Feldmarschalleutnant*, 15, 16
Maffei, Massimiliano, Austrian Lloyd captain, 141
Magenta, battle of (1859), 192
Malta, 8, 21, 110, 121, 122, 123
Manin, Daniele, Venetian revolutionary leader, 133, 138–40, 155, 160, 161–62
Mantua, 34
Marengo, battle of (1800), 10
Maria Theresa, Queen, 2
Maria Theresa, Archduchess, Queen of Naples, 91, 131
Mariani, Paolo, gunnery mate, 120, 124–25, 126, 145n.22
Mariazell, 243
Marie Louise, Archduchess, Empress of France, 30
Marine-Ober-Kommando. See entries for individual commanders
Marinovich, Johann, Captain: as tutor and aide to Archduke Frederick, 101–2, 115n.20, 124, 126, 127, 135, 180; unpopularity of, 137, 138; murder of, 140

Maroncelli, Pietro, Italian nationalist, 108, 116n.31
Marseilles, 88, 98, 203, 211
Marsich, Giuseppe, Captain, 128
Martini, Anton von, *Feldmarschalleutnant* and Vice Admiral: background of, 137; appointed *Marine-Ober-Kommandant,* 137–38, 148n.50; and Venetian Revolution of 1848, 140–41; as prisoner of rebels, 141, 150, 156; resumes command of navy, 156–58; as ambassador to Naples, 159, 165, 185
Matticola, Luigi, Captain, 128, 129, 138
Maximilian, Emperor of Mexico. *See* Ferdinand Max, Archduke
Mazzini, Giuseppe, Italian revolutionary, 105, 107–12, 118, 123, 134, 141
Mazzuchelli, Ippolito, Ensign, 110, 111, 146n.28
Meaussé, Chevalier Jean Charles de, Habsburg navy commander, 3
Mediterranean Sea: Italian as trading language of, 4; during Napoleonic wars, 8, 19; and role of postwar Austrian navy, 42–43; Austrian respect for British strength in, 66; early steamship traffic in, 95; Austrian trade in western basin of, 203–4. *See also* Austrian Lloyd; Levant; individual countries and cities on Mediterranean coastline
Mehemet Ali, Pasha of Egypt, 69, 70, 80, 94, 102–4

Menabrea, Luigi, Italian general and politician, 212–13, 219–21
Mensdorff-Pouilly, Count Alexander, *General der Kavallerie* and foreign minister, 242–43, 245, 247–48, 249
Merchant marine, Austrian: attacks against, and defense of, 7, 12, 13, 18, 19, 23, 41–42, 70–71, 79; rebuilding and expansion of, 46, 74, 265–68 *passim,* 269n.5. *See also* Austrian Lloyd
Merchant marine, Venetian, 1–3
Merchant ships:
Carolina, Austrian steamer, 95;
Ferdinando I, Neapolitan steamer, 95;
Imperatore, Austrian (Lloyd) steamer, 120;
Veloce, Austrian brig, 74–75.
See also Warships
Merton, Louis, English arms dealer, 224–25
Metternich, Count (later Prince) Clemens von, foreign minister, chancellor: negotiates for outlet to Adriatic after 1809, 30; and armed mediation of 1813, 29; and War of Liberation, 31; and postwar schemes to sell warships, 41, 44–46, 62, 65; and commercial life of Venice, 50; and Neapolitan Revolution of 1820, 51, 57, 59; and Greek War for Independence, 63, 65, 69–71; and Moroccan campaign (1828–30), 74; and Italian revolutions of 1831–32, 78, 79; and Treaty of Münchengrätz (1833), 80–81; and Polish exiles, 88–89; and succession of Ferdi-

nand, 90; and D.D.S.G., 95; and Austrian Lloyd, 96–98, 100; and Near Eastern Crisis of 1839–40, 93–94, 101, 104; and Bandiera brothers, 119, 121, 123, 125; and steam-powered warships, 130; and base at Pola, 131; and Suez Canal project, 133; and pre-1848 precautions, 135; evolving views of, on Austrian sea power, 42, 48, 51–52, 61, 86, 112, 265
Mexico, 45, 226–27, 245, 248
Micciarelli, Tito Vespasiano, Italian revolutionary, 111, 118–19
Michelangelo Buonarroti, 173
Michieli, Count Carlo, Captain, 180, 196n.20
Milan, 35, 135, 138, 150, 152, 155, 187, 192
Mincio River, 251
Minghetti, Marco, Italian minister-president, 221–22
Miramar, 212, 244; Convention of (1864), 226
Modena, 78, 200, 201
Mogniat de Pouilly, Count Charles, Lieutenant: expedition against Morocco, 14, 75
Moltke, Helmut von, Prussian general and chief of staff, 250, 253
Montenegro, 179, 189, 205
Morari, Antonio, Captain, 122, 128
Moravia, 88
Möring, Karl, Major General: as army engineer, 174, 195n.3; opposes ironclad fleet, 215–17; and Wüllerstorf, 241–42; negotiates armistice with Italy (1866), 257–58

Moro, Domenico, Ensign: decorated for bravery in 1840, 108; as messenger to Mazzini, 109–10; desertion of, 122–23; on expedition to Calabria, 124–25; execution of, 126
Morocco, 14, 74–75, 76, 77, 81, 88
Münchengrätz, Treaty of (1833), 80, 104
Murat, Joachim, King of Naples, 32, 34, 47

N

Nabresina (Aurisina), 253
Nádasdy, Count Mihaly, finance minister, 68
Nantes, 221
Naples, kingdom of: under Habsburg rule, 2, 22; conquered by Bourbons, 2; during Napoleonic wars, 8, 10, 17, 32, 34, 47; Bourbon restoration in, 47; Revolution of 1820 in, 45, 51, 57–60, 61–62, 67; visited by Archduke Frederick, 91, 131; state-owned steamship company of, 96, 97, 115n.17; and Bandiera brothers, 111, 125–26; Revolution of 1848 in, 152–53; Austrian attempt to buy warships from, 161; Ferdinand Max's report on, 184–85; and War of 1859, 200; collapse of (1860), 202, 205. *See also* Neapolitan navy
Napoleon I, Emperor of the French: conquers Venetian Republic, 1, 4–5; and subsequent

warfare, 9, 17, 18–19, 20, 21, 29, 32; and the Illyrian provinces, 30; defeat of, 34; and the Hundred Days, 47
Napoleon III, Emperor of the French: and Treaty of Plombières, 189; and War of 1859, 192; and unification of Italy, 201, 204, bans armor exports, 211; and Ferdinand Max's accession to Mexican throne, 226; before and during War of 1866, 247, 249, 253, 258
Napoleonic kingdom of Italy. *See* Italy, Napoleonic kingdom of
Nationality problem. *See* entries to specific nationalities
Naval academy: opened in Venice (1802), 13; reopened (1814), 38; Italian as language of instruction, 13, 38, 107; curriculum of, 106–7, 115n.29, 129; Mazzinian influences in, 107–8, 111; reorganization and purge of (1844), 128–29; reopened in Trieste (1852), 177; German as language of instruction, 177; moved to Rijeka (1855), 186; closed in favor of *Venus* school ship, 238; reopened in Rijeka (1866), 246
Navale Adriatico. *See* Stabilimento Navale Adriatico
Navarino Bay, battle of (1827), 70–71, 72
Navy Law of 1850, 163–64, 171n.34, 175, 177; navy exceeds spending limits of, 185, 188, 207; revision of (1858), 188; and naval commission of 1862, 216–17
Neapolitan navy: under Habsburg control, 2; after Revolution of 1820, 59–60; against Barbary pirates, 75–76; during Greek War for Independence, 84n.43; against Austria in 1848, 153–54; and technological developments, 130, 173, 176; mutiny and collapse of (1860), 202
Near East. *See* Levant
New York, 88, 89, 90, 108, 172; construction of Italian ironclads in, 219, 223–24
Nicolotti, Venetian clan, 138
Nikolsburg, Peace of (1866), 257
North Sea, 189, 239–40, 243
Novara, battle of (1821), 61
Novara, battle of (1849), 160
Nugent, Count Laval, Field Marshal, 31, 32, 53n.7, 91–92, 266

O

October Diploma (1860), 209
Odessa, 18, 73
Orient. *See* China; Far East; Japan
Otranto, 8, 10, 125
Otto, Prince of Bavaria, King of Greece, 79, 102, 226, 239
Ottoman Empire, 2; during Napoleonic wars, 8, 19; and Greek War for Independence, 63, 69, 70–73; at war with Egypt (1832–41), 80, 94, 98, 101–4; Austrian attempt to buy warships from, 158, 161; and Mon-

tenegro, 179, 189; navy, and strength of, 65, 94, 102, 189. *See also* Russo-Turkish wars; Crimean War

P

Padua, 67
Palffy, Count Alois, governor of Venice, 139–41
Palmerston, Henry John Temple, Viscount, British foreign secretary and prime minister, 101, 103, 204–5, 240
Panfilli shipyard, Trieste, 94, 100, 170n.32, 182, 196n.23
Papal legations, 78, 80. *See also* Romagna
Papal State: offered surplus Austrian warships, 44; invaded by Austria (1821), 60; Revolution of 1831–32 in, 77–78, 88; and Bandiera brothers, 110, Revolution of 1848–49 in, 160; and War of 1859, 200–201; and unification of Italy (1860), 203. *See also* Roman Republic; Rome and Roman Question
Parma, 200, 201
Pasqualigo, Nicolo, Captain: commander in Adriatic, 9, 47; as provisional second-in-command of navy, 16; seniority of, after Napoleonic wars, 39–40; commands expedition to Brazil, 49, 89; death of, 57
Paul, Tsar of Russia, 9
Paulucci delle Roncole, Marquis Amilcare, Vice Admiral: background of, 57–58, 81n.2; as special inspector of navy, 58, 64; during Neapolitan Revolution, 58–61; returns to *Hofkriegsrat*, 66–67; named *Marine-Ober-Kommandant*, 67; and ship sales, 68; and expansion of fleet, 68–69, 76–77, 81; attitude of, regarding discipline and regulations, 69–70, 107; and budget cuts, 86; relationship with Dandolo, 87–88, 113n.2; attitude toward technological change, 91, 93, 113, 172; opposes base at Pola, 92, 131; and Austrian Lloyd, 96; and Bandiera brothers, 120–24; retirement of, 126; death of, 149n.56; mentioned, 157
Paulucci delle Roncole, Antonio, Major, 116n.30, 139–40, 144n.16, 162
Pepe, Guglielmo, Neapolitan general, 60
Perry, Matthew, American commodore, 246
Persano, Count Carlo Pellion de, Sardinian-Italian admiral: background of, 233n.42; during unification of Italy, 202, 203, 205; as navy minister, 219–21; and War of 1866, 250, 252–56; postwar trial of, 264n.43
Pesaro, 93
Pest, 16, 95
Petitti, Agostino, Italian general, 258
Petz, Anton von, Rear Admiral, 255
Piracy, 4. *See also* Barbary pirates; Privateering
Piraeus, 130, 132, 141

Pirano (Piran), 78, 92
Pius IX, Pope, 131, 133, 134
Plener, Ignaz von, finance minister, 207–8, 209, 212, 213, 214–15, 217, 232n.30, 244, 245, 246
Plombières, Treaty of (1858), 189, 192
Po River, 33, 34, 35, 47, 203, 251
Pöck, Friedrich von, Rear Admiral, 246, 248
Pola: as potential site for naval base, 92; favored by Radetzky, 92; opposed by Paulucci, 92, 131; favored by Metternich, 131; development and use of, under Frederick, 131, 135; during Revolution of 1848–49, 140–41, 150–53, 156; and Navy Law of 1850, 163–64; site opposed by Dahlerup, 186, 197n.30; and War of 1859, 190, 191, 193; and War of 1864, 239, 241; and War of 1866, 248, 252, 254, 256
Pola Arsenal: construction of, 186; shipbuilding and renovations in, 188, 214
Polish refugees: deportation of, aboard Austrian warships, 88–89
Pöltl, Seraphim von, Captain, 49–50
Porcia, Prince Alphons, governor of Küstenland, 78–79
Porte. *See* Ottoman Empire
Porto Ré (Kraljevica), 3, 32, 91
Portugal: offered surplus Austrian warships, 44, 45; strength of navy, 48, 65
Pressburg, Treaty of (1805), 17, 19, 29, 39

Privateering, in Adriatic: by French during Napoleonic wars, 9, 12, 14–15, 17; by British during Napoleonic wars, 48
Prokesch von Osten, Count Anton, 67–68
Prussia: in Napoleonic wars, 29; and Treaty of Münchengrätz (1833), 80; and Near Eastern crisis of 1839–40, 102; and Schleswig-Holstein war of 1848, 159; and War of 1859, 190, 192; and War of 1864, 237–38, 239, 242–43; in Italian strategic considerations, 244, 247; alliance with Italy (1866), 247; encourages Italian ambitions in Adriatic, 247, 251, 253; negotiates with Hungarian revolutionaries, 249; blocks Krupp delivery to Austrian navy, 249; army of, in War of 1866, 253–54; urges Italy to accept armistice, 256
Prussian navy: during War of 1864, 238, 240; and proposal to build Prussian ironclads in Trieste, 243; ridiculed by Tegetthoff, 260n.6
Pula. *See* Pola
Putzer, Johann von, ironworks owner and *Reichsrat* member, 213, 224–25, 232n.30

Q

Quadrilateral fortresses, 192
Querini, Andrea, commander of Habsburg navy, 6, 7, 11, 12

R

Radetzky, Count Joseph, Field Marshal: and Italian campaign of 1832, 78, 79; opinion of, on Austrian sea power, 92–93; and Austrian Lloyd, 96; and War Scare of 1840, 102; and Bandiera brothers, 118–19, 121; and occupation of Ferrara, 134; receives reinforcements, 135, 139; and Martini, 137; concerns of, for loyalty of navy, 138–39; and Revolutions of 1848–49, 139, 150, 155, 160; and rebuilding of navy, 158–59, 164, 181; retirement of, 186–87; mentioned, 251, 266

Ragusa (Dubrovnik), 34, 59

Rainer, Archduke, viceroy of Lombardy-Venetia, 122, 246

Rainer, Archduke, minister-president, 235n.59

Rattazzi, Urbano, Italian minister-president, 220–21

Ravenna, 93

Rechberg, Count Johann von, foreign minister, 201, 205, 211, 213, 214, 216–18, 237–38, 240, 242, 265

Reich. See Holy Roman Empire

Reichsrat: initial expansion of (1860), 206, 208; under the October Diploma (1860), 209; under the February Patent (1861), 209; boycotts of, by various nationalities, 212, 231n.26, 244; and navy budget of 1862, 211, 212, 214, 218–19; and subsequent navy budgets, 218, 225, 245; dissolved (1865), 245; under dual monarchy, after 1867, 267

Ressel, Josef, inventor, 174, 194n.2

Revolution of 1848–49, 138–41, 150–62

Rhine River, 1, 11–12

Ricasoli, Bettino, Italian minister-president, 220, 251–52, 253–54, 256–57, 259

Ricciotti, Nicola, Italian revolutionary, 124, 126, 145n.20

Rieti, battle of (1821), 60

Rijeka (Fiume): during Napoleonic wars, 4, 19–21, 30–33; and campaign against Naples (1821), 59; trade of, 23, 33, 73–74; and naval contracts, 223, 267; in Italian war plans and aims (1866), 251; Italian annexation of (1918), 268. *See also* Naval academy; Stabilimento Tecnico Fiume

Rimini, 17, 93

Rio do Janeiro, 48, 49

Romagna, 88, 131, 201, 251. *See also* Papal legations; Papal State

Romako, Joseph, naval engineer, 210, 225

Roman Republic (1848–49), 160

Rome and Roman Question, 221, 222, 244. *See also* Papal State

Roon, Albrecht von, Prussian general, war and navy minister, 243

Rothschild, House of, 62, 207

Rothschild, Solomon, financier, 65, 68, 95, 96–97

Russell, Lord John, British foreign secretary, 240

Russia: during Napoleonic wars, 9, 10, 15, 17, 18–19, 29–30; grain trade of, 24n.7, 52, 73; and Greek War for Independence, 70; and Treaty of Münchengrätz (1833), 80; and Polish exiles in Austria, 88; and D.D.S.G., 100; and Near Eastern crisis of 1839–40, 102, 104; crushes Hungarian revolution (1849), 161; British-built steamers of, sought by Austria, 170n.29; and Crimean War, 179, 183–84; and Montenegrin crisis (1858), 189

Russian navy: in Mediterranean (1799–1800), 8–10; with British at Naples (1805), 17; interned at Lisbon and Trieste (1807), 19, 20, 27–28n.45; during Greek War for Independence, 70–71

Russo-Turkish wars: of 1787–92, 4; of 1806–12, 19; of 1828–29, 72. *See also* Crimean War

S

St. Petersburg, 165
Salonika (Thessaloniki), 95
Sandfort, Eugène, naval engineer, 188, 210
San Marco wharves. *See* Stabilimento Navale Adriatico
San Rocco wharves. *See* Stabilimento Tecnico Triestino
Santa Lucia, battle of (1848), 155
Sardinian navy: offered surplus Austrian warships, 44; during Revolution of 1821, 60; against Barbary pirates, 75–76; during Greek War for Independence, 84n.43; against Austria in 1848–49, 154–55, 157, 160, 166; and technological developments, 130, 173, 176; during Crimean War, 184; during War of 1859, 190–91; academy at Genoa, 191; during unification of Italy (1860–61), 202, 203, 205. *See also* Italian navy

Sardinia-Piedmont: Revolution of 1821 in, 60–61; Austrian occupation of, 61; protests Austrian occupation of Ferrara (1846), 134–35; army of, in Revolution of 1848–49, 150, 155, 160; and Crimean War, 184; and War of 1859, 189–93, 200; annexes central Italian duchies, 201; and Garibaldi's conquests (1860), 202; invades Papal State, 203. *See also* Italy, kingdom of

Sava River, 21, 73, 115n.19
Saxony, 32
Scandinavians, in Austrian naval officer corps, 162, 165
Scheffer, Karl, naval engineer, 162, 188
Schiarino Rizzino, armistice of (1814), 34–35
Schleswig-Holstein question: in 1848–49, 159; in 1863–64, 237–38, 242–43. *See also* War of 1864
Schmerling, Anton von, minister of state, 209, 213, 214, 245, 265

Schönbrunn, Treaty of (1809), 21–22, 29
Schwarzenberg, Prince Felix zu: as ambassador to Naples, 131, 152–53; as minister-president and foreign minister, 157–58; and Dahlerup, 160; and Navy Law of 1850, 164; mentioned, 265
Schwarzenberg, Prince Karl zu, Field Marshal, 31, 43, 137, 266
Scopinich, Johann, Rear Admiral, 192
Screw propeller, 173–75
Scuola dei cadetti di marina. See Naval academy
Sedlnitzky, Count Joseph, police director, 125
Senj, 17, 20, 73
September Convention (1864), 222, 243
Septinsular Republic. *See* Ionian Islands
Serbia, 30, 205
Shipbuilding: development of paddle steamer, 172–73; and screw propeller, 173–75; and armor plating, 184, 209–10. *See also* Panfilli shipyard, Trieste; Pola Arsenal; Stabilimento Navale Adriatico; Stabilimento Tecnico Fiume; Stabilimento Tecnico Triestino; Venice Arsenal
Sicily, 2, 58–59, 62, 111, 202. *See also* Naples, kingdom of
Sidon, 103, 108, 109
Singapore, 49
Skagerrak, 241
Slavonia, 73

Slovenes: in Austrian army, 139; in Austrian navy, 178. *See also* South Slavs
Smith, Francis, English naval engineer, 174
Smyrna (Izmir), 63, 72, 95, 103, 108, 109, 111, 118, 120, 123, 124, 127, 165
Solferino, battle of (1859), 192
Sourdeau, Baron August von, Rear Admiral, 157–58, 159, 165
South America, 88. *See also* Brazil
South Slavs: in Austrian naval officer corps, 13, 22, 38, 129, 151, 178–79, 195n.14. *See also* Croatians
South Tyrol, 247, 251, 257, 259
Spain: during Napoleonic wars, 20; and sale of surplus Austrian warships, 44, 45, 68; Revolution of 1820 in, 45; and Italian fear of Austro-Spanish alliance, 219–20; recognizes kingdom of Italy, 222
Spanish navy, 16, 23n.2, 65, 221
Spanish Succession, War of (1701–14), 2
Spannochi, Baron Lelio, Tuscan seaman, 11
Spezzia, 71
Stabilimento Navale Adriatico, 162–63, 170n.32, 182, 210–11, 230n.23, 243. *See also* Tonello
Stabilimento Tecnico Fiume, 210, 214, 223, 230n.22. *See also* Whitehead
Stabilimento Tecnico Triestino, 210, 214, 230n.22. *See also* Strudthoff
Stadion, Count Franz, governor of Trieste, 99–100, 133

Stadion, Count Johann Philipp: as foreign minister, 18, 20; as finance minister, 41, 42–43, 48, 61, 62; death of, 68; mentioned, 207, 265

Staatskanzlei (State Chancellery), 68. *See also* Metternich

Steamships, 172–75. *See also* Austrian Lloyd; entries for individual navies; names of individual vessels under Merchant ships and Warships

Sterneck, Maximilian von, Captain, 138, 248, 252

Stopford, Robert, British admiral, 103–5, 109

Straits Convention (1841), 104

Strudthoff, Wilhelm, owner of Stabilimento Tecnico Triestino, 210, 230n.22

Stürmer, Count Bartholomäus von, ambassador to Turkey, 119, 121

Styria and Styrians, 139, 140, 178, 211, 213, 224, 243, 249

Südbahn (Vienna-Trieste railway), 183, 210, 257

Suez Canal: project for, 133, 183, 246; opening of (1869), 266

Sweden, 189

Sylvester Patent (1851), 181

Syria, 102–4

T

Tangier, 89

Taranto, 250, 253

Tegetthoff, Baron Wilhelm von, Vice Admiral: and War of 1859, 202; on duty in Levant, 202, 223, 226, 239; joins ironclad debate against Möring, 232n.35; and War of 1864, 239–42; appointed squadron commander, 242; and Archduke Leopold, 246; and projected Far Eastern cruise, 247, 248; appointed fleet commander, 248; prepares for War of 1866, 248–49, 252; and sortie to Ancona, 252–53; at Battle of Lissa, 255–56; postwar disillusionment of, 258, 266–67; appointed *Marine-Kommandant*, 267, 268n.3

Thiers, Adolphe, French prime minister, 102, 104

Thugut, Baron Franz Amadeus, Habsburg minister, 5–10, 23, 265

Tilsit, Treaty of (1807), 19

Tirpitz, Alfred von, German admiral, 208

Tommaseo, Niccolò, Venetian revolutionary leader, 133, 138–40, 155, 162

Tonello, Giuseppe, owner of Stabilimento Navale Adriatico, 211, 230n.23

Toulon, 65, 89, 184; construction of Italian ironclads in, 201, 209, 221

Trafalgar, battle of (1805), 16

Trebizond, 132

Trieste: acquired by Austria (1382), 2; granted free port status, 2; and piracy, 8, 41; trade of, 2–3, 4, 12, 18, 19, 23, 26n.25, 50, 74, 96, 97, 132, 183, 196n.24,

204, 266, 268n.1; defense of, 4, 8, 19, 92, 93, 252; under French occupation (1805, 1809–13), 4, 20–21, 30, 33; Russian warships in (1807–10), 19, 20, 27–28n.45; reacquired by Austria (1813–14), 32–33, 35; and campaign against Naples (1821), 59; and Italian revolutions of 1831–32, 78; and early steamship traffic, 94–95; loyalty of Italians living in, 132; rail connections of, to interior, 132–33, 183; and Suez Canal project, 133, 183; during Revolution of 1848–49, 150–56; and Navy Law of 1850, 163–64, 166; and War of 1859, 192; and unification of Italy, 204; represented in *Reichsrat*, 212; plan to build Confederate ironclads in, 224–25; and Italian irredentists, 244; in Italian war plans and aims (1866), 250–54, 257, 259; Italian annexation of (1918), 268. *See also* Austrian Lloyd; Stabilimento Tecnico Triestino; Stabilimento Navale Adriatico
Triple Alliance (1882), 267
Tripoli (Lebanon), 103
Tripoli (Libya): 41, 48, 75
Troppau, Congress of (1820), 51, 57
Tunis, 76, 122
Turin, 60–61
Turkey. *See* Ottoman Empire
Turkish straits. *See* Bosporus; Dardanelles; Straits Convention

Türr, Stefan, Hungarian revolutionary, 205, 208
Tuscany, 200, 201
Two Sicilies, kingdom of the. *See* Naples, kingdom of
Tyre, 103
Tyrol, 249, 254. *See also* South Tyrol

U

Udine, 1
Ulm, battle of (1805), 16
United States: offered surplus Austrian warships, 44; accepts Polish and Italian exiles, 88–90; and steamship technology, 172, 174; and Koszta Affair (1853), 196n.17; and *Novara* cruise, 197n.31; possible Austrian warship construction in, 196n.22, 229n.14. *See also* American Civil War
Unkiar-Skelessi, Treaty of (1833), 80, 104

V

Valerio, Lorenzo, Sardinian commissioner in Marches, 204
Venetia: coveted by Austria, 1; during Napoleonic wars, 5, 16, 17, 20, 32; strength of army in, 139; and War of 1859, 192, 193; boycotts *Reichsrat* (1861), 212; annexation sought by Italy, 220, 221, 244, 247; offered to Italy in return for neutrality

(1866), 248; cession to Italy via France arranged, 249, 253; in Italian war plans and aims, 249, 251; during War of 1866, 252, 254, 256–57; ceded to Italy, 258
Venetian navy, 1–2, 24–25n.13; acquired by Austria, 5–7. *See also* Merchant marine, Venetian
Venetian Republic: and Austria, 2; and Barbary pirates, 7; dissolution of, 1; restoration of, proclaimed (1848), 140
Venetians: in Austrian navy and officer corps, 13, 16, 38–40, 58, 65–66, 68, 87, 106, 134, 178, 242; in Sardinian navy (after 1849), 191, 198n.39; in Italian navy, 250
Venice: and piracy, 7–8; trade of, 2–3, 12, 18, 23, 50, 133; defense of, 7, 8, 16–18, 42, 43, 92, 93, 134; Austrian evacuation of (1805), 17; Austrian reacquisition of (1814), 32, 34–35; and Italian revolutions of 1831–32, 79; and early steamship traffic, 94–95; and Austrian Lloyd, 96; and Bandiera brothers, 121, 134; Revolution of 1848–49 in, 118, 138–41, 150–62 *passim;* and War of 1859, 191; Italian plans to attack, 221–22; and War of 1866, 248, 252
Venice Arsenal: history of, 5–6; under early Austrian rule, 5–6, 14; under Napoleonic kingdom of Italy, 18, 50; postwar condition and resources of, 35, 36, 42, 44; and fire of 1814, 43, 45; Paulucci's inspection of (1819), 58; during campaign against Naples (1821), 59–61; shipbuilding in, 77, 109, 130–31; convicts working in, 134, 140; Frederick's reforms of, 134; Marinovich as commander of, 138, 140; Dahlerup hesitates to use, 162; construction in, under Ferdinand Max, 182; stripped of materiel (1859), 190
Veracruz, 228, 245
Victor Emmanuel I, King of Sardinia-Piedmont, 60
Victor Emmanuel II, King of Sardinia-Piedmont and Italy, 202, 205, 243, 251, 257
Victoria, Queen of England, 109, 110
Vienna: Congress of (1814–15), 41, 42, 44; revolution in (1848), 139–40, 152, 157; Treaty of (1864), 242; in Italian war plans, 249, 254; defense of (1866), 254; Treaty of (1866), 258
Villafranca, armistice of (1859), 192, 193, 201, 206
Visconti Venosta, Emilio, Italian war minister, 254

W

Wagram, battle of (1809), 21
Walker, Baldwin ("Walker Bey"), British captain, Turkish rear admiral, 104, 145n.25

Wallis, Count Olivier,
  Feldzeugmeister, 5, 6
War ministry (*Kriegsministerium*): replaces *Hofkriegsrat*, 153; subordinated to *Armee-Ober-Kommando*, 181
War of 1859, 190–93
War of 1864, 237–42
War of 1866: preparations for, 247–51; on land, 251–52, 256–58; at sea, 252–56
Warships, Austrian:
  Abbondanza, corvette, 78;
  Adria (II), corvette, 89, 108, 110, 122–23, 128;
  Adria (III), screw-frigate, 188, 189, 211;
  Augusta, frigate, 49, 64, 69, 77;
  Austria, frigate, 49, 59, 63, 64, 69, 77;
  Bellona, ex-*Severo*, frigate, 66, 69–71, 73, 77, 87;
  Bellona (II), frigate, 109–12, 120, 124, 126, 127, 131, 135;
  Carolina, corvette and frigate, 49–50, 54n.20, 64–66, 69, 70;
  Carolina (II), corvette, 91, 94, 165;
  Carolina (III), corvette, 186, 189;
  Clemenza, corvette, 103, 110. See also *Minerva*, corvette;
  Dandolo, 188, 224, 245, 248;
  Diana, ex-*Veloce*, corvette, 165;
  Donau, screw-frigate, 188, 211;
  Drache, armored frigate, 211, 213, 241;
  Ebe, frigate, 65, 69, 77, 88, 131;
  Erzherzog Friedrich, screw-frigate, 188, 189, 224, 241, 243, 248;
  Ferdinand Max, armored frigate, 243, 252, 255, 256;
  Guerriera, frigate, 77, 88, 89, 91, 94, 103–4, 108, 135, 152–53, 156;
  Habsburg, armored frigate, 243, 252;
  Italiano, ship of the line and frigate, 61–62, 64–66, 69, 77;
  Juan d'Austria, armored frigate, 241, 261n.8;
  Kaiser, ship of the line, 188, 190, 193, 223, 241, 255, 256;
  Kaiserin Elisabeth, paddle steamer, 207, 241;
  Kaiser Max, armored frigate, 241, 243, 261n.8;
  Lipsia, frigate, 63, 64, 69, 77;
  Lipsia (II), corvette, 88–89, 103, 108, 163;
  Marianna, paddle steamer, 91, 96, 132, 173;
  Medea, frigate, 75, 77, 88, 91, 103, 108;
  Minerva, frigate, 131, 163. See also *Novara*, frigate;
  Minerva, ex-*Clemenza*, corvette, 180;
  Novara, frigate, 163, 179, 186, 189, 190, 193, 206, 213;
  Novara (II), screw-frigate, 214, 226, 227, 245;
  Orione, brig, 69–70;
  Prinz Eugen, armored frigate, 241, 261n.8;
  Radetzky, screw-frigate, 175, 176, 182, 188, 189, 224, 239;
  Salamander, armored frigate, 211, 213, 241;
  Schwarzenberg, frigate, 179, 213;
  Schwarzenberg (II), screw-frigate, 214, 239, 240;

Seehund, gunboat, 239, 240;
Seemöve, yacht, 175;
Severo, ship of the line, 61–62, 64–66;
Tritone, brig, 110;
Ussaro, brig, 89–90, 113n.5;
Veloce (II), corvette, 122, 124. See also *Diana*, corvette;
Venere, frigate, 77, 135, 163. See also *Venus*, frigate;
Venus, ex-*Venere*, frigate, 164, 179, 238, 246, 260;
Vulcano, paddle steamer, 131, 152–53, 158, 163.
See also Merchant ships; appendixes A and B
Warships, foreign:
Affondatore, Italian armored ram, 255, 256;
Capri, Neapolitan ship of the line, 59;
Carlo Alberto, Sardinian screw-frigate, 176, 184;
Egiziana, Egyptian frigate. See *Reschid*;
Fulton, ex-*Demologos*, American paddle steamer, 172;
Gloire, French armored frigate, 209–10;
Monitor, American ironclad, 218, 220, 221;
Palestro, Italian armored gunboat, 256;
Princeton, American screw-sloop, 174;
Re d'Italia, Italian armored frigate, 224, 255, 256;
Re di Portogallo, Italian armored frigate, 224;
Reschid, ex-*Egiziana*, Egyptian frigate, 72–73, 170n.29;

Suffren, French ship of the line, 78;
Virginia, Confederate ironclad, 218, 220;
Warrior, British armored frigate, 210
Webb, William, American shipbuilder, 212–13
Whitehead, Robert, owner of Stabilimento Tecnico Fiume, 210
Wickenburg, Count Matthias von, trade and navy minister, 214–18, 226
Wiener Neustadt Military Academy, 137
William, Archduke, 181, 225, 232n.32
Williams, James Ernest, Lieutenant Colonel, commander of "Trieste Navy," 6–8, 12
Wilson, John, English ship broker, 68
Wimpffen, Count Franz von, *Feldmarschalleutnant*, 165, 166, 175–79, 182
Wissiak, Alphons von, Rear Admiral, 215–17, 224, 239
Wüllerstorf, Bernhard von, Vice Admiral: background of, 177, 195n.8; and naval committee of 1850, 163; as Wimpffen's adjutant, 177, 178; and *Novara* cruise, 186–87, 193; and Bourguignon, 187, 197n.32; as squadron commander, 202, 203; represents navy before *Reichsrat*, 212, 214; commands fleet in War of 1864, 239, 241–42; as trade minister, 245, 247

Y

Young Italy, 108, 109, 110, 134. *See also* Mazzini, Giuseppe

Z

Zach, Anton von, Colonel, 7
Zadar. *See* Zara
Zagreb, 21
Zahrtmann, Christian, Danish vice admiral, 159
Zara (Zadar), 34, 192
Zeltweg, 211
Zichy, Count Ferdinand, *Feldmarschalleutnant,* fortress commandant of Venice: criticizes naval academy, 115n.29; critical of Paulucci, 116n.30, 121; critical of Admiral Bandiera, 117n.38; and Bandiera brothers, 121, 123, 125–26; and Baldiserotto trial, 128, 138; and revolutionary threat to Venice, 134; and Venetian Revolution of 1848, 139–40, 149n.59
Zucchi, Count Carlo, Italian revolutionary, 78
Zurich, Peace of (1859), 201

COLLEGE